The Twofish Encryption Algorithm

A 128-Bit Block Cipher

Bruce Schneier
John Kelsey
Doug Whiting
David Wagner
Chris Hall
Niels Ferguson

WILEY COMPUTER PUBLISHING

WILEY

John Wiley & Sons, Inc.

New York • Chichester • Weinheim • Brisbane • Singapore • Toronto

Published by John Wiley & Sons, Inc. Published simultaneously in Canada.

This publication is designed to provide accurate and authoritative information in regard to the subject matter covered. It is sold with the understanding that the publisher is not engaged in professional services. If professional advice or other expert assistance is required, the services of a competent professional person should be sought.

Library of Congress Cataloging-in-Publication Data:

ISBN 0-471-35381-7
Printed in the United States of America.

10 9 8 7 6 5 4 3 2 1

Preface

AES

NIST, the National Institute of Standards and Technology, is replacing the DES encryption algorithm. The new algorithm will be called AES (Advanced Encryption Standard), will have a longer key length (128-, 192-, and 256-bit) and a larger block size (128-bit), be faster than triple DES (and probably DES), and hopefully will remain strong for a long, long time.

The process is an interesting one. In 1997, NIST sent out a request for candidate algorithms. They received fifteen submissions by the June 1998 deadline, five from the U.S. and ten from other countries. In the weeks that followed, most of the submitters posted their algorithms on the World Wide Web. In August 1998, all the submitters presented their algorithms to the world at the First AES Candidate Conference.

There will be a Second AES Candidate Conference in Rome in March 1999, where people will present papers analyzing the algorithms. Through June 1999, NIST is soliciting public comment. Then NIST will choose about five algorithms to go into the second round and, after another comment period and a third conference (sometime in mid-2000), they will choose one to turn into the standard. Then, NIST will write a FIPS, a Federal Information Processing Standard for the new algorithm, and hopefully the AES will be adopted by other standards bodies throughout the world.

All fifteen algorithms are new. Existing ones, like triple-DES, IDEA, RC5, and Blowfish, were not eligible because their block sizes were too small. Skipjack was not eligible because its block and key size were both too small.

The NSA did not submit any algorithm. They had one ready, but NIST preferred to use them as an independent evaluator. Of course, their classified analysis will not be made public, but NIST hopes that the public comments will recommend the same algorithms that the NSA's analysis does.

NIST required that all submitters state that if their algorithm was chosen as AES, they would give up all patent rights. Some submitters have given up patent rights regardless, others are holding on to their patent rights until they are chosen (and will keep them if they are not chosen). Some people chose not to submit their algorithms under these circumstances, stating that they do not want to give up the ability to charge for their algorithms. But since NIST received some very high-quality designs from groups that were willing to give them away for free, it seems NIST was correct in demanding patent-free submissions.

Cryptographers are busily analyzing the submissions for security. It's tempting to think of the process as a big demolition derby: everyone submits their algorithms and then attacks all the others... the last one standing wins. Really, it won't be like that.

At the time of writing (November 1998), there has been some pretty devastating cryptanalysis against three of the weaker candidates. (One was broken minutes after it was presented.) By the end of the first comment period, we expect there to be weaknesses found in only a few others. We strongly believe that at the end of the process most of the candidates will be unbroken. The winner will be chosen based on other factors: performance, flexibility, suitability.

AES will have to work in a variety of current and future applications, doing all sorts of different encryption tasks. Specifically:

- AES will have to be able to encrypt bulk data quickly on top-end 32-bit CPUs and 64-bit CPUs. The algorithm will be used to encrypt streaming video and audio to the desktop in real time.

- AES will have to be able to fit on small 8-bit CPUs in smart cards. To a first approximation, all DES implementations in the world are on small CPUs with very little RAM. It's in burglar alarms, electricity meters, pay-TV devices, and smart cards. Sure, some of these applications will get 32-bit CPUs as those get cheaper, but that just means that there will be another set of even smaller 8-bit applications.

- AES will have to be efficient on the smaller, weaker, 32-bit CPUs. Smart cards won't be getting Pentium-class CPUs for a long time. The first 32-bit smart cards will have simple CPUs with a simple instruction set. 16-bit CPUs will be used in embedded systems that need more power than an 8-bit CPU, but can't afford a 32-bit CPU.

- AES will have to be efficient in hardware, in not very many gates. There are lots of encryption applications in dedicated hardware: contactless cards for fare payment, for example.

- AES will have to be key agile. There are many applications where small amounts of text are encrypted with each key, and the key changes frequently. This is a very different optimization problem than encrypting a lot of data with a single key.

- AES will have to be able to be parallelized. Sometimes you have a lot of gates in hardware, and raw speed is all you care about.

- AES will have to work on DSPs. Sooner or later, your cell phone will have proper encryption built in. So will your digital camera and your digital video recorder.

- AES will need to be secure as a hash function. There are many applications where DES is used both for encryption and authentication; there just isn't enough room for a second cryptographic primitive. AES will have to serve these same two roles.

- AES needs to be secure for a long time. Infrastructure is hard to update. Like DES, AES hardware is likely to be installed and used for decades. A radical new algorithm, with interesting and exciting ideas, just doesn't make sense. A conservative algorithm is what is needed.

Choosing a single algorithm for all these applications is not easy, but that's what we have to do. It might make more sense to have a family of algorithms, each tuned to a particular application, but there will be only one AES. And when AES becomes a standard, customers will want their encryption products to be "buzzword compliant." They'll demand it in hardware, in desktop computer software, on smart cards, in electronic-commerce terminals, and in other places we never thought it would be used. Anything we pick for AES has to work in all those applications.

We designed Twofish with this in mind. It's the fastest submission on the Pentium, second fastest on the Pentium Pro/Pentium II, efficient on RAM-poor smart cards (some other algorithms can't even fit on some smart cards), implementable in hardware at either high speeds or low gate count, and suitable to be used in a hash function. It's flexible enough for implementations where one key encrypts megabytes, and for implementations where the key changes with each block.

For more information on the AES process, visit the NIST AES home page at `http://www.nist.gov/slash aes`. A general performance comparison of all the AES candidates can be found at `http://www.counterpane.com/aes-performance.html` [SKW+99a]; see also Brian Gladman's work at `http://www.seven77.demon.co.uk/aes.htm`. For a summary of the most recent attacks against the different candidates, see Lars Knudsen's summary at `http://www.ii.uib.no/~larsr/aes.html`.

This Book

This book contains all the details about Twofish, from the design criteria to the best cryptanalysis at the time of writing (November 1998). It is based on the original Twofish AES submission [SKW+98a], but also includes the first three Twofish Technical Reports [Fer98b, WW98, WS98] and the various Twofish articles and papers [SKW+98b, Sch98, SKW+99b].

This book does not contain information about the other fourteen AES submissions, or any comparisons of Twofish with them. Since this book is about the design of Twofish, which was completed without seeing the other AES submissions (except for LOKI97 and a preliminary version of Serpent, which were published early), we felt that it would be inappropriate to discuss the other submissions in this book.

As analysis progresses, more will become known about Twofish. The latest information can always be found on the Twofish web site:

http://www.counterpane.com/twofish.html

The web site also contains downloadable Twofish source code:

- Reference C implementation.
- Optimized C for the Intel Pentium, Pentium Pro, and Pentium II.
- Assembly code for the Intel Pentium, Pentium Pro, and Pentium II.
- 6805 assembly code.

Additional implementations will be added when they become available.

The authors would like to thank Carl Ellison, Nina Fefferman, Paul Kocher, and Randy Milbert, who read and commented on drafts of the original AES submission, and Beth Friedman, who copyedited the manuscript twice (both the original AES submission and this book). Additionally, the authors would like to thank NIST for initiating the AES process, Miles Smid, Jim Foti, and Ed Roback for putting up with a never-ending stream of questions and complaints about its details, and all the other AES candidates for submitting their algorithms, and making the AES selection process so interesting. We know how much effort they all went through.

This work has been funded by Counterpane Systems and Hi/fn Inc.

Table of Contents

List of Figures

List of Tables

1. Introduction

In 1972 and 1974, the National Bureau of Standards (now the National Institute of Standards and Technology, or NIST) issued the first public request for an encryption standard. The result was DES [NBS77], arguably the most widely used and successful encryption algorithm in the world.

Despite its popularity, DES has been plagued with controversy. Some cryptographers objected to the "closed-door" design process of the algorithm. The debate about whether DES' key is too short for acceptable commercial security has raged for many years [DH79], but recent advances in distributed key search techniques have left no doubt in anyone's mind that its key is simply too short for today's security applications [Wie94, BDR+96, Koc98b]. Triple-DES has emerged as an interim solution in many high-security applications, such as banking, but it is too slow for some uses. More fundamentally, the 64-bit block length shared by DES and most other well-known ciphers opens it up to attacks when large amounts of data are encrypted under the same key.

In response to a growing desire to replace DES, NIST announced the Advanced Encryption Standard (AES) program in 1997 [NIST97a].

NIST solicited comments from the public on the proposed standard, and eventually issued a call for algorithms to satisfy the standard [NIST97b]. The intention is for NIST to make all submissions public and eventually, through a process of public review and comment, choose a new encryption standard to replace DES.

NIST's call requested a block cipher. Block ciphers can be used to design stream ciphers with a variety of synchronization and error extension properties, one-way hash functions, message authentication codes, and pseudo-random number generators. Because of this flexibility, they are the workhorse of modern cryptography.

NIST specified several other design criteria: a longer key length, larger block size, faster speed, and greater flexibility. While no single algorithm can be optimized for all needs, NIST intends AES to become the standard symmetric algorithm of the next decade.

Twofish is our submission to the AES selection process. It meets all the required NIST criteria—128-bit block; 128-, 192-, and 256-bit keys; efficient on various platforms; etc.—and some strenuous design requirements, performance as well as cryptographic, of our own.

Specifically, Twofish is a 128-bit block cipher that accepts a variable-length key up to 256 bits. The cipher is a 16-round Feistel network with a bijective F function made up of four key-dependent 8-by-8-bit S-boxes, a fixed 4-by-4 maximum distance separable matrix over $GF(2^8)$, a pseudo-Hadamard transform, bitwise rotations, and a carefully designed key schedule. A fully optimized implementation of Twofish encrypts on a Pentium Pro at 16.1 clock cycles per byte, and an 8-bit smart card implementation encrypts at 1660 clock cycles per byte. Twofish can be implemented in hardware in 8000 gates. The design of both the round function and the key schedule permits a wide variety of tradeoffs between speed, software size, key setup time, gate count, and memory. We have extensively cryptanalyzed Twofish; our best attack breaks six rounds (without the whitening) with 2^{41} chosen plaintexts and 2^{232} effort.

Twofish can:

- Encrypt data at 258 clock cycles per block on a Pentium Pro, after an 8600 clock-cycle key setup, or after a 6500 clock-cycle key setup if 256 Kbytes of tables are available.

- Encrypt data at 860 clock cycles per block on a Pentium Pro, after a 1250 clock-cycle key setup.

- Encrypt data at 26500 clock cycles per block on a 6805 smart card, after a 1750 clock-cycle key setup, using only 60 bytes of RAM.

2. Twofish Design Goals

Twofish was designed to meet NIST's design criteria for AES [NIST97b]. Specifically, they are:

- A 128-bit symmetric block cipher.

- Key lengths of 128 bits, 192 bits, and 256 bits.

- No weak keys.

- Efficiency, both on the Intel Pentium Pro and other software and hardware platforms.

- Flexible design: e.g., accept additional key lengths; be implementable on a wide variety of platforms and applications; and be suitable for a stream cipher, hash function, and MAC.

- Simple design, both to facilitate ease of analysis and ease of implementation.

Additionally, we imposed the following performance criteria on our design:

- Encrypt data in less than 500 clock cycles per block on an Intel Pentium, Pentium Pro, and Pentium II for a fully optimized version of the algorithm.

- Be capable of setting up a 128-bit key (for optimal encryption speed) in less than the time required to encrypt 32 blocks on a Pentium, Pentium Pro, and Pentium II.

- Encrypt data in less than 5000 clock cycles per block on a Pentium, Pentium Pro, and Pentium II, with no key setup time.

- Not contain any operations that make it inefficient on other 32-bit microprocessors.

- Not contain any operations that make it inefficient on 8-bit and 16-bit microprocessors.

- Not contain any operations that reduce its efficiency on existing and proposed 64-bit microprocessors; e.g., Merced.

- Not include any elements that make it inefficient in hardware.

- Have a variety of performance tradeoffs with respect to the key schedule.

- Encrypt data in less than 10 milliseconds on a commodity 8-bit microprocessor.

- Be implementable on an 8-bit microprocessor with only 64 bytes of RAM.

- Be implementable in hardware using less than 20000 gates.

Our cryptographic goals were as follows:

- 12-round Twofish (without whitening) should have no chosen-plaintext attack requiring fewer than 2^{80} chosen plaintexts and less than 2^N time, where N is the key length.

- 12-round Twofish (without whitening) should have no related-key attack requiring fewer than 2^{64} chosen plaintexts, and less than $2^{N/2}$ time, where N is the key length.

Finally, we imposed the following flexibility goals:

- Accept any key length up to 256 bits.

- Have variants with a variable number of rounds.

- Have a key schedule that can be precomputed for maximum speed, or computed on the fly for maximum agility and minimum memory requirements. Additionally, it should be suitable for dedicated hardware applications: e.g., no large tables.

- Be suitable as a stream cipher, one-way hash function, MAC, and pseudo-random number generator, using well-understood construction methods.

- Have a family-key variant to allow for different, non-interoperable versions of the cipher.

We feel we have met all of these goals in the design of Twofish.

3. Twofish Building Blocks

3.1 Feistel Networks

A *Feistel network* is a general method of transforming any function (usually called the F function) into a permutation. It was invented by Horst Feistel [FNS75] in his design of Lucifer [Fei73], and popularized by DES [NBS77].

All commonly used symmetric block ciphers are product ciphers; they are strong ciphers constructed by many iterations of a round function, which is itself a kind of weak cipher. In a Feistel cipher, the round function consists of taking one part of the data being encrypted, feeding it into some key dependent function F, and then XORing (or otherwise combining) the result into another part of the block. If the part of the data used as input to the F function and the part of the data combined with output from the F function are each half of the block, then the cipher is a "balanced" Feistel network [SK96].

This is the basis of most block ciphers published since then, including FEAL [SM88], GOST [GOST89], Khufu and Khafre [Mer91], LOKI [BPS90, BKPS93], CAST-128 [Ada97a], Blowfish [Sch94], and RC5 [Riv95].

Two rounds of a Feistel network are collectively called a "cycle" [SK96]. In one cycle, every bit of the text block has been modified once.[1] Twofish is a 16-round Feistel network with a bijective F function, which corresponds to eight cycles.

3.2 Whitening

Whitening, the technique of XORing key material before the first round and after the last round, was used by Ralph Merkle in Khufu/Khafre, and independently invented by Ron Rivest for DES-X [KR96a].

---

[1] The notion of a cycle allows balanced Feistel networks to be compared with unbalanced Feistel networks [SK96, ZMI90] such as MacGuffin [BS95] (cryptanalyzed in [RP95a]) and Bear/Lion [AB96a], and with SP-networks (also called uniform transformation structures [Fei73]) such as SAFER and Shark [RDP+96] (see also [YTH96]). Thus, 8-cycle (8-round) SAFER is comparable to 8-cycle (16-round) DES and 8-cycle (32-round) Skipjack [NSA98].

In [KR96a], it was shown that whitening substantially increases the difficulty of keysearch attacks against the remainder of the cipher. In our attacks on reduced-round Twofish variants, we discovered that whitening substantially increased the difficulty of attacking the cipher by hiding from an attacker the specific inputs to the first and last rounds' F functions.

Twofish XORs 128 bits of subkey before the first Feistel round, and another 128 bits after the last Feistel round. These subkeys are calculated in the same manner as the round subkeys, but are not used anywhere else in the cipher.

3.3 S-boxes

An S-box is a table-driven non-linear substitution operation used in most block ciphers. S-boxes vary in both input size and output size, and can be created either randomly or algorithmically. S-boxes were first used in Lucifer, then DES, and afterwards in most encryption algorithms.

Twofish uses four different, bijective, key-dependent, 8-by-8-bit S-boxes. Each S-box is constructed using two fixed 8-by-8-bit permutations and several bytes of key material. These S-boxes can either be precomputed for a specific key, or computed on the fly for every required value. This provides a lot of flexibility and tradeoffs both in hardware and software.

3.4 MDS Matrices

A maximum distance separable (MDS) code over a field is a linear mapping from a field elements to b field elements, producing a composite vector of $a + b$ elements, with the property that the minimum number of non-zero elements in any non-zero vector is at least $b + 1$ [MS77].[2] Put another way, the "distance" (i.e., the number of elements that differ) between any two distinct vectors produced by the MDS mapping is at least $b + 1$. It can easily be shown that no mapping can have a larger minimum distance between two distinct vectors, hence the term maximum distance separable. MDS mappings can be represented by an MDS matrix consisting of $a \times b$ elements. Reed-Solomon (RS) error-correcting codes are known to be MDS. A necessary and sufficient condition for an $a \times b$ matrix to be MDS is that all possible square submatrices, obtained by discarding rows or columns, are non-singular.

Serge Vaudenay first proposed MDS matrices as a cipher design element [Vau95]. Shark [RDP+96] and Square [DKR97] use MDS matrices (see also

---

[2] We describe only the normal form of a linear MDS code. Any MDS code can be converted to an equivalent code in normal form.

[YMT97]), although we first saw the construction used in the unpublished cipher Manta [Fer96].[3]

MDS matrices are useful building blocks for ciphers because they guarantee a certain degree of diffusion. If one of the input elements is changed, all the output elements must change. If two input elements are changed, all but one of the output elements must change, etc. Twofish uses a single 4-by-4 MDS matrix over $GF(2^8)$. This is one of the two main diffusion elements of Twofish. (There is also an RS-code with the MDS property used in the key schedule; this doesn't add diffusion to the cipher, but does add diffusion to the key schedule.)

3.5 Pseudo-Hadamard Transforms

A pseudo-Hadamard transform (PHT) is a simple mixing operation that is very efficient in software. Given two inputs, a and b, the 32-bit PHT is defined as:

$$a' = a + b \bmod 2^{32}$$
$$b' = a + 2b \bmod 2^{32}$$

SAFER [Mas94] uses 8-bit PHTs extensively for diffusion.

Twofish uses a 32-bit PHT to mix the outputs from its two parallel 32-bit g functions. This PHT can be executed in two opcodes on most modern microprocessors, including the Pentium family. This is the second main diffusion element in Twofish.

3.6 Key Schedule

The key schedule is the means by which the key bits are turned into round keys that the cipher can use. The requirements call for a variable-length key. The easiest way of using this is to have a key schedule that expands a variable-length key to a fixed set of expanded key values.

Twofish needs a lot of key material, and has a complicated key schedule. To facilitate analysis, the key schedule uses the same primitives as the round function. Except for two additional rotations, each pair of expanded key words is constructed by applying the Twofish round function (with key-dependent S-boxes) to a fixed input.

---

[3] Manta is a block cipher with a large block size and an emphasis on long-term security rather than speed. It uses an SP-like network with DES as the S-boxes and MDS matrices for the permutations.

4. Twofish

Figure 4.1 shows an overview of the Twofish block cipher. Twofish uses a 16-round Feistel-like structure with additional whitening of the input and output. The only non-Feistel elements are the 1-bit rotates. The rotations can be moved into the F function to create a pure Feistel structure, but this requires an additional rotation of the words just before the output whitening step.

The plaintext is split into four 32-bit words. In the input whitening step, these are XORed with four key words. This is followed by 16 rounds. In each round, the two words on the left are used as input to the g functions. (One of them is rotated by 8 bits first.) The g function consists of four byte-wide key-dependent S-boxes, followed by a linear mixing step based on an MDS matrix. The results of the two g functions are combined using a Pseudo-Hadamard Transform (PHT), and two round key words are added. These two results are then XORed into the words on the right (one of which is rotated left by one bit first, the other is rotated right by one bit afterwards). The left and right halves are then swapped for the next round. After all the rounds, the swap of the last round is reversed, and the four words are XORed with four more key words to produce the ciphertext.

More formally, the 16 bytes of plaintext $p_0, \ldots, p_{15}$ are first split into four words $P_0, \ldots, P_3$ of 32 bits each using the little-endian convention.

$$P_i = \sum_{j=0}^{3} p_{(4i+j)} \cdot 2^{8j} \qquad i = 0, \ldots, 3$$

In the input whitening step, these words are XORed with four words of the expanded key.

$$R_{0,i} = P_i \oplus K_i \qquad i = 0, \ldots, 3$$

In each of the 16 rounds, the first two words are used as input to the function F, which also takes the round number as input. The third word is XORed with the first output of F and then rotated right by one bit. The fourth word is rotated left by one bit and then XORed with the second output word of F. Finally, the two halves are exchanged. Thus,

$$(F_{r,0}, F_{r,1}) \quad = \quad F(R_{r,0}, R_{r,1}, r)$$

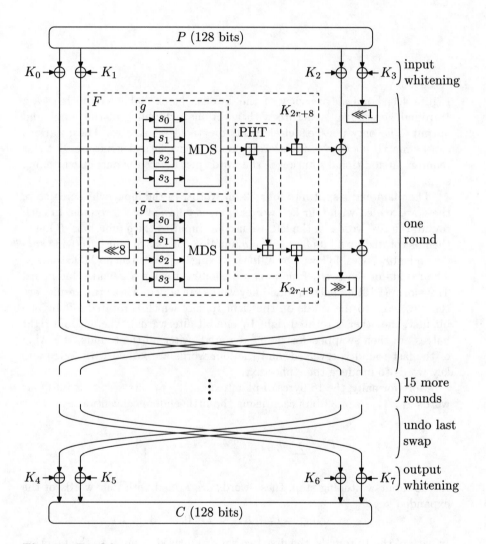

Fig. 4.1. Twofish

$$\begin{aligned}
R_{r+1,0} &= \text{ROR}(R_{r,2} \oplus F_{r,0}, 1) \\
R_{r+1,1} &= \text{ROL}(R_{r,3}, 1) \oplus F_{r,1} \\
R_{r+1,2} &= R_{r,0} \\
R_{r+1,3} &= R_{r,1}
\end{aligned}$$

for $r = 0, \ldots, 15$ and where ROR and ROL are functions that rotate their first argument (a 32-bit word) left or right by the number of bits indicated by their second argument.

The output whitening step undoes the "swap" of the last round, and XORs the data words with four words of the expanded key.

$$C_i = R_{16,(i+2) \bmod 4} \oplus K_{i+4} \qquad i = 0, \ldots, 3$$

The four words of ciphertext are then written as 16 bytes $c_0, \ldots, c_{15}$ using the same little-endian conversion used for the plaintext.

$$c_i = \left\lfloor \frac{C_{\lfloor i/4 \rfloor}}{2^{8(i \bmod 4)}} \right\rfloor \bmod 2^8 \qquad i = 0, \ldots, 15$$

4.1 The Function F

The function F is a key-dependent permutation on 64-bit values. It takes three arguments: two input words R_0 and R_1, and the round number r used to select the appropriate subkeys. R_0 is passed through the g function, which yields T_0. R_1 is rotated left by eight bits and then passed through the g function to yield T_1. The results T_0 and T_1 are then combined using a PHT and two words of the expanded key are added.

$$\begin{aligned}
T_0 &= g(R_0) \\
T_1 &= g(\text{ROL}(R_1, 8)) \\
F_0 &= (T_0 + T_1 + K_{2r+8}) \bmod 2^{32} \\
F_1 &= (T_0 + 2T_1 + K_{2r+9}) \bmod 2^{32}
\end{aligned}$$

where (F_0, F_1) is the result of F. We also define the function F' for use in our analysis. F' is identical to the F function, except that it does not add any key blocks to the output. (The PHT is still performed.)

4.2 The Function g

The function g forms the heart of Twofish. The input word X is split into four bytes. Each byte is run through its own key-dependent S-box. Each S-box is an 8-bit permutation: it takes eight bits of input and produces eight bits of output. The four results are interpreted as components of a vector of length 4 over $GF(2^8)$, and multiplied by the 4×4 MDS matrix (using the field $GF(2^8)$ for the computations).

The resulting vector is interpreted as a 32-bit word which is the result of g.

$$x_i = \lfloor X/2^{8i} \rfloor \bmod 2^8 \qquad i = 0, \ldots, 3$$
$$y_i = s_i[x_i] \qquad i = 0, \ldots, 3$$

$$\begin{pmatrix} z_0 \\ z_1 \\ z_2 \\ z_3 \end{pmatrix} = \begin{pmatrix} \cdot & \cdots & \cdot \\ \vdots & \text{MDS} & \vdots \\ \cdot & \cdots & \cdot \end{pmatrix} \cdot \begin{pmatrix} y_0 \\ y_1 \\ y_2 \\ y_3 \end{pmatrix}$$

$$Z = \sum_{i=0}^{3} z_i \cdot 2^{8i}$$

where s_i are the key-dependent S-boxes and Z is the result of g. For this to be well-defined, we need to specify the correspondence between byte values and the field elements of $GF(2^8)$. We represent $GF(2^8)$ as $GF(2)[x]/v(x)$, where $v(x) = x^8 + x^6 + x^5 + x^3 + 1$ is a primitive polynomial of degree 8 over $GF(2)$. The field element $a = \sum_{i=0}^{7} a_i x^i$ with $a_i \in GF(2)$ is identified with the byte value $\sum_{i=0}^{7} a_i 2^i$. This is in some sense the "natural" mapping; addition in $GF(2^8)$ corresponds to a XOR of the bytes.

The MDS matrix is given by:

$$\text{MDS} = \begin{pmatrix} 01 & EF & 5B & 5B \\ 5B & EF & EF & 01 \\ EF & 5B & 01 & EF \\ EF & 01 & EF & 5B \end{pmatrix}$$

where the elements have been written as hexadecimal byte values using the above-defined correspondence.

4.3 The Key Schedule

The key schedule has to provide 40 words of expanded key $K_0, \ldots, K_{39}$, and the 4 key-dependent S-boxes used in the g function. Twofish is defined for keys of length $N = 128$, $N = 192$, and $N = 256$.

We define $k = N/64$. The key M consists of $8k$ bytes $m_0, \ldots, m_{8k-1}$. The bytes are first converted into $2k$ words of 32 bits each

$$M_i = \sum_{j=0}^{3} m_{(4i+j)} \cdot 2^{8j} \qquad i = 0, \ldots, 2k - 1$$

and then into two word vectors of length k.

$$
\begin{aligned}
M_e &= (M_0, M_2, \ldots, M_{2k-2}) \\
M_o &= (M_1, M_3, \ldots, M_{2k-1})
\end{aligned}
$$

A third word vector of length k is also derived from the key. This is done by taking the key bytes in groups of eight, interpreting them as a vector over $\mathrm{GF}(2^8)$, and multiplying them by a 4×8 matrix derived from an RS code. Each result of four bytes is then interpreted as a 32-bit word. These words make up the third vector.

$$
\begin{pmatrix} s_{i,0} \\ s_{i,1} \\ s_{i,2} \\ s_{i,3} \end{pmatrix} = \begin{pmatrix} \cdot & \cdots & \cdot \\ \vdots & \mathrm{RS} & \vdots \\ \cdot & \cdots & \cdot \end{pmatrix} \cdot \begin{pmatrix} m_{8i} \\ m_{8i+1} \\ m_{8i+2} \\ m_{8i+3} \\ m_{8i+4} \\ m_{8i+5} \\ m_{8i+6} \\ m_{8i+7} \end{pmatrix}
$$

$$
S_i = \sum_{j=0}^{3} s_{i,j} \cdot 2^{8j}
$$

for $i = 0, \ldots, k-1$, and

$$
S = (S_{k-1}, S_{k-2}, \ldots, S_0)
$$

Note that S lists the words in "reverse" order. For the RS matrix multiply, $\mathrm{GF}(2^8)$ is represented by $\mathrm{GF}(2)[x]/w(x)$, where $w(x) = x^8 + x^6 + x^3 + x^2 + 1$ is another primitive polynomial of degree 8 over $\mathrm{GF}(2)$. The mapping between byte values and elements of $\mathrm{GF}(2^8)$ uses the same definition as used for the MDS matrix multiply. Using this mapping, the RS matrix is given by:

$$
\mathrm{RS} = \begin{pmatrix} 01 & A4 & 55 & 87 & 5A & 58 & DB & 9E \\ A4 & 56 & 82 & F3 & 1E & C6 & 68 & E5 \\ 02 & A1 & FC & C1 & 47 & AE & 3D & 19 \\ A4 & 55 & 87 & 5A & 58 & DB & 9E & 03 \end{pmatrix}
$$

The three vectors M_e, M_o, and S form the basis of the key schedule.

4.3.1 Additional Key Lengths

Twofish can accept keys of any byte length up to 256 bits. For key sizes that are not defined above, the key is padded at the end with zero bytes to the

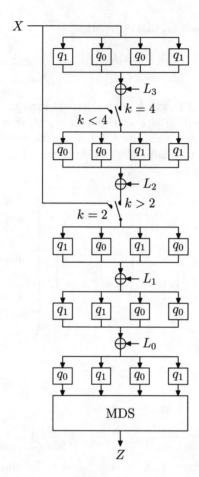

Fig. 4.2. The Function h

next larger length that is defined. For example, an 80-bit key $m_0, \ldots, m_9$ would be extended by setting $m_i = 0$ for $i = 10, \ldots, 15$ and treating it as a 128-bit key. Every key of non-standard length is thus equivalent to exactly one key of a standard length.

We have not defined Twofish for keys whose length is not an integral number of bytes. Although this can be done trivially, we see no reason to do so. Keys that span only part of a byte create a lot of extra software complexity that can easily lead to implementation bugs. There is very little to be gained from the use of such odd-sized keys.

4.3.2 The Function h

Figure 4.2 shows an overview of the function h. This is a function that takes two inputs—a 32-bit word X and a list $L = (L_0, \ldots, L_{k-1})$ of 32-bit words of length k—and produces one word of output. This function works in k stages. In each stage, the four bytes are each passed through a fixed S-box and then XORed with a byte derived from the list. Finally, the bytes are once again passed through a fixed S-box, and the four bytes are multiplied by the MDS matrix just as in g. More formally: we split the words into bytes.

$$
\begin{aligned}
l_{i,j} &= \left\lfloor L_i/2^{8j} \right\rfloor \bmod 2^8 \\
x_j &= \left\lfloor X/2^{8j} \right\rfloor \bmod 2^8
\end{aligned}
$$

for $i = 0, \ldots, k-1$ and $j = 0, \ldots, 3$. Then the sequence of substitutions and XORs is applied.

$$
y_{k,j} = x_j \qquad j = 0, \ldots, 3
$$

If $k = 4$ we have

$$
\begin{aligned}
y_{3,0} &= q_1[y_{4,0}] \oplus l_{3,0} \\
y_{3,1} &= q_0[y_{4,1}] \oplus l_{3,1} \\
y_{3,2} &= q_0[y_{4,2}] \oplus l_{3,2} \\
y_{3,3} &= q_1[y_{4,3}] \oplus l_{3,3}
\end{aligned}
$$

If $k \geq 3$ we have

$$
\begin{aligned}
y_{2,0} &= q_1[y_{3,0}] \oplus l_{2,0} \\
y_{2,1} &= q_1[y_{3,1}] \oplus l_{2,1} \\
y_{2,2} &= q_0[y_{3,2}] \oplus l_{2,2} \\
y_{2,3} &= q_0[y_{3,3}] \oplus l_{2,3}
\end{aligned}
$$

In all cases we have

$$
\begin{aligned}
y_0 &= q_1[q_0[q_0[y_{2,0}] \oplus l_{1,0}] \oplus l_{0,0}] \\
y_1 &= q_0[q_0[q_1[y_{2,1}] \oplus l_{1,1}] \oplus l_{0,1}] \\
y_2 &= q_1[q_1[q_0[y_{2,2}] \oplus l_{1,2}] \oplus l_{0,2}] \\
y_3 &= q_0[q_1[q_1[y_{2,3}] \oplus l_{1,3}] \oplus l_{0,3}]
\end{aligned}
$$

Here, q_0 and q_1 are fixed permutations on 8-bit values that we will define shortly. The resulting vector of y_i's is multiplied by the MDS matrix, just as in the g function.

$$
\begin{pmatrix} z_0 \\ z_1 \\ z_2 \\ z_3 \end{pmatrix} = \begin{pmatrix} \cdot & \cdots & \cdot \\ \vdots & \text{MDS} & \vdots \\ \cdot & \cdots & \cdot \end{pmatrix} \cdot \begin{pmatrix} y_0 \\ y_1 \\ y_2 \\ y_3 \end{pmatrix}
$$

$$
Z = \sum_{i=0}^{3} z_i \cdot 2^{8i}
$$

where Z is the result of h.

4.3.3 The Key-dependent S-boxes

We can now define the S-boxes in the function g by

$$g(X) = h(X, S)$$

That is, for $i = 0, \ldots, 3$, the key-dependent S-box s_i is formed by the mapping from x_i to y_i in the h function, where the list L is equal to the vector S derived from the key.

4.3.4 The Expanded Key Words K_j

The words of the expanded key are defined using the h function. We have

$$
\begin{aligned}
\rho &= 2^{24} + 2^{16} + 2^8 + 2^0 \\
A_i &= h(2i\rho, M_e) \\
B_i &= \text{ROL}(h((2i+1)\rho, M_o), 8) \\
K_{2i} &= (A_i + B_i) \bmod 2^{32} \\
K_{2i+1} &= \text{ROL}((A_i + 2B_i) \bmod 2^{32}, 9)
\end{aligned}
$$

for $i = 0, \ldots, 19$. The constant ρ is used here to duplicate bytes; it has the property that for $i = 0, \ldots, 255$, the word $i\rho$ consists of four equal bytes, each with the value i. The function h is applied to words of this type. For A_i the byte values are $2i$, and the second argument of h is M_e. B_i is computed similarly using $2i + 1$ as the byte value and M_o as the second argument, with an extra rotate over eight bits. The values A_i and B_i are combined in a PHT. One of the results is further rotated by nine bits. The two results form two words of the expanded key.

4.3.5 The Permutations q_0 and q_1

The permutations q_0 and q_1 are fixed permutations on 8-bit values. They are constructed from four different 4-bit permutations each. For the input value x, we define the corresponding output value y as follows:

$$
\begin{aligned}
a_0, b_0 &= \lfloor x/16 \rfloor, x \bmod 16 \\
a_1 &= a_0 \oplus b_0 \\
b_1 &= a_0 \oplus \text{ROR}_4(b_0, 1) \oplus 8a_0 \bmod 16 \\
a_2, b_2 &= t_0[a_1], t_1[b_1] \\
a_3 &= a_2 \oplus b_2 \\
b_3 &= a_2 \oplus \text{ROR}_4(b_2, 1) \oplus 8a_2 \bmod 16 \\
a_4, b_4 &= t_2[a_3], t_3[b_3] \\
y &= 16\, b_4 + a_4
\end{aligned}
$$

where ROR$_4$ is a function similar to ROR that rotates 4-bit values. First, the byte is split into two nibbles (1 nibble = 4 bits). These are combined in a bijective mixing step. Each nibble is then passed through its own 4-bit fixed S-box. This is followed by another mixing step and S-box lookup. Finally, the two nibbles are recombined into a byte. For the permutation q_0 the 4-bit S-boxes are given by

$$t_0 = [\ 8\ \ 1\ \ 7\ D\ 6\ F\ 3\ 2\ 0\ B\ 5\ 9\ E\ C\ A\ 4\ ]$$
$$t_1 = [\ E\ C\ B\ 8\ 1\ 2\ 3\ 5\ F\ 4\ A\ 6\ 7\ 0\ 9\ D\ ]$$
$$t_2 = [\ B\ A\ 5\ E\ 6\ D\ 9\ 0\ C\ 8\ F\ 3\ 2\ 4\ 7\ 1\ ]$$
$$t_3 = [\ D\ 7\ F\ 4\ 1\ 2\ 6\ E\ 9\ B\ 3\ 0\ 8\ 5\ C\ A\ ]$$

where each 4-bit S-box is represented by a list of the entries using hexadecimal notation. (The entries for the inputs $0, 1, \ldots, 15$ are listed in order.) Similarly, for q_1 the 4-bit S-boxes are given by

$$t_0 = [\ 2\ 8\ B\ D\ F\ 7\ 6\ E\ 3\ 1\ 9\ 4\ 0\ A\ C\ 5\ ]$$
$$t_1 = [\ 1\ E\ 2\ B\ 4\ C\ 3\ 7\ 6\ D\ A\ 5\ F\ 9\ 0\ 8\ ]$$
$$t_2 = [\ 4\ C\ 7\ 5\ 1\ 6\ 9\ A\ 0\ E\ D\ 8\ 2\ B\ 3\ F\ ]$$
$$t_3 = [\ B\ 9\ 5\ 1\ C\ 3\ D\ E\ 6\ 4\ 7\ F\ 2\ 0\ 8\ A\ ]$$

4.4 Round Function Overview

Figure 4.3 shows a more detailed view of how the function F is computed each round when the key length is 128 bits. Incorporating the S-box and round-subkey generation makes the Twofish round function look more complicated, but is useful for visualizing exactly how the algorithm works.

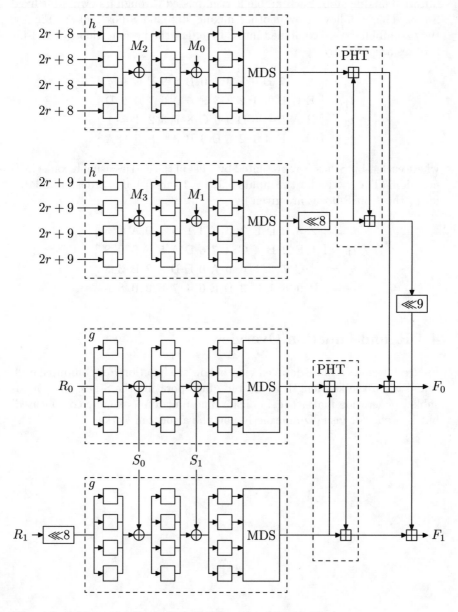

Fig. 4.3. A View of a Single Round F Function (128-bit Key)

5. Performance of Twofish

Twofish has been designed from the start with performance in mind. It is efficient on a variety of platforms: 32-bit CPUs, 8-bit smart cards, and dedicated VLSI hardware. More importantly, though, Twofish has been designed to allow several layers of performance tradeoffs, depending on the relative importance of encryption speed, key setup, memory use, hardware gate count, and other implementation parameters. The result is a highly flexible algorithm that can be implemented efficiently in a variety of cryptographic applications.

All these options are interoperable; these are simply implementation tradeoffs and do not affect the mathematics of Twofish. One end of a communication could use the fastest Pentium II implementation, and the other the cheapest hardware implementation.

5.1 Performance on Large Microprocessors

Table 5.1 gives Twofish's performance, encryption or decryption, for different key scheduling options and on several modern microprocessors using different languages and compilers. This table shows our results for many different implementations. Each implementation is presented on a single line. The first column gives the CPU the implementation was run on (PPro/II = Pentium Pro/Pentium II, U-SPARC = Ultra-SPARC, PPC = Power PC). The second column is the programming language (ASM = assembly language, MS C = Microsoft Visual C++ 4.2, BC = Borland C 5.0, C = standard C compiler). The keying options are explained below. The code size column contains the approximate total code size (in bytes) of the routines for encryption, decryption, and key setup, where available. All remaining numbers in the row are in clock cycles. For each key size we show the number of clock cycles required for the key setup, and the number of clock cycles required to encrypt a single block. The times for encryption and decryption are identical in assembly, and encryption is slightly slower than decryption in C; only the encryption (i.e., the larger) number is given. There is no time required to set up the algorithm except for key setup. The time required to change a key is the same as the time required to set up a key.

For example, on a Pentium Pro a fully optimized assembly-language version of Twofish can encrypt or decrypt data in 258 clock cycles per block, or

Processor	Lang	Keying Option	Code Size	Clocks to Key			Clocks to Encrypt		
				128	192	256	128	192	256
PPro/II	ASM	Comp.	9000	8600	11300	14100	258	258	258
PPro/II	ASM	Full	8500	7600	10400	13200	315	315	315
PPro/II	ASM	Part.	10700	4900	7600	10500	460	460	460
PPro/II	ASM	Min.	13600	2400	5300	8200	720	720	720
PPro/II	ASM	Zero	9100	1250	1600	2000	860	1130	1420
PPro/II	MS C	Full	11200	8000	11200	15700	600	600	600
PPro/II	MS C	Part.	13200	7100	9700	14100	800	800	800
PPro/II	MS C	Min.	16600	3000	7800	12200	1130	1130	1130
PPro/II	MS C	Zero	10500	2450	3200	4000	1310	1750	2200
PPro/II	BC	Full	14100	10300	13600	18800	640	640	640
PPro/II	BC	Part.	14300	9500	11200	16600	840	840	840
PPro/II	BC	Min.	17300	4600	10300	15300	1160	1160	1160
PPro/II	BC	Zero	10100	3200	4200	4800	1910	2670	3470
Pentium	ASM	Comp.	9100	12300	14600	17100	290	290	290
Pentium	ASM	Full	8200	11000	13500	16200	315	315	315
Pentium	ASM	Part.	10300	5500	7800	9800	430	430	430
Pentium	ASM	Min.	12600	3700	5900	7900	740	740	740
Pentium	ASM	Zero	8700	1800	2100	2600	1000	1300	1600
Pentium	MS C	Full	11800	11900	15100	21500	630	630	630
Pentium	MS C	Part.	14100	9200	13400	19800	900	900	900
Pentium	MS C	Min.	17800	3800	11100	16900	1460	1460	1460
Pentium	MS C	Zero	11300	2800	3900	4900	1740	2260	2760
Pentium	BC	Full	12700	14200	18100	26100	870	870	870
Pentium	BC	Part.	14200	11200	16500	24100	1100	1100	1100
Pentium	BC	Min.	17500	4700	12100	19200	1860	1860	1860
Pentium	BC	Zero	11800	3700	4900	6100	2150	2730	3270
U-SPARC	C	Full		16600	21600	24900	750	750	750
U-SPARC	C	Part.		8300	13300	19900	930	930	930
U-SPARC	C	Min.		3300	11600	16600	1200	1200	1200
U-SPARC	C	Zero		1700	3300	5000	1450	1680	1870
PPC 750	C	Full		12200	17100	22200	590	590	590
PPC 750	C	Part.		7800	12200	17300	780	780	780
PPC 750	C	Min.		2900	9100	14200	1280	1280	1280
PPC 750	C	Zero		2500	3600	4900	1030	1580	2040
68040	C	Full	16700	53000	63500	96700	3500	3500	3500
68040	C	Part.	18100	36700	47500	78500	4900	4900	4900
68040	C	Min.	23300	11000	40000	71800	8150	8150	8150
68040	C	Zero	16200	9800	13300	17000	6800	8600	10400

Table 5.1. Twofish Performance with Different Key Lengths and Options

16.1 clock cycles per byte, after a 12700-clock key setup (equivalent to encrypting 45 blocks). On a 200 MHz Pentium Pro microprocessor, this translates to a throughput of just under 90 Mbits/sec.

5.1.1 Keying Options

We implemented four different keying options. All of our keying options precompute K_i for $i = 0, \ldots, 39$ and use 160 bytes of RAM to store these constants. The differences occur in the way the function g is implemented. There are several other possible keying options, each with slightly different setup/throughput tradeoffs, but the examples listed below are representative of the range of possibilities.

Full Keying. This option performs the full key precomputations. Using 4 Kbytes of table space, each S-box is expanded to a 8-by-32-bit table that combines both the S-box lookup and the multiply by the column of the MDS matrix. Using this option, a computation of g consists of four table lookups, and three XORs. Encryption and decryption speeds are constant regardless of key size.

Partial Keying. For applications where few blocks are encrypted with a single key, it may not make sense to build the complete key schedule. The partial keying option precomputes the four S-boxes in 8-by-8-bit tables, and uses four fixed 8-by-32-bit MDS tables to perform the MDS multiply. This reduces the key-schedule table space to 1 Kbyte. For each byte, the last of the q-box lookups is in fact incorporated into the MDS table, so only k of the q-boxes are incorporated into the 8-by-8-bit S-box table that is built by the key schedule. Encryption and decryption speeds are again constant regardless of key size.

Minimal Keying. For applications where very few blocks are encrypted with a single key, there is a further possible optimization. Compared to partial keying, one less layer of q-boxes is precomputed into the S-box table, and the remaining q-box is done during the encryption. For the 128-bit key this is particularly efficient, as precomputing the S-boxes now consists of copying the table of the appropriate q-box and XORing it with a constant (which can be done word-by-word instead of byte-by-byte). This option uses a 1 Kbyte table to store the partially precomputed S-boxes. The necessary key bytes from S are of course precomputed, as they are needed in every round.

Zero Keying. The zero keying option does not precompute any of the S-boxes, and thus needs no extra tables. Instead, every entry is computed on the fly. The key setup time consists purely of computing the K_i values and S. For an application that cannot have any key setup time, the time it takes to encrypt one block is the sum of the key setup time and encryption time for the zero keying option.

Compiled. In this option, available only in assembly language, the subkey constants are directly embedded into a key-specific copy of the code, saving memory fetches and allowing the use of the Pentium LEA opcode to perform both the PHT and the subkey addition all in a single clock cycle. Some additional setup time is required, as well as about an extra 5000 bytes of memory to hold the "compiled" code, but this option allows the fastest execution time of 258 clocks per block on the Pentium Pro. The setup time for a Pentium more than doubles over the full keying case because of its smaller cache size, but the Pentium MMX setup time is still comparable to the Pentium Pro setup time. However, almost all the extra time required is consumed merely in copying the code; the table does not reflect the fact that, once a single key has been initialized, future keys can be compiled at a cost of only a few hundred more clocks than full key schedule time.

5.1.2 Code and Data Size

As shown in Table 5.1, the code size for a fully optimized Twofish implementation on a Pentium Pro ranges from about 8450 bytes in assembler to 14100 bytes in Borland C. In assembler, the encryption and decryption routines are each about 2250 bytes in size; the remaining 4000 bytes of code are in the key scheduling routines, but about 2200 bytes of that total can be discarded if only 128-bit keys are needed. In Borland C, the encryption and decryption routines are each about 4500 bytes in length, and the key schedule routine is slightly less than 5000 bytes. Note that each routine fits easily within the code cache of a Pentium or a Pentium Pro. These sizes are larger than Blowfish but very similar to a fully optimized assembly language version of DES. Note that, with the exception of the zero keying option, the code sizes in the table are for fully unrolled implementations; in either C or assembler, it is possible to achieve significantly smaller code sizes using loops with round counters, at a cost in performance.

In addition to the code, there are about 4600 bytes of fixed tables for the MDS matrix, q_0 and q_1 required for key setup, and each key requires about 4300 bytes of key-dependent data tables for the full keying option. During encryption or decryption, these tables fit easily in the Pentium data cache. The other keying options use less data and table space, as discussed above.

5.1.3 Large Memory Implementations

For machines with sufficient RAM and a good memory cache subsystem, large precomputed tables can be used to reduce the key setup time for Twofish even further. For example, in compiled, full, or partial keying modes, the first two levels of q_0 and q_1 lookups with one key byte can be precomputed for all four S-boxes, requiring 256 Kbytes of table (four tables of 64 Kbytes each). This approach saves roughly 2000 clocks per key setup on the Pentium Pro in

Processor	Lang	Keying Option	Code Size	Clocks to Key			Clocks to Encrypt		
				128	192	256	128	192	256
PPro/II	ASM	Comp.	271,200	6500	9200	11900	258	258	258
PPro/II	ASM	Full	270,600	5300	8000	11000	315	315	315
PPro/II	ASM	Part.	272,900	2600	5300	8200	460	460	460
PPro/II	MS C	Full	273,300	7300	11200	15700	600	600	600

Table 5.2. Twofish Performance with Large Fixed Tables

assembly language; details are shown in Table 5.2. For instance, the compiled mode key setup for 128-bit keys on a Pentium Pro can be reduced from 8700 clocks to 6500 clocks. Unfortunately, the savings on Pentium and Pentium MMX CPUs seems to depend on the performance of the L2 cache subsystem (which is included in the Pentium Pro and thus is more predictable); the gain seems to range from 500 clocks down to nothing. Implementing this "big table" version in C also leads to savings of about 1000 clocks per key setup on the Pentium Pro, depending on the quality of the compiler; again, Pentium performance gains are minimal.

For the ultimate in key agility, a full 256 Mbytes of precomputed tables could comprise all four S-boxes for the final two stages of q_0, q_1, covering all 2^{16} key byte possibilities for the 128-bit key case, and including the MDS matrix multiply. With a good memory subsystem, such a version should cut another 1000 clocks or so out of the above key setup times. Clearly, this is a fairly expensive solution (at least with today's technology), but it illustrates the flexibility of Twofish very nicely.

5.1.4 Total Encryption Times

Any performance measures that do not take key setup into account are only valid for asymptotically large amounts of text. For shorter messages, performance is the sum of key setup and encryption. For very short messages, the key setup time can overwhelm the encryption speed.

Table 5.3 gives Twofish's performance on the Pentium Pro (assembly-language version), both 128-bit key setup and encryption, for a variety of message lengths. This table assumes the best of our implementations (not including the large-memory implementations) for the particular length of text.

5.1.5 Hash Function Performance

Hash functions built from block ciphers generally require the algorithm to be uniquely keyed for each text block [Pre93, Sch96]. Assuming the chaining variables are the plaintext and ciphertext, and the block to be hashed is the

Plaintext (bytes)	Keying Option	Clocks to Key	Clocks to Encrypt	Total Clocks per Byte
16	Zero	1250	860	131.9
32	Zero	1250	1720	92.8
64	Zero	1250	4690	73.3
128	Minimal	2400	6880	63.5
256	Partial	4900	7360	47.9
512	Compiled	8600	8256	32.9
1K	Compiled	8600	16512	24.5
2K	Compiled	8600	33024	20.3
4K	Compiled	8600	66048	18.2
8K	Compiled	8600	132096	17.2
16K	Compiled	8600	264192	16.7
32K	Compiled	8600	528384	16.4
64K	Compiled	8600	1056768	16.3
1M	Compiled	8600	270532608	16.1

Table 5.3. Best Speed to Encrypt a Message with a New 128-bit Key on a Pentium Pro

key, Twofish can hash text at a rate of 175 clock cycles per byte on a Pentium, assuming a 128-bit key, and 132 clock cycles per byte on a Pentium Pro/II.

5.1.6 Language, Compiler, and Processor Choice

As with most algorithms, the choices of language and compiler can have a huge impact on performance. It is clear that the Borland C 5.0 compiler chosen as the standard AES reference is not the best optimizing compiler. For example, the Microsoft Visual C++ 4.2 compiler generates Twofish code that is at least 20 percent faster than Borland on a Pentium computer, with both set to optimize for speed (630 clocks per block for Microsoft Visual C++ 4.2 versus 870 clocks per block for Borland C 5.0); on a Pentium Pro/II, the difference between the compilers is not quite as large (e.g., 600 clocks/block vs. 640 clocks/block), but it is still significant. Part of the difference stems from the inability of the Borland C compiler to generate intrinsic rotate instructions, despite documentation claiming that it is possible. This problem alone accounts for nearly half of the speed difference between Borland and Microsoft. The remaining speed difference comes simply from poorer code generation. The Borland C compiler is uniformly slower than Microsoft's compiler. The encryption speed in Microsoft C of 40 Pentium clocks per byte (i.e., 630 clocks/block at 16 bytes/block) is over ten percent faster than the best known DES assembly language implementation on the same platform. However, coding the Twofish algorithm in assembly language achieves speeds of 258 clocks, achieving a very significant speedup over any of the C implementations.

To make matters even more complicated, the assembly language that optimizes performance on a Pentium (or Pentium MMX) is drastically different from the assembly language required to maximize speed on a Pentium Pro or Pentium II, even though the final code size and speed achieved on each platform are almost identical. For example, the Pentium Pro/II CPUs can perform only one memory read per clock cycle, while the Pentium and Pentium MMX can perform two. However, the Pentium Pro/II can perform two ALU operations per clock in addition to memory accesses, while the Pentium can process only a total of two ALU operations or memory accesses per clock. These (and other) significant architectural differences result in the fact that running the optimal Pentium Twofish encryption code on a Pentium Pro results in a slowdown of nearly 2:1—and vice versa! Fortunately, it is relatively simple to detect the CPU type at run-time and select which version of the assembly code to use. Another anomaly is that the key schedule setup time is considerably faster (43 percent) on the Pentium MMX than on the Pentium, not because the key schedule uses any MMX instructions, but simply because of the larger cache size of the MMX chip.

Empirically, there also seems to be some anomalous behavior of the C compilers. In almost all cases, the encryption and decryption routines in C achieved speeds within a few percent of each other. However, there were cases in the table where the two speeds differed by considerably more than ten percent (we used the larger number in the table), which is very odd because the "inner loop" C code used is virtually identical. We also noted several cases where compiler switches that seemed unrelated to performance optimization sometimes caused very large changes in timings.

It should be noted that performance numbers for Pentium II processors are almost identical in all cases to those for a Pentium Pro, which is not surprising since Intel claims they have the same core. The Pentium and Pentium MMX achieve almost identical speeds for encryption and decryption, although, as noted above, the MMX key setup times are faster, due mainly to the larger cache size.

The bottom line is that, when comparing the relative performance of different algorithms, using the same language and compiler for all implementations helps to make the comparison meaningful, but it does not guarantee a valid measure of the relative speeds. We have listed many different software performance metrics across platforms and languages to facilitate speed comparisons between Twofish and other algorithms. Our belief is that, on any given platform (e.g., Pentium Pro), the assembly-language performance numbers are the best numbers to use to gauge absolute performance, since they are unaffected by the vagaries and limitations of the compiler (e.g., inability to produce rotate opcodes). High-level languages (e.g., C, Java) are also important because of the ease of porting to different platforms, but once

RAM, ROM, or EEPROM for Key	Working RAM	Code and Table Size	Clocks per Block	Time per Block @ 4MHz
24	36	2200	26500	6.6 msec
24	36	2150	32900	8.2 msec
24	36	2000	35000	8.7 msec
24	36	1750	37100	9.3 msec
184	36	1900	15300	3.8 msec
184	36	1700	18100	4.5 msec
184	36	1450	19200	4.8 msec
1208	36	1300	12700	3.2 msec
1208	36	1100	15500	3.9 msec
1208	36	850	16600	4.2 msec
3256	36	1000	11900	3.0 msec

Table 5.4. Twofish Performance on a 6805 Smart Card

an algorithm becomes standardized, it will ultimately be coded in assembly for the most popular platforms.

5.2 Performance on Smart Cards

Twofish is ideally suited for smart cards. It can fit on the smallest smart cards while exhibiting reasonable performance, and can take advantage of more RAM or more powerful processors with increased performance. It can operate efficiently in environments that require rapid key changes, and can be implemented in dedicated hardware in only a few gates.

We implemented Twofish on a 6805 CPU, which is a typical smart card processor, with several different space–time tradeoff options [SKW+99b]. Our results are shown in Table 5.4. The code size includes both encryption and decryption.[1] The block encryption and decryption times are almost identical. If only encryption is required, minor improvements in code size and speed can be obtained. The only key schedule precomputation time required in this implementation is the Reed-Solomon mapping used to generate the S-box key material S from the key M, which requires slightly over 1750 clocks per key. This setup time can be made considerably shorter at the cost of two additional 256-byte ROM tables. It should also be observed that the lack of a second index register on the 6805 has a significant impact on the code size and performance, so a different CPU with multiple index registers (e.g., 6502) might be a better fit for Twofish.

---

[1] For comparison purposes: DES on a 6805 takes about 1K code, 23 bytes of RAM, and 20000 clock cycles per block.

5.2.1 RAM Usage

For any encryption algorithm, memory usage can be divided into two parts: that required to hold the expanded key, and that required as working space to encrypt or decrypt text (including the text block). In applications where a smart card holds a single key for a long period of time, the key can be put into EEPROM or even ROM, greatly reducing RAM requirements. Most applications, however, require the smart card to encrypt using session keys, which change with each transaction. In these situations, the expanded key must be stored in RAM, along with working space to perform the encryption.

Twofish—the 128-bit key version—can be implemented in a smart card in 60 bytes of RAM. This includes the text block, key, and working space. If a slightly expanded key (16 bytes of the key plus another eight bytes of the Reed-Solomon results (S)) can be stored in ROM or EEPROM, then Twofish can be implemented in only 36 bytes of RAM. In either case, there is zero key setup time for the next encryption operation with the same key.[2]

Larger key sizes require more RAM to store the larger keys: 36 bytes for 192-bit keys and 48 bytes for 256-bit keys. If these applications can store key material in ROM or EEPROM, then these key lengths can be implemented on smart cards with only 36 bytes of RAM. All of this RAM can be reused for other purposes between block encryption operations.

For smart cards with larger memory to hold key-dependent data, encryption speed can increase considerably. This is because the round keys can be precomputed as part of the expanded key, requiring a total of 184 bytes of key memory. As shown in Table 5.4, this option nearly halves the encryption time. If the smart card has enough additional memory available to hold 1 Kbyte of precomputed S-box in either RAM, ROM, or EEPROM (for a total of 1208 bytes), performance improves further. Finally, as shown in the final row of Table 5.4, if the entire precomputed S-box plus MDS table can be held in memory (3256 bytes), the speed can again be increased slightly more. It should be noted that some of these "large RAM" implementations save 512 bytes of code space by assuming that certain tables are not required in ROM, with the entire precomputation being performed instead on the host that sets the key in the smart card. If the smart card has to perform its own key expansion the code size will increase. This increase has its own space/time tradeoff options.

This flexibility makes Twofish well-suited for both small and large smart-card processors: Twofish works in the most RAM-poor environments, while at the same time it is able to take advantage of both moderate-RAM cards and large-RAM cards.

---

[2] All of our implementations leave the key intact so that it can be used again.

5.2.2 Encryption Speed and Key Agility

On a 6805 with only 60 bytes of RAM, Twofish encrypts at speeds of 26500 to 37100 clocks per block, depending on the amount of ROM available for the code. On a 4 MHz chip, this translates to 6.6 msec to 9.3 msec per encryption. In these implementations, the key-schedule precomputation time is minimal: slightly over 1750 clocks per key. This setup time could be cut considerably at the cost of two additional 512-byte ROM tables, which would be used during the key schedule.

If ROM is expensive, Twofish can be implemented in less space at slower speeds. The space–speed tradeoffs are of two types: unrolling loops and implementing various lookup tables. By far, the latter has the larger impact on size and speed. For example, Twofish's MDS matrix can be computed in three different ways:

- Full table lookups for the multiplications by EF and 5B. This is the fastest, and requires 512 bytes of ROM for tables.

- Single table lookup for the multiplications by α^{-1}. This is slower, but only requires 256 bytes of ROM for the table.

- No tables, all multiplies done with shifts and XORs. This is the slowest, and the smallest.

Longer keys are slower, but only slightly so. For the small memory versions, Twofish's encryption time per block increases by less than 2600 clocks per block for 192-bit keys, and by about 5200 clocks per block for 256-bit keys. Similarly, the key schedule precomputation increases to 2550 clocks for 192-bit keys, and to 3400 clocks for 256-bit keys.

As shown in Table 5.4, in smart card CPUs with sufficient additional RAM storage to hold the entire set of subkeys, the throughput improves significantly, although the key setup time also increases. The time savings per block is over 11000 clocks, cutting the block encryption time down to about 15000 clocks; i.e., nearly doubling the encryption speed. The key setup time increases by roughly the same number of clocks, thus making the key setup time comparable to a single block encryption. This approach also cuts down the code size by a few hundred bytes. It should be noted further that, in fixed-key environments, the subkeys can be stored along with the key bytes in EEPROM, cutting the total RAM usage down to 36 bytes while maintaining the higher speed.

As another tradeoff, if another 1 Kbyte of RAM or EEPROM is available, all four 8-bit S-boxes can be precomputed. Clearly, this approach has relatively low key agility, but the time required to encrypt a block decreases by roughly 6000 clocks. When combined with precomputed subkeys as discussed in the previous paragraph, the block encryption time drops to about 12000 clocks, nearly three times the best speed for "low RAM" implementations. In most cases, this approach would be used only where the key is fixed, but it does allow for very high throughput. Similarly, if 3 Kbytes of RAM or EEPROM is available for tables, throughput can be further improved slightly.

The wide variety of possible speeds again illustrates Twofish's flexibility in these constrained environments. The algorithm does not have one speed; it has many speeds, depending on available resources.

5.2.3 Code Size

Twofish code is very compact: 1760 to 2200 bytes for minimal RAM footprint, depending on the implementation. The same code base can be used for both encryption and decryption. If only encryption is required, minor improvements in code size can be obtained (on the order of 150 bytes). The extra code required for larger keys is fairly negligible: less than 100 extra bytes for a 192-bit key, and less than 200 bytes for a 256-bit key.

Observe that it is possible to save further ROM space by computing q_0 and q_1 lookups using the underlying 4-bit construction, as specified in Section 4.3.5. Such a scheme would replace 512 bytes of ROM table with 64 bytes of ROM and a small subroutine to compute the full 8-bit q_0 and q_1, saving perhaps 350 bytes of ROM; unfortunately, encryption speed would decrease by a factor of ten or more. Thus, this technique is only of interest in smart card applications for which ROM size is extremely critical but performance is not. Nonetheless, such an approach illustrates the implementation flexibility afforded by Twofish.

5.3 Performance on the Alpha

The 64-bit Alpha 21164 CPU can run up to 600 MHz using only a 0.35 micron CMOS process, compared to the 0.25 micron technology used in a Pentium II. The Alpha is widely regarded as the fastest general purpose processor available today. Its architecture and performance are expected to remain at the leading edge of technology for the foreseeable future. It has a 4-way superscalar architecture, which is fairly close in many respects to a Pentium II. Twofish should run on an Alpha in roughly the same number of clocks as on a Pentium Pro (i.e., 300).

5.4 Performance on Future Microprocessors

Given the ever-advancing capabilities of CPUs, it is worthwhile to make some observations about how the Twofish algorithm will run on future processors, including Intel's Merced. Not many details are known about Merced, other than that it includes an Explicitly Parallel Instruction Computing (EPIC) architecture, as well the ability to run existing Pentium code. EPIC is related to VLIW architectures that allow many parallel opcodes to be executed at once, while the Pentium allows only two opcodes in parallel, and the Pentium Pro/Pentium II may process up to three opcodes per clock. However, access to memory tables is limited in most VLIW implementations to only a few parallel operations, and we expect similar restrictions to hold for Merced. For example, an existing Philips VLIW CPU can process up to five opcodes in parallel, but only two of the opcodes can read from memory.

Since Twofish relies on 8-bit non-linear S-boxes, it is clear that table access is an integral part of the algorithm. Thus, Twofish might not be able to take advantage of all the parallel execution units available on a VLIW processor. However, there is still plenty of parallelism in Twofish that can be well-utilized in an optimized VLIW software implementation. Equally important, the alternative of not using large S-boxes, while it may allow greater parallelism, also naturally involves less non-linearity and thus generally requires more rounds. For example, Serpent [BAK98], based on "inline" computation of 4-bit S-boxes, may experience a relatively larger speedup than Twofish on a VLIW CPU, but Serpent also requires 32 rounds, and is considerably slower to start with.

It should also be noted that, as with most encryption algorithms, the primitive operations used in Twofish could very easily be added to a CPU instruction set to improve software performance significantly. Future mainstream CPUs may include such support for the new AES standard. However, it is also worthwhile to remember that DES has been a standard for more than twenty years, and no popular CPU has added instruction set support for it, even though DES software performance would benefit greatly from such features.

5.5 Hardware Performance

No actual logic design has been implemented for Twofish, but estimates in terms of gates for each building block have been made. As in software, there are many possible space–time tradeoffs in hardware implementations of Twofish. Thus, it is not meaningful to give just one figure for the speed and size attributes of Twofish in hardware. Instead, we will try to outline several of the options and give estimates for speed and gate count of several different architectures.

For example, the round subkeys could be precomputed and stored in a RAM, or they could be computed on the fly. If computed on the fly, the h function logic could be time-multiplexed between subkeys and the round function to save size at a cost in speed, or the logic could be duplicated, adding gates but perhaps running twice as fast. If the subkeys were precomputed, the h function logic would be used during a key setup phase to compute the subkeys, saving gates but adding a startup time roughly equal to one block encryption time. Similarly, a single h function logic block could be time-multiplexed between computing T_0 and T_1, halving throughput but saving even more gates.

As another example of the possible tradeoffs, the S-boxes could be pre-computed and stored in on-chip RAMs, allowing faster operation because there is no need to ripple through several layers of key material XORs and q permutations. The addition of such RAMs (e.g., eight 256-byte RAMs) would perhaps double or triple the size of the logic, and it would also impose a significant startup time on key change to initialize the RAMs. Despite these disadvantages, such an architecture might raise the throughput by a factor of two or more (particularly for the larger key sizes), so for high-performance systems with infrequent re-keying, this option may be attractive.

The construction method specified in Section 4.3.5 for building the 8-bit permutations q_0 and q_1 from four 4-bit permutations was selected mainly to minimize gate count in many hardware implementations of Twofish. These permutations can be built either directly in logic gates or as full 256-byte ROMs in hardware, but such a ROM is usually several times larger than the direct logic implementation. Since each full h block in hardware (see Figure 4.2) involves six q_0 blocks and six q_1 blocks (for $N = 128$), the gate savings mount fairly quickly. The circuit delays in building q_0 or q_1 using logic gates are typically at least as low as those using ROMs, although this metric is certainly somewhat dependent on the particular silicon technology and circuit library available.

It should also be noted that the Twofish round structure can be very nicely pipelined to break up the overall function into smaller and much faster blocks (e.g., q's, key XORs, MDS, PHT, subkey addition, Feistel XOR). None of these operations individually is slow, but trying to run all of them in a single clock cycle does affect the cycle time. In ECB mode, counter mode, or an interleaved chaining mode, the throughput can be dramatically increased by pipelining the Twofish round structure. As a very simple example of two-level pipelining, we could compute the q_i's, key XORs, and MDS multiply for one block during "even" clocks, while the PHT, subkey addition, and Feistel XOR would be computed on the "odd" clocks; a second block is processed in parallel on the alternate clock cycles. Using careful balancing of circuit delays between the two clock phases, this approach allows us to cut the logic delay in half, thus running the clock at twice the speed of an unpipelined approach. Such an approach does not require duplicating the entire Twofish round function logic, but merely the insertion of one extra layer of clocked storage elements (128 bits). Thus, for a very modest increase in gate count, throughput can be doubled, assuming that the application can use one of these cipher modes. It is clear that this general approach can be applied with more levels of pipelining to get higher throughput, although diminishing re-turns are achieved past a certain point. For even higher levels of performance, multiple independent engines can be used to achieve linear speedups at a lin-

Gate Count	h Blocks	Clocks/ Block	Interleave Levels	Clock Speed	Throughput (Mbits/sec)	Startup Clocks
8000	0.25	324	1	80 MHz	32	20
14000	1	72	1	40 MHz	71	4
19000	1	32	1	40 MHz	160	40
23000	2	16	1	40 MHz	320	20
26000	2	32	2	80 MHz	640	20
28000	2	48	3	120 MHz	960	20
30000	2	64	4	150 MHz	1200	20
80000	2	16	1	80 MHz	640	300

Table 5.5. Hardware Tradeoffs (128-bit Key)

ear cost in gates. We see no problem meeting NSA's requirement to "be able to encrypt data at a minimum of 1 Gb/s, pipelined if necessary, in existing technology" [McD97].

Table 5.5 gives hardware size and speed estimates for the case of 128-bit keys. The first line of the table is a "byte serial" implementation. It uses one clock per S-box lookup, and four clocks per h function (including the MDS). We allow two clocks for the PHT and key addition. With four h functions per round, each round requires 18 clock cycles.

The next line uses a fully wired h function, but still computes the round keys on the fly. The other versions all precompute the round subkeys. The last line is a version that precomputes the S-boxes in to dedicated RAM instead of computing the S-boxes on the fly. Depending on the architecture, the logic will grow somewhat in size for larger keys, and the clock speed (or startup time) may increase, but it is believed that a 128-bit AES scheme will be acceptable in the market long enough that most vendors will choose to implement that recommended key length.

These estimates are all based on existing 0.35 micron CMOS technology. All the examples in the table are actually quite small in today's technology, except the final (highest performance non-pipeline) instance, but even that is very doable today and will become fairly inexpensive as the next generation silicon technology (0.25 micron) becomes the industry norm.

6. Twofish Design Philosophy

In the design of Twofish, we tried to stress the following principles:

Performance. When comparing different options, compare them on the basis of relative performance.

Conservativeness. Do not design close to the edge. In other words, leave a margin for error and provide more security than is provably required. Also, try to design against attacks that are not yet known.

Simplicity. Do not include ad hoc design elements without a clear reason or function. Try to design a cipher whose details can be easily kept in one's head.

These principles were applied not only to the overall design of Twofish, but to the design of the S-boxes and the key schedule.

6.1 Performance-Driven Design

The goal of performance-driven design is to build and evaluate ciphers on the basis of performance [SW97]. The early post-DES cipher designs would often compete on the number of rounds in the cipher. The original FEAL paper [SM88], for example, discussed the benefits of a stronger round function and fewer rounds. Other cipher designs of the period—REDOC-II [CW91], LOKI89 [BPS90] and LOKI91 [BKPS93], IDEA [LM91, LMM91]—only considered performance as an afterthought. Khufu/Khafre [Mer91] was the first published algorithm that explicitly used operations that were efficient on 32-bit microprocessors; SEAL [RC94, RC98] is a more recent example. RC2 [Riv97, KRRR98] and Jeroboam [CM98] were designed for 16-bit microprocessors, SOBER [Ros98] for 8-bit ones. Other, more recent designs, do not seem to take performance into account at all. Two 1997 designs, SPEED [Zhe97][1] and Zhu-Guo [ZG97], are significantly slower than alternatives that existed years previous.

   Arbitrary metrics, such as the number of rounds, are not good measures of performance. What is important is the cipher's speed: the number of clock

---

[1] SPEED has been cryptanalyzed in [HKSW98, UTK98, HKR+98].

cycles per byte encrypted. When ciphers are analyzed according to this property, the results can be surprising [SW97]. RC5 might have twice the number of rounds of DES,[2] but since its round function is more than twice as fast as DES', RC5 is faster than DES on most microprocessors.

Even when cryptographers made efforts to use efficient 32-bit operations, they often lacked a full appreciation of low-level software optimization principles associated with high-performance CPUs. Thus, many algorithms are not as efficient as they could be. Minor modifications in the design of Blowfish [Sch94], SEAL [RC94, RC98], and RC4 [Sch96] could improve performance without affecting security [SW97] (or, alternatively, increase the algorithms' complexity without affecting performance). In designing Twofish, we tried to evaluate all design decisions in terms of performance.

Since NIST's platform of choice was the Intel Pentium Pro [NIST97b], we concentrated on that platform. However, we did not ignore performance on other 32-bit CPUs, as well as 8-bit and 16-bit CPUs. If there is any lesson from the past twenty years of microprocessors, it is that the high end gets better and the low end never goes away. Yesterday's top-of-the-line CPUs are currently in smart cards. Today's CPUs will eventually be in smart cards, while the 8-bit microprocessors will move to devices even smaller. The only thing we did not consider in our performance metrics is bitslice implementations [Bih97, SAM97, NM97], since these can only be used in very specialized applications and often require unrealistic implementations; e.g., 32 simultaneous ECB encryptions, or 32 interleaved IVs.[3]

6.1.1 Performance-driven Tradeoffs

During our design, we constantly evaluated the relative performance of different modifications to our round function. Twofish's round function encrypts at about 20 clock cycles; 16 rounds translates to about 320 clock cycles per block encrypted. When we contemplated a change to the round function, we evaluated it in terms of increasing or decreasing the number of rounds to keep performance constant. For example:

- We could have added a data-dependent rotation to the output of the two MDS matrices in each round. This would add 10 clock cycles to the round function on the Pentium (two on the Pentium Pro). To keep the performance constant, we would have to reduce the number of rounds to 11. The question to ask is: Are 11 rounds of the modified cipher more or less secure than 16 rounds of the unmodified cipher?

---

[2] Here we use the term "round" in the traditional sense: as it was defined by DES [NBS77] and has been used to describe Feistel-network ciphers ever since. The RC5 documentation [Riv95] uses the term "round" differently: one RC5-defined round equals two Feistel rounds.

[3] One AES submission, Serpent [BAK98], uses ideas from bitslice implementations to create a cipher that is optimized for 32-bit processors while sacrificing performance on 8-bit processors.

- We could have removed the one-bit rotation. This would have saved clocks equivalent to one Twofish round. Are 17 rounds of this new round function more or less secure than 16 rounds of the old one?

- We could have defined the key-dependent S-boxes using the whole key, instead of half of it. This would have doubled key setup time on high-end machines, and halved encryption speed on memory-poor implementations (where the S-boxes could not be precomputed). On memory-poor machines, we would have to cut the number of rounds in half to be able to afford this. Are 8 rounds of this improved cipher better than 16 rounds of the current design?

This analysis is necessarily dependent on the microprocessor architecture the algorithm is being compared on. While we focused on the Intel Pentium architecture, we also tried to keep 8-bit smart card and hardware implementations in mind. For example, we considered using an 8-by-8 MDS matrix over $GF(2^4)$ to ensure a finer-grained diffusion, instead of a 4-by-4 MDS matrix over $GF(2^8)$; the former would have been no slower on a Pentium but at least twice as slow on a low-memory smart card.

6.2 Conservative Design

In the last decade there has been considerable research in designing ciphers to be resistant to known attacks [Nyb91, Nyb93, OCo94a, OCo94b, OCo94c, Knu94a, Knu94b, Nyb94, DGV94b, Nyb95, NK95, Mat96, Nyb96], such as differential [BS93], linear [Mat94], and related-key cryptanalysis [WH87, Bih94, KSW96, KSW97]. This research has culminated in strong cipher designs—CAST-128 [Ada97a] and MISTY [Mat97] are probably the most noteworthy—as well as some excellent cryptanalytic theory.

However, it is dangerous to rely solely on theory when designing ciphers. Ciphers provably secure against differential cryptanalysis have been attacked with higher-order differentials [Lai94, Knu95b] or the interpolation attack [JK97]: KN-cipher [NK95] was attacked in [JK97, SMK98], Kiefer [Kie96] in [JK97], and a version of CAST in [MSK98a]. The CAST cipher cryptanalyzed in [MSK98a] is not CAST-128, but it does illustrate that while the CAST design procedure [AT93, HT94a] can create ciphers resistant to differential and linear cryptanalysis, it does not create ciphers resistant to whatever form of cryptanalysis comes next. SNAKE [LC97], another cipher provably secure against differential and linear cryptanalysis, was successfully broken using the interpolation attack [MSK98b]. When designing a cipher, it is prudent to assume that new attacks will be developed in order to break it.

We took a slightly different approach in our design. Instead of trying to optimize Twofish against known attacks, we tried to make Twofish strong against both known and unknown attacks. While it is impossible to optimize a cipher design for resisting attacks that are unknown, conservative design and overengineering can instill some confidence.

Many elements of Twofish reflect this philosophy. We used well-studied design elements throughout the algorithm. We started with a Feistel network, probably the most studied block-cipher structure, instead of something newer like an unbalanced Feistel network [SK96, ZMI90] or a generalized Feistel network [Nyb96].

We did not implement multiplication mod $2^{16} + 1$ (as in IDEA or MMB [DGV93]) or data-dependent rotations (as in Madryga [Mad84] and RC5[4] or Akelarre [AGMP96][5]) for non-linearity. The most novel design elements we used—MDS matrices and PHTs—are only intended for diffusion (and are used in Square [DKR97] and SAFER, respectively).

We used key-dependent S-boxes because they offer adequate protection against known statistical attacks and are likely to offer protection to any unknown similar attacks. We defined Twofish at 16 rounds, even though our analysis cannot break anywhere near that number. We added one-bit rotations to prevent potential attacks that relied solely on the byte structure. We designed a very thorough key schedule to prevent related-key and weak-key attacks.

6.3 Simple Design

A guiding design principle behind Twofish is that the round function should be simple enough for us to keep in our heads. Anecdotal evidence from algorithms like FEAL [SM88], CAST, and Blowfish indicates that complicated round functions are not always better than simple ones. Also, complicated round functions are harder to analyze and rely on more ad hoc arguments for security (e.g., REDOC-II [CW91]).

However, with enough rounds, even bad round functions can be made to be secure.[6] Even a simple round function like TEA's [WN95] or RC5's seems secure after 32 rounds [BK98]. In Twofish, we tried to create a simple round function and then iterate it more than enough times for security.

---

[4] RC5's security is almost wholly based on data-dependent rotations. Although initial cryptanalysis was promising [KY95] (see also [Sel98]), subsequent research [KM97, BK98] suggests that there is considerably more to learn about the security properties of data-dependent rotations.

[5] Akelarre was severely broken in [FS97, KR97].

[6] Student cryptography projects bear this observation out. At 16 rounds, the typical student cipher fares rather badly against a standard suite of statistical tests. At 32 rounds, it looks better. At 128 rounds, even the worst designs look very good.

6.3.1 Reusing Primitives

One of the ways to simplify a design is to reuse the same primitives in multiple parts of a cipher. Cryptographic design does not lend itself to the adage of not putting all your eggs in one basket. Since any particular "basket" has the potential of breaking the entire cipher, it makes more sense to use as few baskets as possible—and to scrutinize those baskets intensely.

To that end, we used essentially the same construction (8-by-8-bit key-dependent S-boxes consisting of alternating fixed permutations and subkey XORs followed by an MDS matrix followed by a PHT) in both the key schedule and the round function. The differences were in the key material used (the round function's g function uses a list of key-derived words processed by an RS code; the key schedule's h function uses individual key bytes directly) and the rotations. The rotations represent a performance-driven design trade-off: putting the additional rotations into F would have unacceptably slowed down the cipher performance on high-end machines. The use of the RS code to derive the key material for g adds substantial resistance to related-key attacks.

While many algorithms reuse the encryption operation in their key schedule (e.g., Blowfish, Panama [DC98a, DC98b], RC4, CRISP [Lee96], YTH [YTH96]), and several alternative DES key schedules reuse the DES operation [Knu94b, BB96], we are unaware of any that reuse the same primitives in exactly this manner.[7] We feel that doing so greatly simplifies the analysis of Twofish, since the same kinds of analysis can apply to the cipher in two different ways.

6.3.2 Reversibility

While it is essential that any block cipher be reversible, so that ciphertext can be decrypted back into plaintext, it is not necessary that the identical function be used for encryption and decryption. Some block ciphers are reversible with changes only in the key schedule (e.g., DES, IDEA, Blowfish), while others require different algorithms for encryption and decryption (e.g., SAFER, Serpent, Square).

The Twofish encryption and decryption round functions are slightly different, but are built from the same blocks. That is, it is simple to build a hardware or software module that does both encryption and decryption without duplicating much functionality, but the exact same module cannot both encrypt and decrypt.

Note that having the cipher work essentially the same way in both directions is a nice feature in terms of analysis, since it lets analysts consider

---

[7] The closest idea is an alternate DES key schedule that uses the DES round function, both the 32-bit block input and 48-bit key input, to create round subkeys [Ada97b].

chosen-plaintext and chosen-ciphertext attacks at once, rather than considering them as separate attacks with potentially radically different levels of difficulty [Cop98].

6.4 S-boxes

The security of a cipher can be very sensitive to the particulars of its S-boxes: size, number, values, usage. Ciphers invented before the public discovery of differential cryptanalysis sometimes used arbitrary sources for their S-box entries.

Randomly constructed known S-boxes are unlikely to be secure. Khafre uses S-boxes taken from the RAND tables [RAND55], and it is vulnerable to differential cryptanalysis [BS92]. NewDES[8] [Sco85], with S-boxes derived from the Declaration of Independence [Jeff+76], could be made much stronger with good S-boxes. DES variants with random fixed S-boxes are very likely to be weak [BS93, Mat95], and CMEA was weakened extensively because of a poor S-box choice [WSK97].

Some cipher designers responded to this threat by carefully crafting S-boxes to resist known attacks—DES [Cop94], s^nDES [KPL93, Knu93c, KLPL95], CAST [MA96, Ada97a]—while others relied on random key-dependent S-boxes for security—Khufu, Blowfish, WAKE [Whe94].[9] The best existing attack on Khufu breaks 16 rounds [GC94], while the best attack on Blowfish breaks only four [Rij97]. Serpent [BAK98] reused the DES S-boxes.

GOST [GOST89] navigated a middle course: each application has different fixed S-boxes, turning them into an application-specific family key.

6.4.1 Large S-boxes

S-boxes vary in size, from GOST's 4-by-4-bit S-boxes to Tiger's 8-by-64-bit S-boxes [AB96b]. Large S-boxes are generally assumed to be more secure than smaller ones—a view we share—but at the price of increased storage requirements; DES' eight 6-by-4-bit S-boxes require 256 bytes of storage, while Blowfish's four 8-by-32-bit S-boxes require 4 Kbytes. Certainly input size matters more than output size; an 8-by-64-bit S-box can be stored in 2 Kbytes, while a 16-by-16-bit S-box requires 128 Kbytes. (Note that there is a limit to the advantages of making S-boxes bigger. S-boxes with small input size and very large output size tend to have very good linear approximations; S-boxes with sufficiently large outputs relative to input size are *guaranteed* to have at least one perfect linear approximation [Bih95].)

---

[8] Despite the algorithm name, NewDES is neither a DES variant nor a new algorithm based on DES.

[9] The WAKE design has several variants [Cla97, Cla98]; neither the basic algorithm nor its variants have been extensively cryptanalyzed.

Twofish used the same solution as Square: mid-sized S-boxes (8-by-8-bit) used to construct a large S-box (8-by-32-bit).

6.4.2 Algorithmic S-boxes

S-boxes can either be specified as large tables, like DES, Khufu/Khafre, and YLCY [YLCY98], or derived algebraically, like FEAL, LOKI89/LOKI91 (and LOKI97 [Bro98]), IDEA, and SAFER. The advantage of the former is that there is no mathematical structure that can potentially be used for cryptanalysis. The advantage of the latter is that the S-boxes are more compact, and can be more easily implemented in applications where the ROM or RAM for large tables is not available.

Algebraic S-boxes can result in S-boxes that are vulnerable to differential cryptanalysis: [Mur90] against FEAL, and [Knu93a, Knu93b] against LOKI. Higher-order differential cryptanalysis is especially powerful against algorithms with simple algebraic S-boxes [Knu95b, JK97, SMK98].

Both tabular and algebraic techniques, however, can be used to generate S-boxes with given cryptographic properties simply by testing the results of the generation algorithm. There has been much written about testing S-boxes for their resistance to different statistical attacks, starting from the work done on DES [AT90, AT93, Cop94, Ada97a, Mor98].

In Twofish we tried to do both: we chose to build our 8-by-8-bit S-boxes algorithmically out of 4-by-4-bit S-boxes. However, we chose the 4-by-4-bit S-boxes randomly and then extensively tested the resulting 8-by-8-bit S-boxes against the cryptographic properties we required. This idea is similar to the one used in CS-Cipher [SV98].

6.4.3 Key-dependent S-boxes

S-boxes are either fixed for all keys or key dependent. It is our belief that ciphers with key-dependent S-boxes are, in general, more secure than fixed S-boxes.

There are two different philosophies regarding key-dependent S-boxes. In some ciphers, the S-box is constructed specifically to ensure that no two entries are identical—Khufu and WAKE—while others simply create the S-box randomly and hope for the best: REDOC-II [CW91] and Blowfish [Sch94]. The latter results in a simpler key schedule, but may result in weaknesses (e.g., a weakness in reduced-round variants of Blowfish [Vau96a]). Another strategy is to generate key-dependent S-boxes from a known secure S-box and a series of strict mathematical rules: e.g., Biham-DES [BB94].

Most key-dependent S-boxes are created by some process completely orthogonal to the underlying cipher. SEAL, for example, uses SHA [NIST93] to create its key-dependent S-boxes. Blowfish uses repeated iterations of itself. The results are S-boxes that are effectively random, but the cost is an enormous performance penalty in key setup time.[10]

An alternative is to build the S-boxes using fairly simple key-dependent operations from fixed S-boxes. This results in a much faster key setup, but unless the creation algorithm is extensively cryptanalyzed together with the encryption algorithm, unwanted synergies could lead to attacks on the resulting cipher.

To avoid differential (as well as high-order differential, linear, and related-key) attacks, we made the small S-boxes key dependent. It is our belief that while random key-dependent S-boxes can offer acceptable security if used correctly, the benefits of a surjective S-box are worth the additional complexities that constructing them entails. So, to avoid attacks based on non-surjective round functions [BB95, RP95b, RPD97, CWSK98], we made the 8-by-8-bit S-boxes bijective.

This construction is similar to Skipjack's use of a single fixed 8-by-8-bit S-box, four key bytes, and a 4-round Feistel structure to create five different 16-by-16-bit key-dependent S-boxes [NSA98].

However, there is really no such thing as a key-dependent S-box. Twofish uses a complex multi-stage series of S-boxes and round subkeys that are often precomputed as key-dependent S-boxes for efficiency purposes. (For example, see Figure 4.3 on page 18.) We often used this conceptualization when carrying out our own cryptanalysis against Twofish.

6.5 The Key Schedule

An algorithm's key schedule is the mechanism that distributes key material to the different parts of the cipher that need it, expanding the key material in the process. This is necessary for three reasons:

- There are fewer key bits provided as input to the cipher than are needed by the cipher.

- The key bits used in each round must be unique to the round in order to avoid "slide" attacks [Wag95b].

- The cipher must be secure against an attacker with partial knowledge or control over some key bits.

When key schedules are poorly designed, they often lead to strange cipher properties: large classes of equivalent keys, self-inverse keys, and so forth. These properties can often aid an attacker in a real-world attack. For example, the DES weak (self-inverse) keys have been exploited in many attacks on larger cryptographic mechanisms built from DES [Knu95a], and the S-1

---

[10] For example, setting up a single Blowfish key takes as much time as encrypting 520 blocks, or 4160 bytes, of data.

[Anon95] cipher was broken due to a bad key-schedule design [Wag95a]. Even worse, they can make attacks on the cipher easier, and some attacks on the cipher will be focused directly at the key schedule, such as related-key differential attacks [KSW96, KSW97]. These attacks can be especially devastating when the cipher is used in a hash function construction.

Key schedules can be divided into several broad categories [CDN98]. In some key schedules, knowledge of a round subkey uniquely specifies bits of other round subkeys. In some ciphers the bits are just reused, as in DES, IDEA, and LOKI; and in others some manipulation of the round subkeys is required to determine the other round subkeys: e.g., CAST and SAFER. Other key schedules are designed so that knowledge of one round subkey does not directly specify bits of other round subkeys. Either the round subkey itself is used to generate the other round subkeys in some cryptographically secure manner, as in RC5 and CS-Cipher [SV98], or a one-way function is used to generate the round subkeys (sometimes the block cipher itself): e.g., Blowfish, Serpent [BAK98], ICE[11] [Kwa97], and Shark.

Some simple design principles guided our development of the key schedule for Twofish:

Design the Key Schedule for the Cipher. This is not simply a cryptographic PRNG or hash function grafted onto the cipher; the Twofish key schedule is instead an integral part of the whole cipher design.

Reuse the Same Primitives. The Twofish key schedule's subkey generation mechanism, h, is built from the same primitives as the Twofish round function. This allowed us to apply much of the same analysis to both the round function and the subkey generation. This also makes for a relatively simple picture of the cipher and key schedule together. It is reasonable to consider one round's operations and the derivation of its subkeys at the same time.

Use All Key Bytes the Same Way. All key material goes through h (or g, which is the same function). That is, the only way a key bit can affect the cipher is after it defines a key-dependent S-box. This allows us to analyze the properties of the key schedule in terms of the properties of the byte permutations.

Make It Hard to Attack Both S-box and Subkey Generation. The key material used to derive the key-dependent S-boxes in g is derived from the key using an RS code having properties similar to those of the MDS matrix. Deriving the key material in this way maximizes the difficulties of an attacker's trying to mount any kind of related-key attack on the cipher, by giving him conflicting requirements between controlling the S-box keys and controlling the subkeys.

---

[11] ICE was cryptanalyzed in [RKR98].

The key schedule design of some other ciphers has led to various undesirable properties. These properties, such as the existence of equivalent keys; DES-style weak, semi-weak, and quasi-weak keys; and DES-style complementation properties do not necessarily make the cipher weak. However, they tend to make it harder to use the cipher securely. With our key schedule, we can make convincing arguments that none of these properties exists.

6.5.1 Performance Issues

Key schedules vary widely in performance. The DES key schedule can be computed in less than the time required to do one encryption. The Blowfish key schedule requires the time equivalent to 521 encryptions to complete. Most other algorithms fall somewhere in the middle.

For large messages, performance of the key schedule is minor compared to performance of the encryption and decryption functions. For smaller messages, key setup can overwhelm encryption speed. In the design of Twofish, we tried to balance these two items. Our performance criteria included:

- The key schedule must be precomputable for maximal efficiency. This involves trying to minimize the amount of storage required to keep the precomputed key material.

- The key schedule must work "on the fly," deriving each block of subkey material as it is needed, with as little required memory as possible.

- The key schedule must be reasonably efficient for hardware implementations.

- The key schedule must have minimal latency for changing keys.[12]

If security were not an issue, we would design a simple key schedule where the key bits were used in some natural order, like Skipjack, or with some minimal shuffling, like DES and IDEA. However, these key schedules cause weaknesses when the block cipher is used as a one-way hash function.

If performance were not an issue, it would make sense to simply use a one-way hash function to expand the key into the subkeys and S-box entries, as is done in Khufu, Blowfish, and SEAL. However, the AES efficiency requirements make such an approach unacceptable.

Balancing these two requirements led us to design a relatively simple key schedule with a very complicated analysis.

---

[12] In its comments on the AES criteria, the NSA suggested that "a goal should be that two blocks could be enciphered with different keys in virtually the same time as two blocks could be enciphered with the same key" [McD97]. The cynical reader would immediately conclude that the NSA is concerned with the efficiency of their brute-force keysearch machines. However, there are implementations where key agility is a valid concern. Key-stretching techniques can always be used to frustrate brute-force attacks [QDD86, KSHW98]. A better defense, of course, is to always use keys too large to make a brute-force search practicable, and to generate them randomly.

7. The Design of Twofish

7.1 The Round Structure

An n-bit block cipher with a k-bit key uses its key to select among 2^k possible different permutations on the 2^n possible inputs/outputs to the cipher. This can be imagined as an enormous (virtual) codebook; each possible n-bit plaintext block leads to only one possible n-bit ciphertext block under a given key. Data is encrypted in n-bit chunks, with each n-bit chunk's encryption independent of other encryptions. This can be contrasted with a stream cipher, where different parts of the message are treated differently. The goal for a block cipher is to be impossible in practice to distinguish from a random permutation family on n-bit blocks.

DES is a 64-bit cipher, and most block ciphers in the literature are also 64-bit ciphers; AES, on the other hand, requires a 128-bit block cipher.

A product cipher (sometimes called an iterative block cipher) is a block cipher made by iterating a fairly simple round function many times, each time with its own key. Thus, a 4-round product cipher would look like

$$E_K(X) = R_{K_3}(R_{K_2}(R_{K_1}(R_{K_0}(X))))$$

where $K_{0...3}$ are functions of K.

Each round function, $R_K()$, is actually a weak block cipher. It implements the basic Shannon principles of encryption, confusion and diffusion [Sha49], and can be viewed as a key-dependent transformation of plaintext into ciphertext. It is weak in the sense that if an attacker knows much about the plaintext (such as simple plaintext statistics), he can quickly break the round function and recover its round key.

Even a very weak round function is resistant to attack when the sequence of inputs to the function is random and unknown to the attacker. Iterating the round function many times makes the input to the last round very hard for an attacker to guess; this prevents the attacker from being able to attack the last round, and thus prevents him from attacking the cipher as a whole. An increased number of rounds means a decrease in the throughput of a cipher, but an attack effective against an n-round version of a particular algorithm might be ineffective against an $n + 1$-round version. Some of the best cipher analysis shows how to break reduced-round variants of the design and why each attack cannot be extended to a greater number of rounds.

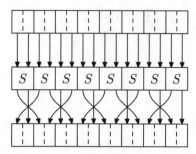

Fig. 7.1. A Simple SP-network Construction

7.1.1 Common Block Cipher Structures

All well-known block ciphers use this iterated round structure, and given the number of different algorithms that have been proposed over the years, there are surprisingly few round-function structures.

SP Networks. These were named by Horst Feistel [Fei73, FNS75], although the ideas are much older. "SP" stands for "substitution-permutation," and one round of an SP-network consists of a substitution layer followed by a permutation layer. These two layers are meant to capture C. Shannon's fundamental notions in cipher design of confusion and diffusion [Sha49]. The substitution layer confuses the statistics of the input by breaking it up into smaller pieces and performing substitutions on those pieces. The permutation layer diffuses the statistics of the input by rearranging the bits output from the substitution layer, each of which should be a function of more than one input bit. Figure 7.1 gives a simple SP-network construction (which is not secure).

SP-networks have been well-studied in the cryptographic literature; examples of SP-network designs are SAFER [Mas94], Shark [RDP+96], and Square [DKR97].[1] Rotor machines can be viewed as SP networks: the rotor is a substitution layer, and the key-dependent stepping of the rotor is the permutation.

Feistel Networks. These were invented by Horst Feistel [FNS75] in his design of Lucifer[Fei73]. The fundamental building block of a Feistel network is the F function, a key-dependent mapping of an input string onto an output string. An F function is always non-linear and possibly non-surjective[2]

$$F : \{0,1\}^{n/2} \times \{0,1\}^k \mapsto \{0,1\}^{n/2}$$

where n is the block size of the Feistel network, and F is a function taking $n/2$ bits of the block and k bits of a key as input, and producing an output of

---

[1] See also [HT94b].

[2] A non-surjective F function is one in which not all outputs in the output space can occur.

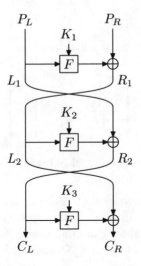

Fig. 7.2. A 3-round Feistel Network

length $n/2$ bits. In each round, the "source block" is the input to F, and the output of F is XORed with the "target block," after which these two blocks swap places for the next round. Feistel networks are the most studied block cipher structure, and are the basis for most of the algorithms proposed in the literature.

Figure 7.2 shows a 3-round Feistel network. Here (P_L, P_R) is the plaintext, (C_L, C_R) is the ciphertext, (L_1, R_1) and (L_2, R_2) are intermediate values, and K_1, K_2, and K_3 are round-dependent subkeys.

In order to decrypt the ciphertext (C_L, C_R) one starts at the tail end of the network and works backwards. It is important to understand that data flows the same direction through F even during decryption and that the reversibility of the network comes from the property that $\alpha \oplus \alpha = 0$ for any α. This is easy to see if we compute the ciphertext as a function of the plaintext:

$$
\begin{aligned}
(L_1, R_1) &= (P_L, P_R \oplus F(P_L)) \\
(L_2, R_2) &= (R_1, L_1 \oplus F(R_1)) \\
(C_L, C_R) &= (R_2, L_2 \oplus F(R_2))
\end{aligned}
$$

Then reversing the network we find:

$$
\begin{aligned}
(L_2, R_2) &= (C_R \oplus F(C_L), C_L) \\
(L_1, R_1) &= (R_2 \oplus F(L_2), L_2) \\
(P_L, P_R) &= (R_1 \oplus F(L_1), L_1)
\end{aligned}
$$

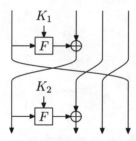

Fig. 7.3. An Incomplete 2-round Feistel Network

Incomplete Feistel Networks. This is a variant of the Feistel network where the F-function has an input and output size that is some fraction of n other than $n/2$. Skipjack, for example, has an F-function whose input and output is one-quarter the block size [NSA98]:

$$F : \{0,1\}^{n/4} \times \{0,1\}^k \mapsto \{0,1\}^{n/4}$$

Figure 7.3 shows a 2-round variant of an incomplete Feistel network whose F-function also has an input and output of one-quarter the block size. In each round, the source block is the input into F, and is XORed with the target block; the other bits are unused in the round (hence the name "incomplete Feistel network").[3] Then, the subblocks are rotated among each other, so that each subblock becomes the source and target in subsequent rounds. The first incomplete Feistel networks in the literature were Khufu and Khafre [Mer91], although their similarities to shift-register–based stream ciphers (common in military cryptographic hardware) make it likely that there is a significant amount of classified literature on their design and analysis.

Source-heavy Feistel Networks. In this variant of the Feistel network, the source and target blocks are of different size, with the source block larger than the target block. Both RC2 [Riv97] and MacGuffin [BS95] have a 48-by-16-bit source-heavy structure; the F-function takes a 48-bit input and produces a 16-bit output. The underlying block cipher in MD4 [Riv91] and MD5 [Riv92] are 96-by-32-bit structures. SHA-1 [NIST93] is a 128-by-32-bit structure. Figure 7.4 shows a source-heavy 2-round Feistel network.

Target-heavy Feistel Networks. These are the opposite: Feistel-type networks where the F-function has a larger output than input. Tiger [AB96b] uses a 64-by-192-bit target-heavy structure. Figure 7.5 shows a target-heavy 2-round Feistel network.

Other Variants. There are other round function structures, which are variants of the above. IDEA [LMM91] is a variant of an SP-network, for example. In "fenced" constructions, multiple parallel implementations of the same structure are separated by specially constructed mixing operations [Rit96].

---

[3] A taxonomy of these Feistel-network variants can be found in [SK96].

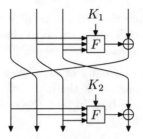

Fig. 7.4. A Source-heavy 2-round Feistel Network

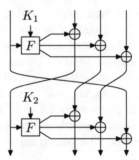

Fig. 7.5. A Target-heavy 2-round Feistel Network

Although there has been some analysis of incomplete, source-heavy, and target-heavy Feistel networks [SK96], they are not nearly as well-understood as Feistel and SP networks. Given the current state of analysis, we discarded any of the newer structures.

Our Choice. Twofish was designed as a Feistel network, primarily because it is one of the most studied block-cipher building blocks, but also because the Feistel structure takes care of its own inverse. The structure of a Feistel network means that the F function need only be calculated in one direction.[4] This means that we were able to use operations in our F function that are inefficient in the other direction, and make do with tables and constants for one direction only. Contrast this with an SP-network, which must execute its encryption function in both the forward and backward directions.

7.2 The Key-dependent S-boxes

A fundamental component of Twofish is the set of four key-dependent S-boxes. These must have several properties:

- The four different S-boxes actually need to be different.

---

[4] In fact, the F function can be non-surjective, as it is in DES or Blowfish.

- Few or no keys may cause the S-boxes used to be "weak," in the sense of having high-probability differential or linear characteristics, or in the sense of having a very simple algebraic representation.

- There should be few or no pairs of keys that define the same S-boxes. That is, changing even one bit of the key used to define an S-box should always lead to a different S-box. In fact, these pairs of keys should lead to extremely different S-boxes.

7.2.1 The Fixed Permutations q_0 and q_1

The construction method for building q_0 and q_1 from 4-bit permutations (specified in Section 4.3.5) was chosen because it decreases hardware and memory costs for some implementations, as discussed previously, without adding any apparent weaknesses to the cipher. It is helpful to recall that these individual fixed-byte permutations are used only to construct the key-dependent S-boxes, which, in turn, are used only within the h and g functions. In particular, the individual characteristics of q_0 and q_1 are not terribly relevant (except perhaps in some related-key attacks), because Twofish always uses at least three of these permutations in series together with at least two XORs with key material bytes.

Consideration was initially given to using random full 8-bit permutations for q_0 and q_1, as well as algebraically derived permutations (e.g., multiplicative inverses over $GF(2^8)$) that have slightly better individual permutation characteristics, but no substantial improvement was found when composite keyed S-boxes were constructed and compared to the q_0 and q_1 used in Twofish.

The construction of q_0 and q_1 is a basically a 2-round SP network. We investigated several possible constructions. The main alternative was a 3- or 4-round Feistel network. We chose the SP network, as it has a lower circuit-depth. This reduces the propagation delay in a hardware implementation of the q-box. As several q-boxes are used in series, an increase in propagation delay has significant effects on the hardware speed of the cipher.

The q_0 and q_1 permutations were constructed by performing a random search for the 4-bit permutations t_0, t_1, t_2, and t_3. Using the notation of Matsui [Mat96], we define

$$\mathrm{DP}_{\max}(q) = \max_{a \neq 0, b} \Pr_X[q(X \oplus a) \oplus q(X) = b]$$

and

$$\mathrm{LP}_{\max}(q) = \max_{a, b \neq 0} \left(2 \Pr_X[X \cdot a = q(X) \cdot b] - 1\right)^2$$

where q is the mapping $\mathrm{DP}_{\max}$ and $\mathrm{LP}_{\max}$ are being computed for, the probabilities are taken over a uniformly distributed X, and the operator $\cdot$ computes the overall parity of the bitwise-AND of its two operands. Only fixed permutations with $\mathrm{DP}_{\max} \leq 10/256$, $\mathrm{LP}_{\max} \leq 1/16$, and fewer than three fixed points[5] were accepted as potential candidates. These criteria alone rejected over 99.8 percent of all randomly chosen permutations of the given construction. Pairs of permutations meeting these criteria were then evaluated as potential (q_0, q_1) pairs, computing various metrics when combined with key material into Twofish's S-box structure, as described below.

The actual q_0 and q_1 chosen were one of several pairs with virtually identical statistics that were found with only a few tens of hours of searching on Pentium class computers. Each permutation has $\text{DP}_{\max} = 10/256$ and $\text{LP}_{\max} = 1/16$; q_0 has one fixed point, while q_1 has two fixed points.

7.2.2 The S-boxes

Each S-box is defined with two, three, or four bytes of key material, depending on the Twofish key size. This is done as follows for 128-bit Twofish keys:

$$
\begin{aligned}
s_0(x) &= q_1[q_0[q_0[x] \oplus s_{0,0}] \oplus s_{1,0}] \\
s_1(x) &= q_0[q_0[q_1[x] \oplus s_{0,1}] \oplus s_{1,1}] \\
s_2(x) &= q_1[q_1[q_0[x] \oplus s_{0,2}] \oplus s_{1,2}] \\
s_3(x) &= q_0[q_1[q_1[x] \oplus s_{0,3}] \oplus s_{1,3}]
\end{aligned}
$$

where the $s_{i,j}$ are the bytes derived from the key bytes using the RS matrix. Note that if $s_{0,i} = s_{0,j}$ and $s_{1,i} = s_{1,j}$ for $i \neq j$, then $s_i(x) \neq s_j(x)$ for most values of x. In fact, as each S-box uses a unique order of q-boxes, it is extremely unlikely that two different S-boxes could produce the identical mapping.

Note that when all $s_{i,j} = 0$, then $s_0(x) = q_1[s_1(q_1^{-1}[x])]$. Similar relationships hold between other S-boxes. We have not been able to find any weaknesses resulting from this, as long as q_0 and q_1 have no high-probability differential characteristics.

In some sense this construction is similar to a rotor machine [PB92, DK85, Bau93, Bau97], with two different types of rotor (q_0 and q_1). The first rotor is fixed, and the fixed offset between two rotors is specified by a key byte. We did not find any useful cryptanalysis from this parallel, but someone else might.

For the 128-bit key, we have experimentally verified that each $N/8$-bit key used to define a byte permutation results in a distinct permutation. For example, in the case of a 128-bit key, the S-box s_0 uses 16 bits of key material. Each of the 2^{16} s_0 permutations defined is distinct, as is also the case for s_1, s_2, and s_3. We have not yet exhaustively tested longer key lengths, but we conjecture that all S-boxes generated by our construction are distinct. We also conjecture that this would be the case for almost all choices of q_0 and q_1 meeting the basic criteria discussed above.

---

[5] A fixed point for a function f is a value x such that $f(x) = x$.

Key Size	Max Value	$-\log_2(\Pr(\mathrm{DP}_{\max} = x/256))$								
		$x =$	8	10	12	14	16	18	20	22	24
128 bits	18/256		15.4	1.3	0.9	4.1	8.0	12.0			
192 bits	24/256		15.2	1.3	0.9	4.1	8.0	12.2	16.5	20.8	25.0
256 bits*	22/256		15.1	1.3	0.9	4.1	8.0	12.2	16.7	22.0	

Table 7.1. $\mathrm{DP}_{\max}$ Over All Keys

7.2.3 Exhaustive and Statistical Analysis

Given the fixed permutations q_0 and q_1, and the definitions for how to construct s_0, s_1, s_2, and s_3 from them, we have performed extensive testing of the characteristics of these key-dependent S-boxes. In the 128-bit key case, all testing has been performed exhaustively, which is feasible because each S-box uses only 16 bits of key material. In many cases, however, only statistical (i.e., Monte Carlo) testing has been possible for the larger key sizes. In this section, we present and discuss these results. It is our hope to complete exhaustive testing over time for the larger key sizes where feasible, but the probability distributions obtained for the statistical tests give us a fairly high degree of confidence that no surprises are in store.

Computing $\mathrm{DP}_{\max}$ Over All Keys. Table 7.1 shows the $\mathrm{DP}_{\max}$ distribution for the various key sizes. A detailed explanation of the format of this table will also help in understanding the other tables in this section. An asterisk (*) next to a key size in the tables discussed in this section indicates that the entries in that row are a statistical distribution using Monte Carlo sampling of key bits, not an exhaustive test. For example, in Table 7.1, only the 256-bit key row uses statistical sampling; the 128-bit and 192-bit cases involve an exhaustive test. Clearly, the maximum value from a statistical sample is not a guaranteed maximum.

Note that, for 128-bit keys, each S-box has a $\mathrm{DP}_{\max}$ value no larger than 18/256. The remaining columns give the distribution of observed $\mathrm{DP}_{\max}$ values. Each entry is expressed as the negative base-2 logarithm of the fraction of S-boxes with the given value (or value range), with blank entries indicating that no value in the range was found. For example, in the $N = 128$ case only one of every $2^{12.0}$ key-dependent S-boxes has $\mathrm{DP}_{\max} = 18/256$, while over half (1 in $2^{0.9}$) have $\mathrm{DP}_{\max} = 12/256$. These statistics are taken over all four S-boxes (s_0, s_1, s_2, s_3), so a total of 4×2^{16} (i.e., 256K) S-boxes were evaluated for the 128-bit key case. Each Monte Carlo sampling involves at least 2^{16} S-boxes, but in many cases the number is considerably larger.

Computing $\mathrm{LP}_{\max}$ Over All Keys. Table 7.2 shows the distribution of $\mathrm{LP}_{\max}$ for the various key sizes. Observe that the vast majority of Twofish S-boxes have $\mathrm{LP}_{\max} < (88/256)^2$, although there is a small fraction of S-boxes with larger values. For 128-bit keys, no Twofish S-box has an $\mathrm{LP}_{\max}$ value

Key size	Max Value	$-\log_2(\Pr(\text{LP}_{\max} = (x/256)^2))$						
		$x=$ 56..63	64..71	72..79	80..87	88..95	96..103	104..111
128 bits	$(100/256)^2$	9.3	1.0	1.2	4.2	8.0	12.4	
192 bits*	$(104/256)^2$	9.3	1.0	1.2	4.2	8.2	12.2	17.0
256 bits*	$(108/256)^2$	9.4	1.0	1.2	4.2	8.1	12.5	17.4

Table 7.2. $\text{LP}_{\max}$ Over All Keys.

Key Size	Max Value	$-\log_2(\Pr(\# \text{ fixed points} = x))$										
		$x=$ 0	1	2	3	4	5	6	7	8	9	10
128 bits	8	1.4	1.4	2.4	4.1	6.0	8.2	11.1	14.1	17.0		
192 bits	10	1.4	1.4	2.4	4.0	6.0	8.4	10.9	13.8	16.8	19.8	23.4
256 bits*	10	1.4	1.4	2.4	4.0	6.0	8.4	10.9	13.7	16.8	21.0	21.0
random		1.4	1.4	2.4	4.0	6.0	8.3	10.9	13.7	16.7	19.9	23.2

Table 7.3. Number of Fixed Points Over All Keys

greater than $(100/256)^2$, while the maximum value is somewhat higher for larger key sizes. Monte Carlo statistics are given for the larger two key sizes, since the computational load for computing $\text{LP}_{\max}$ is roughly a factor of 15 higher than for $\text{DP}_{\max}$.

Counting Fixed Points Over All Keys. The distribution of the number of permutation fixed points for various key sizes is given in Table 7.3. A fixed point of an S-box s_i is a value x for which $x = s_i(x)$. This metric does not necessarily have any direct cryptographic significance. However, it is a useful way to verify that the S-boxes are behaving similarly to random S-boxes, since it is possible to compute the theoretical distribution of fixed points for random S-boxes. The probabilities for random bijective S-boxes is given in the last row. (The probability of n fixed points is approximately $e^{-1}/n!$.) The Twofish S-box distributions of fixed points over all keys match theory fairly well.

Differences between S-boxes. The metrics discussed so far give us a fair level of confidence that the Twofish method of constructing key-dependent S-boxes does a reasonable job of approximating a random set of S-boxes, when viewed individually. Another possible concern is how different the various Twofish S-boxes are from each other, for a given key length. This issue is of particular interest in dealing with related-key attacks, but it also has an important bearing on the ability of an attacker to model the S-boxes. Despite the fact that the Twofish S-boxes are key dependent, if the entire set (or large subsets) of S-boxes, taken as a black box, are very closely related, the benefit of key dependency is severely weakened. As a pathological example, consider a fixed 8-bit permutation $q[x]$ which has very good $\text{DP}_{\max}$ and $\text{LP}_{\max}$ values, but which is used as a key-dependent family of S-boxes simply by defining

$s_k(x) = q[x] \oplus k$. It is true that each s_k permutation also has good individual metrics, but the class of s permutations is so closely related that conventional differential and linear cryptanalysis techniques can probably be effectively applied without knowing the key k. The Twofish S-box structure has been carefully designed with this issue in mind.

For example, if an attacker wants to perform a differential attack that is not key dependent, then he can view each S-box as a series of q-boxes and XORs with key bytes. The direct consequence is that he needs to use 3 to 5 differential characteristics of q-boxes per S-box, which makes the probability of any differential characteristic much smaller.

In one class of related-key attacks, an attacker attempts to modify the key bytes in such a way as to minimize the differences in the round subkey values A_i, B_i. Since the Twofish S-box structure is used in computing A_i and B_i, with M_e and M_o as key material, respectively, a measure of the differential characteristics of A_i (or B_i) across keys M will help us understand both how different the S-boxes are from each other and how likely such an attack is to succeed.

To this end, let us first look at how many consecutive values of A_i with a fixed XOR difference can be generated for two different keys. That is, if A_i is the sequence for the key M and A_i' is the sequence for the key M', then we want to examine how many consecutive A_i, A_i' satisfy $A_i \oplus A_i' = \delta$ for some fixed XOR difference δ. A nearly identical argument holds for the B_i, so we can restrict our attention to the A_i, and furthermore, we can consider only those changes which affect M_e, the key material used by the S-boxes when computing A_i.

If we let y_i be the output sequence for one S-box used in generating the A_i, and y_i' the output sequence for the same S-box when generating the A_i', then we can consider the difference sequence $y_i^* = y_i \oplus y_i'$. For example, in the 128-bit key case, with 16 bits of key material per S-box, there are about 2^{31} distinct pairs of keys for each S-box, so there would be 2^{31} such difference sequences, each of length 20. We can then consider the probability of having a "run" of n consecutive equal values in the sequence. If n can be made to approach 20, then a related-key attack might be able to control the entire sequence of A_i values, and, even worse, our belief in the independence of the key-dependent S-boxes must be called seriously into question. Note that an attacker has exactly 16 bits of freedom for a single S-box in the 128-bit key case, so intuitively it seems unlikely that he should be able to force a given difference sequence that is very long.

Table 7.4 shows the distribution of run lengths of the same XOR difference y_i^* for consecutive i. For random byte sequences, we would theoretically expect that $\Pr(\text{XOR run length} = n)$ should be roughly $2^{-8(n-1)}$, which matches quite nicely with the behavior observed in the table. It can be seen that the probability of injecting a constant difference into more than five consecutive subkey entries is extremely low, which is reassuring.

Key Size	Max Value	$-\log_2(\Pr(\text{XOR run length} = n))$				
		$n =$ 1	2	3	4	5
128 bits	5	0.01	7.98	15.95	23.89	30.00
192 bits*	4	0.01	7.98	15.93	23.69	
256 bits*	5	0.01	7.98	15.93	24.02	30.29

Table 7.4. Subkey XOR Difference Run Lengths

Key Size	Max Value	$-\log_2(\Pr(\text{max \# equal XOR differences} = n))$						
		$x =$ 1	2	3	4	4	6	7
128 bits	7	1.1	0.9	5.9	11.6	17.6	23.9	31.0
192 bits*	7	1.1	0.9	5.9	11.7	17.8	23.9	29.0
256 bits*	7	1.1	0.9	5.9	11.7	17.7	23.8	29.3

Table 7.5. "Mini"-DP_{max} Subkey Distribution

Table 7.5 shows the results of measuring this same property in a different way. Instead of requiring a run of n consecutive identical differences, this metric is similar to a "mini"-DP_{max}, computed over only the 20 input values used in the subkey generation (e.g., $0, 2, 4, \ldots, 38$). The quantity measured is the maximum number of equal differences out of the 20 values generated, across key pairs. In other words, while it may be difficult to generate a large run, it may be possible to generate equal values in a large (non-consecutive) fraction of the set of differences. However, the results are again very encouraging, showing that it is extremely difficult to force more than five or six differences to be identical. This also shows that it is not possible to influence only a few A_i, as that would require many zero differences.

Comparison to Random S-boxes. For every metric discussed here, a similar distribution using randomly generated 8-bit permutations has been generated for purposes of comparison. For example, DP_{max} was computed for a set of 2^{16} randomly generated permutations, and the resulting distribution of DP_{max} values was compared to that of the Twofish key-dependent S-boxes. For each metric, the probability distributions looked virtually identical to those obtained for the Twofish set of key-dependent S-boxes, except for small fluctuations on the tail ends of the distribution, as should be expected. This similarity is comforting, as is the fact that the probability distributions for each metric look quite similar across key sizes. These results help confirm our belief that, from a statistical standpoint, the Twofish S-box sets behave largely like a randomly chosen set of permutations.

7.3 MDS Matrix

The four bytes output from the four S-boxes are multiplied by a 4-by-4 MDS matrix over $GF(2^8)$. This matrix multiply is the principal diffusion mechanism in Twofish. The MDS property guarantees that the number of changed input bytes plus the number of changed output bytes is at least five. In other words, any change in a single input byte is guaranteed to change all four output bytes; any change in any two input bytes is guaranteed to change at least three output bytes; and so forth. More than 2^{127} such MDS matrices exist, but the Twofish MDS matrix is also carefully chosen with the property of preserving the number of bytes changed even after the rotation in the round function.

7.3.1 Non-key-dependent Coefficients

The MDS matrix used in Twofish has fixed coefficients. Initially, some thought was given to making the matrix itself key dependent, but such a scheme would require the verification that the key-dependent values in fact formed an MDS matrix, adding a non-trivial computational load to the key selection and key scheduling process. However, it should be noted that there are many acceptable MDS matrices, even with the extended properties discussed below.

7.3.2 Implementation Issues

For software implementation on a modern microprocessor, the MDS matrix multiply is normally implemented using four lookup tables, each consisting of 256 32-bit words, so the particular coefficients used in the matrix do not affect performance. This works because the actual transformation defined by the MDS matrix is purely linear over $GF(2)$. That is, each of the output bits is the XOR of a subset of the input bits and hence we can XOR four table lookups together to compute the entire 32-bit word. However, for smart cards and in hardware, "simple" coefficients, as in Square [DKR97], can make implementations cheaper and faster.

7.3.3 Preserving Diffusion Properties after Rotation

Unlike the MDS matrix used in Square, Twofish does not use the inverse matrix for decryption because of its Feistel structure, nor is there a requirement that the matrix be a circulant matrix. However, because of the rotation applied after the XOR within the round function, it is desirable to select the MDS matrix carefully to preserve the diffusion properties even after the rotation. For both encryption and decryption, a right rotation by one bit occurs after the XOR. This direction of rotation is chosen to preserve the MDS property with respect to the PHT addition $a + 2b$, since the rotation undoes the shift applied to b as part of the PHT. It is true that the most significant bit of b is still "lost" in this half of the PHT, but the MDS properties for three of the bytes are still fully guaranteed with respect to b, and they are met with probability 254/255 for the fourth byte.

The effect of the rotation on the unshifted PHT additions also needs to be addressed. A single byte input change to the MDS matrix will change all four output bytes, which affect the round function output, but after rotation there is no such guarantee. If a byte value difference of 1 is one output from the matrix multiply, performing a 32-bit rotate on the result will shift in one bit from the next byte in the 32-bit word and shift out the only non-zero bit. The MDS matrix coefficients in Twofish are carefully selected so that, if a byte difference 1 is output from the matrix multiply with a single byte input change, the next highest byte is guaranteed to have its least significant bit changed as well. Thus, if the rotation shifts out the only original flipped bit, it will also shift in a flipped bit from the next byte.

The construction used to preserve this property after rotation is actually very simple. The idea is to choose a small set of non-zero elements of $GF(2^8)$ with the property that, for each pair x, y in the set, if $x * a = 1$, then $y * a$ (i.e., y/x) has the least significant bit set. We then use such a set as the coefficients to construct an MDS matrix. Observe that this property is reflexive; i.e., if $x = y$, then $y/x = 1$, so the property holds. It is intuitively obvious (and empirically verified) that the probability that two random field elements satisfy this property is roughly one half, so it should not be difficult to find such sets of elements. Also, since over 75 percent of all 4-by-4 matrices over $GF(2^8)$ are MDS, the hope of finding such a matrix sounds reasonable.

A computer search was executed over all primitive polynomials of degree eight, looking for sets of three "simple" elements x,y,z with the above property. Simple in this context means that $x * a$ for arbitrary a can be easily computed using at most a few shifts and XORs. Several dozen sets of suitable values were found, each of which allowed several MDS matrices with the three values. The primitive polynomial $v(x) = x^8 + x^6 + x^5 + x^3 + x^0$ was selected, together with the field elements 01, EF, and 5B (using hexadecimal notation and the field element to byte value correspondence of Chapter 4). The element EF is actually $\beta^{-2} + \beta^{-1} + 1$, where β is a root of $v(x)$, and 5B is $\beta^{-2} + 1$, so multiplication by these elements consists of two LFSR right shifts mod $v(x)$, plus a few byte XORs.

Alternate Constructions. It should also be noted that a very different type of construction could be used to preserve MDS properties on rotation. Use of an 8-by-8 MDS matrix over $GF(2^4)$ will guarantee eight output nibble changes for every input nibble change. Because the changes now are nibble-based, a 1-bit rotation may shift the only non-zero bit of a nibble out of a byte, but the other nibble remains entirely contained in the byte. In fact, it can easily be seen that this construction preserves the MDS property nicely even for multi-bit rotations. Unfortunately, 8-by-8 MDS matrices over $GF(2^4)$

Hamming Weight	Number of Occurrences	Number with MSB Set
8	7/1020	1
9	23/1020	4
10	42/1020	15

Table 7.6. Hamming Weight Distribution of MDS Output after 1-byte Input Change

are nowhere near as plentiful as 4-by-4 matrices over $GF(2^8)$, so very little freedom is available to pick simple coefficients. The best construction for such a matrix seems to be an extended RS-(15,7) code over $GF(2^4)$, which requires considerably more gates in hardware and more tables in smart card firmware than the Twofish matrix. Because of this additional cost, we decided not to use an 8-by-8 MDS matrix over $GF(2^4)$.

7.3.4 Rotational Uniqueness of Output Vectors

Another constraint imposed on the Twofish MDS matrix is that no row (or column) of the matrix be a rotation of another row (or column) of the matrix. This property guarantees that all single-byte input differences result in unique output differences, even when rotations over eight bits are applied to the output, as is done in generating the round subkeys. This constraint did not seem to limit the pool of candidate matrices significantly. In fact, the Twofish MDS matrix actually exhibits a much stronger property: all 1020 MDS output differences for single-byte input changes are distinct from all others, even under bitwise rotations by each of the rotation values in the range 6..26. The subkey generation routine takes advantage of this property to help thwart related-key differential attacks. For all single-byte input changes, the rotation of the output 32-bit word B by eight bits has an output difference that is guaranteed to be unique from output differences in the unrotated A quantity.

7.3.5 Maximizing the Minimal Hamming Distance

There are many MDS matrices containing only the three elements 01, EF, and 5B. The particular Twofish matrix was also chosen to maximize the minimum binary Hamming weight of the output differences over all single-byte input differences. The Twofish MDS matrix guarantees that any single-byte input change will produce an output Hamming difference of at least eight bits, in addition to the property that all four output bytes will be affected. In fact, as shown in Table 7.6, only seven of the 1020 possible single-byte input differences result in output differences with Hamming weight difference 8; the remaining 1013 differences result in higher Hamming weights. Also, only one of the seven outputs with Hamming weight 8 has its most significant bit set, meaning that at least eight bits will be affected even in the PHT term $T_0 + 2T_1$ for 1019 of the 1020 possible single-byte input differences. Input differences in two bytes are guaranteed to affect three output bytes, and they can result in an output Hamming difference of only three bits, with probability 0.000018; the probability that the output difference Hamming weight is less than eight bits for 2-byte input differences is only 0.00125, which is less than the corresponding probability (0.0035) for a totally random binomial distribution.

There are many other MDS matrices, using either the same or another set of simple field elements, that can guarantee the same minimum output Hamming difference, and the particular matrix chosen is representative of the class. No higher minimum Hamming weight was found for any matrices with such simple elements.

7.4 PHT

The PHT operation, including the addition of the round subkeys, was chosen to facilitate very fast operation on the Pentium CPU family using the LEA (load effective address) opcodes. The LEA opcodes allow the addition of one register to a shifted (by 1,2,4,8) version of another register, along with a 32-bit constant, all in a single clock cycle, with the result placed in an arbitrary Pentium register. For best performance, a version of the encryption and decryption code can be "compiled" for a given key, with the round subkeys inserted as constant values in LEA opcodes in the instruction stream. This is what was done for the "compiled" keying option explained in section 5.1.1. This approach requires a full instantiation in memory of the code for each key in use, but it provides a speedup for bulk encryption.

7.4.1 Eliminating the PHT

Instead of using four key-dependent S-boxes, a 4-by-4 MDS matrix, and the PHT, we could have used eight key-dependent S-boxes and an 8-by-8 MDS matrix over $GF(2^8)$, hence eliminating the PHT. Such a construction would be easier to analyze and would have nicer properties, but it is much slower in virtually all implementations and would not be worth it.

7.4.2 Diffusion and the Least Significant Bit

One disadvantage of the PHT is that it does not provide complete diffusion for the special case of the least significant bit of $T_0 + 2T_1$. In particular, the least significant bit of $T_0 + 2T_1$ depends only on the least significant bit of T_0, and thus depends only on half of the input bits to the Feistel function. This means that F does not exhibit complete diffusion: there is one output bit which is not affected by all input bits. In fact, we use this property in our differential attack in Section 9.2.

We could have replaced the PHT with a variant that exhibits better diffusion; however, this would have incurred a significant performance penalty. Is it better to eliminate this weakness, if the price is that we must reduce the number of rounds to retain the same performance?

We believe that the PHT yields an excellent bang-for-the-buck ratio. In practice, the PHT's incomplete diffusion to the least significant bit of $T_0 + 2T_1$ should not be a problem, because full diffusion will be easily achieved in the next two rounds; also, the 1-bit rotation prevents the least significant bits from lining up across multiple rounds, which seems to prevent attacks based on analyzing least significant bits.

7.5 Key Addition

As noted in the previous section, the round subkeys are combined with the PHT output via addition to enable optimal performance on the Pentium CPU family. From a cryptographic standpoint, an XOR operation could have been used, but it would reduce the best Pentium software performance for bulk encryption. It should be noted that using addition instead of XOR does impose a minor gate count and speed penalty in hardware, but this additional overhead was considered to be well worth the extra performance in software. On a smart card, using addition instead of XOR has virtually no impact on code size or speed.

7.6 Feistel Combining Operation

Twofish uses XOR to combine the output of F with the target block. This is done primarily for simplicity; XOR is the most efficient operation in both hardware and software. We chose not to use addition (used in MD4 [Riv91], MD5 [Riv92], RIPE-MD [RIPE92], HAVAL [ZPS93], RIPEMD-160 [DBP96], and SHA [NIST93]), or a more complicated combining function like Latin squares (used in DESV [CDN95]). We also did not implement dynamic swapping [KKT94] or other additional complexities.

7.7 Use of Different Groups

By design, the general ordering of operations in Twofish alternates as follows: 8-by-8 S-box, MDS matrix, PHT with subkey addition, and XOR. The underlying algebraic operations thus alternate between non-linear table lookup, a GF(2)-linear combination of the bits by the MDS matrix, integer addition mod 2^{32}, and GF(2) addition (XOR). Within the S-boxes, several levels of alternating XOR and 8-by-8 permutations are applied. The goal of this ordering is to help destroy any hope of using a single algebraic structure as the basis of an attack. No two consecutive operations use the same structure, except for the PHT and the key addition that are designed to be merged for faster implementations.

7.8 Diffusion in the Round Function

There are two major mechanisms for providing diffusion in the round function. The first is the MDS matrix multiply, which ensures that each output byte depends on all input bytes. The two outputs of the g functions (T_0 and T_1) are then combined using a PHT so that both of them will affect both 32-bit Feistel XOR quantities. The half of the PHT involving the quantity $T_0 + 2T_1$ will lose the most significant bit of T_1 due to the multiply by 2. This bit could be regained using some extra operations, but the software performance would be significantly decreased, with very little apparent cryptographic benefit. In general, the most significant byte of this PHT output will still have a non-zero output difference with probability 254/255 over all 1-byte input differences.

7.8.1 Changes Induced by F

We cannot guarantee that a single byte input change to the F function will change seven or eight of the output bytes of F. The reason is that the carries in the addition of the PHT can remove certain byte differences. For example, an addition with a constant might turn a difference of 00000180_{16} into 00000080_{16}. The chances of this happening depend on the distance between the two bits that influence each other. A large reduction in the number of changed bytes is very unlikely.

7.9 One-bit Rotation

Within each round, both of the 32-bit words that are XORed with the round function results are also rotated by a single bit. One word is rotated before the XOR, and one after the XOR. This structure provides symmetry for decryption in the sense that the same software pipeline structure can be applied in either direction. By rotating a single bit per round, each 32-bit quantity is used as an input to the round function twice in each of the eight possible bit alignments within the byte.

7.9.1 Reason for Rotations

These rotations in the Twofish round functions were included specifically to help break up the byte-aligned nature of the S-box and MDS matrix operations, which we feared might otherwise permit attacks using statistics based on strict byte alignment. For example, Square uses an 8-by-8-bit permutation and an MDS matrix in a fashion fairly similar to Twofish, but without any rotations. An early draft of the Square paper proposed a very simple and powerful attack, based solely on such byte statistics, that forced the authors to increase the number of rounds from six to eight. Also, an attack against SAFER is based on the cipher's reliance on a byte structure [Knu95c].

Choosing a rotation by an odd number of bits ensures that each of the four 32-bit words are used as input to the g function in each of the eight possible bit positions within a byte. Rotating by only one bit position helps optimize performance on the Pentium CPU (which, unlike the Pentium Pro, has a one-clock penalty for multi-bit rotations) and on smart card CPUs (which generally do not have multi-bit rotate opcodes for 32-bit words). Limiting rotations to single-bit also helps minimize hardware costs, since the wiring overhead of fixed multi-bit rotations is not negligible.

7.9.2 Downsides to Rotations

There are three downsides to the rotations in Twofish. First, there is a minor performance impact (less than 7 percent on the Pentium) in software due to the extra rotate opcodes. Second, the rotations make the cipher nonsymmetric in that the encryption and decryption algorithms are slightly different, thus requiring distinct code for encryption and decryption. It is only the rotations that separate Twofish from having a "reversible" Feistel structure. Third, the rotates make it harder to analyze the cipher for security against differential and linear attacks. In particular, they make the simple technique of merely counting active S-boxes quite a bit more complicated. On the other hand, it is much harder for the attacker to analyze the cipher. For instance, it is much harder to find iterative characteristics, since the bits do not line up. The rotates also make it harder to use the same high-probability characteristic several times, because the bits get rotated out of place. On the whole, the advantages were considered to outweigh the disadvantages.

7.9.3 Converting to a Pure Feistel Structure

It is possible to convert Twofish to a pure Feistel structure by incorporating round-dependent rotation amounts in F, and adding some fixed rotations just before the output whitening. This might be a useful view of the cipher for analysis purposes, but we do not expect any implementation to use such a structure.

The rotations were also very carefully selected to work together with the PHT and the MDS matrix to preserve the MDS difference properties for single byte input differences to g. In particular, for both encryption and decryption, the one-bit right rotation occurs after the Feistel XOR with the PHT output. The MDS matrix was chosen to guarantee that a 32-bit word rotate right by one bit will preserve the fact that all four bytes of the 32-bit word are changed for all single input byte differences. Thus, placing the right rotation after the XOR preserves this property. However, during decryption, the rotate right is done after the XOR with the Feistel quantity involving $T_0 + 2T_1$. Note that, in this case, the rotate right puts the $2T_1$ quantity back on its byte boundary, except that the most significant bit has been lost. Therefore, given a single input byte difference that affects only T_1, the least significant three bytes of the Feistel XOR output are guaranteed to change after the rotation, and the most significant byte will change with probability 254/255.

The fact that the rotate left by one bit occurs before the Feistel XORs during encryption guarantees that the same relative ordering (i.e., rotate right after XOR) occurs during decryption, preserving the difference-property for both directions. Also, performing one rotation before and one after the Feistel XOR imposes a symmetry between encryption and decryption that helps guarantee very similar software performance for both operations on the Pentium CPU family, which has only one ALU pipeline capable of performing rotations.

7.10 The Number of Rounds

Sixteen rounds corresponds to eight cycles, which seems to be the norm for block ciphers. DES, IDEA, and Skipjack all have eight cycles. Twofish was defined to have eight cycles (16 rounds) primarily out of pessimism. Although our best non-related-key attack only breaks five rounds of the cipher, we cannot be sure that undiscovered cryptanalysis techniques do not exist that can do better. Hence, we consider 16 rounds to be a good balance between our natural skepticism and our desire to optimize performance. Even so, we took pains to ensure that the Twofish key schedule works with a variable number of rounds. It is easy to define Twofish variants with more or fewer rounds.

8. Design of the Twofish Key Schedule

The key schedule for Twofish is a really a huge piece by itself. While it reuses many of the components of the cipher, it also required a significant amount of independent engineering. This chapter addresses the issues we came across in designing the key schedule.

To understand the design of the key schedule, it is necessary to consider how key material is used in Twofish:

The Whitening Subkeys. A whitening subkey of 128 bits is XORed into the plaintext block before encryption, and another 128 bits subkey after encryption. Since the rest of the encryption is a permutation, this can be seen as selecting among as many as 2^{256} different (but closely related) 128-bit to 128-bit permutations for the whole cipher. This key material has the effect of making many cryptanalytic attacks a little more difficult at a very low cost. Note that nearly all the added strength against cryptanalytic attack is added by the XOR of subkeys into the input to the first and last rounds' F functions.

The Round Subkeys. Each round, 64 bits of key material are combined into the output of the F function using addition modulo 2^{32}. The F function without the round subkey addition is a permutation on 64-bit values; the round subkey selects among one of 2^{64} closely related permutations in each round. These subkeys must be slightly different per round to prevent a slide attack, as will be discussed below.

The Key-dependent S-boxes. To create the S-boxes, the key is mapped down to a block of data half its size, S, and that block of data is used to specify the S-boxes for the whole cipher. As discussed earlier, the key-dependent S-boxes are derived by alternating fixed S-box lookups with XORs of key material. The key-dependent S-boxes define one of $2^{L/2}$ possible permutations for the g function, where L is the number of bits in the cipher key. Unlike the other keys used, different S values typically lead to radically different g functions.

8.1 Round Subkeys

8.1.1 Equivalence of Round Subkeys

In this section, we discuss whether different sequences of subkeys can give equivalent encryption functions. Recall that F' is the F function without the addition of the round subkeys, which takes two 32-bit words as input and produces two 32-bit words as output. For this analysis we keep the function F' constant. That is, we only vary the subkeys K_i and not S.

The properties of a Feistel cipher ensure that no pair of 2-round subkey sequences can be equivalent for all inputs. It is natural to ask next whether any pairs of three sequential rounds' subkeys can exist that cause exactly the same encryption.

For a pair of subkey sequences, (k_0, k_1, k_2) and (k_0^*, k_1^*, k_2^*), to be equivalent in their effects, every input block (L_0, R_0) must encrypt to the same output block (L_1, R_2) for both sequences of subkeys. Note that $k_0 \neq k_0^*$ and $k_2 \neq k_2^*$, as we would otherwise have two sequences of 2-round keys that would define the same 2-round encryption function. We have the following equalities:

$$
\begin{aligned}
R_1 &= R_0 \oplus (k_0 + F'(L_0)) \\
R_1^* &= R_0 \oplus (k_0^* + F'(L_0)) \\
L_1 &= L_0 \oplus (k_1 + F'(R_1)) \\
L_1 &= L_0 \oplus (k_1^* + F'(R_1^*)) \\
R_2 &= R_1 \oplus (k_2 + F'(L_1)) \\
R_2 &= R_1^* \oplus (k_2^* + F'(L_1))
\end{aligned}
$$

where $\oplus$ represents bitwise XORing, and $+$ represents 32-bit componentwise addition. Using the two equations for L_1 we get

$$
\begin{aligned}
k_1 + F'(R_1) &= k_1^* + F'(R_1^*) \\
\delta_1 &= F'(R_1) - F'(R_1^*)
\end{aligned}
$$

where $\delta_1 = k_1^* - k_1$ is fixed. Let $T = F'(L_0) + k_0$ and observe that when L_0 goes over all possible values, so does T. We get

$$
\delta_1 = F'(R_0 \oplus T) - F'(R_0 \oplus (T + \delta_0)) \tag{8.1}
$$

where $\delta_0 = k_0^* - k_0$. Note that δ_1 and δ_0 depend only on the round keys, and that the equation must hold for all values of R_0 and T. Set $T = 0$ and look at the cases $R_0 = 0$ and $R_0 = \delta_0$. We get

$$
F'(0) - F'(\delta_0) = \delta_1 = F'(\delta_0) - F'(0) = -\delta_1
$$

The subtraction here is modulo 2^{32} for each of the two 32-bit words. That leaves us with the following possible values for δ_1:

$$\delta_1 \in \{(0,0), (0,2^{31}), (2^{31},0), (2^{31},2^{31})\}$$

These are the possible difference values at the output of F' in equation 8.1. We can easily convert them to difference values at the input of the PHT of F'. Each of the possible values for δ_1 corresponds to exactly one possible value for $(\delta_{T_0}, \delta_{T_1})$:

$$(\delta_{T_0}, \delta_{T_1}) \in \{(0,0), (0,2^{31}), (2^{31},0), (2^{31},2^{31})\}$$

We can write down the analogue to equation 8.1 for g:

$$\delta_{T_0} = g(R' \oplus T') - g(R' \oplus (T' + \delta_0'))$$

for all R' and T' and where δ_0' is the appropriate half of δ_0. Observe that for the specific values of δ_{T_0} that are possible, subtraction and XOR are the same. For $T' = 0$ this translates in a simple differential equation

$$\delta_{T_0} = g(R') \oplus g(R' \oplus \delta_0')$$

for all R'. We know that g has only one perfect differential: $0 \mapsto 0$, so we conclude that $\delta_0' = 0$. Similarly, we can conclude that the other half of δ_0 must also be zero, and thus $\delta_0 = 0$. This is a contradiction, as $k_0 \neq k_0^*$.

We conclude that there are no two sets of 3-round subkey sequences that result in the same encryption function.

A Conjecture about Equivalent Subkeys in Twofish. We believe that, for up to 16 rounds of Twofish, there are no pairs of round subkeys that (with the same F' function) result in the same encryption function. There simply do not appear to be enough degrees of freedom in choosing the different subkeys to make pairs of equivalent subkey sequences in as few as 16 rounds. However, we have been unable to prove this.

Note that this conjecture does not hold for an arbitrary number of rounds. Any fixed round function is an element of the permutation group on 128-bit values $S_{2^{128}}$. The order of this group is $(2^{128})! \approx 2^{2^{134}}$, and the order of any group element must be a divisor of the order of the group. Thus, *any* round function when iterated $(2^{128})!$ times, results in the identity mapping.[1] For this number of rounds there are thus many equivalent round subkeys.

8.1.2 Equivalent keys

Can two keys generate the same sequence of round subkeys? We have performed exhaustive tests to show this is not the case. To generate the same round subkeys, the two keys will have to generate the same set of A_i and B_i.

---

[1] In fact, this property holds for any bijective function, including the complete Twofish encryption and the AES block cipher (irrespective of which candidate is chosen).

We observe that $A_i = h(2\rho i, M_e)$, where the h function consists of applying the MDS matrix multiplication to the four values $(y0, y1, y2, y3)$ obtained by running the value $2i$ through $1 + N/64$ levels of q_0 and q_1, XORing with bytes from M_e. Since the MDS matrix is non-singular, it is easily seen that to generate the same sequence of A_i values, the keys must generate the same sequence of values for y_0, y_1, y_2, and y_3.

The sequence of y_0 values for 256-bit keys is

$$q_1[q_0[q_0[q_1[q_1[i] \oplus k_3] \oplus k_2] \oplus k_1] \oplus k_0]$$

where the k_j are different bytes from M_e. Smaller keys result in similar equations with fewer key bytes, so the analysis is almost identical. The question at hand is whether two distinct sets of four key bytes can result in an identical sequence of 20 y_0 values. In fact, we exclude the input and output whitening values to concentrate solely on the round subkeys, so only 16 values are included in our test (one per round). Clearly, there are 2^{32} such sequences. However, this number can be reduced for the purposes of our search by noting that, since the "outer" mapping q_1 is bijective, it can be removed from the equation, leaving us with

$$q_0[q_0[q_1[q_1[i] \oplus k_3] \oplus k_2] \oplus k_1] \oplus k_0$$

Now the outer XOR term k_0 can be effectively removed by creating a related sequence with only 15 values, where the y_0 values for $i = 5, \ldots, 19$ are XORed with the $i = 4$ value. The k_0 terms thus cancel out, so there are only 2^{24} equivalence classes of sequences, speeding up the search dramatically. If all these sequences (each with 15*8 = 120 bits) are unique, then the y_0 sequence is also guaranteed to be unique.

For 192-bit keys, the y_0 sequence is

$$q_1[q_0[q_0[q_1[i] \oplus k_2] \oplus k_1] \oplus k_0]$$

and for 128-bit keys, it is

$$q_1[q_0[q_0[i] \oplus k_1] \oplus k_0]$$

In a manner identical to that discussed for 256-bit keys, the outer q_1 permutation can be removed for these smaller keys, and the outer k_0 term can similarly be removed by creating the related XOR sequence. The number of the remaining sequences is 2^{16} and 2^8, respectively. All these sequences can then be compared across key sizes (with a total of $N_s = 2^{24} + 2^{16} + 2^8$ sequences) to verify uniqueness.

A computer search has been performed over y_0, y_1, y_2, and y_3, for all sequences across all key lengths. It turns out that only 64 bits of each sequence were sufficient to distinguish the sequences. This fact is actually quite encouraging, since there are 120 bits in each sequence, giving some heuristic comfort that the sequences are in fact quite different. Each search requires slightly more than 128 MB of memory (i.e., $8N_s$ bytes) to hold all the sequences, which are then sorted and compared to adjacent values to guarantee uniqueness. The test was run on a Pentium computer with only 32 MB of memory, so the search was actually performed in multiple passes, running through all the N_s values several times, on each pass selecting only those values falling into certain bins. For example, using approximately 8 MB of memory, there are 16 passes, with the mth pass discarding all sequence values for which a fixed 4-bit field of the sequence does not equal to m.

Similar arguments apply to the B_i sequence, and the same empirical verification has been performed for both sequences. Note that, since the operations used to compute K_{2i} and K_{2i+1} from A_i and B_i are reversible, proving that the A_i and B_i sequences are distinct is more than sufficient to prove that the K_j sequences are distinct.

The definitive result from these tests is that there are no two distinct keys of any size for which the same sequence of A_i and B_i values is obtained. Thus, the round subkey sequence K_j is unique across keys.

8.2 Controlling Changes in Round Subkeys

In a related-key attack, one is concerned about introducing controlled differences into key material that will produce predictable effects that depend on the pair of keys. The basic intuition is that if one can observe the difference in behavior produced by two keys known to have a particular mathematical difference, then one might be able to discern information about the true value of the two keys. Normally one does not limit the attack to pairs of keys and instead may consider subsets of keys instead. Either way, this is a natural attack in many environments where multiple encryption keys are used which are not truly independent of each other.

One very natural notion of mathematical difference is the XOR difference of two values. In this section we consider the problem of trying to produce two sequences of round subkeys $\{K_i\}$ and $\{K_i'\}$ that have a desired difference (either additive or XOR). Recall that the K_i (and K_i') are computed as a function of the sequences A and B (respectively A' and B'). Therefore we consider the problem of trying to produce two sequences $A = \{A_i\}$ and $A' = \{A_i'\}$ such that individual elements have a desired difference $\delta_i = A_i \oplus A_i'$ (a similar discussion holds for $B = \{B_i\}$). A and B are generated using four 8-bit, key-dependent S-boxes in parallel followed by multiplication by a 4-by-4 MDS matrix over $GF(2^8)$, where each S-box output is treated as one component of a four-dimensional vector over $GF(2^8)$. Due to the linearity of the MDS matrix multiply, it is very natural to consider attacks that introduce XOR differences between A and A', since it is very easy to pass XOR differences through the MDS matrix.

8.2.1 XOR Difference Sequences in A and B

Let A and A' be sequences for two keys M and M' respectively. If we have a specific difference sequence, $\delta = \{\delta_i\}$, we want to see in A (i.e., $\delta_i = A_i \oplus A'_i$), we are faced with an interesting problem: since the MDS matrix multiply is XOR-linear, each desired output XOR from the matrix multiply uniquely determines the input XOR. This means that:

1. Any input difference δ_i^I to the MDS matrix corresponds to an output difference for each of the four S-boxes. Hence a difference sequence δ induces four XOR-difference sequences δ^j for the four S-boxes. For any difference sequence $\delta^j = \{\delta_i^j\}$, each value is an 8-bit value instead of a 32-bit value. As a result, we will sometimes refer to these sequences as difference byte sequences.

2. The zero sequence δ can occur *only* when each difference byte sequence δ^j is the zero sequence.

3. Only 1020 possible output differences (out of the 2^{32}) in δ_i can occur with a single "active" (altered) S-box (i.e., only one δ^j is a non-zero sequence). Most differences require all four S-boxes to be active and hence all δ^j to be non-zero sequences.

The above analysis is of course also valid for the B sequence.

Given that any desired difference sequence δ corresponds to four difference byte sequences δ^j, we need to examine the properties of the S-boxes to determine the difficulty of generating specific δ^j.

8.2.2 Byte Sequences with Given Difference

In generating A and A' with a specific difference δ, one must generate four pairs of byte sequences (σ^j, σ'^j), each with a specific difference δ^j, where $\sigma^j = \{\sigma_i^j\}$ and $\sigma'^j = \{\sigma_i'^j\}$. The inputs to the four S-boxes used to produce these values are $\{0, 2, 4, \ldots, 38\}$ (whereas they are $\{1, 3, 5, \ldots, 39\}$ for B). Therefore our byte sequences are given by $\sigma_i^j = s_j[2i]$ and $\sigma_i'^j = s'_j[2i]$. Hence any questions about difference byte sequences reduce to questions about the sequences

$$\{s_j[0], s_j[2], \ldots, s_j[38]\}, \quad \{s'_j[0], s'_j[2], \ldots, s'_j[38]\}$$

For a given δ^j we will estimate the chance that there exists a pair (σ^j, σ'^j) with that difference sequence.

We can model each byte sequence generated by a key-dependent S-box as a randomly selected non-repeating byte sequence of length 20. This allows us to make many useful predictions about the likelihood of finding keys or pairs of keys with various interesting properties. Because we will be analyzing the key schedule using this assumption in the remainder of this section, we should discuss how reasonable it is to treat this byte sequence as randomly generated. As discussed in Section 7.2.3, we have not found any statistical deviations between our key-dependent S-boxes and the random model in any of our extensive statistical tests.

Not all byte sequences are possible; due to the bijectivity of the S-boxes we know that all the bytes in the sequence are distinct. There are 256!/236! of those sequences, which is close to 2^{159}.

Each key-dependent S-box uses $N/8$ bits of key material; hence, if the S-boxes were truly random we would expect two 20-byte sequences to create the desired difference with probability roughly $2^{N/4-1} \cdot 2^{-160}$. (There are $2^{N/4-1}$ pairs of byte sequences, and each has a 2^{-160} chance of being a match.) For example, for $N = 256$ we expect with probability 2^{-97} that there exists a pair of our S-boxes that produces the desired difference sequence. Note that this probability is for any specific difference sequence. There are many such possible difference sequences, and of course some of those actually occur. Attacks requiring a specific difference sequence seem more likely than attacks requiring any of a class of 2^{97} usable difference sequences.

Most difference sequences in A will require that all four δ^j are non-zero. For a randomly chosen difference δ in the A sequence we thus expect that there are two keys that generate exactly this difference with probability about 2^{-388}.

8.2.3 Identical Byte Sequences

As discussed in section 8.1.2, we have empirically verified that there are no equivalent S-box keys that generate the same sequence of 20 bytes. That holds for our specific choice of q_0 and q_1. This section analyzes the probability of two identical sequences occurring for arbitrary q-boxes.

The estimate of section 8.2.2 holds for the special case of δ^j being the all-zero sequence. If we are a little more careful, then we can actually improve the estimate for this case. While this result shows that the S-boxes are not uniformly distributed throughout the space of all possible 8-bit S-boxes, it shows that the S-boxes display better than average differences in this particular case.

To improve the estimate, we peel off one layer of our q construction and assume the rest of the construction is random. Without loss of generality we look at[2]:

$$s_1(x) = q_0[q_0[q_1[q_1[q_0[x] \oplus k_0] \oplus k_1] \oplus k_2] \oplus k_3]$$

Identical sequences are possible only if the inputs to the last q_0 fixed permutation are identical for both sequences. That means that the task of finding

---

[2] For ease of discussion, we number the key bytes as $k_0, \ldots, k_3$ going into one S-box. The actual byte ordering for s_0 and a 256-bit key's subkey-generating S-box is k_0, k_8, k_{16}, k_{24}. The numbering of the key bytes has no effect on the security arguments in this section.

a pair of identical sequences comes down to a simpler task: finding a pair of (k_0, k_1, k_2) byte values that leads to a pair of sequences before the XOR with k_3 that have a fixed XOR difference. Then, k_3 can be changed to include the XOR difference, and identical sequences of inputs will go into the last q_0 S-box.

Let

$$t[i] := q_0[q_1[q_1[q_0[i] \oplus k_0] \oplus k_1] \oplus k_2]$$

The goal is to find a pair of $t[i]$ sequences such that

$$t[i] \oplus t^*[i] = \text{constant}$$

Let us assume that t generates a random sequence (with the restriction that all byte values must be distinct). The chances of any pair of t, t^* generating such a constant difference is about 2^{-151}. (The domain in which we are searching for collisions is the set of all 19-byte sequences with non-repeated values. There are $256!/237!$ of these sequences, which is close to 2^{151}.) This brings the chance of finding a pair with such a constant difference down to $2^{47} \cdot 2^{-151} = 2^{-104}$.

8.2.4 The A and B Sequences

From the properties of the byte sequences, we can discuss the properties of the A and B sequences generated by each key M.

$$A_i = \text{MDS}(s_0(2i, M_e), s_1(2i, M_e), s_2(2i, M_e), s_3(2i, M_e))$$

Since the MDS matrix multiply is invertible, and since i is different for each round's subkey words generated, we can see that no A or B value can repeat itself.

Similarly, we can see from the construction of h that each key byte affects exactly one S-box used to generate A or B. Changing a single key byte always alters every one of the 20 bytes of output from that S-box; the MDS matrix ensures that every byte of every word in the 20-word A or B sequence to which this key byte contributes is altered.

Consider a single byte of output from one of the S-boxes. If we cycle any one of the key bytes that contributes to that S-box through all 256 possible values, the output of the S-box will also cycle through all 256 possible values. If we take four key bytes that contribute to four different S-boxes, and we cycle those four bytes through all possible values, then the result of h will also cycle through all possible values. This proves that A and B are uniformly distributed for all key lengths, assuming the key M is uniformly distributed.

8.2.5 The Sequence (K_{2i}, K_{2i+1})

As A_i and B_i are uniformly distributed (over all keys), so are all the K_i. As all pairs (A_i, B_i) are distinct, all the pairs (K_{2i}, K_{2i+1}) are distinct, although it might happen that $K_i = K_j$ for any pair of i and j.

8.2.6 Difference Sequences in the Subkeys

Difference sequences in A and B translate into difference sequences in (K_{2i}, K_{2i+1}). However, while it is natural to consider A and B difference sequences in terms of XOR differences, subkeys can reasonably be considered either as XOR differences or as differences modulo 2^{32}. Thus, we may discuss difference sequences:

$$D[i, M, M^*] = K_{i,M} - K_{i,M^*}$$
$$X[i, M, M^*] = K_{i,M} \oplus K_{i,M^*}$$

where the difference is computed between the key value M and M^*.

XOR Differences in the Subkeys. Each round, the subkeys are added to the results of the PHT of two g functions, and the results of those additions are XORed into half of the cipher block. An XOR difference in the subkeys has a fairly high probability of passing through the addition operation and ending up in the cipher block. (The probability of this is determined by the Hamming weight of the XOR difference, not counting the highest-order bit.) However, to get into the subkeys, an XOR difference must first pass through the first addition.

Consider

$$x + y = z$$
$$(x \oplus \delta_0) + y = z \oplus \delta_1$$

Let k be the number of bits set in δ_0, not counting the highest-order bit. Then, the highest probability value for δ_1 is δ_0, and the probability that this will hold is 2^{-k}. This is true because addition and XOR are very closely related operations. The only difference between the two is the carry between bit positions. If flipping a given bit changes the carry into the next bit position, this alters the output XOR difference. This happens with probability $1/2$ per bit. The situation is more complex for multiple adjacent bits, but the general rule still holds: for every bit in the XOR difference not in the high-order bit position, the probability that the difference will pass through correctly is cut in half.

For the subkey generation, consider an XOR difference, δ_0, in A. This affects two subkey words:

$$K_{2i} = A_i + B_i$$
$$K_{2i+1} = \text{ROL}(A_i + 2B_i, 9)$$

where the additions are modulo 2^{32}. If we assume these XOR differences propagate independently in the two subkeys (which appears to be the case), we see that this leads to an XOR difference of δ_0 in the even subkey word with probability 2^{-k}, and the XOR difference $\text{ROL}(\delta_0, 9)$ in the odd subkey with the same probability. The most probable XOR difference in the round's subkey block thus occurs with probability 2^{-2k}. A desired XOR difference sequence for all 20 pairs of subkey words is thus quite difficult to get to work when $k \geq 3$, assuming the desired XOR difference sequence can be created in the A sequence at all.

When the XOR difference is in B, the result is slightly more complicated; the most probable XOR difference in a round's pair of subkey words may be either $2^{-(2k-1)}$ or 2^{-2k}, depending on whether or not the XOR difference in B covers the next-to-highest-order bit.

Additive Differences in the Subkeys. An XOR difference in A or B is easy to analyze in terms of additive differences modulo 2^{32}: a XOR difference with k active bits has 2^k equally likely additive differences. Note that if we have an additive difference in A, we get it in both subkey words, just rotated left nine bits in the odd subkey word. Thus, k-bit XOR differences lead to a given additive difference in a pair of subkey words with probability 2^{-2k}. (The rotation does not really complicate things much for the attacker, who knows where the changed bits are.)

8.3 The Round Function

The round function F takes a 64-bit input and produces a 64-bit output; and F is characterized by the four S-boxes s_i and the round keys K_{2r+8}, K_{2r+9}. The S-boxes depend on $N/2$ bits of key material S. We show that all the F functions generated in this way are distinct. Our test for distinctness of the round functions concentrates on only a single bit of the output, which will be sufficient to prove uniqueness.

In particular, consider the value

$$F_1 = (T_0 + 2T_1 + K_{2r+9}) \bmod 2^{32}$$

where $T_0 = g(R_0)$ and $T_1 = g(\text{ROL}(R_1, 8))$. Because the g function involves an MDS matrix multiply, which uses the XOR operation, it is difficult to analyze the full F_1 value due to the interaction between operations of different algebraic groups (i.e., XOR and addition). However, if we examine only the least significant bit (lsb) of F_1, we can ignore carries, so the operation can be analyzed entirely using XOR. Note that this bit does not depend on R_1, due to the multiplication by 2 in the PHT. Further, the MDS matrix element that maps the S-box output is a simple linear transformation (i.e., multiplication by a $\text{GF}(2^8)$ field element). Thus, for each S-box, the effect of the final fixed permutation (q_0 or q_1) of the S-box and the MDS multiply on the lsb of F_1 is a simple fixed mapping from eight bits to one bit.

Now, consider two keys with distinct values for S. Since the S values are different, at least one of the four S-boxes must have different key material under the two different keys. To prove uniqueness, we simply fix the inputs to the remaining three S-boxes, so that their XOR "contribution" to the lsb of F_1 is fixed. Up to a fixed XOR constant (based on K_{2r+9} and the other three S-boxes), we are then left with a simple function involving a single S-box that maps eight bits to one bit, with $N/8$ bits of key material used in the S-box. We can remove dependence on the fixed constant by constructing sequences consisting of the XOR of two bits in the S-box/MDS lsb output sequence, similar to the method discussed in section 8.1.2. If this sequence of bits is unique across the all $2^{N/8}$ possible key material values for the S-box, then the F function is unique with respect to that S-box. If all four S-boxes are unique in this way, then the F function is unique for each distinct value of S.

To remove the dependence on the constant bit, we performed our search on a modified sequence in which each bit was the XOR of two lsbs of the S-box/MDS output values. Since the s_i mapping has 256 inputs, this limits the sequence down to only 255 values, which is still easily sufficient to distinguish between F functions. Let us first consider the 256-bit key case, which obviously involves the longest search. Note, for example,

$$s_0(x) = q_1[q_0[q_0[q_1[q_1[x] \oplus k_3] \oplus k_2] \oplus k_1] \oplus k_0]$$

where the k_j bytes are a subset of the bytes in S. There are 2^{32} such functions, but, unfortunately, since we are dealing only with the lsb, there is no obvious method to cut down the search time by a factor of 256, as we were able to do in section 8.1.2. Similar sequences were produced for the smaller key sizes, with all sequences for each S-box combined across key sizes in the test, for a total of $N_F = 2^{32} + 2^{24} + 2^{16}$ sequences per S-box.

To avoid a "birthday surprise" collision with N_F sequences, we require more than 64 bits of each sequence. Even with only 64 bits, however, a total of over 32 GB of memory would be required, a size far beyond the budget of this experiment. Thus, this test was also performed in multiple passes, with each pass generating all N_F sequences but discarding those values not falling into the selected bin for the particular pass, as before. It was found empirically that the performance time was roughly proportional to the number of passes; in other words, the sort/compare time for a given pass was considerably shorter than the $O(2^{32})$ time required to generate the "filtered" list. For example, on a 200 MHz Pentium computer with slightly over 256MB of available RAM, 128 passes are required, which empirically were completed for a single S-box in slightly less than three days. Each sequence value in the list consisted of 64 bits, with additional sequence bits used to filter out values not to be used in a given pass. For a 128-pass test, this means that seven extra bits were used to help avoid a birthday surprise collision. The filtering code (in C) was carefully optimized so that most of the values to be filtered on each pass were quickly rejected. Since 127 of every 128 values were filtered out on each pass, this simple optimization sped up performance considerably, without requiring particularly fast generation of the 64-bit sequence values to be included.

The test was run on several Pentium computers with various amounts of RAM over a period of about ten days. The results showed that, for each of the four S-boxes, all N_F mappings have a unique lsb sequence. Thus, each F function is unique for each distinct value of S.

8.4 Properties of the Key Schedule and Cipher

One NIST requirement is that the AES candidates have no weak keys. Here we argue that Twofish has none.

8.4.1 Equivalent Keys

A pair of equivalent keys, M, M^*, is a pair of keys that encrypts all plaintexts into the same ciphertexts. We are almost certain that there are no equivalent keys in Twofish. As shown in section 8.1.2, there is no pair of keys, M, M^*, that gives the same subkey sequence $\{K_i\}$. Section 8.3 showed that for two keys to generate the same round function in any one round, they must generate the same S.

It is conceivable that different sequences of subkeys and different S-boxes in g could end up producing the same encryption function, thus giving equivalent keys. This appears to be extremely unlikely, but we cannot prove that such equivalent keys do not exist.

A Conjecture about Equivalent Keys in Twofish. We conjecture that there are no pairs of Twofish keys that lead to identical encryptions for all inputs.

8.4.2 Self-Inverse Keys

Self-inverse keys are keys for which encrypting a block of data twice with the same key gives back the original data. We do not believe that self-inverse keys exist for Twofish. Keys cannot generate a self-inverse sequence of subkeys, because the same round subkey value can never appear more than once in the cipher. Again, it is conceivable that some keys are self-inverse despite using different subkeys at different points, but again this is extremely unlikely. Self-inverse DES keys are sometimes referred to as "weak keys."[3]

8.4.3 Pairs of Inverse Keys

A pair of inverse keys is a pair of keys M_0, M_1, such that $E_{M_0}(E_{M_1}(X)) = X$, for all X. We cannot see any way for this to occur. Encryption and decryption

---

[3] The term "weak key" is used in conflicting ways in the literature. DES' weak keys are fundamentally different from the weak keys of IDEA or Blowfish.

are slightly different processes, because of the one-bit rotations, so even if M_0, M_1 generate a pair of subkey sequences that are reversed, we still do not get pairs of inverse keys.

Consider a Twofish variant without those one-bit rotations. Can we find M_0, M_1 that lead to reversed subkey sequences? That is, can we find a pair of keys whose subkeys appear in the opposite position—the pre-XOR subkeys for M_0 are the post-XOR subkeys for M_1, the first round subkeys for M_0 are the last round subkeys for M_1, etc. To get reversed subkeys, we need to get reversed byte sequences from each of the eight byte-wide key-scheduling S-boxes. Finding a pair of byte sequences that are one another's reverse sequences is the same difficulty as finding a collision in the whole byte sequence, and thus the same difficulty as finding a difference sequence in all 20 output byte positions. By the same arguments as we used above regarding difference sequences, then, this kind of reversed subkey sequence almost certainly doesn't exist for *any* pair of keys M_0, M_1. For these reasons, we do not believe that there are pairs of inverse keys for Twofish. Note that pairs of inverse keys in DES are sometimes referred to as "semi-weak keys."

8.4.4 Simple Relations

A key complementation property exists when

$$E_M(P) = C \quad \Rightarrow \quad E_{M'}(P') = C'$$

where P', C', and K' are the bitwise complement of P, C, and K, respectively. No such property has been observed for Twofish.

More generally, a simple relation [Knu94b] is defined as

$$E_M(P) = C \quad \Rightarrow \quad E_{f(M)}(g(P, M)) = h(C, M)$$

where f, g, and h are simple functions. We have found no simple relations for Twofish, and strongly doubt that they exist.

8.5 Key-dependent Characteristics and Weak Keys

The concept of a key-dependent characteristic seems to have been introduced in [BB93] in their cryptanalysis of Lucifer, and also appears in [DGV94a] in an analysis of IDEA.[4] The idea is that certain iterative properties of the block cipher useful to an attacker become more effective against the cipher for a specific subset of keys.

A differential attack on Twofish may consider XOR-based differences, additive differences, or both. If an attacker sends XOR differences through the PHT and subkey addition steps, his differential characteristic probabilities

---

[4] See [Haw98] for further cryptanalysis of IDEA weak keys.

will be dependent on the subkey values involved. In general, low-weight sub-keys will give an attacker some advantage, but this advantage is relatively small. (Zero bits in the subkeys improve the probabilities of cleanly getting XOR-based differential characteristics through the subkey addition.) Since there appears to be no special way to choose the key to make the subkey sequence especially low weight, we do not believe this kind of key-dependent differential characteristic will have any relevance in attacking Twofish.

A much more interesting issue in terms of key-dependent characteristics is whether the key-dependent S-boxes are ever generated with especially high-probability differential or high-bias linear characteristics. The statistical analysis presented earlier shows that the best linear and differential characteristics over all possible keys are still quite unlikely.

Note that the structure of both differential and linear attacks in Twofish is such that such attacks appear to generally require good characteristics through at least three of the four key-dependent S-boxes (if not all four), so a single high-probability differential or linear characteristic for one S-box will not create a weakness in the cipher as a whole.

8.6 Reed-Solomon Code

The RS structure helps defend against many possible related-key attacks by diffusing the key material in a direction "orthogonal" to the flow used in computing the 8-by-8-bit S-boxes of Twofish. For example, a single byte change in the key is guaranteed to affect all four key-dependent S-boxes in g. Since RS codes are MDS [MS77], the minimum number of different bytes between distinct 12-byte vectors generated by the RS code is guaranteed to be at least five. Notice that any attempt in a related-key attack to affect only a single byte in the computation of A or B is guaranteed to affect all four bytes in the computation of T_0 and T_1. The S-box keys are used in reverse order from the associated key bytes so that related-key material is used in a different order in the round function than in the subkey generation.

The reversible RS code used in Twofish was chosen via computer search to minimize implementation cost. The code generator polynomial is

$$x^4 + (\alpha + \frac{1}{\alpha})x^3 + \alpha x^2 + (\alpha + \frac{1}{\alpha})x + 1$$

where α is a root of the primitive polynomial $w(x)$ used to define the field.

Because all of these coefficients are "simple," this RS computation is easily performed with no tables, using only a few shifts and XOR operations; this is particularly attractive for smart cards and hardware implementations. This computation is only performed once per key schedule setup per 64 bits of key, so the concern in choosing an RS code with such simple coefficients was not the performance overhead, but saving ROM space or gates. Precomputing the RS remainders requires only eight bytes of RAM on a smart card for 128-bit keys.

To take advantage of the simple coefficients of the polynomial, the RS matrix multiply should not be implemented as a direct matrix multiply but as a loop over the input bytes, where each iteration uses the coefficients of the polynomial once.

9. Cryptanalysis of Twofish

We have spent over one thousand man-hours cryptanalyzing Twofish. A summary of our successful attacks is as follows:

- On Twofish with fixed S-boxes, no 1-bit rotations, and no whitening, we have a meet-in-the-middle attack on eleven rounds requiring 2^{225} memory, 256 known plaintexts, and 2^{232} work, and a differential attack breaking nine rounds, requiring 2^{41} memory, 2^{41} chosen plaintexts, and 2^{254} work.

- On standard Twofish, we have a 4-round meet-in-the-middle attack requiring 256 known plaintexts, but 2^{225} memory and 2^{232} work. We also have a differential attack which breaks five rounds of full Twofish with 2^{232} work and 2^{41} chosen-plaintext queries.

- We have a chosen-key attack. This attack involves choosing 160 bits of a pair of keys, K, K^*, with the remaining bits to be found. The attack requires 2^{34} work, 2^{32} chosen-plaintext queries, and 2^{12} adaptive chosen-plaintext queries, in order to break 10 rounds without the whitening.

- We have a related-key attack against 10-round Twofish without whitening. This attack requires 2^{155} related-key queries, 2^{187} work, and for each of the 2^{155} keys it requires 2^{32} chosen plaintexts and 2^{12} adaptive chosen plaintexts.

The fact that Twofish seems to resist related-key attacks well is arguably the most interesting result, because related-key attacks give the attacker the most control over the cipher's inputs. Conventional cryptanalysis allows an attacker to control both the plaintext and ciphertext inputs into the cipher. Related-key cryptanalysis gives the attacker an additional way into a cipher: the key schedule. A cipher that is resistant to attacks with related keys is necessarily resistant to simpler techniques that only involve the plaintext and ciphertext.[1]

Based on our analysis, we conjecture that there exists no more efficient attack on Twofish than brute force. That is, we conjecture that the most efficient attack against Twofish with a 128-bit key has a complexity of 2^{128};

---

[1] We have discussed the relevance of related-key attacks to practical implementations of a block cipher in [KSW96, KSW97]. Most importantly, related-key attacks affect a cipher's ability to be used as a one-way hash function.

Cipher variant	Rounds	Work	Memory
256-bit key, Fixed S, no whitening, no rotations	11	2^{232}	2^{225}
256-bit key, Fixed S, no whitening	10	2^{232}	2^{225}
256-bit key, Fixed S	6	2^{232}	2^{225}
256-bit key, Full Twofish	4	2^{232}	2^{225}

Table 9.1. Attack Results for Our Meet-in-the-Middle Attack

the most efficient attack against Twofish with a 192-bit key has a complexity of 2^{192}; and the most efficient attack against Twofish with a 256-bit key has a complexity of 2^{256}.

9.1 A Meet-in-the-Middle Attack on Twofish

9.1.1 Results of the Attack

Table 9.1 summarizes our attack results. One notable feature of this attack is that it demonstrates the impact of adding the pre- and post-whitening and the key-dependent S-boxes. Without these two features, we would have an extremely simple attack on 10 out of the 16 rounds of our cipher—enough to raise questions about its ultimate security. With these two features, however, the attack extends to only four rounds. Resistance to meet-in-the-middle attacks comes from quickly getting every bit of the key involved in every bit of the block being encrypted.

9.1.2 Overview of the Attack

In a meet-in-the-middle attack, we try to derive some intermediate state inside the cipher, using only part of the key material from both the plaintext and the ciphertext. For each possible value that the part of the key that we guessed can take, we derive that intermediate value from the plaintext and also from the ciphertext. We get two huge lists of possible intermediate values. We then sort the two lists, and check them for matching values. A matching value of more bits than we would expect to occur randomly indicates that our guesses were correct. This kind of attack is important to consider because the AES candidates are using large keys, which imply a very high security level. A user expecting 256 bits worth of security should be concerned by attacks that involve guessing 200 bits of key in each direction. Also, it is easy for cipher designers used to thinking in terms of 64-bit blocks and 128-bit keys to design ciphers that do not get all 256 bits of key involved in the encryption process quickly enough.

9.1.3 Attacking Twofish with Fixed S and no Whitening

In this Twofish variant, all key material is in the round subkeys. We acquire about 256 plaintext/ciphertext pairs from this Twofish variant with ten rounds.

We label the four words of the data during the encryption as A, B, C, and D. From the plaintext side, we guess the round subkeys for the first three rounds, for a total of 192 bits. We also guess one subkey (used to determine the value XORed into A) in the fourth round. We thus know the value of the low-order bit of D after the fifth round, because (1) we knew the value of D after the third round, (2) we know the value of A going into the fifth round, and (3) we know that the low-order bit of the value XORed into D is dependent only on A and one bit of the fifth round's subkey. For each of the 2^{225} possibilities for these key values, we compute this bit for all 256 plaintexts we have. We store these in a list, and sort them.

From the ciphertext side, we guess the round keys for the tenth, ninth, and eighth rounds, and we guess the subkey from the seventh round that affects the value XORed into D. We use this to derive the high-order bit from D going into the seventh round, which was rotated from its position as the low-order bit of D after the fifth round. Again, for all 2^{224} possible key values guessed, we compute this bit for each of the 256 ciphertexts we have. Again, we sort this list.

We now merge the two sorted lists, and thus search for matches. This ought to take on the order of 2^{232} work total. Thus, we use 2^{225} blocks of memory, and about 2^{232} work to break ten rounds of Twofish with fixed S-boxes and no whitening.

Note that without the one-bit rotations in the cipher, we would have needed to know only the low-order bit of the F-function output in the seventh round. This would actually allow us to attack one more round. This is evidence that the one-bit rotations do, in fact, provide some resistance against real attacks.

9.1.4 Attacking Twofish with Fixed S

With the whitening added, the attack becomes much harder. From the plaintext side, we must guess all four pre-whitening subkeys, allowing us to get our known low-order bit only into the output of the third round. Similarly, from the ciphertext side, we must guess all four post-whitening subkeys and the last round's subkeys, and one subkey word from the next-to-last round. We can thus attack only six rounds in this case.

9.1.5 Attacking Normal Twofish

Attacking the full Twofish is still harder. From the plaintext side, we must guess the 128 bits of S, the round subkey that determines the value that is

Key Length	Variant	Rounds	Chosen Texts	Work
128	No whitening, fixed S	7	2^{41}	2^{126}
192	No whitening, fixed S	8	2^{41}	2^{190}
256	No whitening, fixed S	9	2^{41}	2^{254}
128	No whitening, no one-bit rotates	6	2^{41}	2^{126}
192	No whitening, no one-bit rotates	6	2^{41}	2^{158}
256	No whitening, no one-bit rotates	7	2^{41}	2^{254}
256	Normal Twofish	5	2^{41}	2^{232}

Table 9.2. Attack Results for Our Differential Attack

XORed into C in the first round, and the pre-whitening subkey for C. This allows us to predict the low-order bit of B after the second round XORed with an unknown constant (i.e., we predict that this bit will take on a sequence of values or the negation of that sequence). A similar approach is used from the ciphertext side, allowing only four rounds to be attacked.

9.2 Differential Cryptanalysis

9.2.1 Results of the Attack

Table 9.2 summarizes our attack results against several variants of Twofish.

9.2.2 Overview of the Attack

The attack uses two different differential properties of the F function:

1. If the input difference into the F function is $(0, X)$, where X represents any non-zero difference at all, then the output difference of the F function can be expressed additively as $(+Y, +2Y)$, where Y is some other unknown difference. Unfortunately, these additive differences do not always translate cleanly into XOR differences. However, the low-order bit of the second word of F's output is always unchanged, since $2Y$ always has its low-order bit clear. This happens with probability 1.

2. If the same XOR difference comes out of the two g functions during the F function computation, and this difference has k bits not in the high-order position, then with probability 2^{-k}, the F function will generate an output difference of $(0, X)$, where X is some unknown difference.

Our attack works by first trying to force the second event described above to occur in the second round, in a batch of several pairs of plaintexts. If it occurs, then the first event described above occurs in the next round with probability one, resulting in a single bit whose difference is known in the output of the fourth round. This allows an attack on reduced-round Twofish.

The attack requires that we get a specific, predictable difference sequence. We choose

r	$\Delta_{R_{r,0}}$	$\Delta_{R_{r,1}}$	$\Delta_{R_{r,2}}$	$\Delta_{R_{r,3}}$
0	0	0	a'	b'
1	a	b	0	0
2	0	?	a	b
3	?	$(?,1)$	0	?
4	?	?	?	$(?,1)$
5	?	?	?	?

where the table gives the difference patterns for the round values for each of the 5 rounds, and where $a' = \mathrm{ROL}(a,1)$, $b' = \mathrm{ROR}(b,1)$, and $(?,1)$ represents a 32-bit difference of which one bit is known. To recognize right pairs, we shall (roughly speaking) guess enough of the key to decrypt up one round, checking whether the low-order bit of the difference is as expected.

The only critical event for this attack occurs at $r = 1$, where we need the characteristic $(a, b) \to (0, X)$ to happen with high probability. Based on the properties of the MDS matrix, we know that there are three single-byte output XORs for s_0 that lead to an output XOR of g with Hamming weight of only 8. If the same one of those differences goes into the MDS matrix in both g computations in the second round, then, with probability 2^{-8}, we get an offsetting pair of values in the two g outputs; one g output has some value added to it modulo 2^{32}, and the other output has the same value subtracted from it. When the outputs go through the PHT, they lead to only one output word from the whole F being changed, which is what makes this attack possible. Therefore, we choose $a = (\alpha, 0, 0, 0)$ to be a single-byte difference in s_0, and $b = \mathrm{ROR}(a, 8)$ so that the single-byte difference into the second g computation in round 2 lines up with the single-byte difference in a.

In this attack, we will consider N batches of 256 plaintext pairs, of which at least one is expected to consist of all right pairs. We must choose the inputs to the cipher to allow ourselves to later form such batches. We will then guess some part of the key as needed to check the one known bit of difference going into the fifth round. That key guess will be used to test each batch. Batches that are not made up of right pairs will typically be distinguished after a small number of pairs are checked, because the one-bit difference will be wrong with probability 1/2 in each wrong pair checked with the right key, and in each pair checked with the wrong key. The attack thus consists of the following steps:

1. Request the encryptions of plaintext blocks necessary to form at least one batch of 256 plaintext pairs that has a very high probability of being made up of only right pairs.

2. Guess the smallest amount of key material that will let us see the one bit of difference we know in right pairs.

3. For each such guess, check each batch until one batch turns out to be made of only right pairs.

If there are N batches to be checked, and each takes on average about two trial decryptions' worth of work, then we end up with $2N$ work we must do for each guess of key material necessary to see whether the known difference is as we expect it to be.

9.2.3 Building the Batches

Overview. We break the problem into three parts, here. First, we describe how to take a single right pair and generate 255 other right pairs from it. Then, we describe how to take a pair that gets the same 8-bit XOR difference out of both g functions, and use it to generate enough pairs that it is likely that at least one is an actual right pair; i.e., the differences from the two g functions cancel out in the first addition of the PHT. Finally, we describe how to choose pairs so that we are very likely to get at least one pair that gets the same 8-bit XOR difference from both g functions.

Let us suppose we must choose n_0 pairs before we get a pair such that both g functions get the same 8-bit XOR difference. (That is, we must choose n_0 pairs to get our differential through half of the second round.) We have no way to know which pair has the desired differential, so we must treat all of them as potentially right pairs.

Let us also suppose that given a pair whose differential survives through half of the second round, we must choose n_1 related pairs before we find one pair that survives through the whole second round. The rest of the differential occurs with probability one, so one of these pairs is a right pair. We must apply this process to all the potential right pairs to be nearly certain of getting a right pair. Thus, we now have $n_0 n_1$ pairs to deal with.

Finally, let us suppose that, given a right pair, we must expand it into n_2 batches of 256 pairs each before we will be able to detect it. We must do this to all potential right pairs, meaning that we end up with $n_0 n_1 n_2$ batches total, each of 256 pairs. Thus, we need to request a total of $n_0 n_1 n_2 256$ pairs of plaintexts for encryption.

This tells us about the chosen text requirements, but not the workload for the attack. Suppose we have to guess k bits, and that given a guessed partial key, we can check a batch with an average of work equivalent to n_3 encryptions. Then the total work factor is $2^k n_0 n_1 n_2 n_3$. As we discuss below, $n_3 \approx 1$, $n_2 = 2^{16}$, $n_1 = 2^8$, and $n_0 = 2^8$.

Amplifying Right Pairs. The greatest difficulty in this attack is determining a sequence of inputs that gives us at least one batch of 256 pairs of plaintexts that contains all right pairs. This is necessary because we know only that one bit of difference in the output from the fourth round. Essentially, what we need to do is to "magnify" the effects of a right pair so that a single right pair generates 256 right pairs.

To see how this can be done, let us consider a pair of inputs to the F-function,

$$
\begin{aligned}
X &= (C, D) = (c_0, c_1, c_2, c_3), (d_0, d_1, d_2, d_3) \\
X^* &= (C^*, D^*) = (c_0, c_1^*, c_2, c_3), (d_0, d_1^*, d_2, d_3)
\end{aligned}
$$

such that we know that we have a right pair; i.e., that the two g functions have the same XOR difference after processing X and X^*, that these XOR differences have Hamming weights of eight bits only, and that the two XOR differences cancel out during the first addition in the PHT, leading to an output difference of $(0, ?)$. We want to find a way to choose related input pairs that will also be right pairs. To do this, we must consider some details of how right pairs really work. When we compute $F(C, D)$, we find

$$
\begin{aligned}
f_0 &= g(C) + g(D) \\
f_1 &= g(C) + 2g(D)
\end{aligned}
$$

When we apply an XOR difference to a value, this has the effect of flipping k bits, where k is the Hamming weight of the XOR difference. In terms of mod 2^{32} addition, flipping bit j means adding 2^j or subtracting it, depending on whether the bit was on or off. If X, X^* is a right pair, it means that $g(C), g(D)$ both got the same 8-bit difference, and that each bit of C covered by a bit of that XOR difference was different than the corresponding bit of D covered by that bit of the difference. In other words, the XOR difference must result in subtracting from $g(C)$ whatever it adds to $g(D)$, so that $g(C) + g(D)$ will be unchanged. This means that simply changing $g(C)$ at random won't generally produce more right pairs from this one.

There are two ways to make more right pairs from this right pair:

1. Find a way to change one or more inactive bytes $(c_0, c_2, c_3, d_0, d_2, d_3)$ such that the 8 bits that are changed in $g(C), g(D)$ in the original pair aren't changed. Since we don't know which bits those are, this looks hard to do.

2. Find a way to change those inactive bytes that leads to the same XOR difference being applied to $g(C)$ and $g(D)$. If the same bits are flipped in $g(C)$ and $g(D)$, then the resulting pair will also be a right pair. This is our approach.

Our solution is as follows: If we flip the same bits in $g(C)$ as in $g(D)$, then the sum $g(C) + g(D)$ will be unchanged, and as a result, the effect of the input difference in c_1, d_1 will also be unchanged. Let x_3, y_3 be the bytes that actually go into the S-box s_3 in the two g functions. We control c_3, d_3, but their values are XORed with some unknown bytes before being used as x_3, y_3. Thus,

$$x_3 = c_3 \oplus z_3$$
$$y_3 = d_3 \oplus z_4$$

We need to be able to choose c_3, d_3 so that $x_3 = y_3$. If we ever did that, then we could generate 255 additional cases where $y_3 = z_3$, simply by XORing $1, \ldots, 255$ into both c_3 and d_3. Now, if we knew $z_3 \oplus z_4$, we could choose any c_3 value we liked, and then set $d_3 = c_3 \oplus z_3 \oplus z_4$, giving us $x_3 = y_3$. We thus try all 256 possible values for $z_3 \oplus z_4$. One of those values is right; we can use it to take a single right pair, and produce 255 more just like it. This is done by keeping A and B constant, and by choosing

$$C = (c_0, c_1, c_2, c_3 \oplus i)$$
$$D = (d_0, d_1, d_2, d_3 \oplus i \oplus z_3 \oplus z_4)$$
$$C^* = (c_0, c_1^*, c_2, c_3 \oplus i)$$
$$D^* = (d_0, d_1^*, d_2, d_3 \oplus i \oplus z_3 \oplus z_4)$$

where c_1, d_1 and c_1^*, d_1^* are the bytes changed in the original right pair. For each potential right pair, we thus generate 256 pairs of text according to the above formula for each guess about $z_3 \oplus z_4$. This means that each potential right pair generates 256 batches of 256 pairs of plaintexts (and corresponding pairs of ciphertexts), or a total of 2^{16} plaintext pairs. Thus, $n_0 = 256$.

Deriving a Right Pair from a Partial Right Pair. Suppose we have a pair of texts, $(C, D), (C^*, D^*)$, such that $g(C) \oplus g(C^*) = g(D) \oplus g(D^*)$, with that XOR difference having Hamming weight of 8. In most (255/256) cases, this won't be a right pair, because $g(C) + g(D) \neq g(C^*) + g(D^*)$. To turn this into a right pair, some of the bits in $g(C)$ which are covered by the XOR difference need to be flipped. We thus choose the available bytes, c_0 and c_2, and vary both bytes randomly in different texts. After about 256 different random c_0, c_2 choices, we expect to derive a real right pair from the partial right pair. Naturally, most of the pairs we generate will not be right pairs, and we won't be able to distinguish them from wrong pairs until we mount the attack.

We thus determine that $n_1 = 256$.

Finding a Single Partial Right Pair. A partial right pair can be found by getting the same XOR difference out from the S-box determined by c_1 and also by d_1. We don't know the S-box these are going through, but simulations show that if we try $i, i \oplus \delta$ as a pair of inputs into a random 8-bit-wide bijective S-box, s, we have a probability of $1/2$ of getting any desired output XOR difference. If there are three XOR differences that lead, after the MDS matrix is applied, to 8-bit XOR differences, then the probability is thus $7/8$ that this approach will work to find a partial right pair.

We have the same complications we did above: we control c_1, d_1, but we need to control $x_1 = c_1 \oplus z_1, y_1 = d_1 \oplus z_2$, the inputs to the S-boxes in the two g functions. Similarly to the way we dealt with this above, we end up guessing $z_1 \oplus z_2$. The result is that we generate 2^{16} plaintext pairs, of which at least one is almost certainly a partial right pair. Thus, $n_2 = 2^{16}$.

Testing a Batch of Plaintext Pairs. We generate $n_0 n_1 n_2 = 2^8 2^8 2^{16} = 2^{32}$ batches of plaintext pairs. During our attack, we must guess as much of the key material as is required, and for each guess, we must test each batch to see if it is made up of only right pairs. The probability of a randomly-selected key giving us a "false positive"—that is, a batch that appears to be right but is not—is 2^{-256}. This probability is low enough that we never expect a single false positive.

We now consider the difficulty of testing one such batch of plaintext pairs. The question is how many trial partial decryptions we must do for each batch, on average, before determining that the batch is not made up of only right pairs. For a guessed partial key, each batch will yield a sequence of 256 bits; in the batch of right pairs, they will all be the expected bit. However, for each batch, we can stop searching as soon as we find a single bit that is different than the others. The expected number of trial partial decryptions required per batch is thus

$$2 \cdot 1/2 + 3 \cdot 1/4 + 4 \cdot 1/8 + \cdots + (n+1) \cdot 1/2^n \approx 3$$

Each partial decryption is less work than a full encryption. We take $n_3 = 1$ for our estimates, which corresponds to each partial decryption being one-third as much work as a full encryption.

9.2.4 Mounting the Attack

To mount the attack, we must determine what key material must be guessed to check our batches. Consider a 5-round Twofish variant without whitening and without the 1-bit rotations. In this case, we need only guess S. Recall that in a right pair, we know the difference in only one bit—the low-order bit of D in this case—at the input to the fifth round. After guessing S, we can compute the value of the g function that uses A as its input in the fifth round. The low-order bit of this is XORed with the low-order bit of the corresponding subkey, and then XORed into the bit whose difference we know. Knowledge of the low-order bit of that g output thus gives us the desired bit difference.

To extend this another round, we must also guess the subkey in the sixth round that affects the value XORed into A. Because we only have to get the low bit of D, we need not compute the B value input into the fifth round's F function at all. This requires 2^{32} additional work.

To extend this one more round, we must guess the whole set of round subkeys in the next round. This requires 2^{64} additional work.

Five-round Twofish consists of ten g computations and a little extra work. To be conservative, we can consider each g computation to be $1/8$ of a trial encryption.

Key Length	Rounds	Work (equiv. trial encs.)
128	5	$2^{30} \cdot 2^{64} = 2^{94}$
128	6	$2^{30} \cdot 2^{96} = 2^{126}$
192	5	$2^{30} \cdot 2^{96} = 2^{126}$
192	6	$2^{30} \cdot 2^{128} = 2^{158}$
256	5	$2^{30} \cdot 2^{128} = 2^{158}$
256	6	$2^{30} \cdot 2^{160} = 2^{190}$
256	7	$2^{30} \cdot 2^{224} = 2^{254}$

Table 9.3. Differential Attack Results against a Variant with No Whitening and No Rotations

Key Length	Rounds	Work (equiv. trial encs.)	
128	5	$2^{30} \cdot 2^{74} = 2^{104}$	
128	6	$2^{30} \cdot 2^{138} = 2^{166}$	(No longer useful.)
192	5	$2^{30} \cdot 2^{106} = 2^{136}$	
192	6	$2^{30} \cdot 2^{170} = 2^{200}$	(No longer useful.)
256	5	$2^{30} \cdot 2^{138} = 2^{168}$	
256	6	$2^{30} \cdot 2^{202} = 2^{232}$	
256	7	$2^{30} \cdot 2^{266} = 2^{296}$	(No longer useful.)

Table 9.4. Differential Attack Results against a Variant with No Whitening

Thus, for five- to seven-round Twofish with no whitening and no 1-bit rotates, we have the results summarized in Table 9.3.[2] (Note that all of these results are for 2^{41} chosen plaintexts.)

When we add back in the 1-bit rotates, the attacks grow substantially harder. (Interestingly, though we put the 1-bit rotates in because of concerns about the byte structure, so far, the 1-bit rotates have complicated several attacks based on exploiting properties of the low bit of one of the PHT words.) We must now learn both g function outputs in the fifth round, as well as guessing the high-order 10 or so bits of round subkey used to alter the value XORed into D in the fifth round. We list the resulting attack complexities in Table 9.4.

The whitening also adds a little difficulty. When combined with the 1-bit rotates, we get the results summarized in Table 9.5. We note that there are straightforward differential attacks on four rounds that work despite the 1-bit

---

[2] We are indebted to Eli Biham for the suggestion of guessing the whole last round's subkeys for the 256-bit key.

Key Length	Rounds	Work (equiv. trial encs.)	
128	5	$2^{30} \cdot 2^{128} = 2^{158}$	(No longer useful.)
192	5	$2^{30} \cdot 2^{170} = 2^{200}$	(No longer useful.)
256	5	$2^{30} \cdot 2^{202} = 2^{232}$	

Table 9.5. Differential Attack Results against Reduced Rounds

Key Length	Rounds	Work (equiv. trial encs.)
all	6	$2^{30} \cdot 2^{32} = 2^{62}$
all	7	$2^{30} \cdot 2^{96} = 2^{126}$
192 & 256	8	$2^{30} \cdot 2^{160} = 2^{190}$
256	9	$2^{30} \cdot 2^{224} = 2^{254}$

Table 9.6. Differential Attack Results on a Variant with Known S and No Rotations

rotations and whitening, but they involve using only the $(0, X) \to (?, (?, 1))$ differential.

Finally, we can consider the difficulty of this attack on a Twofish variant with a fixed, known S value and no 1-bit rotates. In this case, we have the difficulties results listed in Table 9.6.

Again, this demonstrates how the additional key material in the key-dependent S-boxes adds to the practical difficulty of an attack. Additionally, with fixed S-boxes, it may be possible for the attacker to get a substantial improvement, perhaps by as much as a factor of 256, on the number of plaintext batches he must request. This would reduce the plaintext requirement and the work factors on all these attacks by the same factor.

9.2.5 Lessons from the Analysis

We have learned three important lessons from this analysis:

1. The 1-bit rotates really do add difficulty to some attacks.

2. The key-dependent S-boxes add a great deal of security to the cipher against some attacks.

3. The whitening adds a fair amount of security to the cipher at essentially no cost.

9.3 Extensions to Differential Cryptanalysis

9.3.1 Higher-Order Differential Cryptanalysis

Higher-order differential cryptanalysis looks at higher order relations (e.g., quadratic) between pairs of plaintext and ciphertexts [Lai94, Knu95b]. These attacks seem to work best against algorithms with simple algebraic functions, only a few rounds, and poor short-term diffusion. In particular, we are not aware of any higher-order differential attack reported in the open literature that is successful against more than six rounds of the target cipher. We cannot find any higher-order differentials that can be exploited in the cryptanalysis of Twofish.

9.3.2 Truncated Differentials

Attacks using truncated differentials apply a differential attack to only a partial block [Knu95b]. We have not found any truncated attacks against Twofish. The almost complete diffusion within a round function makes it very difficult to isolate a portion of the block and ignore the rest of the block. Truncated differential attacks are most often successful when most of the cipher's internal components operate on narrow bit paths; Twofish's 64-bit-wide F function seems to make truncated differential characteristics hard to find. We believe that Twofish is secure against truncated differential attacks. For example, our differential attack, described above, is properly classified as a truncated differential attack, and it can successfully attack only five rounds of the full Twofish.

9.4 Search for the Best Differential Characteristic

One aspect of our analysis work is a search for an upper bound on the probability of a differential characteristic. This section contains our results to date. We expect to continue this work and achieve significant improvements over our current results.

The first choice we have to make in differential cryptanalysis is what type of differences to use. Twofish contains S-boxes, an MDS matrix multiply, addition modulo 2^{32}, XORs, and rotations. There are two types of differences that we think could be useful: a XOR difference, and a difference mod 2^{32}. When we use a XOR difference we have to use approximations for the S-boxes and the additions modulo 2^{32}; when we use a differences modulo 2^{32} we have to use approximations for the S-boxes, the MDS matrix multiply, the XORs, and the rotations.

The XOR and addition operations are fairly closely related, and either operation can be approximated with reasonable success in the group of the other operation. In the comparison we will ignore the S-boxes; we assume they are equally hard to approximate in each of the groups. An XOR differential has to approximate two addition operations in each round. An additive differential has to approximate the MDS matrix, a single XOR, and a rotation. We estimate that it is about as difficult to approximate an addition for an XOR differential as it is to approximate an XOR for an additive differential. The rotations are relatively simple to approximate in both cases, so we ignore them for this comparison. Thus, if we ignore the MDS matrix, it would seem that additive differentials are more attractive.

For our analysis, the MDS matrix multiply is best written as a linear function: each output bit is the XOR of several input bits. This is very easy from the point of view of an XOR difference; no approximation is necessary and any given input difference leads to precisely one output difference. For an additive difference this is much harder. There do not seem to be any good approximations of the MDS matrix for an additive difference. Therefore, we estimate that XOR-based differentials are much more effective than additive differentials. In the rest of this paper we will look only at XOR-based differentials.

We use the following notations: Let $\mathcal{B}$ be the set of all possible byte values. Let G be the F-function without the key-dependent S-boxes. Thus G consists of two MDS matrix multiplies, the PHT, and the subkey addition.

9.4.1 Differentials of the S-boxes

In this section we look at differential characteristics of the S-boxes. Each S-box consists of a sequence of q-mappings and XORs with a key byte. For q_0 and q_1 the probability of each differential can easily be computed by trying all possible pairs of inputs.

We define $p_i(a, b)$ to be the probability that q_i has an output difference of b, given an input difference of a. In other words,

$$p_i(a, b) := \Pr_{x \in \mathcal{B}} [q_i(x \oplus a) = q_i(x) \oplus b] \qquad i = 0, 1$$

We now look at the first two stages of an S-box. This consists of a q-mapping, followed by an XOR with a key byte, followed by another q-mapping. As usual, we assume uniform random distributions of the input values and the key bytes. We define $p_{ij}(a, b)$ to be the probability that this construction gives an output difference b given an input difference a, where i is the number of the first q-mapping, and j is the number of the second q-mapping. It is easy to see that

$$p_{ij}(a, b) \quad = \quad \sum_{d \in B} p_i(a, d) p_j(d, b) \tag{9.1}$$

for $i, j \in \{0, 1\}$, and we can extend this definition to arbitrary long chains of q-mappings and key-byte XORs. In general, it holds that

S-box	128-bit Key	192-bit Key	256-bit Key
0	$1.0649 \cdot 2^{-8}$	$1.0084 \cdot 2^{-8}$	$1.0043 \cdot 2^{-8}$
1	$1.0566 \cdot 2^{-8}$	$1.0087 \cdot 2^{-8}$	$1.0043 \cdot 2^{-8}$
2	$1.0533 \cdot 2^{-8}$	$1.0097 \cdot 2^{-8}$	$1.0045 \cdot 2^{-8}$
3	$1.0538 \cdot 2^{-8}$	$1.0088 \cdot 2^{-8}$	$1.0044 \cdot 2^{-8}$

Table 9.7. Best Differential Probabilities of the S-boxes under Random Key

$$p_{ij\ldots m}(a, b) = \sum_{d \in B} p_i(a, d) p_{j\ldots m}(d, b)$$

for $i, j, \ldots, m \in \{0, 1\}$. This allows us to compute the exact probabilities for each of the S-boxes in Twofish. Table 9.7 gives the probabilities of the best differential of each of the S-boxes for each key length. From this point of view the S-boxes are very good; there are no high-probability differentials. (Note that the average differential probability is $1/255 = 1.0039 \cdot 2^{-8}$, as we know that the S-boxes are permutations, and thus the output differential 0 does not occur in non-trivial cases. The best differential probability must be at least as large as the average.)

Note that the numbers in this table hold only when the key bytes are chosen at random. In our analysis we assumed that the probabilities in each q-stage were independent. If we try a differential many times, each time with random input and key byte values, then we expect to get the numbers in the table. However, for any particular set of key bytes there are differentials with a much higher probability (as shown in section 7.2.3). Our computations are no longer valid, because for any fixed key byte, the differential probabilities of p_i and p_j in equation 9.1 are no longer independent of each other.

Twofish uses the same S-boxes in each round. When analyzing a multi-round differential characteristic, the differential probabilities of each of the round functions are not independent either. This makes the analysis of the probability of a differential characteristic more difficult.

9.4.2 Differentials of F

The function F takes a 64-bit input and produces a 64-bit output. Thus there are a total of about 2^{128} possible differentials. It is clearly not possible to compute or list all of them. To alleviate this problem we will group the differentials in sets, and for every set compute upper bounds on the probability of the differentials in that set.

We split the 2^{128} different differential patterns into a number of subsets. The input difference is classified by the set of input bytes that are non-zero. There are 256 different classifications of input differences. The output difference too is classified by the set of output bytes that are non-zero. We group differentials with the same input and output classification in the same set. There are therefore 2^{16} different sets of differentials, each containing between 1 and 255^{16} elements.

We will construct differentials of F in two steps. First we use a differential approximation of the S-boxes, and then we use an approximation of the differentials of G.

Differentials of G. The MDS matrix multiply is purely linear, and thus creates no problem for our differential. The PHT and key addition use addition modulo 2^{32} as basic operation. This makes the differentials non-trivial. A theoretical analysis of differential probabilities is difficult, as the probabilities at the result are not independent of each other. We therefore chose to use numerical simulation to establish bounds on the differential probability.

We are trying to derive an upper bound on differential probabilities. Therefore, we are interested in finding good bounds for the most likely differentials of G. We know that for any 128-bit key, the best differential probability of an S-box is 18/256. If we look only at the S-boxes, then the most likely differentials occur when there are a low number of active S-boxes. The most important task is thus to find good bounds on the differential characteristics of G for differentials with a low number of active S-boxes.

We performed numerical simulations of differentials of G. Given an input difference, we generated n random input pairs with that difference and applied the G function (using random keys). We collected the output differences and counted how often each of them appeared. Due to limited resources we could do this analysis only for moderately large n.

From this data we would like to derive a bound on the differential probability. Let us assume a specific differential occurs k times out of n tries. It is obviously not a good idea to use k/n as a bound on the differential probability. Most possible differences occur zero times, but we should not assume that they have a zero probability. If we knew the distribution of the probability we could give some meaningful bound; for example, saying that the probability is less than x with a confidence level of 1 percent. However, in our case we do not know the distribution of the differential probabilities, and it would be dangerous to assume one. We can, however, reverse the process.

Let us assume that a specific differential has a probability p. If we try the input difference n times, we expect to find this differential around $p \cdot n$ times. The number of times this differential is actually observed is binomially distributed. Let X be a stochastic variable that represents the number of times the differential is observed. We have

$$\Pr(X = k) = \binom{n}{k}(1-p)^{n-k}p^k \qquad k = 0, \ldots, n$$

From this distribution we can derive a bound on the lower tail of the binomial distribution [Fer98a]:

$$\Pr(X \leq k) < \Pr(X = k) \frac{p(n - k + 1)}{(p \cdot n - k) + p}$$

for $k \leq p \cdot n$. Given a probability p for the differential, we can say that we have an unlikely event if the differential occurs k times and $\Pr(X \leq k) < \gamma$ where γ would be a small number. This is a normal test for statistical significance.

We use the following rule to derive a bound on a differential that occurs k out of n times. We use a probability p such that $\Pr(X \leq k) < \gamma$ for some global parameter γ (typical values for γ are 0.05 or 0.01). Of course, we try to choose p as low as possible given this condition. This will overestimate p for most differentials, but underestimate the actual p in a few cases.

We ran these simulations for all input differences with a low enough number of active S-boxes. For every differential that we tried, we estimated the probability using this rule. For each set of differentials with the same input and output characterization, we computed the maximum estimated probability. For each differential, there is a small chance that we underestimated the probability. However, it is far less likely that we underestimated the maximum probability of a set of differentials. For our maximum to be too low we have to underestimate the probability of the most likely differential. This by itself is rather unlikely. Not only that, we cannot significantly overestimate the probability of any differential with a probability close to the most likely differential. We therefore feel confident that these approximations are reasonable, and that they most likely will result in our overestimating the actual differential probability quite significantly.

For differentials with too many active S-boxes (for which we did not run the simulations), we simply use an upper bound of 1 on the probability of a differential of G.

To improve efficiency, we generate our input differences using a straightforward structure. This improves our performance and allows us to increase the number of samples that we make. However, the differentials that we try are no longer independent of each other. We have observed that the use of structures significantly increases the peaks in the bounds. The smaller the structures that we use, the lower the maximum probability bound tends to be. Therefore, we try to reduce the use of structures. We hope our next software version will allow us to eliminate structures altogether.

Apart from these numerical results, we know that certain differential patterns cannot occur. For example, if the input difference is restricted to the first input word of G, then the output difference must have active bits in both output words. Similarly, if the input difference is restricted to the second input word of G, then the output difference must have active bits in both halves, except when the output of the MDS matrix has a difference of 0x80000000. In this special case, we know that all four S-boxes in this half must be active (otherwise more than one byte in the output of the MDS matrix must change). Our software generates all these impossible differential patterns and sets the differential probabilities of the associated sets to zero.

Prob.	Differential
2^{-20}	x000 0x00 → 0000 xxxx
2^{-26}	x000 0x00 → 0000 0xxx
2^{-22}	x000 0x00 → xxxx 0000
2^{-26}	000x x000 → 0000 xx0x
2^{-21}	000x x000 → 0000 xxxx
2^{-22}	000x x000 → xxxx 0000
2^{-20}	00x0 000x → 0000 xxxx
2^{-22}	00x0 000x → xxxx 0000
2^{-14}	0x00 0000 → 0x0x 0x0x

Table 9.8. Experimentally Found Differentials of F

Differentials of F. Given the results from the last section, we can now create a table of upper bounds on the differential probabilities of differentials of F. For each set of differentials we know how many active S-boxes there are. Let σ be the maximum probability of a differential of an S-box. We can now bound the probability of each set of differentials by multiplying the bounds that we found in the previous section on the set by the proper power of σ.

The value σ can be set in various ways. We know that most S-boxes have a best differential probability of 12/256. For the time being we will use this value for σ. Other values, especially larger ones, will be discussed later.

Experimental Results. We ran a test for differential characteristics of the F function with one active byte in each 4-byte g input and at most four active bytes at the 8-byte F output. Table 9.8 shows some interesting differentials that we found. The probabilities are very approximate, as they derive from numerical experiments with not too many samples. Note that in all but the last of these, the two active input bytes are going through the same key-dependent S-box due to the 8-bit rotate at the input of the second g function. The leading cause of all of these differentials seems to be that these two bytes generate the same output differential from the S-box, and thus the same differential at the output of the MDS matrix. With some positive probability, the PHT maps this into an output differential where one half is zero. This probability depends on the bit pattern of the differential just before the PHT.

The last characteristic has a different explanation. The input differential results in a differential at the output of the MDS matrix that has a relatively high chance of being converted into a 0x0x pattern after a constant is added to it. For example, the differential 03f2037a$_{16}$ has a fair chance of being converted to a 0x0x pattern after a 32-bit addition.

All of these characteristics have a relatively low probability. We have not found any attack that directly relates to this property, but it provides a useful starting point for further research. In particular, upper bounds on the differential characteristics of F of this type could be used to improve our bound on the best differential characteristic for the full cipher.

9.4.3 Differentials of the Round Function

Once we have derived bounds on the differentials of F, we can do the same for the round function. The differential pattern at the start of the round is characterized by 16 bits; each bit indicates whether the differential pattern in the corresponding byte is non-zero. Given the characterization of the differential pattern at the input of the round, we know exactly which S-boxes are active. We can generate a list of all suitable differential patterns of F with their associated probability bound. Each of these differentials is combined with the other half of the input differential using the rotate and XOR operations. Each choice of the F differential set leads to several possible output differential patterns as the rotate and XORs can lead to different output characterizations depending on the exact differential.

For example, let us look at a differential pattern of 0110 in a 32-bit word. This pattern indicates that only the middle two bytes of the 4-byte word contain active differential bits. After a left rotation, the possible output differential patterns are: 0100, 0110, 1010, 1100, and 1110. XORing two differential patterns can similarly lead to a list of possible results. If we XOR two words, one with a differential pattern of 0101 and one with a differential pattern of 0011, then the possible result patterns are 0110 and 0111.

For each input differential pattern to the round, we can go through all possible F differential patterns, and generate all possible output patterns that can arise. For each possible output pattern of the round, we keep track of the largest upper bound that we generate this way. This produces an upper bound for each of the 2^{32} possible input/output differential patterns of the round function.

9.4.4 Multi-round Patterns

The simplest way of generating multi-round patterns would be to use the list of 2^{32} possible round patterns and a standard search algorithm. We use an algorithm that is somewhat more efficient than that. There are 2^{16} possible differential patterns after r rounds, as each of the 16 data bytes can have a zero or non-zero difference. For each of the 2^{16} possible patterns, we store an upper bound on the probability of any characteristic that has this difference pattern after r rounds. Furthermore, we store the list of differential patterns of F, and a precomputed table of how the rotates and XORs can propagate patterns. For each difference pattern after $r + 1$ rounds, we use this data to compute an upper bound on the probability of a differential characteristic that has this pattern after $r + 1$ rounds.

Given the output pattern of the round in question, we know the first half of the input pattern. This leaves us with 256 possible differential input patterns, and 256 possible differential patterns of F. Each of the 2^{16} possible combinations is tried to see whether it can yield the required output differential pattern. The process can be speeded up by traversing either the F output patterns or the input patterns in decreasing order of probability and using some simple cut-off logic.

9.4.5 Results

The results depend on the parameters used to estimate the differential probabilities of G, and the values of γ and σ.

Our current results use $n = 2^{11}$ tries for all differentials with one active S-box, and $n = 2^8$ tries for all differentials with 2 active S-boxes. The structure size is 8 and 16 respectively. We use $\gamma = 0.05$, and $\sigma = 12/256$. The full Twofish cipher has 16 rounds. We assume that an adversary can somehow bypass the first round and can mount a 3R-attack. We thus look at the best 12-round differential characteristic.

With these parameters we found an upper bound on the probability of a 12-round differential characteristic of $2^{-102.8}$. This puts a differential attack against Twofish well outside the practical realm.

This upper bound is pessimistic in the following areas:

- The best differential pattern used three active S-boxes in four of the 12 rounds. The probability of passing a differential with three active S-boxes through G is currently taken to be 1. This is clearly overly optimistic, especially since the differential pattern used has both a low input and a low output weight. We believe that extending our simulations to all differentials with three active S-boxes will yield a significant further reduction in probability.

- Many of the rounds in the best differential pattern use fancy transformations of the difference pattern by the rotations. This is to be expected of our algorithm, but any non-trivial transformation poses serious restrictions on the actual difference patterns of that word. This makes it much less likely that our upper bound can actually be approached by an actual differential.

- Our estimates are based on the maximum probability of groups of differentials. It is not clear at all that there exists a differential that has a probability that even approaches our upper bound.

9.4.6 Other Problems for the Attacker

To create an attack, the attacker has to choose a specific differential characteristic. That characteristic uses certain specific differences of each of the S-boxes. To get anywhere near the bound, all of these differences need to have a probability close to our σ. We chose σ equal to the probability of the best differential of most S-boxes. However, a specific differential will not have the same probability under all keys. If the S-box keys are not known, the attacker has two options. First, he can guess the S-box key bits, and construct a differential characteristic based on that assumption. To achieve good differential probabilities in enough S-boxes, he will have to guess the keys of at least two S-boxes (between 32 and 64 bits, depending on the key size). Alternatively, he can try to find a differential that works for all keys. As we saw in section 9.4.1, this leads to very low differential probabilities.

9.4.7 Best S-box Differential

We use $\sigma = 12/256$ while we know that there are keys for which the best S-box differential has probability $18/256$ for a 128-bit key, and even higher for larger key sizes. However, those higher probabilities only occur for a small subset of the keys. We need to address the question of how much we are willing to pay in the size of the keyspace the attack is effective on to get a higher probability. If we have an attack that works for 2^{-28} of the key space, how much more efficient should the attack be before it is a better choice for the attacker?

The most natural way is to look at the expected work for the attacker before recovering a single key. We assume that there are enough keys to attack, and optimize the attacker's strategy to find any one key with the least amount of work. This is a reasonable way of looking at the attacker's problem. After all, we know there is an attack that is effective on a subset of 2^{-64} of the keys with 2^{64} work: a simple exhaustive search of any subset of that size will do. With such a brute-force attack on a subset of the keys, the expected amount of work before a key is found remains the same.

Let us now look at our Twofish differentials. Suppose we want to use a differential of S-box 0 with probability $14/256$; this is possible for about one in eight of all possible keys. We have restricted ourselves to $1/8$ of the set of keys, so the workload of our attack should be reduced by at least a factor of 8 for this to be worthwhile. We ran our search for the best differential characteristic pattern again where S-box 0 had a best differential probability of $14/256$. The resulting differential probability was 4.6 times higher than the result with $\sigma = 12/256$. Is this worth it?

Let us assume a differential has a probability that depends on the key. We have a list of (p_i, k_i) where the probability of the differential is at most p_i for a fraction k_i of all keys. The expected workload of the attacker to get a single right pair is $1/p_i$ for a fraction k_i of the key space, and thus $\sum k_i/p_i$ when taken over all keys. The workload is at least $\max k_i/p_i$. This corresponds to the workload of an attack with a differential with probability $\min p_i/k_i$. In our situation, the minimum occurs when we use the S-box approximation with probability $12/256$. As we currently ignore the $1/k_i$ term, the actual "effective" probability of a real differential is lower than the bound that we have derived.

We conclude that using a higher probability than 12/256 for an S-box approximation is not worth the loss in key space on which the approximation holds. Thus the bounds we presented earlier hold, and are in fact pessimistic.

9.4.8 Other Variants

As an experiment, we ran the same analysis for Twofish with the 1-bit rotations removed. This makes our approximations match the behavior of the differential much better. Our results give an upper bound on the probability of a 12-round differential characteristic of $2^{-104.1}$.

This bound is not much better than we have for full Twofish. However, the sequence of differential patterns that achieves this bound uses far more approximations of F that have three active S-boxes. In all cases it uses differential characteristics of G that have three active input bytes and only a few active output bytes. In practice, such differentials of G will have a far lower probability than the upper bound of 1 that we currently use. Therefore, we expect that our bound can be improved to beyond 2^{-128}.

We have no reason to believe that the 1-bit rotations make Twofish stronger against a differential attack. They were conceived to break up the byte-level structure, but they do not require a separate approximation or increase the avalanche effect of the cipher. We think it is unlikely that the full Twofish has a differential characteristic that is significantly more likely than the version without rotations.

9.4.9 Further Work

We will continue our analysis work to improve the bound and our understanding of the intricacies of Twofish. We have several areas that we plan to improve.

Improved G Differential Estimates. An obvious way to improve our overall bound is to improve our bounds on the differentials of G. We hope to be able to do this in the near future. A larger sample size will improve the accuracy of our estimates. Extending our computations to differentials of G with three active S-boxes should give a great improvement.

More Accurate Patterns. Our current pattern-representation is somewhat coarse. We group differentials only by which bytes contain active bits. Apart from the first and final round, all internal differential patterns in our best result have at most four active bytes (out of 16). A more fine-grained grouping of the differentials could lead to a better upper bound.

For example, there are only a few G differences with one active input byte that have a relatively high probability. Instead of grouping these into the sets, we could treat them separately. This would ensure that our algorithm doesn't magically transform the output of the high-probability difference pattern to one with fewer active bytes by the rotation. The characterization could be extended with special cases for differences that have only a few active nibbles. We expect that this will result in more S-boxes being needed for a full differential characteristic, and thus a lower bound.

Improved Treatment of S-box Differentials. There is still room to improve our approximations of the S-boxes. We can, for example, compute the best differential approximation for each of the output differences separately. This can then be combined with the analysis of G to get a better bound on differentials of F.

The data on the best S-box differentials in section 7.2.3 is merged for all the S-boxes. We plan to test the differentials again and collect information for each S-box separately.

We will also improve our handling of the variation of differential probability over the key-space. This will also result in a better bound.

Additive Differentials. We would like to take a closer look at additive differentials modulo 2^{32}. Although we do not expect these to be more useful, it would be nice to derive some bound in that case too.

9.4.10 Conclusion

For practical purposes, Twofish is immune to differential cryptanalysis. We have shown that any 12-round differential has a probability of at most $2^{-102.8}$. This bound is far from tight, and we expect that any real differential has a much smaller probability.

The Twofish structure is not easy to analyze. The mixing of various operations makes it hard to give a clean analysis and forces us to use approximation techniques. Some aspects, such as the rotates, make the analysis a lot harder and force us to use less accurate approximations, while there is no a priori reason to assume that the rotations would have any significant influence on the differential probabilities.

One can argue whether a cipher with a structure that is easier to analyze would be preferable. On the one hand, a structure that allows easier analysis makes it easier to rule out certain attacks. On the other hand, the very structure that makes it easy to analyze might be used in a future attack. Although differential attacks were obviously considered during the design, Twofish was not specifically strengthened against differential attacks, or designed to allow a simple upper bound on differential probabilities to be derived. This is a result of the design philosophy of Twofish. It was not optimized specifically against known attacks; it is a conservative design that tries to resist both known and unknown attacks.

9.5 Linear Cryptanalysis

We perform a similar analysis to that of Section 9.4 in the context of linear cryptanalysis. The approach is the same, but a simpler model was used.

Our model is much as before: it is centered around the pattern of active bytes. (Here a byte position is considered *active* if any of its bits are active in the linear approximation for that round; i.e., if the mask Γ selects at least one bit from that byte position.) We used a fairly rough approximation of the effect of the PHT. This approximation fails to accurately treat some low-probability approximations for the PHT where there are fewer active bytes at the output than at the input. This analysis also ignores the 1-bit rotations.

Because of the second limitation, our model should be considered only a heuristic; it may fail to capture some important features of the round function.

A search for the best linear characteristics within this model found that every 12-round characteristic has at least 36 active S-boxes. Here is an example of one characteristic we found:

```
 1 FE->FF   (1 active)
 2 FF<-FF   (2 active)
 3 FF->DD   (4 active)
 4 CC<-DD   (6 active)
 5 CC->00   (0 active)
 6 CC<-00   (6 active)
 7 CC->77   (4 active)
 8 00<-77   (0 active)
 9 00->77   (4 active)
10 66<-77   (6 active)
11 66->00   (0 active)
12 66<-00   (3 active)
13 66   07
```

The first few approximations for the F function are $01_{16} \rightarrow FF_{16}$, $22_{16} \rightarrow FF_{16}$, $33_{16} \rightarrow DD_{16}$, and so on.

To translate these results into an estimated attack complexity, we turn to the results of Section 7.2.3. We have $LP_{max} \leq (108/256)^2$, so this suggests an attacker would need at least $(LP_{max})^{-36} \approx 2^{89.6}$ known plaintexts; and such an analysis would only work for a very small class of weak keys (representing about $2^{-49.6}$ of the keyspace for 128-bit keys, or about 2^{-68} of the 192-bit keyspace).

It is much more natural to demand that the attack work for a significant percentage of all keys. In this case, $LP_{max} = (80/256)^2$ is a much more representative value, and thus in this model any linear attack working for a significant fraction of the keyspace would require at least $2^{120.8}$ chosen plaintexts.

These results are only heuristic estimates, and probably overestimate the probability of the best linear characteristic. Nonetheless, they present some useful evidence for the security of Twofish against linear cryptanalysis.

A more thorough analysis along the lines of section 9.4 remains to be performed.

9.5.1 Multiple Linear Approximations

Multiple linear approximations [KR94, KR95] allow one to combine the bias of several high-probability linear approximations. However, it only provides a significant advantage over traditional linear cryptanalysis when there are a number of linear approximations whose bias is close to that of the best linear approximation. In practice, this seems to improve linear attacks by a small constant factor. Hence, we do not feel that Twofish is vulnerable to this kind of cryptanalysis.

9.5.2 Non-linear Cryptanalysis

Another generalization of linear cryptanalysis looks at non-linear relations [KR96b], e.g., quadratic relations. While this attack, combined with the technique of multiple approximations [KR94], managed to improve the best linear attack against DES a minute amount [SK98], we do not believe it can be brought to bear against Twofish for the same reasons that it is immune to linear cryptanalysis.

9.5.3 Generalized Linear Cryptanalysis

This generalization of linear cryptanalysis uses the notion of binary I/O sums [HKM95, Har96, JH96]. An attacker attempts to find a statistical imbalance that can be described as the result of some group operation on some function of the plaintext and some function of the ciphertext. We have not found any such statistical imbalances, and believe Twofish to be immune to this kind of analysis.

9.5.4 Partitioning Cryptanalysis

Partitioning cryptanalysis is another generalization of linear cryptanalysis [Har96, JH96, HM97].[3] An attacker trying to carry out a partitioning attack is generally trying to find some way of partitioning the input and output spaces of the round function so that knowledge of which partition the input to a round is in gives some information about which partition the output from a round is in. This can be seen as a general form of a failure of the block

---

[3] Similar ideas can be found in [Vau96b].

cipher to get good confusion; an attacker after N rounds can distinguish the output from the Nth round from a random block of bits, because the output is somewhat more likely to be in one specific partition than in any of the others. This can be used in a straightforward way to attack the last round of the cipher.[4]

We have been unable to find any useful way to partition the input and output spaces of the Twofish F function or a Twofish round that works consistently across many keys, because of the key-dependent S-boxes. For the 128-bit key case, there are 2^{64} different F functions, presumably each with its own most useful partitioning. We are not aware of any general way to partition F's inputs and outputs to facilitate such attacks.

9.5.5 Differential-linear Cryptanalysis

Differential-linear cryptanalysis uses a combination of techniques from both differential and linear cryptanalysis [LH94]. Due to the need to cover the last part of the cipher with two copies of a linear characteristic, the bias of the linear characteristic is likely to be extremely small unless the linear portion of the attack is confined to just three or four rounds. (The available linear characteristics for Twofish's round function have a relatively low probability, and are very hard to combine due to the MDS and PHT mappings.) This means that the cryptanalyst would need to cover almost all of the rounds with the differential characteristic, making a differential-linear analysis not much more powerful than a purely differential analysis. Therefore, we feel that differential-linear cryptanalysis is unlikely to be successful against the Twofish structure. In our analysis, we have found no differential-linear attacks that work against Twofish.

9.6 Interpolation Attack

The interpolation attack [JK97, MSK98b] is effective against ciphers that use simple algebraic functions. The principle of the attack is simple: if the ciphertext can be represented as a polynomial or rational expression (with N coefficients) of the plaintext, then the polynomial or rational expression can be reconstructed using N plaintext/ciphertext pairs.

However, interpolation attacks are often only workable against ciphers with a very small number of rounds, or against ciphers whose round functions have very low algebraic degree. Twofish's S-boxes already have relatively large algebraic degree, and the combination of operations from different algebraic groups (including both addition mod 2^{32} and XOR) should help increase the degree even further. Therefore, we believe that Twofish is secure against interpolation attacks after even only a small number of rounds.

---

[4] Basic results against reduced-round DES can be found in [HYSK98].

9.7 Partial Key Guessing Attacks

A good key schedule should have the property that, when an attacker guesses some subset of the key bits, he does not learn very much about the subkey sequence or other internal operations in the cipher. The Twofish key schedule has this property.

Consider an attacker who guesses the even words of the key M_e. He learns nothing of the key S to g. For each round subkey block, he now knows A_i. If he guesses K_0, he can compute the corresponding K_1. He can carry this attack out against as many round subkeys as he likes, but each guess takes 32 bits. We can see no way for the attacker to actually test the 96-bit guess that it would take to attack even one round's subkey in this way on the full Twofish.

An alternative is to guess the key input S to g. This is only half the length of the full key M, but provides no information about the round keys K_i. The differential attack described in Section 9.2 is the best way we were able to find to test such a partial key guess. We can see no way to test a guess of S on the full 16-round Twofish.

9.8 Related-key Cryptanalysis

Related-key cryptanalysis [Bih94, KSW96, KSW97] uses a cipher's key schedule to break plaintexts encrypted with related keys. In its most advanced form, differential related-key cryptanalysis, both plaintexts and keys with chosen differentials are used to recover the keys. This type of analysis has had considerable success against ciphers with simplistic key schedules—e.g., GOST [GOST89] and 3-Way [DGV94b, Dae95]—and is a realistic attack in some circumstances. A conventional attack is usually judged in terms of the number of plaintexts or ciphertexts needed for the attack, and the level of access to the cipher needed to get those texts (i.e., known plaintext, chosen plaintext, adaptive chosen plaintext). A related-key attack adds another parameter—number of related keys under which the plaintexts will be encrypted.

9.8.1 Resistance to Related-key Slide Attacks

A "slide" attack occurs in an iterated cipher when the encryption of one block for rounds 1 through n is the same as the encryption of another block for rounds $s + 1$ to $s + n$. An attacker can look at two encryptions, and can slide the rounds forward in one of them relative to another. S-1 [Anon95] can be broken with a slide attack [Wag95a]. Travois [Yuv97] has identical round functions, and can also be broken with a slide attack. Conventional slide attacks allow one to break the cipher with only known- or chosen-plaintext queries; however, as we shall see next, there is a generalization to related-key attacks as well.

Related-key slide attacks were first discovered by Biham in his attack on a DES variant [Bih94]. To mount a related-key slide attack on Twofish, an attacker must find a pair of keys M, M^* such that the key-dependent S-boxes in g are unchanged, but the subkey sequences slide down one round. This amounts to finding, for each of the eight byte-permutations used for subkey generation, a change in the keys such that:

$$s_i(j, M) = s_i(j + 2s, M^*)$$

for n values of j. In total, this requires $8n$ of these relations to hold.

Let us look in more detail for a fixed key M. Let $m \in \{5, \ldots, 8\}$ be the number of S-boxes used to compute the round keys that are affected by the difference between M and M^*. Observe that $m \geq 5$ due to the restriction that S cannot change and the properties of the RS matrix that at least five inputs must change to keep the output constant. There are at most $\binom{8}{m} 2^{32m-128}$ possible choices of M^*. We have a total of nm 8-bit relations that need to be satisfied. The expected number of M^* that satisfy these relations is thus $\binom{8}{m} \cdot 2^{-8nm+32m-128}$. For $n \geq 4$ this is dominated by the case $m = 5$; we will ignore the other cases for now. So for each M we can expect about 2^{38-40n} keys M^* that support a slide attack for $n \geq 4$. This means that any specific key is unlikely to support a slide attack with $n \geq 4$. Over all possible key pairs, we expect $2^{293-40n}$ pairs M, M^* for which a slide of $n \geq 4$ occurs. Thus, it is unlikely that a pair exists at all with $n \geq 8$.

Swapping Key Halves. It is worth considering what happens when we swap key halves. That is, we swap the key bytes so that the values of M_e and M_o are exchanged. In that case, the sequence of A_i and B_i values totally changes because of the different index values used. We can see no useful attack that could come from this.

Permuting the Subkeys. Although there is no known attack stemming from it, it is interesting to ask whether there exist pairs of keys that give permutations of one another's subkeys. There are 20! ways that the rounds' subkey blocks could be permuted. This is almost as large as 2^{64}, and so there may very well be pairs of keys that give permutations of one another's round subkey blocks.

9.8.2 Resistance to Related-key Differential Attacks

A related-key differential attack seeks to mount a differential attack on a block cipher through the key, as well as or instead of through the plaintext/ciphertext port. Against Twofish, such an attack must control the subkey difference sequence for at least the rounds in the middle. For the sake of simplifying discussions of the attack, let us consider an attacker who wants to put a chosen subkey difference into the middle 12 rounds' subkeys. That is, he wants to change M to M^* and control $D[i, M, M*]$ for $i = 12, \ldots, 35$. At the same time, he needs to keep the g function, and thus the key S, from changing. All else being equal, the longer the key, the more freedom an attacker has to mount a related-key differential attack. We thus will assume the use of 256-bit keys for the remainder of this section. Note that a successful related-key attack on 128- or 192-bit keys that gets only zero subkey differences in the rounds whose subkey differences it must control translates directly to an equivalent related-key attack on 256-bit keys.

Consider the position of the attacker if he attempts a related-key differential attack with different S keys. This must result in different g outputs for all inputs, since we know that there are no pairs of S values that lead to identical S-boxes. Assuming the pair of S values does not lead to linearly related S-boxes, it will not be possible to compensate for this change in S with changes in the subkeys in single rounds. If we assume 12 active rounds in the attack, the added difficulty is approximately that of adding 24 active S-boxes to the existing related-key attack. For this reason, we believe that any useful related-key attack will require a pair of keys that keeps S unchanged.

9.8.3 The Zero Difference Case

The simplest related-key attack to analyze is the one that keeps both S and also the middle 12 rounds' subkeys unchanged. It thus seeks to generate identical A and B sequences for 12 rounds, and thus to keep the individual byte sequences used to derive A and B identical.

The RS code used to derive S from M strictly limits the ways an attacker can change M without altering S. The attacker must try to keep the number of active subkey generating S-boxes as low as possible, since each active S-box is another constraint on his attack. The attacker can keep the number of active S-boxes down to five without altering S, so this is what he should do. With only the key bytes affecting these five subkey generation S-boxes active, he can alter between one and four bytes in all five S-boxes; the nature of the RS matrix is that if he needs to alter four bytes in any one of these S-boxes, he must alter bytes in all five. In practice, in order to maximize his control over the byte sequences generated by these S-boxes, he must alter four bytes in all five active S-boxes.

To get zero subkey differences, the attacker must get zero differences in the byte sequences generated by all five active S-boxes. Consider a single such byte sequence: the attacker tries to find a pair of four-byte key inputs such that they lead to identical byte sequences in the middle 12 rounds, which means the middle 12 bytes. There are 2^{63} pairs of key inputs from which to choose, and about 2^{95} possible byte sequences available. If the byte sequences behave more-or-less like random functions of the key inputs, this implies that it is extremely unlikely that an attacker can find a pair of key inputs that will get identical byte sequences in these middle 12 rounds. We discuss this kind of analysis of byte sequences in Section 8.2.3. From this analysis, we would not expect to see a pair of keys for even one S-box with more than eight successive bytes unchanged, and we would expect even eight successive bytes of unchanged byte sequence to require control of all four key bytes into the S-box. We would expect a specific pair of key bytes to be required to generate these similar byte sequences.

To extend this to five active S-boxes, we expect there to be, at best, a single pair of values for the 20 active key bytes that leave the middle eight subkeys unchanged.

9.8.4 Other Difference Sequences

An attacker who has control of the XOR difference sequences in A_i, B_i does not necessarily have great control over the XOR or modulo 2^{32} difference sequence that appears in the subkeys.

First, we must consider the context of a related-key differential attack. The attacker does not generally know all of the key bytes generating either A_i or B_i. Instead, he knows the XOR difference sequence in A_i and B_i.

Consider an A_i value with an XOR difference of δ. If the Hamming weight of δ is k, not including the high-order bit, then the best estimate for the XOR difference that ends up in the two subkey words for a given round generally has probability of about 2^{-2k}. (Control of the A_i, B_i XOR difference sequence does not make controlling the subkey XOR differences substantially easier.)

Consider an A_i value with an XOR difference of δ. If the Hamming weight of δ is k, then the best estimate for the modulo 2^{32} difference of the two subkey words for a given round has probability of about 2^{-k}.

This points out one of the difficulties in mounting any kind of successful related-key attack with non-zero A_i, B_i difference sequences. If an attacker can find a difference sequence for A_i, B_i that keeps $k = 3$, and needs to control the subkey differences for 12 rounds, he has a probability of about 2^{-72} of getting the most likely XOR subkey difference sequence, and about 2^{-36} of getting the most likely modulo 2^{32} difference sequence. After getting the most likely mod 2^{32} difference into the subkeys, however, the attacker must deal with the fact that the output values are XORed into half of the block. Those relatively high-probability mod 2^{32} differences end up back at 2^{-72} probability for any given XOR difference sequence actually being XORed into the successive rounds' target blocks.

9.8.5 Probability of a Successful Attack with One Related-key Query

We consider the use of the RS matrix in deriving S from M to be a powerful defense against related-key differential attacks, because it forces an attacker to keep at least five key generation S-boxes active. Our analysis suggests that any useful control of the subkey difference sequence requires that each active S-box in the attack have all four key bytes changed.

Further, our analysis suggests that, for nearly any useful difference sequence, each active S-box in the attack has a specific pair of defining key bytes it needs to work. An attacker specifying his key relation in terms of bytewise XOR has five pairs of sequences of four key bytes each, which he wants to get. This leaves him with a probability of a pair of keys with his desired relation actually leading to the desired attack of about 2^{-115}, which moves the attack totally outside the realm of practical attacks.

So long as an attacker is unable to improve this, either by finding a way to get useful difference sequences into the subkeys without having so many active key bytes, or by finding a way to mount related-key attacks with different S values for the different keys, we do not believe that any kind of related-key differential attack is feasible.

Note the implication of this: clever ways to control a couple extra rounds' subkey differences are not going to make the attacks feasible, unless they also allow the attacker to use far fewer active key bytes. For reference, note that with one altered key byte per active subkey generation S-box, the attacker ends up with a 2^{-39} probability that a pair of related keys will yield an attack; with two key bytes per active S-box, this increases to 2^{-78}; with three key bytes per active S-box, it increases to 2^{-117}. In practice, this means that any key relation requiring more than one byte of key changed per active S-box appears to be impractical.

9.8.6 Conclusions

Our analysis suggests that related-key differential attacks against the full Twofish are not workable. Note, however, that we have spent less time working on resistance to chosen-key attacks, such as will be available to an attacker if Twofish is used in the straightforward way to define a hash function. For this reason, we recommend that more analysis be done before Twofish is used in the straightforward way as a hash function, and we note that it appears to be much more secure to use Twofish in this way with 128-bit keys than with 256-bit keys, despite the fact that this also slows the speed of a hash function down by a factor of two.

9.9 A Chosen-key Attack

A chosen-key attack is a variant of a related-key attack. Not only are there several keys that are related, the attacker actually gets to choose some parts of these keys. The parts not chosen are unknown to the attacker, and the objective of the attack is to find them.

Attack Type	Rounds	Work Factor	Text Req.	Special Req.
Partial Chosen Key	10	2^{34}	$2^{32};2^{12}$	160 bits of key from K, K^* chosen by attacker
Related-Key	10	2^{187}	$2^{32};2^{12}$	2^{155} related-key queries

Table 9.9. Attack Results for Our Chosen-key Attack

9.9.1 Overview of the Attack

Results. We define a partial chosen key attack on a 10-round Twofish without the pre- or post-whitening. The attack requires us to control 20 selected bytes of the key, and to set them differently for a pair of related keys K, K^*. The remaining 12 bytes of the two keys, which are the same for both keys, are unknown to us; recovering them is the objective of the attack. Our attack results are summarized in Table 9.9.

Note that the text requirements are shown as n;m, where n is the number of chosen plaintexts, and m is the number of adaptive chosen plaintexts. Also note that the related-key version of the attack requires this many chosen and adaptive chosen plaintexts for each of the 2^{155} related-key pairs.

How the Attack Works. The attack works as follows:

1. Choose a pair of keys, K, K^*, with the property that the middle eight round subkeys are the same for both keys, and the S key value is the same for both keys. This leaves us with some knowledge about the differences that make it into the subkeys as well.

2. Request one encryption under K, and 2^{32} encryptions under K^*, trying to find a way to offset the effect of the change in the first round subkey.

3. When we find a likely right pair (detected because of the zero difference in half the ciphertext block), use it to probe the contents of each S-box in turn. This allows us to recover the S key value. This value, given the RS matrix used for its derivation and our starting partial knowledge of the key, allows us to recover the rest of the key algebraically.

9.9.2 Finding a Key Pair

The first step in the attack is finding a pair of keys, K, K^*, with some relationship, such that we get a useful subkey difference sequence, while leaving the S key unchanged. We described above how such keys can exist. Here, we assume the existence of some pair of keys with a subkey XOR difference sequence zero in rounds one through eight but with non-zero XOR subkey differences in rounds zero and nine.

Structure of the Key Pair. Based on the discussion above, we assume that the keys K, K^* differ in 20 bytes, with the changed bytes selected in such a way to leave S unchanged between the two keys, and to change all four key bytes used to define five of the S-boxes used for subkey generation. We note that a random pair of keys chosen to have this property has only a 2^{-155} probability of being the pair of keys that will generate our desired subkey difference sequence. This makes this attack impractical as a differential related-key attack, though an attacker who is able to control the active 20 bytes of key involved in a pair of keys could mount the attack for a chosen pair of keys. (That is, the attacker could choose the values of the active 20 bytes of both K and K^*, while remaining ignorant of the other twelve bytes of K and K^*, which must be identical for both keys. The attacker would then attempt to learn those remaining 12 bytes of key.)

Subkey Differences. We actually care only about the subkey difference in the round subkey words. Recall that the subkey words are generated from a pair of 32-bit words, which are generated from the subkey generation S-boxes. Let's call these values U, V and U^*, V^*. We don't know any of U, V, U^*, V^*, but we do know $U' = U \oplus U^*$ and $V' = V \oplus V^*$.

9.9.3 Choosing the Plaintexts to Request

From U', V', it is possible to generate a set of about 2^{32} XOR difference values that we can expect to see result from the changed subkeys when they're used in the F function in the first round. We thus do the following:

1. Request the encryption of some fixed 128-bit block A, B, C, D under key K.

2. For each of the 2^{32} different 64-bit XOR difference values, X_i, Y_i, we might expect from U', V', request the encryption of 128-bit block $(A, B, C \oplus X_i, D \oplus Y_i)$.

3. Consider only those ciphertexts from the second step that lead to the same right half of ciphertext as the encryption under K in the first step. The goal is to determine the output XOR from the first round's F function when the input is A, B, under the two keys. (The only difference in the output is caused by the difference in round subkeys.) Note that we expect to have about one false positive occur; we simply run the attack on both potential right pairs; the wrong pair will not allow the attacker to find *any* S-box offsetting differences.

9.9.4 Extracting the Key Material

At this point, we know the single XOR difference from the F function. We can now learn the S-boxes in the g function. To do this, we replace the high-order byte of A in the right pair with 256 different values. Thus, we request the encryption of A_j, B, C, D under K^*. This causes one of 256 possible XOR differences in the g function output. We expect to have to try about 512 requests with different XOR difference values X_i, Y_i, where these values are derived from the X_i, Y_i values that generated the original right pair based on the possible XOR differences in g. We thus request 512 plaintexts of the form $A_j, B, C \oplus X_i, D \oplus Y_i)$ to be encrypted under K^*. One of these we expect to be a right pair, which we can recognize, again, by the fact that the right half of the ciphertext is the same for A_j, B, C, D encrypted under K, and for $A_j, B, C \oplus X_i, D \oplus Y_i$ encrypted under K^*.

After carrying this out for each of the A_j, we have good information about the XOR differences being generated from g by the changes between A and A_j as input. In particular, we will note the 14 cases where we probably got 8-bit Hamming weights in the output XOR difference of g. This information should be enough to brute-force this S-box, $s3$. That is, we try all 2^{32} possible S-boxes for $s3$, and expect one to be the best fit for our data.

We repeat the attack for each of the other bytes in A, so that we recover all four S-boxes in g. When we know these S-boxes, this means we know S. Note that at the beginning of the attack, we already know 20 of the 32 key bytes used. More importantly, due to the structure of the RS matrix used to derive S from the raw key bytes, we know all but three bytes used to derive each 4-byte "row" of values in S. This allows us to guess and check the remaining key bytes three bytes at a time, thus recovering the entire key.

9.10 Side-Channel Cryptanalysis and Fault Analysis

Resistance to these attacks was not part of the AES criteria, and hence not a major concern in this design. However, we do have these comments to make on the design.

Side-channel cryptanalysis [KSWH98b] uses information about the cipher in addition to the plaintext or ciphertext. Examples include timing [Koc96], power consumption (including differential power analysis [Koc98a]), NMR scanning, and electronic emanations.[5] With many algorithms it is possible to reconstruct the key from these side channels. While total resistance to side-channel cryptanalysis is probably impossible, we note that Twofish executes in constant time on most processors.

Fault analysis [BDL97, BS97] can be used to successfully cryptanalyze this cipher. Again, we believe that total resistance to fault analysis is an impossible design constraint for a cipher. The resistance to fault analysis of any block cipher can be improved using classical tamper-resistance and fault-tolerance techniques (although see [AK96]).

In most cases, Twofish seems to be inherently resistant to timing analysis. However, it is worth noting that in certain special cases, implementers may

---

[5] The NSA refers to this particular side channel as "TEMPEST."

need to take extra care to avoid the possibility of timing attacks. On platforms with extremely limited memory resources, it is natural to compute the multiplies over $GF(2^8)$ on the fly without the aid of additional tables by using a shift-register–based approach. If this approach is to be followed, beware: timing attacks may be possible. The obvious way to clock a shift register in software is to shift it and then XOR in the feedback polynomial if the bit that shifted out was a one—but this algorithm does not execute in constant time, because the XOR operation is performed only if a certain data bit is set. Thus, this implementation pattern should be avoided. A better approach would be to XOR in either zero or the feedback polynomial, depending on the value of the bit just shifted out, thereby guaranteeing constant-time execution and resistance to timing analysis. This is probably only of concern to smart cards and other computing platforms without much memory.

9.11 Attacking Simplified Twofish

9.11.1 Twofish with Known S-boxes

As discussed above, our differential attack on Twofish with fixed S-boxes works for 6-round Twofish, and requires only 2^{67} effort. A 7-round differential attack requires 2^{131} effort.

Additionally, much of Twofish's related-key attack resistance comes from the derivation of the S-boxes, so a related-key attack is much easier against a known S-box variant.

9.11.2 Twofish without Round Subkeys

We attack a Twofish variant without any subkeys, thus whose whole key material is in the key-dependent S-boxes. The attack requires about 2^{33} chosen plaintexts; it breaks the Twofish variant with about 2^{36} effort, even when the cipher has a 128-bit key. (Note that this is the amount of key material used to define the S-boxes in normal Twofish with a 256-bit key.)

It is obvious that a Twofish variant with fixed S-boxes and no subkeys would be insecure—there would be no key material injected. We develop a slide attack on Twofish with any number of rounds, and a 128-bit key. (The Twofish key would be 256 bits, but since we never use more than 128 bits of key in the key-dependent S-boxes, the effective key size is 128 bits.)

Note that this attack would not work if we used round subkeys that were simply counter values, as would happen if we used the identity permutation for all the key-scheduling S-boxes. We are not currently aware of any attack on such a Twofish variant.

Overview of the Attack. In a slide attack, we attempt to find a pair of plaintexts, (P, P^*), such that P^* has the same value as the intermediate value after one or more rounds of encrypting P. If we can find and expose this value, we gain direct access to the results of a single round of the cipher; we then attack that single round to recover the key.

Our attack has two parts:

1. We must first find a pair of plaintexts, (P, P^*), such that P^* is the result of encrypting P with one round.

2. We use this pair to derive four relations on g and thus determine the specific S-boxes used in g. This yields the effective key of the cipher.

Finding Our Related Pair of Texts. Twofish is a Feistel cipher, operating on two 64-bit halves in each block. We use the representation where the left half of the block is the input to the Feistel function, and the halves are swapped after each round. Let (L_0, R_0) represent a given pair of 64-bit halves input into the cipher, and let (L_N, R_N) represent the resulting ciphertext. To mount this attack, we need to find some (L_0, R_0, L_1) such that L_1 is the value of the left half of the block after the first round. To test whether we have such a pair, we can try encrypting (L_0, R_0) and (L_1, L_0). When we have a triple with the desired properties, we get (L_N, R_N) from the first encryption, and (L_{N+1}, L_N) from the second encryption.

We use a trick by Biham [Bih94] to get such a pair of plaintexts with only 2^{33} chosen plaintexts: we choose a fixed L_0, and encrypt it with 2^{32} randomly selected R_0 values as (L_0, R_0). We then encrypt the same L_0 with 2^{32} random R_1 values, as (R_1, L_0). By the birthday paradox, we expect to see one pair of values for which $R_1 = R_0 \oplus F(L_0)$. To find this pair, we sort the ciphertexts from the first batch of encryptions on their left halves, and the ciphertexts from the second batch of encryptions on their right halves. When we find a match, the probability is good that we have a pair with the desired property.

Extracting g Values. Once we have this triple (L_0, R_0, L_1), we also have two relations on F: $F(L_0) = R_0 \oplus L_1$ and $F(L_N) = R_N \oplus L_{N+1}$. Note, however, that we do not yet have direct g values. Instead, we have two instances of the results of combining two g outputs with a PHT. Since we have the actual PHT output values, we can simply undo the PHT, yielding relations on g. Our pair has given us two relations on F, and thus four relations on g.

Extracting the S-boxes. The g outputs are the result of applying four key-dependent S-boxes to the input bytes, and then combining those bytes with an MDS matrix multiply. Since the MDS multiply is invertible, we invert it to get back the actual S-box outputs for all four different values. If those values are all different, then we have four bytes of output from each S-box. We can try all 2^{32} possible key input values for each S-box, and see which ones are consistent with the results; for most sets byte values, only one or two S-boxes will match them. We thus learn each key-dependent S-box in g, perhaps with a couple of alternative values. We try all possible alternatives against any plaintext/ciphertext values we have available, and very quickly recover the correct S-boxes. Since this is the only key material in this Twofish variant, the attack is done.

9.11.3 Twofish with Non-bijective S-boxes

We decided early in the design process to use purely bijective S-boxes. One rationale was to ensure that the 64-bit round function is bijective. That way, iterative 2-round differential characteristics cannot exist; when they do exist, they often result in the highest-probability multi-round characteristic, so avoiding them should help to reduce the risk of a successful differential attack. Also, attacks based on non-surjective round functions [BB95, RP95b, RPD97, CWSK98] are sure to fail when the 64-bit Feistel round function is bijective.[6]

We argue here that this was a good design decision, by showing that a Twofish variant that uses non-bijective S-boxes is likely to be much easier to break.

Observe that when q_0 and q_1 are non-bijective, their 3-way composition into s_i is likely to be even more non-surjective than either q_0 or q_1 on its own. It is easily seen that the expected size of the range of a random function on eight bits (such as q_0 or q_1) is $r_1 = 1 - (1 - 1/256)^{256} \approx 1 - e^{-1} \approx 0.632$. When we compose such a function twice, its expected range becomes $r_2 = 1 - (1 - 1/256)^{256r_1} \approx 1 - e^{-r_1} \approx 0.469$; and the expected size of the range of a 3-way composition will be $r_3 \approx 1 - e^{-r_2} \approx 0.374$. In other words, we expect that only about $96 = 0.374 \times 256$ of all possible 8-bit values can appear as the output of the S-box. Therefore, the output of the h function can attain only about $2^{26.3} \approx 96^4$ possible values, and the 64-bit Feistel function can attain only about $2^{52.6}$ of all 2^{64} possible outputs. This is certainly a rather large certificational weakness. (This gets worse when the key size grows, since the number of compositions of the q functions gets larger.)

We point out a serious differential attack when using non-bijective random S-boxes. Consider the probability $p_{\Delta x}$ that a given input difference Δx yields a collision in the S-box output; i.e., $\Delta x \mapsto 0$. Let $p = \sum_{\Delta x \neq 0} p_{\Delta x}/255$ be the average probability over all non-zero input differences, and let $m = \max_{\Delta x \neq 0} p_{\Delta x}$ be the maximum probability over all non-zero input differences. We have $\mathbf{E}\, p = 3/256$; also, $\Pr(p \geq 2/256) \approx 0.78$, $\Pr(p \geq 10/256) \approx 0.02$, and $\Pr(p \geq 16/256) \approx 0.0002$. As for the distribution of m, empirically $\mathbf{E}\, m \approx 11.7/256$; experiments suggest $\Pr(m \geq 10/256) \approx 0.975$, $\Pr(m \geq 16/256) \approx .04$, and $\Pr(m \geq 22/256) \approx 0.0002$.

Consider a Twofish variant with random non-bijective S-boxes and no rotations. We obtain a 2-round iterative differential characteristic with probability m, and thus a 13-round differential characteristic with probability m^6.

---

[6] Vaudenay's attack on Blowfish took advantage of non-bijectivity in the Blowfish round function [Vau96a].

We find that, for 97.5 percent of the keys, one can break the variant with about 2^{28} chosen plaintexts; for 4 percent of the keys, it can be broken with 2^{24} chosen plaintexts; and for a class of weak keys consisting of 0.02 percent of the keys, the variant cipher can be broken with roughly 2^{21} chosen plaintexts. (Of course, one can trade off the number of texts needed against the size of the weak key class; the figures given are just examples of points on a smooth curve.)

Next we consider a Twofish variant with random non-bijective S-boxes, but with all rotations left intact. If we look at any 2-round differential characteristic whose first round is the trivial characteristic and whose second round involves just one active S-box, we expect its probability to be about p. One difficulty is that the rotations prevent us from finding an iterative 2-round characteristic. However, we can certainly piece together 6.5 different 2-round differential characteristics (each of the right form so it will have probability about p) to find a 13-round characteristic with expected probability p^6. (The latter probability can probably be improved to about $3p^6$, due to the extra degrees of freedom, but as we are only doing a back-of-the-envelope estimate anyway, we will omit these considerations.) Thus, we can find a differential attack that succeeds with about 2^{39} chosen plaintexts for the majority (about 78 percent) of the keys; also, for 2 percent of the keys, this variant can be broken with 2^{28} chosen plaintexts; and for a class of weak keys consisting of 0.02 percent of the keys, the variant cipher can be broken with roughly 2^{24} chosen plaintexts.

This analysis clearly shows the value of bijective S-boxes in stopping differential cryptanalysis. Also, it helps show the benefit of the rotations: they make short iterative characteristics much harder to find, thereby conferring (we hope) some additional resistance against differential attacks.

9.12 Trap Doors in Twofish

We assert that Twofish has no trap doors. As designers, we have made every effort to make Twofish secure against all known (and unknown) cryptanalysis, and we have made no effort to build in a secret way of breaking Twofish. However, there is no way to prove this, and not much reason for anyone to believe us. We can offer some assurances.

In this book, we have outlined all of the design elements of Twofish and our justifications for including them. We have explained, in great detail, how we chose Twofish's "magic constants": the RS code, q_0, q_1, and the MDS matrix. There are no mysterious design elements; everything has an explicit purpose. Moreover, we feel that the use of key-dependent S-boxes makes it harder to install a trap door into the cipher. As difficult as it is to create a trap door for a particular set of carefully constructed S-boxes, it is much harder to create one that works with all possible S-boxes or even a reasonably useful subset of them (of relative size 2^{-20} or so).

Additionally, any trap door would have to survive 16 rounds of Twofish. It would have to work even though there is almost perfect diffusion in each round. It would have to survive the pre- and post-whitening. These design elements have long been known to make any patterns difficult to detect; trap doors would be no different.

None of this constitutes a proof. Any reasonable proof of general security for a block cipher would also prove $\mathbf{P} \neq \mathbf{NP}$. Rather than outlining the proof here, we would likely skip the AES competition and go collect our Fields Medal.

However, we have made headway towards a philosophical proof. Assume for a moment that, despite the difficulties listed above, we did manage to put a trap door into Twofish. This would imply one of two things:

One, that we have invented a powerful new cryptanalytic attack and have carefully crafted Twofish to be resistant to all known attacks but vulnerable to this new one. We cannot prove that this is not true. However, we can point out that as cryptographers we would achieve much more fame and glory by publishing our powerful new cryptanalytic attack. In fact, we would probably publish it along with this paper, making sure Twofish is immune so that we can profitably attack the other AES submissions.

The other possibility is that we have embedded a trap door into the Twofish magic constants and then transformed them by some means so that finding them would be a statistical impossibility (see [Har96] for some discussion of this possibility). The resulting construction would seem immune to current cryptanalytic techniques, but we as designers would know a secret transformation rule that we could apply to facilitate cryptanalysis. Again, we cannot prove that this is not true. However, it has been shown that this type of cipher, called a "master-key cryptosystem," is equivalent to a public-key cryptosystem [BFL96]. Again, as cryptographers we would achieve far greater recognition by publishing a public-key cryptosystem that is not dependent on factoring [RSA78] or the discrete logarithm problem [DH76, ElG85, NIST94]. And the resulting algorithm's dual capabilities as both a symmetric and public-key algorithm would make it far more flexible than the AES competition requires (and hence an excellent choice for the standard).

There is a large gap between a weakness that is exploitable in theory and one that is exploitable in practice. Even the best attack against DES (a linear-cryptanalysis-like attack combining quadratic approximations and a multiple-approximation method) requires just under 2^{43} plaintext/ciphertext blocks [SK98], which is equivalent to about 64 terabytes of plaintext/ciphertext encrypted under a single key. A useful trap door would need to work with much less plaintext—a few thousand blocks—or it would have to reduce the effective keyspace to something on the order of 2^{72}. We believe that, given the quality of the public cryptanalytic research community, it would be impossible to put a weakness of this magnitude into a block cipher and have it remain undetected through the AES process. And we would be foolish to even try.

10. Using Twofish

10.1 Chaining Modes

All standard block-cipher chaining modes work with Twofish: CBC, CFB, OFB, counter [NBS80]. We are aware of no problems with using Twofish with any commonly used chaining mode. (See [Sch96] for a detailed comparison of the various modes of operation.) A cryptanalyst considering OFB-, CFB-, or CBC-mode encryption with Twofish may collapse the pre- and post-whitening of key material into a single XOR, but he does not appear to benefit much from this.

10.2 One-Way Hash Functions

It is not hard to build a one-way hash function out of Twofish [Win84]. We suggest the following construction, taken from [Pre93]:

$$H_i = M_i \oplus E_{H_{i-1}}(M_i)$$

This mode seems to be somewhat preferable to Davies-Meyer, because it gives the cryptanalyst less control over the value entering the key port and thus may provide more robust protection in case there are any related-key attacks on Twofish.

We believe that Twofish, with its strong key schedule, can be used securely in any of these formats. Note, however, that the key schedule has been analyzed mainly for related-key attacks, not for the class of chosen-key attack that hash functions must resist. Additionally, the 128-bit block size makes straightforward use of this construction useful only when collision-finding attacks can be expected to be unable to try 2^{64} trial hashes to find a collision.

As keys that are non-standard sizes have equivalent keys that are longer, any use of Twofish in a hashing construction must ensure that only a single key length is used. We recommend using 128-bit keys for hashing constructions.

10.3 Message Authentication Codes

Twofish can be easily used to build a very strong message authentication code using the CBC-MAC construction [BKR94]. In fact, [BKR94] gives formal proofs of security for the CBC-MAC approach, assuming that the underlying cipher is secure. We feel that this makes Twofish-CBC-MAC a very strong candidate for use in message authentication applications.

Alternatives include using Twofish as a hash function, and then constructing a MAC out of the hash function [BCK96].

10.4 Pseudorandom Number Generators

Twofish can also be used as a primitive in a pseudorandom number generator suitable for generating session keys, public-key parameters, protocol nonces, and so on [Plu94, KSWH98a, Gut98, KSWH98c].

10.5 Larger Keys

Even though it would be straightforward to extend the Twofish key schedule scheme to larger key sizes, there is currently no definition of Twofish for key lengths greater than 256 bits. We urge caution in trying to extend key lengths; our experience with Twofish has taught us that extending the key length can have important security implications.

10.6 Additional Block Sizes

There is no definition of Twofish for block lengths other than 128 bits. While it may be theoretically possible to extend the construction to larger block sizes, we have not evaluated these constructions at all. We urge caution in trying to extend the block size; many of the constructions we use may not scale well to 256 bits, 512 bits, or larger blocks.

10.7 More or Fewer Rounds

Twofish is defined to have 16 rounds. We designed the key schedule to allow natural extensions to more or fewer rounds if and when required. We strongly advise against reducing the number of rounds. We believe it is safe to increase the number of rounds, although we see no need to do so. Note that the key schedule cannot support more than 124 rounds, as the 8-bit input counter to the key schedule S-boxes overflows.

Algorithm	Key Length	Width (bits)	Rounds	Cycles	Clocks/ Byte
Twofish	variable	128	16	8	16.1
Blowfish	variable	64	16	8	19.8
Square	128	128	8	8	20.3
RC5-32/16	variable	64	32	16	24.8
CAST-128	128	64	16	8	29.5
DES	56	64	16	8	43
Serpent	128, 192, 256	128	32	32	45
SAFER (S)K-128	128	64	8	8	52
FEAL-32	64, 128	64	32	16	65
IDEA	128	64	8	8	74
Triple-DES	112	64	48	24	116

Table 10.1. Performance of Different Block Ciphers (on a Pentium)

More and more recent ciphers are being defined with a variable number of rounds; e.g., SAFER-K64 [Mas94], RC5 [Riv95], and SPEED [Zhe97]. This means that it is impossible to categorically state that a given cipher construction is insecure: there might always be a number of rounds n for which the cipher is still secure. However, while this might theoretically be true, this is not a useful engineering definition of "secure." After all, the user of the cipher actually has to choose how many rounds to use. In a performance-driven model, it is useful to compare ciphers of equal speed, and compare their security, or compare ciphers of equal security and compare their speeds. For example, FEAL-32 is secure against both differential and linear attacks. Its speed is 65 clock cycles per byte of encryption, which makes it less desirable than faster, also secure, alternatives. As speed is relatively easy to measure and quantify, the simplest way of comparing ciphers in a performance-driven model is to choose the number of rounds in such a way as to make the two ciphers equally fast. The hard question of "which cipher is more secure" then remains, but at least that is a clearly defined problem.

With that in mind, Table 10.1 gives performance metrics for block and stream ciphers on the Pentium processor.[1] Similar comparisons are being done for the AES candidates [SKW+99a], and will presumably be one of the criteria in the selection process.

---

[1] These metrics are based on theoretical analyses of the algorithms and actual hand-tooled assembly-language implementations [SW97, PRB98a, PRB98b].

10.8 Family Key Variant: Twofish-FK

We often see systems that use a proprietary variant of an existing cipher, altered in some hopefully security-neutral way to prevent that system from interoperating with standard implementations of the cipher. A family key is a way of designing this into the algorithm: each different family key is used to define a different variant of the cipher. In some sense, the family key is like an additional key to the cipher, but in general, it is acceptable for the family key to be very computationally expensive to change. We would expect nearly all Twofish implementations that used any family key to use only one family key.

Our goals for the family key algorithm are as follows:

- No family key variant should be substantially weaker than the original cipher.

- Related-key attacks between different unknown but related family keys, or between a known family key and the original cipher, should be hard to mount.

- The family key should not merely reorder the set of 128-by-128-bit permutations provided by the cipher, it should change that set.

A Twofish family key is simply a 256-bit random Twofish key. This key, FK, is used to derive several blocks of bits, as follows:

1. Preprocessing Step:
   This step is done once per family key.
   a) $T_0 = FK$.
   b) $T_1 = (E_{FK}(0), E_{FK}(1)) \oplus FK$.
   c) $T_2 = E_{FK}(2)$.
   d) $T_3 = E_{FK}(3)$.
   e) $T_4 = $ First 8 bytes of $E_{FK}(4)$.
   Note that, using our little-endian convention, the small integers used as plaintext inputs should occur in the first plaintext byte.

2. Key Scheduling Step: This step is done once per key used under this family key.
   a) Before subkey generation, T_0 is XORed into the key, using as many of the leading bytes of T_0 as necessary.
   b) After subkey generation, T_2 is XORed into the pre-whitening subkeys, T_3 is XORed into the post-whitening subkeys, and T_4 is XORed into each round's 64-bit subkey block.
   c) Before the cipher's S-boxes are derived, T_1 is XORed into the key. Once again, we use as many of the leading bytes of T_1 as we need. Each byte of the key is then passed through the byte permutation q_0, and the result is passed through the RS matrix to get S. Note

that the definition of T_1 means that the effect of the first XOR of FK into the key is undone.

Note the properties of the alterations made by any family key:

- The keyspace is simply permuted for the initial subkey generation.

- The subkeys are altered in a simple way. However, there is strong evidence that this alteration cannot occur by changing keys, based on the same difference sequence analysis used in discussing related-key attacks on Twofish.

- The S-boxes used in the cipher are altered in a powerful way, but one which does not alter the basic required properties of the key schedule. Getting no changes in the S-boxes used in the cipher still requires changing at least five bytes of key, and those five bytes of key must change five of the S-boxes used for subkey generation.

10.8.1 Analysis

Effects of Family Keys on Cryptanalysis. We are not aware of any substantial difference in the difficulty of cryptanalyzing the family key version of the cipher rather than the regular version. The cipher's operations are unchanged by the family key; only subkey and S-box generation are changed. However, they are changed in simple ways; the S-boxes are generated in exactly the same way as before, but the key material provided to them is processed in a simple way first; the round subkeys are generated in the same way as before (again, with the key material processed in a simple way first), and then have a constant 64-bit value XORed in. Related-key attacks of the kind we have been able to consider are made slightly harder, rather than easier, by this 64-bit value. The new constants XORed into the whitening subkeys simply permute the input and output space of the cipher in a very simple way.

Related Keys across Family Keys. Related-key attacks under the same family key appear, as we said above, to be at least as hard as related-key attacks in normal Twofish. There is still the question, however, of whether there are interesting related keys across different family keys. It is hard to see how such related keys would be used, but the analysis may be worth pursuing anyway.

An interesting question, from the perspective of an attacker, is whether there are pairs of keys that give identical subkeys except for the constant values XORed into them, and that also give identical S-boxes. By allowing an attacker to put a constant XOR into all round subkeys, such pairs of keys would provide a useful avenue of attack.

This can be done by finding a pair of related family keys, FK, FK^*, that are identical in their first 128 bits, and a pair of 128-bit cipher keys,

M, M^*, such that M generates the same set of S-boxes with FK that M^* does with FK^*. For a random pair of M, M^* values, this has probability 2^{-64} of happening. Thus, an attacker given complete control over M, M^* and knowledge of FK, FK^* can find such a pair of keys and family keys. However, this does not seem to translate into any kind of clean related-key attack; the attacker must actually choose the specific keys used.

We do not consider this to be a valid attack against the system. In general, related-key attacks between family keys seem unrealistic, but one which also requires the attacker to be able to choose specific key values he is trying to recover is also pointless.

A Valid Related-key Attack. An attacker can also try to find quadruples FK, FK^*, M, M^* such that the subkey generation and the S-box generation both get identical values. This requires that

$$T_0 \oplus M = T_0^* \oplus M^*$$
$$T_1 \oplus M = T_1^* \oplus M^*$$

If FK, FK^* have the property that

$$T_0 \oplus T_0^* = T_1 \oplus T_1^* = \delta$$

then related-key pairs $M, M \oplus \delta$ will put a fixed XOR difference into every round subkey, and may allow some kind of related-key attack. Again, we do not think this is an interesting attack; the attacker must force the family keys to be chosen this way, since the probability that any given pair of family keys will work this way is (for 128-bit cipher keys) 2^{-128}. We do not expect such relationships to occur by chance until about 2^{64} family keys are in use.

11. Historical Remarks

Twofish originated from an attempt to take the original Blowfish design and modify it for a 128-bit block. We wanted to leverage the speed and good diffusion of Blowfish, while also improving it where we could. We wanted the new cipher to have a bijective F function, a much more efficient key schedule, and to be implementable in custom hardware and smart cards in addition to 32-bit processors (i.e., have smaller tables). And we wanted it to be even faster than Blowfish (per byte encrypted), if possible.

Initial thoughts were to have the Blowfish round structure operate on the four 32-bit subblocks in a circular structure (an incomplete Feistel network), but there were problems getting the diffusion to work in both the encryption and decryption directions. Having two parallel Blowfish round functions and letting them interact via a two-dimensional Feistel structure ran into the same problems. Our solution was to have a single Feistel structure with two Blowfish-like 32-bit round functions and to combine them using a PHT (an idea stolen from SAFER). This idea also provided nearly complete avalanche during the round.

Round subkeys are required to avoid slide attacks against identical round functions. We used addition instead of XOR to take advantage of the Pentium LEA opcode and implement them in effectively zero time.

We used 8-by-8-bit S-boxes and an MDS matrix (an idea stolen from Square, although Square uses a single fixed S-box) instead of random 8-by-32-bit S-boxes, both to simplify the key schedule and ensure that the g function is bijective. This construction ensured that Twofish would be efficient on 32-bit processors (by precomputing the S-boxes and MDS matrix into four 8-by-32-bit S-boxes) while still allowing it to be computed on the fly in smart cards. And since our MDS matrix is only ever computed in one direction, we did not have to worry about the matrix's efficiency in the reverse direction (which Square had to consider).

The construction also gave us considerable performance flexibility. We worked hard to keep this flexibility, so implementers would have a choice of how much key pre-processing to do depending on the amount of plaintext to be encrypted. And we tried to maintain these tradeoffs for 32-bit microprocessors, 8-bit microprocessors, and custom hardware.

Since one goal was to be able to keep the complete design in our heads, any complication that did not have a clear purpose was deleted. Additional complications we chose not to introduce were key-dependent MDS matrices or round-dependent variations on the byte ordering and the PHT. We also toyed with the idea of swapping 32-bit words within the Feistel halves (something we called the "twist"), but abandoned it because we saw no need for the additional complexity.

We did keep in the one-bit rotations of the target block, primarily to reduce the vulnerability to any attack based on byte boundaries. The particular manifestation of this one-bit rotation was due to a combination of performance and cryptanalytic concerns. Larger rotations would be slower in some implementations, and simpler constructions were less secure.

We considered using all the key bytes, rather than just half, to define the key-dependent S-boxes. Unfortunately, this made the key setup time for high-end machines unreasonably large, and also made encryption too slow on low-end machines. By dropping this to half the key bits, these performance figures were improved substantially. By carefully selecting how the key bytes were folded down to half their size before being used to generate the cipher's S-boxes, we were able to ensure that pairs of keys with the same S-boxes would have very different subkey sequences.

The key schedule gave us the most trouble. We had to resist the temptation to build a cryptographic key schedule like the ones used by Blowfish, Khufu, and SEAL, because low-end implementations needed to be able to function with minimal additional memory and, if necessary, to compute the subkeys as needed by the cipher. However, a simple key schedule can be an important weak point in a cipher design, leaving the whole cipher vulnerable to partial-key guessing attacks, related-key attacks, or to attacks based on waiting for especially weak keys to be selected by a user. Though our final key schedule is rather complex, it is conceptually much simpler than many of our intermediate designs. Reusing many of the primitives of the cipher (each round's subkeys are generated by a computation nearly identical to the one that goes on inside the round function, except for the specific inputs involved) made it possible to investigate properties of both the key schedule and of the cipher at the same time.

We spent considerable time choosing q_0 and q_1. Since these provide the primary non-linearity in the cipher, they had to be strong. We wanted to be able to construct them algebraically for applications where storing 512 bytes of fixed tables was not possible. In the end, we built permutations from random parameters, and tested the permutations against our required criteria.

The name "Twofish" reared its head late in the design process. We tried various names beginning with "Blow" or ending with "fish." The name Twofish was chosen for several reasons: it is traditional to name ciphers after sea creatures, and animals in general; no one liked "Blowfish II"; the round function originally derived from two Blowfish round functions in parallel; and of course, there is Dr. Seuss [Seu60].[1]

And finally, we cryptanalyzed Twofish. We cryptanalyzed and cryptanalyzed and cryptanalyzed, right up to the morning of the submission deadline. Since then we have cryptanalyzed more, and are continuing to do so. There's no stopping.

---

[1] For readers who did not grow up in North America: Dr. Seuss was a famous writer of children's books, one of which is called *One Fish, Two Fish, Red Fish, Blue Fish*. The marketing tie-ins were too lucrative to ignore.

12. Conclusions and Further Work

We have presented Twofish, the rationale behind its design, and the results of our initial cryptanalysis. Design and cryptanalysis go hand in hand—it is impossible to do one without the other—and it is only in the analysis that the strength of an algorithm can be demonstrated.

During the design process, we learned several lessons about cipher design:

- The encryption algorithm and key schedule must be designed in tandem; subtle changes in one affect the other. It is not enough to design a strong round function and then to graft a strong key schedule onto it (unless you are satisfied with an inefficient and inelegant construction like Blowfish has); both must work together.

- There is no such thing as a key-dependent S-box, only a complicated multistage non-linear function that is implemented as a key-dependent S-box for efficiency.

- Keys should be as short as possible. It is much harder to design an algorithm with a long key than an algorithm with a short key. Throughout our design process, we found it easier to design and analyze Twofish with a 128-bit key than Twofish with a 192- or 256-bit key.

- Build a cipher with strong local encryption and let the round function handle the global diffusion. Designing Twofish in this manner made it very hard to mount any statistical cryptanalytical attacks.

- Consider performance at every stage of the design. Having a code optimization guru on our team from the beginning drastically changed the way we looked at design tradeoffs, to the ultimate benefit of Twofish.

- Analysis can go on forever. Even after the 15 June 1998 AES submission deadline, we are still cryptanalyzing Twofish.

We believe Twofish to be an ideal algorithm choice for AES. It is efficient on large microprocessors, smart cards, and dedicated hardware. The multiple layers of performance tradeoffs in the key schedule make it suitable for a variety of implementations. And the attention to cryptographic detail in the design—both the encryption function and the key schedule—make it suitable as a codebook, output-feedback and cipher-feedback stream cipher, one-way hash function (using standard techniques for converting block ciphers into hash functions), and pseudorandom number generator.

We welcome any new cryptanalysis from the cryptographic community. We plan on continuing to evaluate Twofish all through the AES selection process and beyond. Specifically:

- Whether the number of rounds can safely be reduced. At this point our best non-related-key attack—a differential attack—can only break five rounds. If no better attacks are found after a few years, it may be safe to reduce the number of rounds to 14 or even 12. 12-round Twofish can encrypt and decrypt data at about 220 clock cycles per block on a Pentium, Pentium Pro, and Pentium II.

- Whether there are alternative fixed tables that increase security. We have chosen both the MDS matrix and the fixed permutations, q_0 and q_1, to meet our mathematical requirements. In the event we find better constants that make Twofish even harder to cryptanalyze, we may want to revise the algorithm.

- Whether we can define a Twofish variant with fixed S-boxes. This variant would have a faster key setup time than the algorithm presented here—about 1200 clock cycles on a Pentium Pro—and the same encryption and decryption speeds. Although we cannot break Twofish with fixed S-boxes, further research is required on what the fixed S-boxes would look like, and how much data could be safely encrypted with this variant.

- Whether we can improve our lower bounds on the complexity of a differential attack and a linear attack.

Developing Twofish was a richly rewarding experience, and one of our most satisfying cryptographic projects to date. There is an enormous gap between simply creating a cryptographic primitive and completing a full design process, and we have learned much by completing the process.

References

[AB96a]   R. Anderson and E. Biham, "Two Practical and Provably Secure Block Ciphers: BEAR and LION," *Fast Software Encryption, Third International Workshop Proceedings*, Springer-Verlag, 1996, pp. 113–120. [Page 5]

[AB96b]   R. Anderson and E. Biham, "Tiger: A Fast New Hash Function," *Fast Software Encryption, Third International Workshop Proceedings*, Springer-Verlag, 1996, pp. 89–97. [Pages 38, 46]

[Ada97a]   C. Adams, "Constructing Symmetric Ciphers Using the CAST Design Procedure," *Designs, Codes and Cryptography*, v.12, n.3, Nov 1997, pp. 71–104. [Pages 5, 35, 38, 39]

[Ada97b]   C. Adams, "DES-80," *Workshop on Selected Areas in Cryptography (SAC '97) Workshop Record*, School of Computer Science, Carleton University, 1997, pp. 160–171. [Page 37]

[AGMP96]   G. Álvarez, D. De la Guia, F. Montoya, and A. Peinado, "Akelarre: A New Block Cipher Algorithm," *Workshop on Selected Areas in Cryptography (SAC '96) Workshop Record*, Queens University, 1996, pp. 1–14. [Page 36]

[AK96]   R. Anderson and M. Kuhn, "Tamper Resistance — A Cautionary Note," *Proceedings of the Second USENIX Workshop on Electronic Commerce*, USENIX Press, 1996, pp. 1–11. [Page 111]

[Anon95]   Anonymous, "this looked like it might be interesting," sci.crypt Usenet posting, 9 Aug 1995. [Pages 41, 104]

[AT90]   C.M. Adams and S.E. Tavares, "The Structured Design on Cryptographically Good S-Boxes," *Journal of Cryptology*, v. 3, n. 1, 1990, pp. 27–41. [Page 39]

[AT93]   C.M. Adams and S.E. Tavares, "Designing S-boxes for Ciphers Resistant to Differential Cryptanalysis," *Proceedings of the 3rd Symposium on State and Progress of Research in Cryptography*, Rome, Italy, 15–16 Feb 1993, pp. 181–190. [Pages 35, 39]

[BAK98]   E. Biham, R. Anderson, and L. Knudsen, "Serpent: A New Block Cipher Proposal," *Fast Software Encryption, 5th International Workshop Proceedings*, Springer-Verlag, 1998, pp. 222–238. [Pages 30, 34, 38, 41]

[Bau93]   F.L. Bauer, *Kryptologie*, Springer-Verlag, 1993. (In German.) [Page 49]

[Bau97]   F.L. Bauer, *Decrypted Secrets*, Springer-Verlag, 1997. [Page 49]

[BB93]   I. Ben-Aroya and E. Biham, "Differential Cryptanalysis of Lucifer," *Advances in Cryptology — CRYPTO '93 Proceedings*, Springer-Verlag, 1994, pp. 187–199. [Page 75]

[BB94]   E. Biham and A. Biryukov, "How to Strengthen DES Using Existing Hardware," *Advances in Cryptology — ASIACRYPT '94 Proceedings*, Springer-Verlag, 1994, pp. 398–412. [Page 39]

[BB95]   E. Biham and A. Biryukov, "An Improvement of Davies' Attack on DES," *Advances in Cryptology — EUROCRYPT '94 Proceedings*, Springer-Verlag, 1995, pp. 461–467. [Pages 40, 114]

[BB96]   U. Blumenthal and S. Bellovin, "A Better Key Schedule for DES-Like Ciphers," *Pragocrypt '96 Proceedings*, 1996, pp. 42–54. [Page 37]

[BCK96]   M. Bellare, R. Canetti, and H. Karwczyk, "Keying Hash Functions for Message Authentication," *Advances in Cryptology — CRYPTO '96 Proceedings*, Springer-Verlag, 1996, pp. 1–15. [Page 120]

[BDL97]   D. Boneh, R.A. DeMillo, and R.J. Lipton "On the Importance of Checking Cryptographic Protocols for Faults," *Advances in Cryptology — EUROCRYPT '97 Proceedings*, Springer-Verlag, 1997, pp. 37–51. [Page 111]

[BDR+96]   M. Blaze, W. Diffie, R. Rivest, B. Schneier, T. Shimomura, E. Thompson, and M. Weiner, "Minimal Key Lengths for Symmetric Ciphers to Provide Adequate Commercial Security," Jan 1996. [Page 1]

[BFL96]   M. Blaze, J. Feigenbaum, and F. T. Leighton, *Master-Key Cryptosystems*, DIMACS Technical Report 96-02, Rutgers University, Piscataway, 1996. [Page 116]

[Bih94]   E. Biham, "New Types of Cryptanalytic Attacks Using Related Keys," *Journal of Cryptology*, v. 7, n. 4, 1994, pp. 229–246. [Pages 35, 104, 105, 113]

[Bih95]   E. Biham, "On Matsui's Linear Cryptanalysis," *Advances in Cryptology — EUROCRYPT '94 Proceedings*, Springer-Verlag, 1995, pp. 398–412. [Page 38]

[Bih97]   E. Biham, "A Fast New DES Implementation in Software," *Fast Software Encryption, 4th International Workshop Proceedings*, Springer-Verlag, 1997, pp. 260–271. [Page 34]

[BK98]   A. Biryukov and E. Kushilevitz, "Improved Cryptanalysis of RC5," *Advances in Cryptology — EUROCRYPT '98 Proceedings*, Springer-Verlag, 1998, pp. 85–99. [Page 36]

[BKPS93]   L. Brown, M. Kwan, J. Pieprzyk, and J. Seberry, "Improving Resistance to Differential Cryptanalysis and the Redesign of LOKI," *Advances in Cryptology — ASIACRYPT '91 Proceedings*, Springer-Verlag, 1993, pp. 36–50. [Pages 5, 33]

[BKR94]   M. Bellare, J. Kilian, and P. Rogaway, "The security of the cipher block chaining message authentication code," *Advances in Cryptology—CRYPTO '94*, Springer-Verlag, 1994. [Page 120]

[BPS90]   L. Brown, J. Pieprzyk, and J. Seberry, "LOKI: A Cryptographic Primitive for Authentication and Secrecy Applications," *Advances in Cryptology — AUSCRYPT '90 Proceedings*, Springer-Verlag, 1990, pp. 229–236. [Pages 5, 33]

[Bro98]   L. Brown, "Design of LOKI97," draft AES submission, 1998. [Page 39]

[BS92]   E. Biham and A. Shamir, "Differential Cryptanalysis of Snefru, Khafre, REDOC II, LOKI, and Lucifer," *Advances in Cryptology — CRYPTO '91 Proceedings*, Springer-Verlag, 1992, pp. 156–171. [Page 38]

[BS93]   E. Biham and A. Shamir, *Differential Cryptanalysis of the Data Encryption Standard*, Springer-Verlag, 1993. [Pages 35, 38]

[BS95]   M. Blaze and B. Schneier, "The MacGuffin Block Cipher Algorithm," *Fast Software Encryption, Second International Workshop Proceedings*, Springer-Verlag, 1995, pp. 97–110. [Pages 5, 46]

[BS97]   E. Biham and A. Shamir, "Differential Fault Analysis of Secret Key Cryptosystems," *Advances in Cryptology — CRYPTO '97 Proceedings*, Springer-Verlag, 1997, pp. 513–525. [Page 111]

[CDN95]   G. Carter, E. Dawson, and L. Nielsen, "DESV: A Latin Square Variation of DES," *Proceedings of the Workshop on Selected Areas in Cryptography (SAC '95)*, Ottawa, Canada, 1995, pp. 158–172. [Page 58]

[CDN98]   G. Carter, E. Dawson, and L. Nielsen, "Key Schedules of Iterative Block Ciphers," *Third Australian Conference, ACISP '98*, Springer-Verlag, to appear. [Page 41]

[Cla97]   C.S.K. Clapp, "Optimizing a Fast Stream Cipher for VLIW, SIMD, and Superscalar Processors," *Fast Software Encryption, 4th International Workshop Proceedings*, Springer-Verlag, 1997, pp. 273–287. [Page 38]

[Cla98]   C.S.K. Clapp, "Joint Hardware/Software Design of a Fast Stream Cipher," *Fast Software Encryption, 5th International Workshop Proceedings*, Springer-Verlag, 1998, pp. 75–92. [Page 38]

[CM98]   H. Chabanne and E. Michon, "JEROBOAM," *Fast Software Encryption, 5th International Workshop Proceedings*, Springer-Verlag, 1998, pp. 49–59. [Page 33]

[Cop94]   D. Coppersmith, "The Data Encryption Standard (DES) and its Strength Against Attacks," *IBM Journal of Research and Development*, v. 38, n. 3, May 1994, pp. 243–250. [Pages 38, 39]

[Cop98]   D. Coppersmith, personal communication, 1998. [Page 38]

[CW91]   T. Cusick and M.C. Wood, "The REDOC-II Cryptosystem," *Advances in Cryptology — CRYPTO '90 Proceedings*, Springer-Verlag, 1991, pp. 545–563. [Pages 33, 36, 39]

[CWSK98]   D. Coppersmith, D. Wagner, B. Schneier, and J. Kelsey, "Cryptanalysis of TWOPRIME," *Fast Software Encryption, 5th International Workshop Proceedings*, Springer-Verlag, 1998, pp. 32–48. [Pages 40, 114]

[Dae95]   J. Daemen, "Cipher and Hash Function Design," Ph.D. thesis, Katholieke Universiteit Leuven, Mar 95. [Page 104]

[DBP96]   H. Dobbertin, A. Bosselaers, and B. Preneel, "RIPEMD-160: A Strengthened Version of RIPEMD," *Fast Software Encryption, Third International Workshop Proceedings*, Springer-Verlag, 1996, pp. 71–82. [Page 58]

[DC98a]   J. Daemen and C. Clapp, "Fast Hashing and Stream Encryption with PANAMA," *Fast Software Encryption, 5th International Workshop Proceedings*, Springer-Verlag, 1998, pp. 60–74. [Page 37]

[DC98b]   J. Daemen and C. Clapp, "The Panama Cryptographic Function," *Dr. Dobbs Journal*, v. 23, n. 12, Dec 1998, pp. 42–49. [Page 37]

[DGV93]   J. Daemen, R. Govaerts, and J. Vandewalle, "Block Ciphers Based on Modular Arithmetic," *Proceedings of the 3rd Symposium on: State and Progress of Research in Cryptography*, Fondazione Ugo Bordoni, 1993, pp. 80–89. [Page 36]

[DGV94a]   J. Daemen, R. Govaerts, and J. Vandewalle, "Weak Keys for IDEA," *Advances in Cryptology — EUROCRYPT '93 Proceedings*, Springer-Verlag, 1994, pp. 159–167. [Page 75]

[DGV94b]   J. Daemen, R. Govaerts, and J. Vandewalle, "A New Approach to Block Cipher Design," *Fast Software Encryption, Cambridge Security Workshop Proceedings*, Springer-Verlag, 1994, pp. 18–32. [Pages 35, 104]

[DH76]   W. Diffie and M. Hellman, "New Directions in Cryptography," *IEEE Transactions on Information Theory*, v. IT-22, n. 6, Nov 1976, pp. 644–654. [Page 116]

[DH79]   W. Diffie and M. Hellman, "Exhaustive Cryptanalysis of the NBS Data Encryption Standard," *Computer*, v. 10, n. 3, Mar 1979, pp. 74–84. [Page 1]

[DK85]   C. Deavours and L.A. Kruh, *Machine Cryptography and Modern Cryptanalysis*, Artech House, Dedham MA, 1985. [Page 49]

[DKR97]   J. Daemen, L. Knudsen, and V. Rijmen, "The Block Cipher Square," *Fast Software Encryption, 4th International Workshop Proceedings*, Springer-Verlag, 1997, pp. 149–165. [Pages 6, 36, 44, 54]

[ElG85]   T. ElGamal, "A Public-Key Cryptosystem and a Signature Scheme Based on Discrete Logarithms," *IEEE Transactions on Information Theory*, v. IT-31, n. 4, 1985, pp. 469–472. [Page 116]

[Fei73]   H. Feistel, "Cryptography and Computer Privacy," *Scientific American*, v. 228, n. 5, May 1973, pp. 15–23. [Pages 5, 44]

[Fer96]   N. Ferguson, personal communication, 1996. [Page 7]

[Fer98a]   N. Ferguson, "Bounds on the tail of binomial distributions," research notes, 1998. [Page 93]

[Fer98b]   N. Ferguson, "Upper Bounds on Differential Characteristics in Two-fish," Twofish Technical Report #1, Counterpane Systems, Aug 1998. [Page v]

[FNS75]   H. Feistel, W.A. Notz, and J.L. Smith, "Some Cryptographic Techniques for Machine-to-Machine Data Communications, *Proceedings on the IEEE*, v. 63, n. 11, 1975, pp. 1545–1554. [Pages 5, 44]

[FS97]   N. Ferguson and B. Schneier, "Cryptanalysis of Akelarre," *Workshop on Selected Areas in Cryptography (SAC '97) Workshop Record*, School of Computer Science, Carleton University, 1997, pp. 201–212. [Page 36]

[GC94]   H. Gilbert and P. Chauvaud, "A Chosen-Plaintext Attack on the 16-Round Khufu Cryptosystem," *Advances in Cryptology — CRYPTO '94 Proceedings*, Springer-Verlag, 1994, pp. 359–368. [Page 38]

[GOST89]   GOST, Gosudarstvennyi Standard 28147-89, "Cryptographic Protection for Data Processing Systems," Government Committee of the USSR for Standards, 1989. [Pages 5, 38, 104]

[Gut98]   P. Gutmann, "Software Generation of Random Numbers for Cryptographic Purposes," *Proceedings of the 1998 USENIX Security Symposium*, USENIX Press, 1998, pp. 243–257. [Page 120]

[Har96]   C. Harpes, *Cryptanalysis of Iterated Block Ciphers*, ETH Series on Information Processing, v. 7, Hartung-Gorre Verlang Konstanz, 1996. [Pages 102, 116]

[Haw98]   P. Hawkes, "Differential-Linear Weak Key Classes of IDEA," *Advances in Cryptology — EUROCRYPT '98 Proceedings*, Springer-Verlag, 1998, pp. 112–126. [Page 75]

[HKM95]   C. Harpes, G. Kramer, and J. Massey, "A Generalization of Linear Cryptanalysis and the Applicability of Matsui's Piling-up Lemma," *Advances in Cryptology — EUROCRYPT '95 Proceedings*, Springer-Verlag, 1995, pp. 24–38. [Page 102]

[HKR+98]   C. Hall, J. Kelsey, V. Rijmen, B. Schneier, and D. Wagner, "Cryptanalysis of SPEED," *Selected Areas in Cryptography*, Springer-Verlag, 1998, to appear. [Page 33]

[HKSW98]   C. Hall, J. Kelsey, B. Schneier, and D. Wagner, "Cryptanalysis of SPEED," *Financial Cryptography '98 Proceedings*, Springer-Verlag, 1998, pp. 309–310. [Page 33]

[HM97]   C. Harpes and J. Massey, "Partitioning Cryptanalysis," *Fast Software Encryption, 4th International Workshop Proceedings*, Springer-Verlag, 1997, pp. 13–27. [Page 102]

[HT94a]   H.M. Heys and S.E. Tavares, "On the Security of the CAST Encryption Algorithm," Canadian Conference on Electrical and Computer Engineering, 1994, pp. 332–335. [Page 35]

[HT94b]   H.M. Heys and S.E. Tavares, "The Design of Substitution-Permutation Networks Resistant to Differential and Linear Cryptanalysis," *2nd ACM Conference on Computer and Communications Security*, ACM Press, 1994, pp. 148–155. [Page 44]

[HYSK98]   T. Hamade, T. Yokoyama, T. Shimada, and T. Kanedo, "On Partitioning Cryptanalysis of DES," *1998 Symposium on Cryptography and Information Security*, 2.2.A. (In Japanese.) [Page 103]

[Jeff+76] T. Jefferson et al., "Declaration of Independence," Philadelphia PA, 4 Jul 1776. [Page 38]

[JH96]   T. Jakobsen and C. Harpes, "Bounds on Non-Uniformity Measures for Generalized Linear Cryptanalysis and Partitioning Cryptanalysis," *Pragocrypt '96 Proceedings*, 1996, pp. 467–479. [Page 102]

[JK97]   T. Jakobsen and L. Knudsen, "The Interpolation Attack on Block Ciphers," *Fast Software Encryption, 4th International Workshop Proceedings*, Springer-Verlag, 1997, pp. 28–40. [Pages 35, 39, 103]

[Kie96]   K. Kiefer, "A New Design Concept for Building Secure Block Ciphers," *Proceedings of the 1st International Conference on the Theory and Applications of Cryptography, Pragocrypt '96*, CTU Publishing House, 1996, pp. 30–41. [Page 35]

[KKT94]   T. Kaneko, K. Koyama, and R. Terada, "Dynamic Swapping Schemes and Differential Cryptanalysis," *IEICE Transactions*, v. E77-A, 1994, pp. 1328–1336. [Page 58]

[KLPL95]   K. Kim, S. Lee, S. Park, and D. Lee, "Securing DES S-boxes Against Three Robust Cryptanalysis," *Proceedings of the Workshop on Selected Areas in Cryptography (SAC '95)*, Ottawa, Canada, 1995, pp. 145–157. [Page 38]

[KM97]   L.R. Knudsen and W. Meier, "Differential Cryptanalysis of RC5," *European Transactions on Communication*, v. 8, n. 5, 1997, pp. 445–454. [Page 36]

[Knu93a]   L.R. Knudsen, "Cryptanalysis of LOKI," *Advances in Cryptology — ASIACRYPT '91*, Springer-Verlag, 1993, pp. 22–35. [Page 39]

[Knu93b]   L.R. Knudsen, "Cryptanalysis of LOKI91," *Advances in Cryptology — AUSCRYPT '92*, Springer-Verlag, 1993, pp. 196–208. [Page 39]

[Knu93c]   L.R. Knudsen, "Iterative Characteristics of DES and s^{2}DES," *Advances in Cryptology — CRYPTO '92*, Springer-Verlag, 1993, pp. 497–511. [Page 38]

[Knu94a]   L.R. Knudsen, "Block Ciphers — Analysis, Design, Applications," Ph.D. dissertation, Aarhus University, Nov 1994. [Page 35]

[Knu94b]   L.R. Knudsen, "Practically Secure Feistel Ciphers," *Fast Software Encryption, Cambridge Security Workshop Proceedings*, Springer-Verlag, 1994, pp. 211–221. [Pages 35, 37, 75]

[Knu95a]   L.R. Knudsen, "New Potentially 'Weak' Keys for DES and LOKI," *Advances in Cryptology — EUROCRYPT '94 Proceedings*, Springer-Verlag, 1995, pp. 419–424. [Page 40]

[Knu95b]   L.R. Knudsen, "Truncated and Higher Order Differentials," *Fast Software Encryption, 2nd International Workshop Proceedings*, Springer-Verlag, 1995, pp. 196–211. [Pages 35, 39, 90]

[Knu95c]   L.R. Knudsen, "A Key-Schedule Weakness in SAFER K-64," *Advances in Cryptology—CRYPTO '95 Proceedings*, Springer-Verlag, 1995, pp. 274–286. [Page 60]

[Koc96]   P. Kocher, "Timing Attacks on Implementations of Diffie-Hellman, RSA, DSS, and Other Systems," *Advances in Cryptology — CRYPTO '96 Proceedings*, Springer-Verlag, 1996, pp. 104–113. [Page 111]

[Koc98a]   P. Kocher, "Differential Power Analysis," available online from `http://www.cryptography.com/dpa/`. [Page 111]

[Koc98b]   P. Kocher, "DES Key Search Project," available online from `http://www.cryptography.com/des/index.html`. [Page 1]

[KPL93]   K. Kim, S. Park, and S. Lee, "Reconstruction of s^2DES S-Boxes and their Immunity to Differential Cryptanalysis," *Proceedings of the 1993 Japan-Korea Workshop on Information Security and Cryptography*, Seoul, Korea, 24–26 October 1993, pp. 282–291. [Page 38]

[KR94]   B. Kaliski Jr. and M. Robshaw, "Linear Cryptanalysis Using Multiple Approximations," *Advances in Cryptology — CRYPTO '94 Proceedings*, Springer-Verlag, 1994, pp. 26–39. [Page 102]

[KR95]   B. Kaliski Jr. and M. Robshaw, "Linear Cryptanalysis Using Multiple Approximations and FEAL," *Fast Software Encryption, Second International Workshop Proceedings*, Springer-Verlag, 1995, pp. 249–264. [Page 102]

[KR96a]   J. Kilian and P. Rogaway, "How to Protect DES Against Exhaustive Key Search," *Advances in Cryptology — CRYPTO '96 Proceedings*, Springer-Verlag, 1996, pp. 252–267. [Pages 5, 6]

[KR96b]   L. Knudsen and M. Robshaw, "Non-Linear Approximations in Linear Cryptanalysis," *Advances in Cryptology — EUCROCRYPT '96*, Springer-Verlag, 1996, pp. 224–236. [Page 102]

[KR97]   L.R. Knudsen and V. Rijmen, "Two Rights Sometimes Make a Wrong," *Workshop on Selected Areas in Cryptography (SAC '97) Workshop Record*, School of Computer Science, Carleton University, 1997, pp. 213–223. [Page 36]

[KRRR98]   L.R. Knudsen, V. Rijmen, R. Rivest, and M. Robshaw, "On the Design and Security of RC2," *Fast Software Encryption, 5th International Workshop Proceedings*, Springer-Verlag, 1998, pp. 206–221. [Page 33]

[KSHW98]   J. Kelsey, B. Schneier, C. Hall, and D. Wagner, "Secure Applications of Low-Entropy Keys," *Information Security. First International Workshop ISW '97 Proceedings*, Springer-Verlag, 1998, 121–134. [Page 42]

[KSW96]   J. Kelsey, B. Schneier, and D. Wagner, "Key-Schedule Cryptanalysis of IDEA, G-DES, GOST, SAFER, and Triple-DES," *Advances in Cryptology — CRYPTO '96 Proceedings*, Springer-Verlag, 1996, pp. 237–251. [Pages 35, 41, 79, 104]

[KSW97]   J. Kelsey, B. Schneier, and D. Wagner, "Related-Key Cryptanalysis of 3-WAY, Biham-DES, CAST, DES-X, NewDES, RC2, and TEA," *Information and Communications Security, First International Conference Proceedings*, Springer-Verlag, 1997, pp. 203–207. [Pages 35, 41, 79, 104]

[KSWH98a]   J. Kelsey, B. Schneier, D. Wagner, and C. Hall, "Cryptanalytic Attacks on Pseudorandom Number Generators," *Fast Software Encryption, 5th International Workshop Proceedings*, Springer-Verlag, 1998, pp. 168–188. [Page 120]

[KSWH98b]   J. Kelsey, B. Schneier, D. Wagner, and C. Hall, "Side Channel Cryptanalysis of Product Ciphers," *ESORICS '98 Proceedings*, Springer-Verlag, 1998, pp 97–110. [Page 111]

[KSWH98c] J. Kelsey, B. Schneier, D. Wagner, and C. Hall, "Yarrow: A Pseudo-random Number Generator," in preparation. [Page 120]

[Kwa97]   M. Kwan, "The Design of ICE Encryption Algorithm," *Fast Software Encryption, 4th International Workshop Proceedings*, Springer-Verlag, 1997, pp. 69–82. [Page 41]

[KY95]   B.S. Kaliski and Y.L. Yin, "On Differential and Linear Cryptanalysis of the RC5 Encryption Algorithm," *Advances in Cryptology— CRYPTO '95 Proceedings*, Springer-Verlag, 1995, pp. 445–454. [Page 36]

[Lai94]   X. Lai, "Higher Order Derivations and Differential Cryptanalysis," *Communications and Cryptography: Two Sides of One Tapestry*, Kluwer Academic Publishers, 1994, pp. 227–233. [Pages 35, 90]

[LC97]   C.-H. Lee and Y.-T. Cha, "The Block Cipher: SNAKE with Provable Resistance Against DC and LC Attacks," *Proceedings of JW-ISC '97*, KIISC and ISEC Group of IEICE, 1997, pp. 3–17. [Page 35]

[Lee96]   M. Leech, "CRISP: A Feistel Network with Hardened Key Scheduling," *Workshop on Selected Areas in Cryptography (SAC '96) Workshop Record*, Queens University, 1996, pp. 15–29. [Page 37]

[LH94]   S. Langford and M. Hellman, "Differential-Linear Cryptanalysis," *Advances in Cryptology — CRYPTO '94 Proceedings*, Springer-Verlag, 1994, pp. 17–26. [Page 103]

[LM91]   X. Lai and J. Massey, "A Proposal for a New Block Encryption Standard," *Advances in Cryptology — EUROCRYPT '90 Proceedings*, Springer-Verlag, 1991, pp. 389–404. [Page 33]

[LMM91]   X. Lai, J. Massey, and S. Murphy, "Markov Ciphers and Differential Cryptanalysis," *Advances in Cryptology — CRYPTO '91 Proceedings*, Springer-Verlag, 1991, pp. 17–38. [Pages 33, 46]

[MA96]   S. Mister and C. Adams, "Practical S-Box Design," *Workshop on Selected Areas in Cryptography (SAC '96) Workshop Record*, Queens University, 1996, pp. 61–76. [Page 38]

[Mad84]   W.E. Madryga, "A High Performance Encryption Algorithm," *Computer Security: A Global Challenge*, Elsevier Science Publishers, 1984, pp. 557–570. [Page 36]

[Mas94]   J.L. Massey, "SAFER K-64: A Byte-Oriented Block-Ciphering Algorithm," *Fast Software Encryption, Cambridge Security Workshop Proceedings*, Springer-Verlag, 1994, pp. 1–17. [Pages 7, 44, 121]

[Mat94]   M. Matsui, "Linear Cryptanalysis Method for DES Cipher," *Advances in Cryptology — EUROCRYPT '93 Proceedings*, Springer-Verlag, 1994, pp. 386–397. [Page 35]

[Mat95]   M. Matsui, "On Correlation Between the Order of S-Boxes and the Strength of DES," *Advances in Cryptology — EUROCRYPT '94 Proceedings*, Springer-Verlag, 1995, pp. 366–375. [Page 38]

[Mat96]   M. Matsui, "New Structure of Block Ciphers with Provable Security Against Differential and Linear Cryptanalysis," *Fast Software Encryption, 3rd International Workshop Proceedings*, Springer-Verlag, 1996, pp. 205–218. [Pages 35, 48]

[Mat97]   M. Matsui, "New Block Encryption Algorithm MISTY," *Fast Software Encryption, 4th International Workshop Proceedings*, Springer-Verlag, 1997, pp. 54–68. [Page 35]

[McD97]   T.J. McDermott, "NSA comments on criteria for AES," letter to NIST, National Security Agency, 2 Apr 97. [Pages 32, 42]

[Mer91]   R.C. Merkle, "Fast Software Encryption Functions," *Advances in Cryptology — CRYPTO '90 Proceedings*, Springer-Verlag, 1991, pp. 476–501. [Pages 5, 33, 46]

[Mor98]   S. Moriai, "How to Design Secure S-boxes Against Different Differential, Liear, Higher Order Differential, and Interpolation Attacks," *1998 Symposium on Cryptography and Information Security*, 2.2.C. (In Japanese.) [Page 39]

[MS77]   F.J. MacWilliams and N.J.A. Sloane, "The Theory of Error-Correcting Codes," North-Holland, Amsterdam, 1977. [Pages 6, 76]

[MSK98a]   S. Moriai, T. Shimoyama, and T. Kaneko, "Higher Order Differential Attack of a CAST Cipher," *Fast Software Encryption, 5th International Workshop Proceedings*, Springer-Verlag, 1998, pp. 17–31. [Page 35]

[MSK98b]   S. Moriai, T. Shimoyama, and T. Kaneko, "Interpolation Attacks of the Block Cipher: SNAKE," *1998 Symposium on Cryptography and Information Security*, 7.2.C. (In Japanese.) [Pages 35, 103]

[Mur90]   S. Murphy, "The Cryptanalysis of FEAL-4 with 20 Chosen Plaintexts," *Journal of Cryptology*, v. 2, n. 3, 1990, pp. 145–154. [Page 39]

[NBS77]   National Bureau of Standards, NBS FIPS PUB 46, "Data Encryption Standard," National Bureau of Standards, U.S. Department of Commerce, Jan 1977. [Pages 1, 5, 34]

[NBS80]   National Bureau of Standards, NBS FIPS PUB 46, "DES Modes of Operation," National Bureau of Standards, U.S. Department of Commerce, Dec 1980. [Page 119]

[NIST93]   National Institute of Standards and Technology, "Secure Hash Standard," U.S. Department of Commerce, May 1993. [Pages 39, 46, 58]

[NIST94]   National Institute of Standards and Technologies, NIST FIPS PUB 186, "Digital Signature Standard," U.S. Department of Commerce, May 1994. [Page 116]

[NIST97a] National Institute of Standards and Technology, "Announcing Development of a Federal Information Standard for Advanced Encryption Standard," *Federal Register*, v. 62, n. 1, 2 Jan 1997, pp. 93–94. [Page 1]

[NIST97b] National Institute of Standards and Technology, "Announcing Request for Candidate Algorithm Nominations for the Advanced Encryption Standard (AES)," *Federal Register*, v. 62, n. 117, 12 Sep 1997, pp. 48051–48058. [Pages 1, 3, 34]

[NK95]   K. Nyberg and L.R. Knudsen, "Provable Security Against Differential Cryptanalysis," *Journal of Cryptology*, v. 8, n. 1, 1995, pp. 27–37. [Page 35]

[NM97]   J. Nakajima and M. Matsui, "Fast Software Implementation of MISTY on Alpha Processors," *Proceedings of JW-ISC '97*, KIISC and ISEC Group of IEICE, 1997, pp. 55–63. [Page 34]

[NSA98]   NSA, "Skipjack and KEA Algorithm Specifications," Version 2.0, National Security Agency, 29 May 1998. [Pages 5, 40, 46]

[Nyb91]   K. Nyberg, "Perfect Nonlinear S-boxes," *Advances in Cryptology — EUROCRYPT '91 Proceedings*, Springer-Verlag, 1991, pp. 378–386. [Page 35]

[Nyb93]   K. Nyberg, "On the Construction of Highly Nonlinear Permutations," *Advances in Cryptology — EUROCRYPT '92 Proceedings*, Springer-Verlag, 1993, pp. 92–98. [Page 35]

[Nyb94]   K. Nyberg, "Differentially Uniform Mappings for Cryptography," *Advances in Cryptology — EUROCRYPT '93 Proceedings*, Springer-Verlag, 1994, pp. 55–64. [Page 35]

[Nyb95]   K. Nyberg, "Linear Approximation of Block Ciphers," *Advances in Cryptology — EUROCRYPT '94 Proceedings*, Springer-Verlag, 1995, pp. 439–444. [Page 35]

[Nyb96]   K. Nyberg, "Generalized Feistel Networks," *Advances in Cryptology — ASIACRYPT '96 Proceedings*, Springer-Verlag, 1996, pp. 91–104. [Pages 35, 36]

[OCo94a]   L. O'Connor, "Enumerating Nondegenerate Permutations," *Advances in Cryptology — EUROCRYPT '93 Proceedings*, Springer-Verlag, 1994, pp. 368–377. [Page 35]

[OCo94b]   L. O'Connor, "On the Distribution of Characteristics in Bijective Mappings," *Advances in Cryptology — EUROCRYPT '93 Proceedings*, Springer-Verlag, 1994, pp. 360–370. [Page 35]

[OCo94c]   L. O'Connor, "On the Distribution of Characteristics in Composite Permutations," *Advances in Cryptology — CRYPTO '93 Proceedings*, Springer-Verlag, 1994, pp. 403–412. [Page 35]

[PB92]   H. Beker and F. Piper, *Cipher Systems*, Northwind Books, 1992. [Page 49]

[Plu94]   C. Plumb, "Truly Random Numbers," *Dr. Dobbs Journal*, v. 19, n. 13, Nov 1994, pp. 113-115. [Page 120]

[PRB98a]   B. Preneel, V. Rijmen, and A. Bosselaers, "Principles and Performance of Cryptographic Algorithms," *Dr. Dobbs Journal*, v. 23, n. 12, Dec 1998, pp. [Page 121]

[PRB98b]   B. Preneel, V. Rijmen, and A. Bosselaers, "Recent Developments in the Design of Conventional Cryptographic Algorithms," *State of the Art and Evolution of Computer Security and Industrial Cryptography, Lecture Notes in Computer Science*, B. Preneel, R. Govaerts, J. Vandewalle, Eds., Springer-Verlag, 1998, to appear. [Page 121]

[Pre93]   B. Preneel, *Analysis and Design of Cryptographic Hash Functions*, Ph.D. dissertation, Katholieke Universiteit Leuven, Jan 1993. [Pages 23, 119]

[QDD86]   J.-J. Quisquater, Y. Desmedt, and M. Davio, "The Importance of 'Good' Key Scheduling Schemes," *Advances in Cryptology — CRYPTO '85 Proceedings*, Springer-Verlag, 1986, pp. 537–542. [Page 42]

[RAND55]   RAND Corporation, *A Million Random Digits with 100,000 Normal Deviates*, Glencoe, IL, Free Press Publishers, 1955. [Page 38]

[RC94]   P. Rogaway and D. Coppersmith, "A Software-Optimized Encryption Algorithm," *Fast Software Encryption, Cambridge Security Workshop Proceedings*, Springer-Verlag, 1994, pp. 56–63. [Pages 33, 34]

[RC98]   P. Rogaway and D. Coppersmith, "A Software-Optimized Encryption Algorithm," *Journal of Cryptology*, v. 11, n. 4, 1998, pp. 273–287. [Pages 33, 34]

[RDP+96]   V. Rijmen, B. Preneel, A. Bosselaers, and E. DeWin, "The Cipher SHARK," *Fast Software Encryption, 3rd International Workshop Proceedings*, Springer-Verlag, 1996, pp. 99–111. [Pages 5, 6, 44]

[Rij97]   V. Rijmen, *Cryptanalysis and Design of Iterated Block Ciphers*, Ph.D. thesis, Katholieke Universiteit Leuven, Oct 1997. [Page 38]

[RIPE92]   Research and Development in Advanced Communication Technologies in Europe, *RIPE Integrity Primitives: Final Report of RACE Integrity Primitives Evaluation (R1040)*, RACE, June 1992. [Page 58]

[Rit96]   T. Ritter, "The Fenced DES Cipher: Stronger than DES but Made from DES," Ritter Software Engineering, 1996. [Page 46]

[Riv91]   R.L. Rivest, "The MD4 Message Digest Algorithm," *Advances in Cryptology — CRYPTO '90 Proceedings*, Springer-Verlag, 1991, pp. 303–311. [Pages 46, 58]

[Riv92]   R.L. Rivest, "The MD5 Message Digest Algorithm," RFC 1321, Apr 1992. [Pages 46, 58]

[Riv95]   R.L. Rivest, "The RC5 Encryption Algorithm," *Fast Software Encryption, 2nd International Workshop Proceedings*, Springer-Verlag, 1995, pp. 86–96. [Pages 5, 34, 121]

[Riv97]   R. Rivest, "A Description of the RC2(r) Encryption Algorithm," Internet-Draft, work in progress, June 1997. [Pages 33, 46]

[RKR98]   B. Van Rompay, L.R. Knudsen, and V. Rijmen, "Differential Cryptanalysis of the ICE Encryption Algorithm," *Fast Software Encryption, 5th International Workshop Proceedings*, Springer-Verlag, 1998, pp. 270–283. [Page 41]

[Ros98]   G. Rose, "A Stream Cipher Based on Linear Feedback over $GF(2^8)$," *Third Australian Conference, ACISP '98*, Springer-Verlag, to appear. [Page 33]

[RP95a]   V. Rijmen and B. Preneel, "Cryptanalysis of MacGuffin," *Fast Software Encryption, Second International Workshop Proceedings*, Springer-Verlag, 1995, pp. 353–358. [Page 5]

[RP95b]   V. Rijmen and B. Preneel, "On Weaknesses of Non-surjective Round Functions," *Proceedings of the Workshop on Selected Areas in Cryptography (SAC '95)*, Ottawa, Canada, 1995, pp. 100–106. [Pages 40, 114]

[RPD97]   V. Rijman, B. Preneel, and E. DeWin, "On Weaknesses of Non-surjective Round Functions," *Designs, Codes, and Cryptography*, v. 12, n. 3, 1997, pp. 253–266. [Pages 40, 114]

[RSA78]   R. Rivest, A. Shamir, and L. Adleman, "A Method for Obtaining Digital Signatures and Public-Key Cryptosystems," *Communications of the ACM*, v. 21, n. 2, Feb 1978, pp. 120–126. [Page 116]

[SAM97]   T. Shimoyama, S. Amada, and S. Moriai, "Improved Fast Software Implementation of Block Ciphers," *Information and Communications Security, First International Conference, ICICS '97 Proceedings*, Springer-Verlag, 1997, pp. 203–207. [Page 34]

[Sch94]   B. Schneier, "Description of a New Variable-Length Key, 64-Bit Block Cipher (Blowfish)," *Fast Software Encryption, Cambridge Security Workshop Proceedings*, Springer-Verlag, 1994, pp. 191–204. [Pages 5, 34, 39]

[Sch96]   B. Schneier, *Applied Cryptography, Second Edition*, John Wiley & Sons, 1996. [Pages 23, 34, 119]

[Sch98]   B. Schneier, "The Twofish Encryption Algorithm," *Dr. Dobbs Journal*, v. 23, n. 12, Dec 1998, pp. 30–38. [Page v]

[Sco85]   R. Scott, "Wide Open Encryption Design Offers Flexible Implementation," *Cryptologia*, v. 9, n. 1, Jan 1985, pp. 75–90. [Page 38]

[Sel98]   A.A. Selçuk, "New Results in Linear Cryptanalysis of RC5," *Fast Software Encryption, 5th International Workshop Proceedings*, Springer-Verlag, 1998, pp. 1–16. [Page 36]

[Seu60]   Dr. Seuss, *One Fish, Two Fish, Red Fish, Blue Fish*, Beginner Books, 1960. [Page 127]

[Sha49]   C. Shannon, "Communication Theory of Secrecy Systems," *Bell Systems Technical Journal*, v. 28, n. 4, 1949, pp. 656–715. [Pages 43, 44]

[SK96]   B. Schneier and J. Kelsey, "Unbalanced Feistel Networks and Block Cipher Design," *Fast Software Encryption, 3rd International Workshop Proceedings*, Springer-Verlag, 1996, pp. 121–144. [Pages 5, 36, 46, 47]

[SK98]   T. Shimoyama and T. Kaneko, "Quadratic Relation of S-box and Its Application to the Linear Attack of Full Round DES," *Advances in Cryptology — CRYPTO '98 Proceedings*, Springer-Verlag, 1998, pp. 200–211. [Pages 102, 116]

[SKW+98a]   B. Schneier, J. Kelsey, D. Whiting, D. Wagner, C. Hall, and N. Ferguson, "Twofish: A 128-Bit Block Cipher," NIST AES Proposal, 15 June 1998. [Page v]

[SKW+98b]   B. Schneier, J. Kelsey, D. Whiting, D. Wagner, C. Hall, and N. Ferguson, "On the Twofish Key Schedule," *Proceedings of the 1998 SAC Conference*, Springer-Verlag, 1998, to appear. [Page v]

[SKW+99a]   B. Schneier, J. Kelsey, D. Whiting, D. Wagner, C. Hall, and N. Ferguson, "Performance Comparison of the AES Submissions," submitted to the 2nd AES Candidate Conference, 1999, to appear. [Pages v, 121]

[SKW+99b]   B. Schneier, J. Kelsey, D. Whiting, D. Wagner, C. Hall, and N. Ferguson, , "Twofish on Smart Cards," *Proceedings of CARDIS 98*, Springer-Verlag, to appear. [Pages v, 26]

[SM88]   A. Shimizu and S. Miyaguchi, "Fast Data Encipherment Algorithm FEAL," *Advances in Cryptology — EUROCRYPT '87 Proceedings*, Springer-Verlag, 1988, pp. 267–278. [Pages 5, 33, 36]

[SMK98]   T. Shimoyama, S. Moriai, and T. Kaneko, "Improving the Higher Order Differential Attack and Cryptanalysis of the KN Cipher," *Information Security. First International Workshop ISW '97 Proceedings*, Springer-Verlag, 1998, pp. 32–42. [Pages 35, 39]

[SV98]   J. Stern and S. Vaudenay, "CS-Cipher," *Fast Software Encryption, 5th International Workshop Proceedings*, Springer-Verlag, 1998, pp. 189–205. [Pages 39, 41]

[SW97]   B. Schneier and D. Whiting, "Fast Software Encryption: Designing Encryption Algorithms for Optimal Speed on the Intel Pentium Processor," *Fast Software Encryption, 4th International Workshop Proceedings*, Springer-Verlag, 1997, pp. 242–259. [Pages 33, 34, 121]

[UTK98]   M. Uemra, H. Tanaka, and T. Kanedo, "On the Weak Keys in SPEED Cipher by Higher Order Differential Attack," *1998 Symposium on Cryptography and Information Security*, 1.2.D. (In Japanese.) [Page 33]

[Vau95]   S. Vaudenay, "On the Need for Multipermutations: Cryptanalysis of MD4 and SAFER," *Fast Software Encryption, Second International Workshop Proceedings*, Springer-Verlag, 1995, pp. 286–297. [Page 6]

[Vau96a]   S. Vaudenay, "On the Weak Keys in Blowfish," *Fast Software Encryption, 3rd International Workshop Proceedings*, Springer-Verlag, 1996, pp. 27–32. [Pages 39, 114]

[Vau96b]   S. Vaudenay, "An Experiment on DES Statistical Cryptanalysis," *3rd ACM Conference on Computer and Communications Security*, ACM Press, 1996, pp. 139–147. [Page 102]

[Wag95a]   D. Wagner, "Cryptanalysis of S-1," sci.crypt Usenet posting, 27 Aug 1995. [Pages 41, 104]

[Wag95b]   D. Wagner, personal communication, 1995. [Page 40]

[WH87]   R. Winternitz and M. Hellman, "Chosen-key Attacks on a Block Cipher," *Cryptologia*, v. 11, n. 1, Jan 1987, pp. 16–20. [Page 35]

[Whe94]   D. Wheeler, "A Bulk Data Encryption Algorithm," *Fast Software Encryption, Cambridge Security Workshop Proceedings*, Springer-Verlag, 1994, pp. 127–134. [Page 38]

[Wie94]   M.J. Wiener, "Efficient DES Key Search," TR-244, School of Computer Science, Carleton University, May 1994. [Page 1]

[Win84]   R.S. Winternitz, "Producing One-Way Hash Functions from DES," *Advances in Cryptology: Proceedings of Crypto 83*, Plenum Press, 1984, pp. 203–207. [Page 119]

[WN95]   D. Wheeler and R. Needham, "TEA, a Tiny Encryption Algorithm," *Fast Software Encryption, 2nd International Workshop Proceedings*, Springer-Verlag, 1995, pp. 97–110. [Page 36]

[WS98]   D. Whiting and B. Schneier "Improved Twofish Implementations," Twofish Technical Report #3, Counterpane Systems, to appear. [Page v]

[WSK97]   D. Wagner, B. Schneier, and J. Kelsey, "Cryptanalysis of the Cellular Message Encryption Algorithm," *Advances in Cryptology — CRYPTO '97 Proceedings*, Springer-Verlag, 1997, pp. 526–537. [Page 38]

[WW98]   D. Whiting and D. Wagner, "Empirical Verification of Twofish Key Uniqueness Properties," Twofish Technical Report #2, Counterpane Systems, 22 Sep 1998. [Page v]

[YLCY98]   X. Yi, K.Y. Lam, S.X. Cheng, and X.H. You, "A New Byte-Oriented Block Cipher," *Information Security. First International Workshop ISW '97 Proceedings*, Springer-Verlag, 1998, 209–220. [Page 39]

[YMT97]   A.M. Youssef, S. Mister, and S.E. Tavares, "On the Design of Linear Transformations for Substitution Permutation Encryption Networks," *Workshop on Selected Areas in Cryptography (SAC '97) Workshop Record*, School of Computer Science, Carleton University, 1997, pp. 40–48. [Page 7]

[YTH96]   A.M. Youssef, S.E. Tavares, and H.M. Heys, "A New Class of Substitution-Permutation Networks," *Workshop on Selected Areas in Cryptography (SAC '96) Workshop Record*, Queens University, 1996, pp. 132–147. [Pages 5, 37]

[Yuv97]   G. Yuval, "Reinventing the Travois: Encryption/MAC in 30 ROM Bytes," *Fast Software Encryption, 4th International Workshop Proceedings*, Springer-Verlag, 1997, pp. 205–209. [Page 104]

[ZG97]   F. Zhu and B.-A. Guo, "A Block-Ciphering Algorithm Based on Addition-Multiplication Structure in $GF(2^n)$," *Workshop on Selected Areas in Cryptography (SAC '97) Workshop Record*, School of Computer Science, Carleton University, 1997, pp. 145–159. [Page 33]

[Zhe97]   Y. Zheng, "The SPEED Cipher," *Financial Cryptography '97 Proceedings*, Springer-Verlag, 1997, pp. 71–89. [Pages 33, 121]

[ZMI90]   Y. Zheng, T. Matsumoto, and H. Imai, "On the Construction of Block Ciphers Provably Secure and Not Relying on Any Unproved Hypotheses," *Advances in Cryptology — CRYPTO '89 Proceedings*, Springer-Verlag, 1990, pp. 461–480. [Pages 5, 36]

[ZPS93]   Y. Zheng, J. Pieprzyk, and J. Seberry, "HAVAL — A One-Way Hashing Algorithm with Variable Length of Output," *Advances in Cryptology — AUSCRYPT '92 Proceedings*, Springer-Verlag, 1993, pp. 83–104. [Page 58]

A. Overview of Symbols

This appendix gives an overview of the symbols used in the definition of Twofish. For data elements, lowercase symbols usually refer to byte values and uppercase symbols usually refer to 32-bit word values.

A	The list of A_i words used in the key schedule. [Page 67]
$A_0, \ldots, A_{19}$	Intermediate values in the key schedule. [Page 16]
$a_0, \ldots, a_4$	Intermediate 4-bit values used in the definition of the q mappings. [Page 16]
B	The list of B_i words used in the key schedule. [Page 67]
$B_0, \ldots, B_{19}$	Intermediate values in the key schedule. [Page 16]
$b_0, \ldots, b_4$	Intermediate 4-bit values used in the definition of the q mappings. [Page 16]
$C_0, \ldots, C_3$	The four 32-bit words of the ciphertext. [Page 11]
$c_0, \ldots, c_{15}$	The bytes of the ciphertext. [Page 11]
$\mathrm{DP}_{\max}(f)$	The probability of the best differential characteristic of f. [Page 48]
$F(X, Y, r)$	The Feistel round function. This function takes the round number r and two data words X and Y as input. It produces two words of output. The round number is used to select the correct words from the expanded key. Note that the definition of F depends on the key. [Page 11]
$F'(X, Y)$	This is the F function without the final addition of two key words. It is thus independent of the round number, but still depends on the key. [Page 11]
$F_{r,0}, F_{r,1}$	The two output words from the F function in round r. [Page 11]
$g(X)$	This function maps a 32-bit word to a 32-bit word. It consists of four S-boxes, and the MDS matrix. It is defined as $g(X) \mapsto h(X, S)$. Note that S depends on the key, so this function depends also on the key. [Page 11]

$h(X, L)$ A function that maps the 32-bit word X to a 32-bit result under control of a list of words L that is derived from the key. This function is used both in the key schedule, and in the round function. [Page 14]

$K_0, \ldots, K_{39}$ The expanded key, consisting of 40 words of 32 bits each. The words $K_0, \ldots, K_3$ are used for the pre-whitening, $K_4, \ldots, K_7$ for the post-whitening, and $K_8, \ldots, K_39$ for the 16 rounds. [Page 16]

k The length of the key divided by 64. [Page 12]

L The list of key-derived words used in h. [Page 14]

$L_0, \ldots, L_{k-1}$ The k words of L. [Page 14]

$l_i, 0, \ldots, l_i, 3$ The four bytes of L_i. [Page 15]

$\text{LP}_{\max}(f)$ The significance-probability of the best linear characteristic of f. [Page 48]

$M_0, \ldots, M_{2k-1}$ The $2k$ 32-bit words of the key. [Page 12]

M_e, M_o Two lists of 32-bit words. The first one consists of the even key words and the second one of the odd key words. [Page 13]

$m_0, \ldots, m_{8k-1}$ The $8k$ bytes of the key. [Page 12]

N The length of the key, in bits. [Page 12]

$P_0, \ldots, P_3$ The four 32-bit words of the plaintext. [Page 9]

$p_0, \ldots, p_{15}$ The bytes of the plaintext. [Page 9]

q_0, q_1 Two distinct fixed bijective functions that map byte values into byte values. [Page 16]

$R_{r,0}, \ldots, R_{r,3}$ The 32-bit words of the data just before round r. The rounds are numbered $0, \ldots, 15$. For $r = 0$ these words are the data just before the first round (but after the whitening). For $r = 16$ they are the data just after the last round (but before the whitening). [Page 9]

r The round number. The rounds are numbered 0 to 15 when encrypting. [Page 11]

$\text{ROL}(X, n)$ A function that rotates a 32-bit value X left by n bits. [Page 11]

$\text{ROR}(X, n)$ A function that rotates a 32-bit value X right by n bits. [Page 11]

S A list of k 32-bit words that is derived from the key using the RS matrix. [Page 13]

$S_0, \ldots, S_{k-1}$ The words that make up S. Note that these are put in reverse order to create S. [Page 13]

$s_0, \ldots, s_3$	The key-dependent S-boxes. Each S-box consists of a sequence of table lookups in a q-table, and XORs with key bytes. [Page 16]
$s_{i,0}, \ldots, s_{i,3}$	The four bytes of S_i. [Page 13]
T_0, T_1	Two intermediate values used in the computation of F. These are the results of the two g functions, just before the PHT. [Page 11]
$t_0, \ldots, t_3$	Four permutations on 4-bit values. One set of four t permutations is used to define q_0, a second set is used to define q_1. [Page 17]
v	The polynomial used to define $GF(2^8)$ for the MDS matrix multiply. [Page 12]
w	The polynomial used to define $GF(2^8)$ for the RS matrix multiply. [Page 13]
x	The input to one of the q mappings. [Page 16]
$x_0, \ldots, x_3$	The four input bytes to g or h. [Page 12]
y	The output of one of the q mappings. [Page 16]
$y_0, \ldots, y_3$	Four intermediate bytes in g or h [Page 12].
$y_{i,j}$	The intermediate values used in the computation of y_i from x_i. [Page 15]
$z_0, \ldots, z_3$	The four output bytes from g or h. [Page 15]
Z	The 32-bit output word from g or h. [Page 12]
ρ	A constant used for notational convenience. [Page 16]

B. Twofish Test Vectors

B.1 Intermediate Values

The following file shows the intermediate values of three Twofish computations. This particular implementation does not swap the halves but instead applies the F function alternately between the two halves.

```
FILENAME:  "ecb_ival.txt"

Electronic Codebook (ECB) Mode
Intermediate Value Tests

Algorithm Name:       TWOFISH
Principal Submitter:  Bruce Schneier, Counterpane Systems


==========

KEYSIZE=128

KEY=00000000000000000000000000000000

;
;makeKey:    Input key           --> S-box key      [Encrypt]
;            00000000 00000000   -->  00000000
;            00000000 00000000   -->  00000000
;            Subkeys
;            52C54DDE 11F0626D   Input whiten
;            7CAC9D4A 4D1B4AAA
;            B7B83A10 1E7D0BEB   Output whiten
;            EE9C341F CFE14BE4
;            F98FFEF9 9C5B3C17   Round subkeys
;            15A48310 342A4D81
;            424D89FE C14724A7
;            311B834C FDE87320
;            3302778F 26CD67B4
;            7A6C6362 C2BAF60E
;            3411B994 D972C87F
;            84ADB1EA A7DEE434
;            54D2960F A2F7CAA8
;            A6B8FF8C 8014C425
;            6A748D1C EDBAF720
;            928EF78C 0338EE13
```

```
;              9949D6BE  C8314176
;              07C07D68  ECAE7EA7
;              1FE71844  85C05C89
;              F298311E  696EA672
;
PT=00000000000000000000000000000000

Encrypt()

R[-1]:x= 00000000 00000000 00000000 00000000.
R[ 0]:x= 52C54DDE 11F0626D 7CAC9D4A 4D1B4AAA.
R[ 1]:x= 52C54DDE 11F0626D C38DCAA4 7A0A91B6.   t0=C06D4949 t1=41B9BFC1
R[ 2]:x= 55A538DE 5C5A4DB6 C38DCAA4 7A0A91B6.   t0=7C4536B9 t1=67A58299
R[ 3]:x= 55A538DE 5C5A4DB6 899063BD 893E49A9.   t0=60DAC1A4 t1=2D84C23D
R[ 4]:x= 2AE61A96 84BC42D3 899063BD 893E49A9.   t0=607AAEAD t1=6ED2DBF9
R[ 5]:x= 2AE61A96 84BC42D3 F14F2618 821B5F36.   t0=067D0B49 t1=318EACB4
R[ 6]:x= 0FFE0AD1 D6B87B70 F14F2618 821B5F36.   t0=58554EDB t1=62585CF7
R[ 7]:x= 0FFE0AD1 D6B87B70 CD0D38A1 C069BD9B.   t0=839B0017 t1=B3A89DB0
R[ 8]:x= A85CE579 DE2661CE CD0D38A1 C069BD9B.   t0=E9BC6975 t1=F0DDA4C3
R[ 9]:x= A85CE579 DE2661CE 7A39754C 973ABD2A.   t0=54687CDF t1=9044BF4B
R[10]:x= 013077D7 B3528BA1 7A39754C 973ABD2A.   t0=77FC927F t1=8B8678CC
R[11]:x= 013077D7 B3528BA1 D57933FD F8EA8B1B.   t0=E3C81108 t1=828E7493
R[12]:x= 64F0EAA1 DA27090C D57933FD F8EA8B1B.   t0=B33C25D6 t1=83068533
R[13]:x= 64F0EAA1 DA27090C F64F1005 99149A52.   t0=A0AA2F81 t1=FFF30DB7
R[14]:x= B0681C46 606D0273 F64F1005 99149A52.   t0=114C17C5 t1=EB143CFF
R[15]:x= B0681C46 606D0273 EB27628F 2C51191D.   t0=677DA87D t1=989D1459
R[16]:x= C1708BA9 9522A3CE EB27628F 2C51191D.   t0=9357B338 t1=AC9926BF
R[17]:x= 5C9F589F 322C12F6 2FECBFB6 5AC3E82A.

CT=9F589F5CF6122C32B6BFEC2F2AE8C35A

Decrypt()

CT=9F589F5CF6122C32B6BFEC2F2AE8C35A


R[17]:x= 5C9F589F 322C12F6 2FECBFB6 5AC3E82A.
R[16]:x= C1708BA9 9522A3CE EB27628F 2C51191D.   t0=9357B338 t1=AC9926BF
R[15]:x= B0681C46 606D0273 EB27628F 2C51191D.   t0=677DA87D t1=989D1459
R[14]:x= B0681C46 606D0273 F64F1005 99149A52.   t0=114C17C5 t1=EB143CFF
R[13]:x= 64F0EAA1 DA27090C F64F1005 99149A52.   t0=A0AA2F81 t1=FFF30DB7
R[12]:x= 64F0EAA1 DA27090C D57933FD F8EA8B1B.   t0=B33C25D6 t1=83068533
R[11]:x= 013077D7 B3528BA1 D57933FD F8EA8B1B.   t0=E3C81108 t1=828E7493
R[10]:x= 013077D7 B3528BA1 7A39754C 973ABD2A.   t0=77FC927F t1=8B8678CC
R[ 9]:x= A85CE579 DE2661CE 7A39754C 973ABD2A.   t0=54687CDF t1=9044BF4B
R[ 8]:x= A85CE579 DE2661CE CD0D38A1 C069BD9B.   t0=E9BC6975 t1=F0DDA4C3
R[ 7]:x= 0FFE0AD1 D6B87B70 CD0D38A1 C069BD9B.   t0=839B0017 t1=B3A89DB0
R[ 6]:x= 0FFE0AD1 D6B87B70 F14F2618 821B5F36.   t0=58554EDB t1=62585CF7
R[ 5]:x= 2AE61A96 84BC42D3 F14F2618 821B5F36.   t0=067D0B49 t1=318EACB4
R[ 4]:x= 2AE61A96 84BC42D3 899063BD 893E49A9.   t0=607AAEAD t1=6ED2DBF9
R[ 3]:x= 55A538DE 5C5A4DB6 899063BD 893E49A9.   t0=60DAC1A4 t1=2D84C23D
R[ 2]:x= 55A538DE 5C5A4DB6 C38DCAA4 7A0A91B6.   t0=7C4536B9 t1=67A58299
R[ 1]:x= 52C54DDE 11F0626D C38DCAA4 7A0A91B6.   t0=C06D4949 t1=41B9BFC1
```

```
R[ 0]:x= 52C54DDE 11F0626D 7CAC9D4A 4D1B4AAA.
R[-1]:x= 00000000 00000000 00000000 00000000.

PT=00000000000000000000000000000000

==========

KEYSIZE=192

KEY=0123456789ABCDEFFEDCBA987654321000011223344556677


;
;makeKey:    Input key              --> S-box key      [Encrypt]
;                EFCDAB89 67452301  --> B89FF6F2
;                10325476 98BADCFE  --> B255BC4B
;                77665544 33221100  --> 45661061
;            Subkeys
;                38394A24 C36D1175  Input whiten
;                E802528F 219BFEB4
;                B9141AB4 BD3E70CD  Output whiten
;                AF609383 FD36908A
;                03EFB931 1D2EE7EC  Round subkeys
;                A7489D55 6E44B6E8
;                714AD667 653AD51F
;                B6315B66 B27C05AF
;                A06C8140 9853D419
;                4016E346 8D1C0DD4
;                F05480BE B6AF816F
;                2D7DC789 45B7BD3A
;                57F8A163 2BEFDA69
;                26AE7271 C2900D79
;                ED323794 3D3FFD80
;                5DE68E49 9C3D2478
;                DF326FE3 5911F70D
;                C229F13B B1364772
;                4235364D 0CEC363A
;                57C8DD1F 6A1AD61E
;
PT=00000000000000000000000000000000

Encrypt()

R[-1]:x= 00000000 00000000 00000000 00000000.
R[ 0]:x= 38394A24 C36D1175 E802528F 219BFEB4.
R[ 1]:x= 38394A24 C36D1175 9C263D67 5E68BE8F.  t0=988C8223 t1=33D1ECEC
R[ 2]:x= C8F5099F 0C4B8F53 9C263D67 5E68BE8F.  t0=E8C880BC t1=19C23B0A
R[ 3]:x= C8F5099F 0C4B8F53 69948F5E E67C030F.  t0=C615F1F6 t1=17AE5B7E
R[ 4]:x= 07633866 59421079 69948F5E E67C030F.  t0=90AB32AA t1=7F56EB43
R[ 5]:x= 07633866 59421079 C015BE79 149B9CEC.  t0=52971E00 t1=F6BC546D
R[ 6]:x= A042B99D 709EF54B C015BE79 149B9CEC.  t0=DAA00849 t1=2D2F5FCE
R[ 7]:x= A042B99D 709EF54B 0CD39FA6 B250BEDA.  t0=EE03FB5B t1=FB5A051C
R[ 8]:x= F7B097FA 9E5C4FF7 0CD39FA6 B250BEDA.  t0=09A1B597 t1=18041948
R[ 9]:x= F7B097FA 9E5C4FF7 77FC8B29 CC2B3F88.  t0=99C9694E t1=F1687F43
```

```
R[10]:x= A279C718 421A8D38 77FC8B29 CC2B3F88.   t0=5D174956 t1=2F7D5E04
R[11]:x= A279C718 421A8D38 5B1A0904 12FEBF99.   t0=5BC40012 t1=78D2617B
R[12]:x= E4409C22 702548A2 5B1A0904 12FEBF99.   t0=C251B3CE t1=4AC0BD46
R[13]:x= E4409C22 702548A2 5DDAA2A1 EFB2F051.   t0=91BC2070 t1=6FC0BBF3
R[14]:x= 8561A604 825D2480 5DDAA2A1 EFB2F051.   t0=A7D24F8E t1=84878F62
R[15]:x= 8561A604 825D2480 5CC6CB7B 62A2CE64.   t0=93690387 t1=0EB8FA83
R[16]:x= 17738CD3 B5142D18 5CC6CB7B 62A2CE64.   t0=5FE8370B t1=F3D5AB78
R[17]:x= E5D2D1CF DF9CBEA9 B8131F50 4822BD92.

CT=CFD1D2E5A9BE9CDF501F13B892BD2248

Decrypt()

CT=CFD1D2E5A9BE9CDF501F13B892BD2248


R[17]:x= E5D2D1CF DF9CBEA9 B8131F50 4822BD92.
R[16]:x= 17738CD3 B5142D18 5CC6CB7B 62A2CE64.   t0=5FE8370B t1=F3D5AB78
R[15]:x= 8561A604 825D2480 5CC6CB7B 62A2CE64.   t0=93690387 t1=0EB8FA83
R[14]:x= 8561A604 825D2480 5DDAA2A1 EFB2F051.   t0=A7D24F8E t1=84878F62
R[13]:x= E4409C22 702548A2 5DDAA2A1 EFB2F051.   t0=91BC2070 t1=6FC0BBF3
R[12]:x= E4409C22 702548A2 5B1A0904 12FEBF99.   t0=C251B3CE t1=4AC0BD46
R[11]:x= A279C718 421A8D38 5B1A0904 12FEBF99.   t0=5BC40012 t1=78D2617B
R[10]:x= A279C718 421A8D38 77FC8B29 CC2B3F88.   t0=5D174956 t1=2F7D5E04
R[ 9]:x= F7B097FA 9E5C4FF7 77FC8B29 CC2B3F88.   t0=99C9694E t1=F1687F43
R[ 8]:x= F7B097FA 9E5C4FF7 0CD39FA6 B250BEDA.   t0=09A1B597 t1=18041948
R[ 7]:x= A042B99D 709EF54B 0CD39FA6 B250BEDA.   t0=EE03FB5B t1=FB5A051C
R[ 6]:x= A042B99D 709EF54B C015BE79 149B9CEC.   t0=DAA00849 t1=2D2F5FCE
R[ 5]:x= 07633866 59421079 C015BE79 149B9CEC.   t0=52971E00 t1=F6BC546D
R[ 4]:x= 07633866 59421079 69948F5E E67C030F.   t0=90AB32AA t1=7F56EB43
R[ 3]:x= C8F5099F 0C4B8F53 69948F5E E67C030F.   t0=C615F1F6 t1=17AE5B7E
R[ 2]:x= C8F5099F 0C4B8F53 9C263D67 5E68BE8F.   t0=E8C880BC t1=19C23B0A
R[ 1]:x= 38394A24 C36D1175 9C263D67 5E68BE8F.   t0=988C8223 t1=33D1ECEC
R[ 0]:x= 38394A24 C36D1175 E802528F 219BFEB4.
R[-1]:x= 00000000 00000000 00000000 00000000.

PT=00000000000000000000000000000000


==========


KEYSIZE=256


KEY=0123456789ABCDEFFEDCBA98765432100011223344556677889AABBCCDDEEFF


;
;makeKey:   Input key          -->  S-box key      [Encrypt]
;           EFCDAB89 67452301  -->  B89FF6F2
;           10325476 98BADCFE  -->  B255BC4B
;           77665544 33221100  -->  45661061
;           FFEEDDCC BBAA9988  -->  8E4447F7
;        Subkeys
;           5EC769BF 44D13C60  Input whiten
;           76CD39B1 16750474
```

```
;                349C294B  EC21F6D6   Output whiten
;                4FBD10B4  578DA0ED
;                C3479695  9B6958FB   Round subkeys
;                6A7FBC4E  0BF1830B
;                61B5E0FB  D78D9730
;                7C6CF0C4  2F9109C8
;                E69EA8D1  ED99BDFF
;                35DC0BBD  A03E5018
;                FB18EA0B  38BD43D3
;                76191781  37A9A0D3
;                72427BEA  911CC0B8
;                F1689449  71009CA9
;                B6363E89  494D9855
;                590BBC63  F95A28B5
;                FB72B4E1  2A43505C
;                BFD34176  5C133D12
;                3A9247F7  9A3331DD
;                EE7515E6  F0D54DCD
;
PT=00000000000000000000000000000000


Encrypt()

R[-1]:x= 00000000 00000000 00000000 00000000.
R[ 0]:x= 5EC769BF 44D13C60 76CD39B1 16750474.
R[ 1]:x= 5EC769BF 44D13C60 D38B6C9F A23B7169.   t0=29C0736C t1=E4D3D68D
R[ 2]:x= 99424DFF FBC14BFC D38B6C9F A23B7169.   t0=9D16BBB3 t1=64AD7A3F
R[ 3]:x= 99424DFF FBC14BFC 698BE047 6A997290.   t0=E66B9D19 t1=B87B2DFD
R[ 4]:x= 2C125DD7 5A526278 698BE047 6A997290.   t0=0BB41F61 t1=3945E62C
R[ 5]:x= 2C125DD7 5A526278 E35CD910 7CB57D06.   t0=D5397903 t1=F35A3092
R[ 6]:x= D5178F25 00D35CC5 E35CD910 7CB57D06.   t0=8C8927A1 t1=C3D8103E
R[ 7]:x= D5178F25 00D35CC5 D8447F91 65C2BD96.   t0=4D8B7489 t1=0B2FC79F
R[ 8]:x= FF92E109 DF621C97 D8447F91 65C2BD96.   t0=C1176720 t1=F301CE95
R[ 9]:x= FF92E109 DF621C97 28BFEFF5 D45666FB.   t0=9F3BEC03 t1=77BD388E
R[10]:x= BB79AD2E AA410F41 28BFEFF5 D45666FB.   t0=8C6DB451 t1=0B8B72BA
R[11]:x= BB79AD2E AA410F41 6576A3ED BFF8215E.   t0=8A317EF8 t1=A1EAEAAE
R[12]:x= 4A6BBAFF 439F4766 6576A3ED BFF8215E.   t0=8F8307AA t1=472014C3
R[13]:x= 4A6BBAFF 439F4766 F7186836 04CA5304.   t0=CEB0BBE1 t1=C12302BE
R[14]:x= CBD3C29D BC31FEBE F7186836 04CA5304.   t0=5CF5C93C t1=C1033512
R[15]:x= CBD3C29D BC31FEBE D4E77B7C 5415D5D3.   t0=853A6BB2 t1=9F09EB26
R[16]:x= 85411C2B 7777DC05 D4E77B7C 5415D5D3.   t0=877AF61D t1=4B61EEC7
R[17]:x= E07B5237 B8342305 CAFC0C9F 20FA7CE8.


CT=37527BE0052334B89F0CFCCAE87CFA20

Decrypt()

CT=37527BE0052334B89F0CFCCAE87CFA20


R[17]:x= E07B5237 B8342305 CAFC0C9F 20FA7CE8.
R[16]:x= 85411C2B 7777DC05 D4E77B7C 5415D5D3. t0=877AF61D t1=4B61EEC7
R[15]:x= CBD3C29D BC31FEBE D4E77B7C 5415D5D3. t0=853A6BB2 t1=9F09EB26
```

```
R[14]:x= CBD3C29D BC31FEBE F7186836 04CA5304. t0=5CF5C93C t1=C1033512
R[13]:x= 4A6BBAFF 439F4766 F7186836 04CA5304. t0=CEB0BBE1 t1=C12302BE
R[12]:x= 4A6BBAFF 439F4766 6576A3ED BFF8215E. t0=8F8307AA t1=472014C3
R[11]:x= BB79AD2E AA410F41 6576A3ED BFF8215E. t0=8A317EF8 t1=A1EAEAAE
R[10]:x= BB79AD2E AA410F41 28BFEFF5 D45666FB. t0=8C6DB451 t1=0B8B72BA
R[ 9]:x= FF92E109 DF621C97 28BFEFF5 D45666FB. t0=9F3BEC03 t1=77BD388E
R[ 8]:x= FF92E109 DF621C97 D8447F91 65C2BD96. t0=C1176720 t1=F301CE95
R[ 7]:x= D5178F25 00D35CC5 D8447F91 65C2BD96. t0=4D8B7489 t1=0B2FC79F
R[ 6]:x= D5178F25 00D35CC5 E35CD910 7CB57D06. t0=8C8927A1 t1=C3D8103E
R[ 5]:x= 2C125DD7 5A526278 E35CD910 7CB57D06. t0=D5397903 t1=F35A3092
R[ 4]:x= 2C125DD7 5A526278 698BE047 6A997290. t0=0BB41F61 t1=3945E62C
R[ 3]:x= 99424DFF FBC14BFC 698BE047 6A997290. t0=E66B9D19 t1=B87B2DFD
R[ 2]:x= 99424DFF FBC14BFC D38B6C9F A23B7169. t0=9D16BBB3 t1=64AD7A3F
R[ 1]:x= 5EC769BF 44D13C60 D38B6C9F A23B7169. t0=29C0736C t1=E4D3D68D
R[ 0]:x= 5EC769BF 44D13C60 76CD39B1 16750474.
R[-1]:x= 00000000 00000000 00000000 00000000.

PT=00000000000000000000000000000000
```

B.2 Full Encryptions

The following file shows a number of (plaintext, ciphertext, key) pairs. These pairs are related, and can easily be tested automatically. The plaintext of each entry is the ciphertext of the previous one. The key of each entry is made up of the ciphertext two and three entries back. We believe that these test vectors provide a thorough test of a Twofish implementation.

```
FILENAME:  "ecb_tbl.txt"

Electronic Codebook (ECB) Mode
Tables Known Answer Test
Tests permutation tables and MDS matrix multiply tables.

Algorithm Name:       TWOFISH
Principal Submitter:  Bruce Schneier, Counterpane Systems

==========

KEYSIZE=128

I=1
KEY=00000000000000000000000000000000
PT=00000000000000000000000000000000
CT=9F589F5CF6122C32B6BFEC2F2AE8C35A

I=2
KEY=00000000000000000000000000000000
PT=9F589F5CF6122C32B6BFEC2F2AE8C35A
CT=D491DB16E7B1C39E86CB086B789F5419
```

```
I=3
KEY=9F589F5CF6122C32B6BFEC2F2AE8C35A
PT=D491DB16E7B1C39E86CB086B789F5419
CT=019F9809DE1711858FAAC3A3BA20FBC3

I=4
KEY=D491DB16E7B1C39E86CB086B789F5419
PT=019F9809DE1711858FAAC3A3BA20FBC3
CT=6363977DE839486297E661C6C9D668EB

I=5
KEY=019F9809DE1711858FAAC3A3BA20FBC3
PT=6363977DE839486297E661C6C9D668EB
CT=816D5BD0FAE35342BF2A7412C246F752

I=6
KEY=6363977DE839486297E661C6C9D668EB
PT=816D5BD0FAE35342BF2A7412C246F752
CT=5449ECA008FF5921155F598AF4CED4D0

I=7
KEY=816D5BD0FAE35342BF2A7412C246F752
PT=5449ECA008FF5921155F598AF4CED4D0
CT=6600522E97AEB3094ED5F92AFCBCDD10

I=8
KEY=5449ECA008FF5921155F598AF4CED4D0
PT=6600522E97AEB3094ED5F92AFCBCDD10
CT=34C8A5FB2D3D08A170D120AC6D26DBFA

I=9
KEY=6600522E97AEB3094ED5F92AFCBCDD10
PT=34C8A5FB2D3D08A170D120AC6D26DBFA
CT=28530B358C1B42EF277DE6D4407FC591

I=10
KEY=34C8A5FB2D3D08A170D120AC6D26DBFA
PT=28530B358C1B42EF277DE6D4407FC591
CT=8A8AB983310ED78C8C0ECDE030B8DCA4

        :
        :
        :

I=48
KEY=137A24CA47CD12BE818DF4D2F4355960
PT=BCA724A54533C6987E14AA827952F921
CT=6B459286F3FFD28D49F15B1581B08E42

I=49
KEY=BCA724A54533C6987E14AA827952F921
PT=6B459286F3FFD28D49F15B1581B08E42
CT=5D9D4EEFFA9151575524F115815A12E0
```

```
==========

KEYSIZE=192

I=1
KEY=000000000000000000000000000000000000000000000000
PT=00000000000000000000000000000000
CT=EFA71F788965BD4453F860178FC19101

I=2
KEY=EFA71F788965BD4453F860178FC191010000000000000000
PT=EFA71F788965BD4453F860178FC19101
CT=88B2B2706B105E36B446BB6D731A1E88

I=3
KEY=EFA71F788965BD4453F860178FC19101000000000000000
PT=88B2B2706B105E36B446BB6D731A1E88
CT=39DA69D6BA4997D585B6DC073CA341B2

I=4
KEY=88B2B2706B105E36B446BB6D731A1E88EFA71F788965BD44
PT=39DA69D6BA4997D585B6DC073CA341B2
CT=182B02D81497EA45F9DAACDC29193A65

I=5
KEY=39DA69D6BA4997D585B6DC073CA341B288B2B2706B105E36
PT=182B02D81497EA45F9DAACDC29193A65
CT=7AFF7A70CA2FF28AC31DD8AE5DAAAB63

I=6
KEY=182B02D81497EA45F9DAACDC29193A6539DA69D6BA4997D5
PT=7AFF7A70CA2FF28AC31DD8AE5DAAAB63
CT=D1079B789F666649B6BD7D1629F1F77E

I=7
KEY=7AFF7A70CA2FF28AC31DD8AE5DAAAB63182B02D81497EA45
PT=D1079B789F666649B6BD7D1629F1F77E
CT=3AF6F7CE5BD35EF18BEC6FA787AB506B

I=8
KEY=D1079B789F666649B6BD7D1629F1F77E7AFF7A70CA2FF28A
PT=3AF6F7CE5BD35EF18BEC6FA787AB506B
CT=AE8109BFDA85C1F2C5038B34ED691BFF

I=9
KEY=3AF6F7CE5BD35EF18BEC6FA787AB506BD1079B789F666649
PT=AE8109BFDA85C1F2C5038B34ED691BFF
CT=893FD67B98C550073571BD631263FC78

I=10
KEY=AE8109BFDA85C1F2C5038B34ED691BFF3AF6F7CE5BD35EF1
PT=893FD67B98C550073571BD631263FC78
```

CT=16434FC9C8841A63D58700B5578E8F67

```
    :
    :
    :
```

I=48
KEY=DEA4F3DA75EC7A8EAC3861A9912402CD5DBE44032769DF54
PT=FB66522C332FCC4C042ABE32FA9E902F
CT=F0AB73301125FA21EF70BE5385FB76B6

I=49
KEY=FB66522C332FCC4C042ABE32FA9E902FDEA4F3DA75EC7A8E
PT=F0AB73301125FA21EF70BE5385FB76B6
CT=E75449212BEEF9F4A390BD860A640941

==========

KEYSIZE=256

I=1
KEY=0000000000000000000000000000000000000000000000000000000000000000
PT=0000000000000000000000000000000000
CT=57FF739D4DC92C1BD7FC01700CC8216F

I=2
KEY=0000000000000000000000000000000000000000000000000000000000000000
PT=57FF739D4DC92C1BD7FC01700CC8216F
CT=D43BB7556EA32E46F2A282B7D45B4E0D

I=3
KEY=57FF739D4DC92C1BD7FC01700CC8216F0000000000000000000000000000000000
PT=D43BB7556EA32E46F2A282B7D45B4E0D
CT=90AFE91BB288544F2C32DC239B2635E6

I=4
KEY=D43BB7556EA32E46F2A282B7D45B4E0D57FF739D4DC92C1BD7FC01700CC8216F
PT=90AFE91BB288544F2C32DC239B2635E6
CT=6CB4561C40BF0A9705931CB6D408E7FA

I=5
KEY=90AFE91BB288544F2C32DC239B2635E6D43BB7556EA32E46F2A282B7D45B4E0D
PT=6CB4561C40BF0A9705931CB6D408E7FA
CT=3059D6D61753B958D92F4781C8640E58

I=6
KEY=6CB4561C40BF0A9705931CB6D408E7FA90AFE91BB288544F2C32DC239B2635E6
PT=3059D6D61753B958D92F4781C8640E58
CT=E69465770505D7F80EF68CA38AB3A3D6

I=7
KEY=3059D6D61753B958D92F4781C8640E586CB4561C40BF0A9705931CB6D408E7FA
PT=E69465770505D7F80EF68CA38AB3A3D6

CT=5AB67A5F8539A4A5FD9F0373BA463466

I=8
KEY=E69465770505D7F80EF68CA38AB3A3D63059D6D61753B958D92F4781C8640E58
PT=5AB67A5F8539A4A5FD9F0373BA463466
CT=DC096BCD99FC72F79936D4C748E75AF7

I=9
KEY=5AB67A5F8539A4A5FD9F0373BA463466E69465770505D7F80EF68CA38AB3A3D6
PT=DC096BCD99FC72F79936D4C748E75AF7
CT=C5A3E7CEE0F1B7260528A68FB4EA05F2

I=10
KEY=DC096BCD99FC72F79936D4C748E75AF75AB67A5F8539A4A5FD9F0373BA463466
PT=C5A3E7CEE0F1B7260528A68FB4EA05F2
CT=43D5CEC327B24AB90AD34A79D0469151

     :
     :
     :

I=48
KEY=2E2158BC3E5FC714C1EEECA0EA696D48D2DED73E59319A8138E0331F0EA149EA
PT=248A7F3528B168ACFDD1386E3F51E30C
CT=431058F4DBC7F734DA4F02F04CC4F459

I=49
KEY=248A7F3528B168ACFDD1386E3F51E30C2E2158BC3E5FC714C1EEECA0EA696D48
PT=431058F4DBC7F734DA4F02F04CC4F459
CT=37FE26FF1CF66175F5DDF4C33B97A205

C. Code

Twofish source code is available on the Twofish web site:

http://www.counterpane.com/twofish.html

The web site also contains the following downloadable Twofish implementations:

- Reference C implementation.
- Optimized C for the Intel Pentium, Pentium Pro, and Pentium II.
- Assembly code for the Intel Pentium, Pentium Pro, and Pentium II.
- 6805 assembly code.

C.1 C Code

This section contains C source code that implements Twofish. This is the code that the authors used during the development of Twofish.

```
/***********************************************************************
  PLATFORM.H  -- Platform-specific defines for TWOFISH code

  Submitters:
    Bruce Schneier, Counterpane Systems
    Doug Whiting,   Hi/fn
    John Kelsey,    Counterpane Systems
    Chris Hall,     Counterpane Systems
    David Wagner,   UC Berkeley
    Niels Ferguson, Counterpane Systems

  Code Author:        Doug Whiting,   Hi/fn

  Version  1.00       April 1998

  Copyright 1998, Hi/fn and Counterpane Systems. All rights reserved.

  Notes:
    *   Tab size is set to 4 characters in this file
```

```
*********************************************************************/

/* use intrinsic rotate if possible */
#define ROL(x,n) (((x) << ((n) & 0x1F)) | ((x) >> (32-((n) & 0x1F))))
#define ROR(x,n) (((x) >> ((n) & 0x1F)) | ((x) << (32-((n) & 0x1F))))

#if (0) && defined(__BORLANDC__) && (__BORLANDC__ >= 0x462)
#error "!!!This does not work for some reason!!!"
#include    <stdlib.h>      /* get prototype _lrotl(), _lrotr() */
#pragma inline __lrotl__
#pragma inline __lrotr__
#undef  ROL                 /* get rid of inefficient definitions */
#undef  ROR
#define ROL(x,n)    __lrotl__(x,n)  /* use intrinsic rotations */
#define ROR(x,n)    __lrotr__(x,n)
#endif

#ifdef _MSC_VER
#include    <stdlib.h>      /* get prototypes rotation functions */
#undef  ROL
#undef  ROR
#pragma intrinsic(_lrotl,_lrotr)    /* use intrinsic rotations */
#define ROL(x,n)    _lrotl(x,n)
#define ROR(x,n)    _lrotr(x,n)
#endif

#ifndef _M_IX86
#ifdef  __BORLANDC__
#define _M_IX86         300     /* ensure defined for Intel CPUs */
#endif
#endif

#ifdef _M_IX86
#define     LittleEndian    1   /* e.g., 1 for Pentium, 0 for 68K */
#define     ALIGN32         0   /* need dword alignment? */
#else   /* non-Intel platforms */
#define     LittleEndian    0   /* (assume big endian) */
#define     ALIGN32         1   /* (assume alignment needed) */
#endif

#if LittleEndian
#define     Bswap(x)        (x) /* NOP for little-endian machines */
#define     ADDR_XOR        0   /* NOP for little-endian machines */
#else
#define     Bswap(x) ((ROR(x,8) & 0xFF00FF00) | (ROL(x,8) & 0x00FF00FF))
#define     ADDR_XOR        3   /* convert byte address in dword */
#endif

/* Macros for extracting bytes from dwords (correct for endianness) */
#define _b(x,N) (((BYTE *)&x)[((N) & 3) ^ ADDR_XOR])

#define     b0(x)           _b(x,0)     /* extract LSB of DWORD */
#define     b1(x)           _b(x,1)
```

```
#define     b2(x)               _b(x,2)
#define     b3(x)               _b(x,3)         /* extract MSB of DWORD */


/* =============================================================== */


/* aes.h */
/* AES Cipher header file for ANSI C Submissions
    Lawrence E. Bassham III
    Computer Security Division
    National Institute of Standards and Technology

    This sample is to assist implementers developing to the
Cryptographic API Profile for AES Candidate Algorithm Submissions.
Please consult this document as a cross-reference.

    ANY CHANGES, WHERE APPROPRIATE, TO INFORMATION PROVIDED IN THIS FILE
MUST BE DOCUMENTED. CHANGES ARE ONLY APPROPRIATE WHERE SPECIFIED WITH
THE STRING "CHANGE POSSIBLE". FUNCTION CALLS AND THEIR PARAMETERS
CANNOT BE CHANGED. STRUCTURES CAN BE ALTERED TO ALLOW IMPLEMENTERS TO
INCLUDE IMPLEMENTATION SPECIFIC INFORMATION.
*/

/* Includes:
    Standard include files
*/

#include    <stdio.h>
#include    "platform.h"                /* platform-specific defines */

/*  Defines:
        Add any additional defines you need
*/

#define DIR_ENCRYPT     0       /* Are we encrpyting? */
#define DIR_DECRYPT     1       /* Are we decrpyting? */
#define MODE_ECB        1       /* Are we ciphering in ECB mode? */
#define MODE_CBC        2       /* Are we ciphering in CBC mode? */
#define MODE_CFB1       3       /* Are we ciphering in 1-bit CFB mode?*/

#define TRUE            1
#define FALSE           0

#define BAD_KEY_DIR        -1   /* Invalid Key direction */
#define BAD_KEY_MAT        -2   /* Key material not of correct length */
#define BAD_KEY_INSTANCE   -3   /* Key passed is not valid */
#define BAD_CIPHER_MODE    -4   /* Params struct is invalid */
#define BAD_CIPHER_STATE   -5   /* Cipher in wrong state */

/* CHANGE POSSIBLE: inclusion of algorithm specific defines */
/* TWOFISH specific definitions */
```

```
#define MAX_KEY_SIZE      64  /* # of chars in key representation */
#define MAX_IV_SIZE       16  /* # of bytes needed to represent an IV */
#define BAD_INPUT_LEN     -6  /* inputLen not a multiple of block size */
#define BAD_PARAMS        -7  /* invalid parameters */
#define BAD_IV_MAT        -8  /* invalid IV text */
#define BAD_ENDIAN        -9  /* incorrect endianness define */
#define BAD_ALIGN32      -10  /* incorrect 32-bit alignment */

#define BLOCK_SIZE       128  /* number of bits per block */
#define MAX_ROUNDS        16  /* max # rounds */
#define ROUNDS_128        16  /* default # of rounds for 128-bit keys*/
#define ROUNDS_192        16  /* default # of rounds for 192-bit keys*/
#define ROUNDS_256        16  /* default # of rounds for 256-bit keys*/
#define MAX_KEY_BITS     256  /* max number of bits of key */
#define MIN_KEY_BITS     128  /* min number of bits of key (zero pad) */
#define VALID_SIG 0x48534946  /* initialization signature ('FISH') */
#define MCT_OUTER        400  /* MCT outer loop */
#define MCT_INNER      10000  /* MCT inner loop */
#define REENTRANT          1  /* forces reentrant code (slightly slower) */

#define INPUT_WHITEN       0    /* subkey array indices */
#define OUTPUT_WHITEN       ( INPUT_WHITEN + BLOCK_SIZE/32)
#define ROUND_SUBKEYS      (OUTPUT_WHITEN + BLOCK_SIZE/32)
#define TOTAL_SUBKEYS      (ROUND_SUBKEYS + 2*MAX_ROUNDS)

/* Typedefs:
    Typedef'ed data storage elements. Add any algorithm specific
    parameters at the bottom of the structs as appropriate.
*/

typedef unsigned char BYTE;
typedef unsigned long DWORD;        /* 32-bit unsigned quantity */
typedef DWORD fullSbox[4][256];

/* The structure for key information */
typedef struct
    {
    BYTE direction;                 /* Encrypting or decrypting? */
#if ALIGN32
    BYTE dummyAlign[3];             /* keep 32-bit alignment */
#endif
    int  keyLen;                    /* Length of the key */
    char keyMaterial[MAX_KEY_SIZE+4];/* Raw key data in ASCII */

    /* Twofish-specific parameters: */
    DWORD keySig;                       /* set to VALID_SIG by makeKey()*/
    int   numRounds;                    /* number of rounds in cipher */
    DWORD key32[MAX_KEY_BITS/32];    /* actual key bits, in dwords */
    DWORD sboxKeys[MAX_KEY_BITS/64];/* key bits used for S-boxes */
    DWORD subKeys[TOTAL_SUBKEYS];    /* whitening & round subkeys */
#if REENTRANT
    fullSbox sBox8x32;               /* fully expanded S-box */
  #if defined(COMPILE_KEY) && defined(USE_ASM)
```

```
#undef   VALID_SIG
#define VALID_SIG      0x504D4F43      /* 'COMP' */
    void *encryptFuncPtr;              /* ptr to asm encrypt function */
    void *decryptFuncPtr;              /* ptr to asm decrypt function */
    DWORD codeSize;                    /* size of compiledCode */
    BYTE  compiledCode[5000];          /* make room for the code */
  #endif
#endif
    } keyInstance;

/* The structure for cipher information */
typedef struct
    {
    BYTE  mode;                        /* MODE_ECB, MODE_CBC, or MODE_CFB1 */
#if ALIGN32
    BYTE dummyAlign[3];            /* keep 32-bit alignment */
#endif
    BYTE  IV[MAX_IV_SIZE];         /* CFB1 iv bytes  (CBC uses iv32) */

    /* Twofish-specific parameters: */
    DWORD cipherSig;                   /* set to VALID_SIG by cipherInit() */
    DWORD iv32[BLOCK_SIZE/32];    /* CBC IV bytes arranged as dwords */
    } cipherInstance;

/* Function protoypes */
int makeKey(keyInstance *key, BYTE direction,
        int keyLen, char *keyMaterial);

int cipherInit(cipherInstance *cipher, BYTE mode, char *IV);

int blockEncrypt(cipherInstance *cipher, keyInstance *key,
            BYTE *input, int inputLen, BYTE *outBuffer);

int blockDecrypt(cipherInstance *cipher, keyInstance *key,
            BYTE *input, int inputLen, BYTE *outBuffer);

/* do key schedule using modified key.keyDwords */
int reKey(keyInstance *key);

/* affect number of rounds for given keyLen (64,128,192, 256) */
int setRounds(int keyLen,int nRounds);

/* API to check table usage, for use in ECB_TBL KAT */
#define   TAB_DISABLE       0
#define   TAB_ENABLE        1
#define   TAB_RESET         2
#define   TAB_QUERY         3
#define   TAB_MIN_QUERY     50
int TableOp(int op);


#define   CONST          /* helpful C++ syntax sugar, NOP for ANSI C */
```

```
#if BLOCK_SIZE == 128           /* optimize block copies */
#define     Copy1(d,s,N)    ((DWORD *)(d))[N] = ((DWORD *)(s))[N]
#define     BlockCopy(d,s)  \
    { Copy1(d,s,0);Copy1(d,s,1);Copy1(d,s,2);Copy1(d,s,3); }
#else
#define     BlockCopy(d,s)  { memcpy(d,s,BLOCK_SIZE/8); }
#endif


/* ================================================================ */

/* DEBUG.H  -- debug assist macros */
#ifdef DEBUG
CONST int debugCompile  =   1;
extern  int debug;
extern  void DebugIO(CONST char *s);    /* display the debug output */

#define DebugDump(x,s,R,XOR,doRot,showT,needBswap)  \
    { if (debug) _Dump(x,s,R,XOR,doRot,showT,needBswap,t0,t1); }
#define DebugDumpKey(key) { if (debug) _DumpKey(key); }
#define IV_ROUND    -100

void _Dump(CONST void *p, CONST char *s, int R, int XOR, int doRot,
        int showT, int needBswap, DWORD t0, DWORD t1)
    {
    char line[512]; /* build output here */
    int  i,n;
    DWORD q[4];

    if (R == IV_ROUND)
        sprintf(line,"%sIV:     ",s);
    else
        sprintf(line,"%sR[%2d]: ",s,R);
    for (n=0;line[n];n++) ;

    for (i=0;i<4;i++)
        {
        q[i]=((CONST DWORD *)p)[i^(XOR)];
        if (needBswap) q[i]=Bswap(q[i]);
        }

    sprintf(line+n,"x= %081X  %081X  %081X  %081X.",
            ROR(q[0],doRot*(R  )/2),
            ROL(q[1],doRot*(R  )/2),
            ROR(q[2],doRot*(R+1)/2),
            ROL(q[3],doRot*(R+1)/2));
    for (;line[n];n++) ;

    if (showT)
        sprintf(line+n,"    t0=%081X. t1=%081X.",t0,t1);
    for (;line[n];n++) ;

    sprintf(line+n,"\n");
```

```
        DebugIO(line);
        }

void _DumpKey(CONST keyInstance *key)
    {
    char    line[512];
    int     i;
    int     k64Cnt=(key->keyLen+63)/64; /* round up */
    int     subkeyCnt = ROUND_SUBKEYS + 2*key->numRounds;

    sprintf(line,
 ";\n;makeKey:   Input key              -->  S-box key      [%s]\n",
            (key->direction == DIR_ENCRYPT) ? "Encrypt" : "Decrypt");
    DebugIO(line);
    for (i=0;i<k64Cnt;i++)  /* display in RS format */
        {
        sprintf(line,";%12s %081X %081X  -->  %081X\n","",
                key->key32[2*i+1],key->key32[2*i],
                key->sboxKeys[k64Cnt-1-i]);
        DebugIO(line);
        }
    sprintf(line,";%11sSubkeys\n","");
    DebugIO(line);
    for (i=0;i<subkeyCnt/2;i++)
        {
        sprintf(line,";%12s %081X %081X%s\n","",
                key->subKeys[2*i],key->subKeys[2*i+1],
                (2*i ==  INPUT_WHITEN) ? "  Input whiten" :
                (2*i == OUTPUT_WHITEN) ? "  Output whiten" :
                (2*i == ROUND_SUBKEYS) ? "  Round subkeys" : "");
        DebugIO(line);
        }
    DebugIO(";\n");
    }
#else
CONST int debugCompile  =   0;
#define DebugDump(x,s,R,XOR,doRot,showT,needBswap)
#define DebugDumpKey(key)
#endif


/* ================================================================= */



/***********************************************************************
  TABLE.H -- Tables, macros, etc. for Twofish S-boxes and MDS matrix

  Submitters:
    Bruce Schneier, Counterpane Systems
    Doug Whiting,   Hi/fn
    John Kelsey,    Counterpane Systems
    Chris Hall,     Counterpane Systems
```

```
        David Wagner,   UC Berkeley
        Niels Ferguson, Counterpane Systems

     Code Author:        Doug Whiting,   Hi/fn

     Version  1.00       April 1998

     Copyright 1998, Hi/fn and Counterpane Systems.  All rights reserved.

     Notes:
        *   Tab size is set to 4 characters in this file
        *   These definitions should be used in optimized and unoptimized
            versions to insure consistency.

     **********************************************************************/

     /* for computing subkeys */
     #define SK_STEP         0x02020202u
     #define SK_BUMP         0x01010101u
     #define SK_ROTL         9

     /* Reed-Solomon code parameters: (12,8) reversible code
         g(x) = x**4 + (a + 1/a) x**3 + a x**2 + (a + 1/a) x + 1
         where a = primitive root of field generator 0x14D */
     #define RS_GF_FDBK      0x14D           /* field generator */
     #define RS_rem(x)       \
      { BYTE  b = (BYTE) (x >> 24);                                          \
        DWORD g2= ((b<<1) ^ ((b&0x80) ? RS_GF_FDBK : 0 )) & 0xFF;           \
        DWORD g3= ((b>>1) & 0x7F) ^ ((b&1) ? RS_GF_FDBK >> 1 : 0 ) ^ g2 ;  \
        x= (x << 8) ^ (g3 << 24) ^ (g2 << 16) ^ (g3 << 8) ^ b;             \
      }


     /*  Macros for the MDS matrix
     *   The MDS matrix is (using primitive polynomial 169):
     *       01  EF  5B  5B
     *       5B  EF  EF  01
     *       EF  5B  01  EF
     *       EF  01  EF  5B
     *-----------------------------------------------------------------
     * More statistical properties of this matrix (from MDS.EXE output):
     *
     * Min Hamming weight (one byte difference)= 8. Max=26. Total = 1020.
     * Prob[8]:   7   23   42   20   52   95   88   94  121  128   91
     *          102   76   41   24    8    4    1    3    0    0    0
     * Runs[8]:   2    4    5    6    7    8    9   11
     * MSBs[8]:   1    4   15    8   18   38   40   43
     * HW=8: 05040705 0A080E0A 14101C14 28203828 50407050 01499101 A080E0A0
     * HW=9: 04050707 080A0E0E 10141C1C 20283838 40507070 80A0E0E0 C6432020
     *       07070504 0E0E0A08 1C1C1410 38382820 70705040 E0E0A080 202043C6
     *       05070407 0A0E080E 141C101C 28382038 50704070 A0E080E0 4320C620
     *       02924B02 089A4508
     * Min Hamming weight (two byte difference)= 3. Max=28. Total = 390150.
     * Prob[3]:   7   18   55  149  270  914 2185 5761 11363 20719
```

```
*               32079 43492 51612 53851 52098 42015 31117 20854 11538   6223
*               2492  1033
* MDS OK, ROR:    6+   7+   8+   9+  10+  11+  12+  13+  14+  15+  16+
*                17+  18+  19+  20+  21+  22+  23+  24+  25+  26+
*/
#define MDS_GF_FDBK     0x169   /* primitive polynomial for GF(256)*/
#define LFSR1(x) ( ((x) >> 1) ^ (((x) & 0x01) ?   MDS_GF_FDBK/2 : 0))
#define LFSR2(x) ( ((x) >> 2) ^ (((x) & 0x02) ?   MDS_GF_FDBK/2 : 0) \
                              ^ (((x) & 0x01) ?   MDS_GF_FDBK/4 : 0))

#define Mx_1(x) ((DWORD)  (x))    /* force to dword so << will work */
#define Mx_X(x) ((DWORD) ((x) ^              LFSR2(x)))    /* 5B */
#define Mx_Y(x) ((DWORD) ((x) ^ LFSR1(x) ^ LFSR2(x)))    /* EF */

#define M00     Mul_1
#define M01     Mul_Y
#define M02     Mul_X
#define M03     Mul_X

#define M10     Mul_X
#define M11     Mul_Y
#define M12     Mul_Y
#define M13     Mul_1

#define M20     Mul_Y
#define M21     Mul_X
#define M22     Mul_1
#define M23     Mul_Y

#define M30     Mul_Y
#define M31     Mul_1
#define M32     Mul_Y
#define M33     Mul_X

#define Mul_1   Mx_1
#define Mul_X   Mx_X
#define Mul_Y   Mx_Y

/* Define the fixed p0/p1 permutations used in keyed S-box lookup.
   By changing the following constant definitions for P_ij, the
   S-boxes will automatically get changed in all the Twofish source
   code. Note that P_i0 is the "outermost" 8x8 permutation applied.
   See the f32() function to see how these constants are to be  used.
*/
#define P_00    1                       /* "outermost" permutation */
#define P_01    0
#define P_02    0
#define P_03    (P_01^1)                /* "extend" to larger key sizes */
#define P_04    1

#define P_10    0
#define P_11    0
#define P_12    1
```

```
#define P_13    (P_11^1)
#define P_14    0

#define P_20    1
#define P_21    1
#define P_22    0
#define P_23    (P_21^1)
#define P_24    0

#define P_30    0
#define P_31    1
#define P_32    1
#define P_33    (P_31^1)
#define P_34    1

#define p8(N)   P8x8[P_##N]          /* some syntax shorthand */

/* fixed 8x8 permutation S-boxes */

/**********************************************************************
 * 07:07:14  05/30/98  [4x4]  TestCnt=256. keySize=128. CRC=4BD14D9E.
 * maxKeyed: dpMax = 18. lpMax =100. fixPt = 8. skXor = 0. skDup =  6.
 *log2(dpMax[6..18])= --- 15.42 1.33 0.89 4.05  7.98 12.05
 *log2(lpMax[7..12])= 9.32  1.01 1.16 4.23 8.02 12.45
 *log2(fixPt[0.. 8])= 1.44  1.44 2.44 4.06 6.01  8.21 11.07 14.09 17.00
 *log2(skDup[0.. 6])= ---   2.37 0.44 3.94 8.36 13.04 17.99
 **********************************************************************/
CONST BYTE P8x8[2][256]=
    {
/*  p0:   */
/*  dpMax     = 10. lpMax     = 64. cycleCnt=   1 1 1 0.     */
/*  817D6F320B59ECA4.ECB81235F4A6709D.
    BA5E6D90C8F32471.D7F4126E9B3085CA. */
    0xA9, 0x67, 0xB3, 0xE8, 0x04, 0xFD, 0xA3, 0x76,
    0x9A, 0x92, 0x80, 0x78, 0xE4, 0xDD, 0xD1, 0x38,
    0x0D, 0xC6, 0x35, 0x98, 0x18, 0xF7, 0xEC, 0x6C,
    0x43, 0x75, 0x37, 0x26, 0xFA, 0x13, 0x94, 0x48,
    0xF2, 0xD0, 0x8B, 0x30, 0x84, 0x54, 0xDF, 0x23,
    0x19, 0x5B, 0x3D, 0x59, 0xF3, 0xAE, 0xA2, 0x82,
    0x63, 0x01, 0x83, 0x2E, 0xD9, 0x51, 0x9B, 0x7C,
    0xA6, 0xEB, 0xA5, 0xBE, 0x16, 0x0C, 0xE3, 0x61,
    0xC0, 0x8C, 0x3A, 0xF5, 0x73, 0x2C, 0x25, 0x0B,
    0xBB, 0x4E, 0x89, 0x6B, 0x53, 0x6A, 0xB4, 0xF1,
    0xE1, 0xE6, 0xBD, 0x45, 0xE2, 0xF4, 0xB6, 0x66,
    0xCC, 0x95, 0x03, 0x56, 0xD4, 0x1C, 0x1E, 0xD7,
    0xFB, 0xC3, 0x8E, 0xB5, 0xE9, 0xCF, 0xBF, 0xBA,
    0xEA, 0x77, 0x39, 0xAF, 0x33, 0xC9, 0x62, 0x71,
    0x81, 0x79, 0x09, 0xAD, 0x24, 0xCD, 0xF9, 0xD8,
    0xE5, 0xC5, 0xB9, 0x4D, 0x44, 0x08, 0x86, 0xE7,
    0xA1, 0x1D, 0xAA, 0xED, 0x06, 0x70, 0xB2, 0xD2,
    0x41, 0x7B, 0xA0, 0x11, 0x31, 0xC2, 0x27, 0x90,
    0x20, 0xF6, 0x60, 0xFF, 0x96, 0x5C, 0xB1, 0xAB,
    0x9E, 0x9C, 0x52, 0x1B, 0x5F, 0x93, 0x0A, 0xEF,
```

```
        0x91, 0x85, 0x49, 0xEE, 0x2D, 0x4F, 0x8F, 0x3B,
        0x47, 0x87, 0x6D, 0x46, 0xD6, 0x3E, 0x69, 0x64,
        0x2A, 0xCE, 0xCB, 0x2F, 0xFC, 0x97, 0x05, 0x7A,
        0xAC, 0x7F, 0xD5, 0x1A, 0x4B, 0x0E, 0xA7, 0x5A,
        0x28, 0x14, 0x3F, 0x29, 0x88, 0x3C, 0x4C, 0x02,
        0xB8, 0xDA, 0xB0, 0x17, 0x55, 0x1F, 0x8A, 0x7D,
        0x57, 0xC7, 0x8D, 0x74, 0xB7, 0xC4, 0x9F, 0x72,
        0x7E, 0x15, 0x22, 0x12, 0x58, 0x07, 0x99, 0x34,
        0x6E, 0x50, 0xDE, 0x68, 0x65, 0xBC, 0xDB, 0xF8,
        0xC8, 0xA8, 0x2B, 0x40, 0xDC, 0xFE, 0x32, 0xA4,
        0xCA, 0x10, 0x21, 0xF0, 0xD3, 0x5D, 0x0F, 0x00,
        0x6F, 0x9D, 0x36, 0x42, 0x4A, 0x5E, 0xC1, 0xE0,
/*  p1:  */
/*  dpMax      = 10.  lpMax      = 64.  cycleCnt=   2 0 0 1.     */
/*  28BDF76E31940AC5.1E2B4C376DA5F908.
    4C75169A0ED82B3F.B951C3DE647F208A.  */
        0x75, 0xF3, 0xC6, 0xF4, 0xDB, 0x7B, 0xFB, 0xC8,
        0x4A, 0xD3, 0xE6, 0x6B, 0x45, 0x7D, 0xE8, 0x4B,
        0xD6, 0x32, 0xD8, 0xFD, 0x37, 0x71, 0xF1, 0xE1,
        0x30, 0x0F, 0xF8, 0x1B, 0x87, 0xFA, 0x06, 0x3F,
        0x5E, 0xBA, 0xAE, 0x5B, 0x8A, 0x00, 0xBC, 0x9D,
        0x6D, 0xC1, 0xB1, 0x0E, 0x80, 0x5D, 0xD2, 0xD5,
        0xA0, 0x84, 0x07, 0x14, 0xB5, 0x90, 0x2C, 0xA3,
        0xB2, 0x73, 0x4C, 0x54, 0x92, 0x74, 0x36, 0x51,
        0x38, 0xB0, 0xBD, 0x5A, 0xFC, 0x60, 0x62, 0x96,
        0x6C, 0x42, 0xF7, 0x10, 0x7C, 0x28, 0x27, 0x8C,
        0x13, 0x95, 0x9C, 0xC7, 0x24, 0x46, 0x3B, 0x70,
        0xCA, 0xE3, 0x85, 0xCB, 0x11, 0xD0, 0x93, 0xB8,
        0xA6, 0x83, 0x20, 0xFF, 0x9F, 0x77, 0xC3, 0xCC,
        0x03, 0x6F, 0x08, 0xBF, 0x40, 0xE7, 0x2B, 0xE2,
        0x79, 0x0C, 0xAA, 0x82, 0x41, 0x3A, 0xEA, 0xB9,
        0xE4, 0x9A, 0xA4, 0x97, 0x7E, 0xDA, 0x7A, 0x17,
        0x66, 0x94, 0xA1, 0x1D, 0x3D, 0xF0, 0xDE, 0xB3,
        0x0B, 0x72, 0xA7, 0x1C, 0xEF, 0xD1, 0x53, 0x3E,
        0x8F, 0x33, 0x26, 0x5F, 0xEC, 0x76, 0x2A, 0x49,
        0x81, 0x88, 0xEE, 0x21, 0xC4, 0x1A, 0xEB, 0xD9,
        0xC5, 0x39, 0x99, 0xCD, 0xAD, 0x31, 0x8B, 0x01,
        0x18, 0x23, 0xDD, 0x1F, 0x4E, 0x2D, 0xF9, 0x48,
        0x4F, 0xF2, 0x65, 0x8E, 0x78, 0x5C, 0x58, 0x19,
        0x8D, 0xE5, 0x98, 0x57, 0x67, 0x7F, 0x05, 0x64,
        0xAF, 0x63, 0xB6, 0xFE, 0xF5, 0xB7, 0x3C, 0xA5,
        0xCE, 0xE9, 0x68, 0x44, 0xE0, 0x4D, 0x43, 0x69,
        0x29, 0x2E, 0xAC, 0x15, 0x59, 0xA8, 0x0A, 0x9E,
        0x6E, 0x47, 0xDF, 0x34, 0x35, 0x6A, 0xCF, 0xDC,
        0x22, 0xC9, 0xC0, 0x9B, 0x89, 0xD4, 0xED, 0xAB,
        0x12, 0xA2, 0x0D, 0x52, 0xBB, 0x02, 0x2F, 0xA9,
        0xD7, 0x61, 0x1E, 0xB4, 0x50, 0x04, 0xF6, 0xC2,
        0x16, 0x25, 0x86, 0x56, 0x55, 0x09, 0xBE, 0x91
        };


/*  ================================================================ */
```

```
/**********************************************************************
   TWOFISH.C   -- C API calls for TWOFISH AES submission

   Submitters:
     Bruce Schneier, Counterpane Systems
     Doug Whiting,   Hi/fn
     John Kelsey,    Counterpane Systems
     Chris Hall,     Counterpane Systems
     David Wagner,   UC Berkeley
     Niels Ferguson, Counterpane Systems

   Code Author:       Doug Whiting,   Hi/fn

   Version  1.00       April 1998

   Copyright 1998, Hi/fn and Counterpane Systems.  All rights reserved.

   Notes:
     *   Pedagogical version (non-optimized)
     *   Tab size is set to 4 characters in this file

**********************************************************************/

#include    "aes.h"
#include    "table.h"

/*
***********************************************************************
*           Constants/Macros/Tables
***********************************************************************/

#define VALIDATE_PARMS  1 /* nonzero --> check all parameters */
#define FEISTEL         0 /* nonzero --> use Feistel version (slow) */

int  tabEnable=0;           /* are we gathering stats? */
BYTE tabUsed[256];          /* one bit per table */

#if FEISTEL
CONST       char *moduleDescription="Pedagogical C code (Feistel)";
#else
CONST       char *moduleDescription="Pedagogical C code";
#endif
CONST       char *modeString = "";

#define P0_USED     0x01
#define P1_USED     0x02
#define B0_USED     0x04
#define B1_USED     0x08
#define B2_USED     0x10
#define B3_USED     0x20
#define ALL_USED    0x3F
```

```
/* number of rounds for various key sizes: 128, 192, 256 */
int        numRounds[4]= {0,ROUNDS_128,ROUNDS_192,ROUNDS_256};

#ifndef DEBUG
#define DEBUG   1                        /* force debug */
#endif
#include   "debug.h"                     /* debug display macros */

extern DWORD Here(DWORD x);            /* return caller's address! */
DWORD TwofishCodeStart(void) { return Here(0); };

/*
+*************************************************************************
*
* Function Name: setRounds
*
* Function:      Set the number of rounds for Twofish
*
* Arguments:     keyLen    = which keyLength to affect (128,192,256)
*                numRounds = how many rounds
*
* Return:        TRUE if the values passed in are valid
*
* Notes: This routine sets global variable(s) which are used in
*        setting up the key schedule.
*
-*************************************************************************/
int setRounds(int keyLen,int nRounds)
    {
    if ((nRounds < 2) || (nRounds > MAX_ROUNDS) || (nRounds & 1))
        return FALSE;

    switch (keyLen)
        {
        case 128:  numRounds[1]=nRounds;    break;
        case 192:  numRounds[2]=nRounds;    break;
        case 256:  numRounds[3]=nRounds;    break;
        default:   return FALSE;
        }

    return TRUE;
    }

/*
+*************************************************************************
*
* Function Name:    TableOp
*
* Function:         Handle table use checking
*
* Arguments:        op =   what to do  (see TAB_* defns in AES.H)
*
```

```
* Return:             TRUE --> done (for TAB_QUERY)
*
* Notes: This routine is for use in generating the tables KAT file.
*
-*********************************************************************/
int TableOp(int op)
    {
    static int queryCnt=0;
    int i;
    switch (op)
        {
        case TAB_DISABLE:
            tabEnable=0;
            break;
        case TAB_ENABLE:
            tabEnable=1;
            break;
        case TAB_RESET:
            queryCnt=0;
            for (i=0;i<256;i++)
                tabUsed[i]=0;
            break;
        case TAB_QUERY:
            queryCnt++;
            for (i=0;i<256;i++)
                if (tabUsed[i] != ALL_USED)
                    return FALSE;
            if (queryCnt < TAB_MIN_QUERY)   /* do a minimum number */
                return FALSE;
            break;
        }
    return TRUE;
    }


/*
+********************************************************************
*
* Function Name:   ParseHexDword
*
* Function:        Parse ASCII hex nibbles and fill in key/iv dwords
*
* Arguments:       bit      =   # bits to read
*                  srcTxt   =   ASCII source
*                  d        =   ptr to dwords to fill in
*                  dstTxt   =   where to make a copy of ASCII source
*                                  (NULL ok)
*
* Return:          Zero if no error. Nonzero --> invalid hex or length
*
* Notes: Note that the parameter d is a DWORD array, not a byte array.
*   This routine is coded to work both for little-endian and big-
*   endian architectures.  The character stream is interpreted as a
```

```
 *    LITTLE-ENDIAN byte stream, since that is how the Pentium works,
 *    but the conversion happens automatically below.
 *
-*******************************************************************/
int ParseHexDword(int bits,CONST char *srcTxt,DWORD *d,char *dstTxt)
    {
    int i;
    DWORD b;
    char c;
#if ALIGN32
    char alignDummy[3]; /* keep dword alignment */
#endif

    union   /* make sure LittleEndian is defined correctly */
        {
        BYTE  b[4];
        DWORD d[1];
        } v;
    v.d[0]=1;
    if (v.b[0 ^ ADDR_XOR] != 1) /* sanity check on switch */
        return BAD_ENDIAN;

#if VALIDATE_PARMS
  #if ALIGN32
    if (((int)d) & 3)
        return BAD_ALIGN32;
  #endif
#endif

    for (i=0;i*32<bits;i++)
        d[i]=0;                        /* first, zero the field */

    for (i=0;i*4<bits;i++)        /* parse one nibble at a time */
        {
        c=srcTxt[i];
        if (dstTxt) dstTxt[i]=c;
        if ((c >= '0') && (c <= '9'))
            b=c-'0';
        else if ((c >= 'a') && (c <= 'f'))
            b=c-'a'+10;
        else if ((c >= 'A') && (c <= 'F'))
            b=c-'A'+10;
        else
            return BAD_KEY_MAT; /* invalid hex character */
        /* works for big and little endian! */
        d[i/8] |= b << (4*((i^1)&7));
        }

    return 0;                        /* no error */
    }


/*
```

```
+**********************************************************************
*
* Function Name: f32
*
* Function:        Run four bytes through keyed S-boxes
*                  and apply MDS matrix
*
* Arguments:       x      =    input to f function
*                  k32    =    pointer to key dwords
*                  keyLen =    total key length (k32 --> keyLey/2 bits)
*
* Return:          The output of the keyed permutation applied to x.
*
* Notes:
*   This function is a keyed 32-bit permutation. It is the major
*   building block for the Twofish round function, including the four
*   keyed 8x8 permutations and the 4x4 MDS matrix multiply.  This
*   function is used both for generating round subkeys and within the
*   round function on the block being encrypted.
*
*   This version is fairly slow and pedagogical, although a smartcard
*   would probably perform the operation exactly this way in firmware.
*   For ultimate performance, the entire operation can be completed
*   with four lookups into four 256x32-bit tables, with three dword
*   xors.
*
*   The MDS matrix is defined in TABLE.H.  To multiply by Mij, just
*   use the macro Mij(x).
*
-**********************************************************************/
DWORD f32(DWORD x,CONST DWORD *k32,int keyLen)
    {
    BYTE  b[4];

    /* Run each byte thru 8x8 S-boxes, xoring with key bytes. */
    /* Note that each byte uses a different combination of S-boxes.*/

    *((DWORD *)b) = Bswap(x);   /* make b[0] = LSB, b[3] = MSB */
    switch (((keyLen + 63)/64) & 3)
        {
        case 0:    /* 256 bits of key */
            b[0] = p8(04)[b[0]] ^ b0(k32[3]);
            b[1] = p8(14)[b[1]] ^ b1(k32[3]);
            b[2] = p8(24)[b[2]] ^ b2(k32[3]);
            b[3] = p8(34)[b[3]] ^ b3(k32[3]);
            /* fall thru, having pre-processed b[0]..b[3] */
        case 3:    /* 192 bits of key */
            b[0] = p8(03)[b[0]] ^ b0(k32[2]);
            b[1] = p8(13)[b[1]] ^ b1(k32[2]);
            b[2] = p8(23)[b[2]] ^ b2(k32[2]);
            b[3] = p8(33)[b[3]] ^ b3(k32[2]);
            /* fall thru, having pre-processed b[0]..b[3] */
        case 2:    /* 128 bits of key */
```

```
        b[0] = p8(00)[p8(01)[p8(02)[b[0]]^b0(k32[1])]^b0(k32[0])];
        b[1] = p8(10)[p8(11)[p8(12)[b[1]]^b1(k32[1])]^b1(k32[0])];
        b[2] = p8(20)[p8(21)[p8(22)[b[2]]^b2(k32[1])]^b2(k32[0])];
        b[3] = p8(30)[p8(31)[p8(32)[b[3]]^b3(k32[1])]^b3(k32[0])];
        }

    if (tabEnable)
        {   /* we could give a "tighter" bound, but this works OK */
        tabUsed[b0(x)] |= (P_00 == 0) ? P0_USED : P1_USED;
        tabUsed[b1(x)] |= (P_10 == 0) ? P0_USED : P1_USED;
        tabUsed[b2(x)] |= (P_20 == 0) ? P0_USED : P1_USED;
        tabUsed[b3(x)] |= (P_30 == 0) ? P0_USED : P1_USED;

        tabUsed[b[0] ] |= B0_USED;
        tabUsed[b[1] ] |= B1_USED;
        tabUsed[b[2] ] |= B2_USED;
        tabUsed[b[3] ] |= B3_USED;
        }

    /* Now perform the MDS matrix multiply inline. */
    return  ((M00(b[0]) ^ M01(b[1]) ^ M02(b[2]) ^ M03(b[3]))         ) ^
            ((M10(b[0]) ^ M11(b[1]) ^ M12(b[2]) ^ M13(b[3])) <<  8) ^
            ((M20(b[0]) ^ M21(b[1]) ^ M22(b[2]) ^ M23(b[3])) << 16) ^
            ((M30(b[0]) ^ M31(b[1]) ^ M32(b[2]) ^ M33(b[3])) << 24) ;
    }


/*
+*****************************************************************
*
* Function Name: RS_MDS_Encode
*
* Function:         Use (12,8) Reed-Solomon code over GF(256) to produce
*                   a key S-box dword from two key material dwords.
*
* Arguments:        k0 =    1st dword
*                   k1 =    2nd dword
*
* Return:           Remainder polynomial generated using RS code
*
* Notes:
*   Since this computation is done only once per reKey per 64 bits of
*   key, the performance impact of this routine is imperceptible. The
*   RS code chosen has "simple" coefficients to allow smartcard/
*   hardware implementation without lookup tables.
*
-*****************************************************************/
DWORD RS_MDS_Encode(DWORD k0,DWORD k1)
    {
    int i,j;
    DWORD r;

    for (i=r=0;i<2;i++)
        {
```

```
        r ^= (i) ? k0 : k1;              /* merge in 32 more key bits */
        for (j=0;j<4;j++)                /* shift one byte at a time */
            RS_rem(r);
        }
    return r;
    }

/*
+*****************************************************************
*
* Function Name:   reKey
*
* Function:        Initialize the Twofish key schedule from key32
*
* Arguments:       key         = ptr to keyInstance to be initialized
*
* Return:          TRUE on success
*
* Notes:
*   Here we precompute all the round subkeys, although that is not
*   actually required.  For example, on a smartcard, the round subkeys
*   can be generated on-the-fly using f32()
*
-*****************************************************************/
int reKey(keyInstance *key)
    {
    int     i,k64Cnt;
    int     keyLen   = key->keyLen;
    int     subkeyCnt = ROUND_SUBKEYS + 2*key->numRounds;
    DWORD   A,B;
    /* even/odd key dwords */
    DWORD   k32e[MAX_KEY_BITS/64],k32o[MAX_KEY_BITS/64];

#if VALIDATE_PARMS
  #if ALIGN32
    if ((((int)key) & 3) || (((int)key->key32) & 3))
        return BAD_ALIGN32;
  #endif
    if ((key->keyLen % 64) || (key->keyLen < MIN_KEY_BITS))
        return BAD_KEY_INSTANCE;
    if (subkeyCnt > TOTAL_SUBKEYS)
        return BAD_KEY_INSTANCE;
#endif

    k64Cnt=(keyLen+63)/64;  /* round up to next multiple of 64 bits */
    for (i=0;i<k64Cnt;i++)
        {                           /* split into even/odd key dwords */
        k32e[i]=key->key32[2*i  ];
        k32o[i]=key->key32[2*i+1];
        /* compute S-box keys using (12,8) RS-code over GF(256) */
        key->sboxKeys[k64Cnt-1-i]=RS_MDS_Encode(k32e[i],k32o[i]);
        }
```

```
    for (i=0;i<subkeyCnt/2;i++) /* compute round subkeys for PHT */
        {
        A = f32(i*SK_STEP        ,k32e,keyLen);
        B = f32(i*SK_STEP+SK_BUMP,k32o,keyLen);
        B = ROL(B,8);
        key->subKeys[2*i  ] = A+  B;            /* combine with a PHT */
        key->subKeys[2*i+1] = ROL(A+2*B,SK_ROTL);
        }

    DebugDumpKey(key);

    return TRUE;
    }
/*
+*************************************************************************
*
* Function Name: makeKey
*
* Function:       Initialize the Twofish key schedule
*
* Arguments:      key        = ptr to keyInstance to be initialized
*                 direction  = DIR_ENCRYPT or DIR_DECRYPT
*                 keyLen     = # bits of key text at *keyMaterial
*                 keyMaterial = ptr to hex ASCII chars representing key
*
* Return:         TRUE on success
*                 else error code (e.g., BAD_KEY_DIR)
*
* Notes:
*   This parses the key bits from keyMaterial. No crypto stuff happens
*   here. The function reKey() is called to actually build the key
*   schedule after the keyMaterial has been parsed.
*
-*************************************************************************/
int makeKey(keyInstance *key, BYTE direction,
        int keyLen,CONST char *keyMaterial)
    {
    int i;

#if VALIDATE_PARMS                  /* first, check parameters */
    if (key == NULL)
        return BAD_KEY_INSTANCE;/* must have a keyInstance to init. */
    if ((direction != DIR_ENCRYPT) && (direction != DIR_DECRYPT))
        return BAD_KEY_DIR;     /* must have valid direction */
    if ((keyLen > MAX_KEY_BITS) || (keyLen < 8))
        return BAD_KEY_MAT;     /* length must be valid */
    if (keyMaterial == NULL)
        return BAD_KEY_MAT;     /* must have some data to work with */
    key->keySig = VALID_SIG;    /* show that we are initialized */
    #if ALIGN32
    if ((((int)key) & 3) || (((int)key->key32) & 3))
        return BAD_ALIGN32;
    #endif
```

```
#endif

    key->direction = direction;      /* set our cipher direction */
    key->keyLen    = (keyLen+63) & ~63;        /* round up */
    key->numRounds = numRounds[(keyLen-1)/64];
    for (i=0;i<MAX_KEY_BITS/32;i++) /* zero unused bits */
            key->key32[i]=0;

    if (ParseHexDword(keyLen,keyMaterial,key->key32,key->keyMaterial))
        return BAD_KEY_MAT;

    key->keyMaterial[MAX_KEY_SIZE]=0;    /* terminate ASCII string */

    return reKey(key);                /* generate round subkeys */
    }


/*
+*********************************************************************
*
* Function Name: cipherInit
*
* Function:       Initialize the Twofish cipher in a given mode
*
* Arguments:      cipher = ptr to cipherInstance to be initialized
*                 mode   = MODE_ECB, MODE_CBC, or MODE_CFB1
*                 IV     = ptr to hex ASCII test representing IV bytes
*
* Return:         TRUE on success
*                 else error code (e.g., BAD_CIPHER_MODE)
*
-*********************************************************************/
int cipherInit(cipherInstance *cipher, BYTE mode,CONST char *IV)
    {
    int i;
#if VALIDATE_PARMS              /* first, check parameters */
    if (cipher == NULL)
        return BAD_PARAMS;      /* must have a cipherInstance to init */
    if ((mode != MODE_ECB) && (mode != MODE_CBC)
        && (mode != MODE_CFB1))
        return BAD_CIPHER_MODE; /* must have valid cipher mode */
    if ((mode != MODE_ECB) && (IV == NULL))
        return BAD_PARAMS;      /* must have IV for CBC and CFB modes */
    cipher->cipherSig   =   VALID_SIG;
  #if ALIGN32
    if ((((int)cipher) & 3) || (((int)cipher->IV) & 3)
        || (((int)cipher->iv32) & 3))
        return BAD_ALIGN32;
  #endif
#endif

    if (mode != MODE_ECB)           /* parse the IV */
        {
```

```
            if (ParseHexDword(BLOCK_SIZE,IV,cipher->iv32,NULL))
                return BAD_IV_MAT;
            for (i=0;i<BLOCK_SIZE/32;i++) /* byte-oriented copy for CFB1*/
                ((DWORD *)cipher->IV)[i] = Bswap(cipher->iv32[i]);
            }

    cipher->mode        =   mode;

    return TRUE;
    }

/*
+****************************************************************************
*
* Function Name: blockEncrypt
*
* Function:      Encrypt block(s) of data using Twofish
*
* Arguments:     cipher    = ptr to already initialized cipherInstance
*                key       = ptr to already initialized keyInstance
*                input     = ptr to data blocks to be encrypted
*                inputLen  = # bits to encrypt (multiple of blockSize)
*                outBuffer = ptr to where to put encrypted blocks
*
* Return:        # bits ciphered (>= 0)
*                else error code (e.g., BAD_CIPHER_STATE, ...)
*
* Notes: The only supported block size for ECB/CBC modes is BLOCK_SIZE
*        bits. If inputLen is not a multiple of BLOCK_SIZE bits in
*        those modes, an error BAD_INPUT_LEN is returned. In CFB1
*        mode, all block sizes can be supported.
*
-****************************************************************************/
int blockEncrypt(cipherInstance *cipher, keyInstance *key,
                CONST BYTE *input, int inputLen, BYTE *outBuffer)
    {
    int    i,n,r;                   /* loop variables */
    DWORD x[BLOCK_SIZE/32];         /* block being encrypted */
    DWORD t0,t1,tmp;                /* temp variables */
    int    rounds=key->numRounds;   /* number of rounds */
    BYTE   bit,ctBit,carry;         /* temps for CFB */
#if ALIGN32
    BYTE alignDummy;                /* keep 32-bit alignment on stack */
#endif

#if VALIDATE_PARMS
    if ((cipher == NULL) || (cipher->cipherSig != VALID_SIG))
        return BAD_CIPHER_STATE;
    if ((key == NULL) || (key->keySig != VALID_SIG))
        return BAD_KEY_INSTANCE;
    if ((rounds < 2) || (rounds > MAX_ROUNDS) || (rounds&1))
        return BAD_KEY_INSTANCE;
    if ((cipher->mode != MODE_CFB1) && (inputLen % BLOCK_SIZE))
```

```
            return BAD_INPUT_LEN;
    #if ALIGN32
        if ( (((int)cipher) & 3) || (((int)key      ) & 3) ||
             (((int)input ) & 3) || (((int)outBuffer) & 3))
             return BAD_ALIGN32;
    #endif
#endif

    if (cipher->mode == MODE_CFB1)
        {   /* use recursion here to handle CFB, one block at a time */
        cipher->mode = MODE_ECB;     /* do encryption in ECB */
        for (n=0;n<inputLen;n++)
            {
            blockEncrypt(cipher,key,cipher->IV,BLOCK_SIZE,(BYTE *)x);
            bit   = 0x80 >> (n & 7);/* which bit position in byte */
            ctBit = (input[n/8] & bit)
                        ^ ((((BYTE *) x)[0] & 0x80) >> (n&7));
            outBuffer[n/8] = (outBuffer[n/8] & ~ bit) | ctBit;
            carry = ctBit >> (7 - (n&7));
            for (i=BLOCK_SIZE/8-1;i>=0;i--)
                {
                bit = cipher->IV[i] >> 7;   /* save next "carry" */
                cipher->IV[i] = (cipher->IV[i] << 1) ^ carry;
                carry = bit;
                }
            }
        cipher->mode = MODE_CFB1;    /* restore mode for next time */
        return inputLen;
        }

    /* here for ECB, CBC modes */
    for (n=0;n<inputLen;n+=BLOCK_SIZE,input+=BLOCK_SIZE/8,
                        outBuffer+=BLOCK_SIZE/8)
        {
#ifdef DEBUG
        DebugDump(input,"\n",-1,0,0,0,1);
        if (cipher->mode == MODE_CBC)
            DebugDump(cipher->iv32,"",IV_ROUND,0,0,0,0);
#endif
        for (i=0;i<BLOCK_SIZE/32;i++)    /* copy and add whitening */
            {
            x[i]=Bswap(((DWORD *)input)[i])
                ^ key->subKeys[INPUT_WHITEN+i];
            if (cipher->mode == MODE_CBC)
                x[i] ^= cipher->iv32[i];
            }

        DebugDump(x,"",0,0,0,0,0);
        for (r=0;r<rounds;r++)           /* main Twofish encryption loop */
            {
#if FEISTEL
            t0   = f32(ROR(x[0],   (r+1)/2),key->sboxKeys,key->keyLen);
            t1   = f32(ROL(x[1],8+(r+1)/2),key->sboxKeys,key->keyLen);
```

```
                                                       /* PHT, round keys */
                x[2]^= ROL(t0 +   t1 + key->subKeys[ROUND_SUBKEYS+2*r  ],
                        r    /2);
                x[3]^= ROR(t0 + 2*t1 + key->subKeys[ROUND_SUBKEYS+2*r+1],
                        (r+2) /2);

                DebugDump(x,"",r+1,2*(r&1),1,1,0);
#else
                t0    = f32(   x[0]    ,key->sboxKeys,key->keyLen);
                t1    = f32(ROL(x[1],8),key->sboxKeys,key->keyLen);

                x[3] = ROL(x[3],1);
                x[2]^= t0 +   t1 + key->subKeys[ROUND_SUBKEYS+2*r  ];
                x[3]^= t0 + 2*t1 + key->subKeys[ROUND_SUBKEYS+2*r+1];
                x[2] = ROR(x[2],1);

                DebugDump(x,"",r+1,2*(r&1),0,1,0);/* use same format */
#endif
                if (r < rounds-1)                /* swap for next round */
                    {
                    tmp = x[0]; x[0]= x[2]; x[2] = tmp;
                    tmp = x[1]; x[1]= x[3]; x[3] = tmp;
                    }
                }
#if FEISTEL
        x[0] = ROR(x[0],8);                      /* "final permutation" */
        x[1] = ROL(x[1],8);
        x[2] = ROR(x[2],8);
        x[3] = ROL(x[3],8);
#endif
        for (i=0;i<BLOCK_SIZE/32;i++)     /* copy out, with whitening */
            {
            ((DWORD *)outBuffer)[i] =
                Bswap(x[i] ^ key->subKeys[OUTPUT_WHITEN+i]);
            if (cipher->mode == MODE_CBC)
                cipher->iv32[i] = Bswap(((DWORD *)outBuffer)[i]);
            }
#ifdef DEBUG
        DebugDump(outBuffer,"",rounds+1,0,0,0,1);
        if (cipher->mode == MODE_CBC)
            DebugDump(cipher->iv32,"",IV_ROUND,0,0,0,0);
#endif
        }

    return inputLen;
    }

/*
+*****************************************************************************
*
* Function Name: blockDecrypt
*
* Function:      Decrypt block(s) of data using Twofish
```

```
*
* Arguments:      cipher   = ptr to already initialized cipherInstance
*                 key      = ptr to already initialized keyInstance
*                 input    = ptr to data blocks to be decrypted
*                 inputLen = # bits to encrypt (multiple of blockSize)
*                 outBuffer = ptr to where to put decrypted blocks
*
* Return:         # bits ciphered (>= 0)
*                 else error code (e.g., BAD_CIPHER_STATE, ...)
*
* Notes: The only supported block size for ECB/CBC modes is BLOCK_SIZE
*        bits. If inputLen is not a multiple of BLOCK_SIZE bits in
*        those modes, an error BAD_INPUT_LEN is returned.  In CFB1
*        mode, all block sizes can be supported.
*
-*****************************************************************/
int blockDecrypt(cipherInstance *cipher, keyInstance *key,
                CONST BYTE *input, int inputLen, BYTE *outBuffer)
    {
    int   i,n,r;                    /* loop counters */
    DWORD x[BLOCK_SIZE/32];         /* block being encrypted */
    DWORD t0,t1;                    /* temp variables */
    int   rounds=key->numRounds;    /* number of rounds */
    BYTE  bit,ctBit,carry;          /* temps for CFB */
#if ALIGN32
    BYTE alignDummy;                /* keep 32-bit alignment on stack */
#endif

#if VALIDATE_PARMS
    if ((cipher == NULL) || (cipher->cipherSig != VALID_SIG))
        return BAD_CIPHER_STATE;
    if ((key == NULL) || (key->keySig != VALID_SIG))
        return BAD_KEY_INSTANCE;
    if ((rounds < 2) || (rounds > MAX_ROUNDS) || (rounds&1))
        return BAD_KEY_INSTANCE;
    if ((cipher->mode != MODE_CFB1) && (inputLen % BLOCK_SIZE))
        return BAD_INPUT_LEN;
  #if ALIGN32
    if ( (((int)cipher) & 3) || (((int)key      ) & 3) ||
         (((int)input)  & 3) || (((int)outBuffer) & 3))
        return BAD_ALIGN32;
  #endif
#endif

    if (cipher->mode == MODE_CFB1)
        {   /* use blockEncrypt to handle CFB, one block at a time */
        cipher->mode = MODE_ECB;    /* do encryption in ECB */
        for (n=0;n<inputLen;n++)
            {
            blockEncrypt(cipher,key,cipher->IV,BLOCK_SIZE,(BYTE *)x);
            bit   = 0x80 >> (n & 7);
            ctBit = input[n/8] & bit;
            outBuffer[n/8] = (outBuffer[n/8] & ~ bit) |
```

```
                              (ctBit ^ ((((BYTE *) x)[0] & 0x80) >> (n&7)));
            carry = ctBit >> (7 - (n&7));
            for (i=BLOCK_SIZE/8-1;i>=0;i--)
                {
                bit = cipher->IV[i] >> 7;   /* save next "carry" */
                cipher->IV[i] = (cipher->IV[i] << 1) ^ carry;
                carry = bit;
                }
            }
        cipher->mode = MODE_CFB1;   /* restore mode for next time */
        return inputLen;
        }

    /* here for ECB, CBC modes */
    for (n=0;n<inputLen;n+=BLOCK_SIZE,input+=BLOCK_SIZE/8,
                    outBuffer+=BLOCK_SIZE/8)
        {
        DebugDump(input,"\n",rounds+1,0,0,0,1);

        for (i=0;i<BLOCK_SIZE/32;i++)    /* copy and add whitening */
            x[i]=Bswap(((DWORD *)input)[i])
                ^ key->subKeys[OUTPUT_WHITEN+i];

        for (r=rounds-1;r>=0;r--)             /* main decryption loop */
            {
            t0   = f32(    x[0]   ,key->sboxKeys,key->keyLen);
            t1   = f32(ROL(x[1],8),key->sboxKeys,key->keyLen);

            DebugDump(x,"",r+1,2*(r&1),0,1,0);
            x[2] = ROL(x[2],1);
            x[2]^= t0 +   t1 + key->subKeys[ROUND_SUBKEYS+2*r  ];
            x[3]^= t0 + 2*t1 + key->subKeys[ROUND_SUBKEYS+2*r+1];
            x[3] = ROR(x[3],1);

            if (r)                    /* unswap, except for last round */
                {
                t0   = x[0]; x[0]= x[2]; x[2] = t0;
                t1   = x[1]; x[1]= x[3]; x[3] = t1;
                }
            }
        DebugDump(x,"",0,0,0,0,0);

        for (i=0;i<BLOCK_SIZE/32;i++)    /* copy out, with whitening */
            {
            x[i] ^= key->subKeys[INPUT_WHITEN+i];
            if (cipher->mode == MODE_CBC)
                {
                x[i] ^= cipher->iv32[i];
                cipher->iv32[i] = Bswap(((DWORD *)input)[i]);
                }
            ((DWORD *)outBuffer)[i] = Bswap(x[i]);
            }
        DebugDump(outBuffer,"",-1,0,0,0,1);
```

```
          }

    return inputLen;
    }


DWORD TwofishCodeSize(void) { return Here(0)-TwofishCodeStart(); };
```

Index

ÉDITRICE: Caty Bérubé

DIRECTRICE DE PRODUCTION: Julie Doddridge

CHEF D'ÉQUIPE PRODUCTION ÉDITORIALE: Isabelle Roy

CHEF D'ÉQUIPE PRODUCTION GRAPHIQUE: Marie-Christine Langlois

CHEFS CUISINIERS: Benoît Boudreau et Richard Houde.

CHARGÉE DE CONTENU: Laurence Roy-Tétreault

AUTEURS: Miléna Babin, Caty Bérubé, Benoît Boudreau, Richard Houde
et Annie Lavoie.

RÉVISEURE: Marilou Cloutier

ASSISTANTE À LA PRODUCTION: Kim Tardif

SPÉCIALISTE EN GRAPHISME D'ÉDITION: Lise Lapierre

CONCEPTRICES GRAPHIQUES: Sonia Barbeau, Annie Gauthier,
Ariane Michaud-Gagnon, Myriam Poulin, Claudia Renaud
et Joëlle Renauld.

INFOGRAPHISTE: Lucie Lévesque-Pageau

SPÉCIALISTE EN TRAITEMENT D'IMAGES ET CALIBRATION PHOTO:
Yves Vaillancourt

PHOTOGRAPHES: Sabrina Belzil et Rémy Germain.

STYLISTES CULINAIRES: Laurie Collin et Christine Morin.

DIRECTEUR DE LA DISTRIBUTION: Marcel Bernatchez

DISTRIBUTION: Éditions Pratico-Pratiques et Messageries ADP.

IMPRESSION: TC Interglobe

DÉPÔT LÉGAL: 1er trimestre 2015
Bibliothèque et Archives nationales du Québec
Bibliothèque et Archives Canada
ISBN 978-2-89658-803-9

Gouvernement du Québec – Programme de crédit d'impôt
pour l'édition de livres – Gestion SODEC

1685, boulevard Talbot, Québec (QC) G2N 0C6
Tél.: 418 877-0259
Sans frais: 1 866 882-0091
Téléc.: 418 780-1716
www.pratico-pratiques.com

Commentaires et suggestions: info@pratico-pratiques.com

CUISINE

minceur en

INGRÉDIENTS 5

15 MINUTES

CUISINE
minceur en 5

INGRÉDIENTS

MINUTES

15

265 recettes
POUR MAIGRIR SANS SE PRIVER
en 5 ingrédients, 15 minutes

 Pratico pratiques

Table des matières

Maigrir en toute simplicité et dans le *plaisir*

Comme la plupart des femmes, j'ai à cœur de garder ma ligne. Avec les années et la naissance de mes enfants, je la surveille encore de plus près. Mais les régimes, très peu pour moi! Commencer à calculer les calories, à peser mes aliments, à réfléchir à ce que je peux ingurgiter ou non... mes journées sont déjà assez remplies comme ça, nul besoin d'en ajouter! Il faut dire que l'épicurienne en moi aurait aussi du mal à se priver de certaines gourmandises. Les plaisirs gustatifs font partie des petits bonheurs de la vie, alors pourquoi s'en passer?

C'est donc dans cet esprit que ce livre *5-15* a été pensé. L'idée? Réunir une sélection des meilleures recettes minceur pour vous aider à perdre du poids ou à le maintenir, sans vous priver et sans vous compliquer la vie au quotidien. Ainsi, au moment de préparer le souper les jours de semaine, vous n'aurez qu'à l'ouvrir pour concocter le plat de votre choix, sans calculatrice, ni balance: tout a été calculé pour vous! Et le plus merveilleux, c'est que chacune des 265 recettes qu'il présente se prépare en 15 minutes ou moins à partir de 5 ingrédients de base. Parmi celles-ci, des repas gourmands, mais faibles en calories, des accompagnements allégés et alléchants ainsi que des recettes maison version minceur de produits du commerce. En prime, 25 astuces pour maigrir sans se priver!

N'oubliez pas qu'il est toujours plus facile d'atteindre nos objectifs dans le plaisir et dans la simplicité!

Caty

25 astuces
pour maigrir sans se priver

Pour tout épicurien de ce monde, bien manger fait partie des plus grands bonheurs de la vie! Cependant, avec les nombreuses tentations et l'obsession de la minceur, s'alimenter dans le plaisir et l'équilibre n'est pas toujours une mince tâche.

La solution? Privilégier des aliments sains, nutritifs, colorés... et appétissants. Adieu mets fades et sans saveur pour garder la ligne: manger des plats gourmands sans culpabilité, c'est possible! Il suffit de faire le plein de recettes hautement savoureuses et peu caloriques. Sachant qu'une personne sédentaire âgée entre 31 et 50 ans devrait consommer en moyenne 2 350 calories par jour pour les hommes et autour de 1 800 pour les femmes, il faut veiller à trouver des compromis pour satisfaire notre appétit sans tomber dans l'excès ni céder aux pulsions du grignotage. Fini la privation et le fameux «effet yoyo»: on adopte des habitudes alimentaires saines sans écarter le plaisir de la bonne chère.

Que vous souhaitiez perdre du poids ou simplement changer vos habitudes alimentaires pour manger plus sainement, voici 25 conseils éprouvés pour vous alimenter de mets alléchants tout en coupant dans les calories.

1 Sauter un repas?

Voilà une action à éviter à tout prix: sauter un repas pourrait au contraire vous faire prendre du poids. Lorsque le corps est en carence, il compense en stockant les graisses. De plus, en étant privé d'un repas, on risque de satisfaire nos petits creux en grignotant. La solution: manger plus souvent, mais en petite quantité. Manger entre cinq à sept petits repas par jour favoriserait même la perte de poids, puisque le corps sécrète moins d'insuline – une hormone qui stocke le glucose – s'il est rassasié toutes les quatre heures. Mais attention: cela ne signifie pas de manger même si on n'a plus faim! Respectez les signaux que votre corps vous envoie: apprenez à vous écouter.

2 Les collations: des alliées minceur

Vous avez l'impression d'avoir toujours faim? Prenez de plus petites portions au déjeuner, au dîner et au souper, tout en ingérant suffisamment de protéines, et misez sur des collations rassasiantes entre les repas. La combinaison à privilégier pour fournir un maximum d'énergie à l'organisme: les glucides et les protéines (pita et houmous, fruits et yogourt, craquelins et fromage, etc.). Un duo gagnant qui permet de stabiliser l'appétit!

3 Repas protéinés

La consommation de protéines à chaque repas est essentielle. Les protéines permettent de maintenir nos muscles en santé, de prévenir la perte de masse musculaire liée à l'âge et de faciliter la perte de poids et son maintien à long terme. Il est donc primordial de consommer suffisamment de protéines chaque jour. Quoi qu'il en soit, assurez-vous d'ingérer un minimum de 15 g de protéines à chaque repas (idéalement de 25 à 30 g de protéines) et d'environ 5 g pour vos collations. Ainsi, vous serez rassasié et n'aurez plus envie de grignoter.

4 Écouter sa satiété

La satiété est la sensation de ne plus éprouver la faim après un repas. C'est elle qui permet d'éviter de grignoter entre les repas et de contrôler notre poids. Ainsi, il importe d'écouter les signaux de notre corps pour éviter d'engloutir notre repas sans écouter notre faim. Voici trois conseils:

- **Manger lentement.** On ressent le signal de satiété après plusieurs minutes. Prenez des pauses entre chaque bouchée.

- **Manger seulement lorsque l'on a faim.** Avant de succomber, prenez le temps de vous demander si vous avez réellement faim.

- **Utiliser de plus petites assiettes.** Plus l'assiette est grande, plus l'on a tendance à ingérer une grosse portion.

5 Allez hop! On bouge!

Ce n'est pas un secret: pour perdre du poids, il faut combiner une saine alimentation à de l'exercice physique. Si vous consommez plus de calories que nécessaire pour combler vos besoins journaliers, vous devrez faire un peu plus d'efforts physiques pour dépenser les calories supplémentaires. Des gestes simples tels que prendre les escaliers plutôt que l'ascenseur et marcher pendant l'heure du dîner peuvent faire une différence notable, tant sur la santé physique que mentale.

6 De l'eau froide, s.v.p. !

Une étude de l'Université de l'Utah démontre que ceux qui boivent entre huit et douze verres d'eau chaque jour profitent d'un métabolisme plus rapide que ceux qui n'en boivent que quatre. De plus, boire de l'eau froide permettrait de stimuler le métabolisme en brûlant des calories (par le processus de régulation de la température du corps). Ainsi, pensez à boire un grand verre d'eau froide au réveil et à traîner une bouteille d'eau avec vous partout. Petit truc pour vous inciter à en boire davantage: y ajouter des petits fruits ou des agrumes.

7 Gare aux calories liquides !

La tentation de consommer boissons gazeuses et boissons énergisantes peut être forte, mais mieux vaut réserver ces liquides très sucrés aux occasions spéciales. En effet, ils font vite grimper le nombre de calories ingérées, d'autant plus qu'on les consomme très rapidement sans ressentir de sensation de satiété. À titre d'exemple, une canette de cola de 355 ml renferme l'équivalent de 50 ml (10 c. à thé) de sucre, tandis qu'une canette de 250 ml de boisson énergisante en contient entre 35 et 45 ml (7 à 9 c. à thé). C'est un pensez-y-bien !

8 Faire l'épicerie le ventre vide : un piège

Évitez d'aller à l'épicerie le ventre vide: vous risquez plus de succomber aux moindres tentations et de faire des achats irréfléchis. Autrement dit, votre panier a plus de chances de contenir davantage de denrées et d'aliments riches, sans parler des risques de sortir avec une facture très salée et de gaspiller! Faites une liste et tenez-vous-en à celle-ci. Vous éviterez ainsi de passer inutilement dans les allées où la tentation pourrait être plus forte. Psst! Si vous faites vos courses entre deux repas, pensez à avaler une poignée d'amandes ou une pomme avant le départ de la maison.

9 Pas de sucreries !

Le meilleur moyen de résister aux friandises à toute heure de la journée: éviter d'en acheter! Votre garde-manger regorge de biscuits au chocolat, de croustilles et d'autres gâteries? Il sera plus facile d'y succomber. Si vous n'avez aucun aliment riche à vous mettre sous la dent, il y a peu de chances que vous sortiez pour en acheter. Vous verrez, un fruit ou un yogourt vous satisferont amplement !

10 Se faire plaisir avec du chocolat

Surveiller sa ligne ne veut surtout pas dire se priver de gourmandises sucrées! Il faut simplement faire les bons choix. Plutôt que de vider une boîte de biscuits, optez pour du chocolat noir. Avec son goût riche et corsé, vous serez satisfait avec un ou deux morceaux – deux morceaux de chocolat noir 70% fournissent 104 calories. De plus, vous remplacerez les calories vides et les ingrédients peu nutritifs par un apport en antioxydants et en minéraux.

11 Vive la popote !

L'avantage quand on cuisine nos mets, c'est que l'on contrôle beaucoup plus facilement les ingrédients qui s'y retrouvent, et donc, le nombre de calories ingérées ! Vous avez l'habitude de manger au resto ou d'acheter des prêts-à-manger pour le dîner ? Même si vous optez pour une salade ou pour un plat d'apparence saine, la nourriture préparée maison demeure toujours la meilleure des options ! La solution : doubler les portions du soir pour avoir un bon lunch le lendemain.

12 Cuissons minceur

Les modes de cuisson à privilégier pour une saine gestion du poids ? Les cuissons dans une poêle antiadhésive, dans un wok et à la vapeur, qui nécessitent l'ajout de peu de matières grasses, voire pas du tout. Petites astuces pour diminuer le nombre de calories lors de la cuisson dans une poêle ou dans un wok : on essuie l'excédent d'huile avec du papier absorbant.

13 Bien assaisonné !

Pour éviter l'ajout de sauces riches en calories, aromatisez vos plats d'assaisonnements au choix. Herbes fraîches ou séchées, mélanges d'épices, ail, gingembre, piment fort... Ces extras apporteront de nouvelles touches de saveur et contenteront tout autant vos papilles, les calories en moins. Usez de créativité et osez !

14 Non aux régimes !

Faire un régime, c'est le meilleur moyen de perdre du poids rapidement... et de le reprendre aussi vite ! Un changement drastique dans nos habitudes et la privation donnent souvent des résultats peu efficaces. La solution : privilégier les petits changements qui auront un impact considérable à long terme. Par exemple, commencez par éliminer le grignotage entre 17 h et 20 h : c'est le moment de la journée où ces pulsions sont les plus néfastes pour la ligne. En intégrant graduellement de saines habitudes à notre quotidien, on en vient à adopter de meilleurs comportements, parfois sans s'en rendre compte ! C'est la somme des petits changements qui fait la différence.

Le saviez-vous ?

Le beurre contient moins de calories que l'huile d'olive. En effet, pour la même quantité, soit 5 ml (1 c. à thé), le beurre fournit 36 calories, comparativement à 44 pour l'huile d'olive.

15 La pomme, bonne à croquer

Vous êtes gourmands et mangez toujours plus qu'à votre faim ? Pensez à croquer une pomme environ 30 minutes avant le repas. La raison : elle contient une fibre naturelle, la pectine, qui gonfle dans l'estomac. Ainsi, vous aurez moins faim au moment de passer à table et risquerez moins de tomber dans l'exagération.

16 À distance des écrans

Une étude publiée dans l'*American Journal Clinical Nutrition* a démontré que ceux qui mangent dans leur bureau absorbent deux fois plus de calories. Le fait d'être distrait en mangeant diminue l'habileté de l'organisme à transformer les calories ingérées. Le même principe s'applique à la maison, devant les écrans du téléviseur ou de l'ordinateur. Ainsi, il est important de prendre au moins 15 minutes pour manger en vous concentrant sur la nourriture.

17 Note sucrée en finale

Si vous ne pouvez envisager de terminer un repas sans une touche sucrée, pourquoi vouloir vous l'interdire? Selon Barbara Rolls, auteure de *The Volumetrics Eating Plan*, le sucre permettrait même de signaler au cerveau que le repas est terminé. L'idée, c'est d'éviter les sources de sucre riches en mauvais gras et en calories. Pensez plutôt à manger un fruit, frais ou sec, ou un yogourt, histoire de ne pas rester sur votre faim!

18 Mâcher de la gomme

Saviez-vous que cette habitude peut être bénéfique pour la ligne? En effet, la mastication diminue la sensation de faim. Voilà une belle façon de diminuer les envies d'encas entre les repas! Et ce n'est pas tout: le fait de mâcher de la gomme permet de dépenser de l'énergie – jusqu'à onze calories par jour –, sans compter les calories en moins si vous n'avez pas grignoté.

19 Garder la ligne avec le thé vert

La réputation des vertus du thé vert n'est plus à faire! Mais saviez-vous qu'il donne aussi un coup de pouce pour brûler les graisses? Consommer de deux à quatre tasses de thé vert par jour permettrait de brûler jusqu'à 50 calories! Comment? Grâce à sa composition en caféine et en catéchines: l'effet de la caféine, reconnue pour favoriser l'élimination des graisses, serait renforcé par celui des catéchines. Ces dernières influencent la répartition des graisses, notamment dans la région abdominale. Voilà une boisson-clé pour la ligne!

20 Debout!

Intégrer de petits gestes simples à votre routine quotidienne pourrait faire une différence! Par exemple, profitez de vos appels téléphoniques pour vous mettre sur la pointe des pieds et conservez cette position aussi longtemps que possible. Cet exercice facile peut vous faire perdre jusqu'à 54 calories en 20 minutes. Efficace!

21 Tenir un journal de bord

En notant tout ce que vous mangez chaque jour, vous serez peut-être surpris de constater tout ce que vous avez ingéré en une journée! Peut-être même réaliserez-vous que vos portions sont plus ou moins bien équilibrées. Rappelez-vous: la quantité de protéines devrait entrer dans la paume de la main, les féculents devraient correspondre à la taille du poing et les légumes devraient tenir dans deux paumes ouvertes.

23 Le plein de calcium

Une bonne raison de consommer un verre de lait écrémé à la fin d'un repas? Des études menées à l'Université de Copenhague démontrent que le calcium permettrait de réduire la quantité de gras saturés absorbée par le corps. En effet, il enroberait les molécules de graisse pour favoriser leur élimination dans l'intestin. Les suppléments de calcium n'ont cependant pas le même effet.

22 Bénéfique, le poisson

Les poissons, riches en fibres et en protéines, agissent comme coupe-faim. Lorsqu'on en consomme souvent, on peut observer une diminution de l'appétit. Les poissons maigres à chair blanche comme le bar, la sole, le flétan et la dorade ont une faible teneur en calories, mais les poissons plus gras comme le saumon ont aussi leurs propriétés minceur: ils sont riches en oméga-3, un bon gras qui empêche le stockage des mauvais lipides et qui est facilement brûlé par l'organisme.

24 Penser aux suppléments

La prise de suppléments d'huile de poisson combinée à de l'exercice physique permettrait de brûler davantage de lipides, selon une étude publiée dans l'*American Journal of Clinical Nutrition*. Il est profitable d'investir dans un produit de qualité qui procure au moins 300 mg d'acides gras EPA et 200 mg d'acides gras DHA par capsule. On conseille de prendre deux capsules juste avant l'entraînement.

25 L'assiette parfaitement équilibrée

Pour que votre assiette fournisse tous les nutriments essentiels à votre organisme, elle doit respecter un ratio particulier: la portion de légumes doit correspondre à 50% de l'assiette – assurez-vous de consommer au moins deux légumes différents pour profiter des bienfaits de plus de nutriments –, tandis que les protéines et les féculents doivent chacun occuper 25% de l'assiette.

Soupes-repas

Les soupes-repas ont le don de revigorer à la fois l'âme et les papilles ! Qu'elles soient faites à base de bouillon de volaille, de bœuf, de légumes ou encore de délicieux produits thaï, on s'en délecte jusqu'à la toute dernière goutte !

Gourganes ①
rincées et égouttées
1 boîte de 540 ml

Bouillon de bœuf ②
1,5 litre (6 tasses)

Carottes ③
coupées en dés
125 ml (½ tasse)

**Haricots verts
et jaunes** ④
coupés en morceaux
125 ml (½ tasse)

Orge perlé ⑤
180 ml (¾ de tasse)

Soupe aux légumes

Préparation : **15 minutes** • Cuisson : **20 minutes** • Quantité : **de 4 à 6 portions**

Préparation

Dans une casserole, déposer tous les ingrédients. Porter à ébullition.

Couvrir et laisser mijoter de 20 à 30 minutes à feu moyen.

Si la soupe devient trop épaisse, ajouter un peu d'eau. Saler et poivrer.

PAR PORTION	
Calories	283
Protéines	18 g
Matières grasses	2 g
Glucides	50 g
Fibres	15 g
Fer	5 mg
Calcium	92 mg
Sodium	920 mg

Au total
329
calories

Idée pour accompagner

Croûtons au pesto

Par croûton : 46 calories

Couper la moitié de 1 baguette de pain en 12 croûtons. Badigeonner les deux côtés des croûtons avec 60 ml (¼ de tasse) de pesto. Déposer sur une plaque de cuisson tapissée d'une feuille de papier parchemin. Faire griller au four de 8 à 10 minutes à 190 °C (375 °F).

Mélange de légumes frais pour soupe
500 ml (2 tasses)

Jus de palourdes
500 ml (2 tasses)

Palourdes
égouttées
4 contenants de 142 g chacun

12 crevettes moyennes (calibre 31/40)
crues et décortiquées

Mélange laitier pour cuisson 5 %
250 ml (1 tasse)

PRÉVOIR AUSSI :
➤ **Beurre léger**
15 ml (1 c. à soupe)
➤ **Ail**
haché
15 ml (1 c. à soupe)
➤ **Farine**
45 ml (3 c. à soupe)

FACULTATIF :
➤ **Bacon**
précuit emmietté
au goût
➤ **Pommes de terre**
taillées en dés
500 ml (2 tasses)
➤ **Homard**
1 paquet de 200 g
de chair cuite

Chaudrée du pêcheur

Préparation : **15 minutes** • Cuisson : **20 minutes** • Quantité : **de 6 à 8 portions**

Préparation

Dans une casserole, faire fondre le beurre à feu moyen. Cuire le mélange de légumes et l'ail de 1 à 2 minutes.

Saupoudrer de farine et cuire quelques secondes en remuant. Incorporer le jus de palourdes et 500 ml (2 tasses) d'eau, puis porter à ébullition.

Si désiré, ajouter les pommes de terre. Saler et poivrer, puis laisser mijoter de 15 à 20 minutes à feu doux-moyen.

Ajouter les palourdes, les crevettes, le mélanger laitier et, si désiré, la chair de homard. Cuire 5 minutes à feu moyen.

Répartir la soupe dans les bols. Si désiré, garnir chacune des portions de morceaux de bacon.

Idée pour accompagner

Rouille à tartiner

Par portion (environ 80 ml - ⅓ de tasse) : 49 calories

Laisser infuser de 4 à 5 pistils de safran dans 10 ml (2 c. à thé) de jus de citron. Dans un bol, fouetter 250 ml (1 tasse) de yogourt nature grec 0 % avec 30 ml (2 c. à soupe) d'huile d'olive. Incorporer 5 ml (1 c. à thé) d'ail haché et le safran infusé.

PAR PORTION	
Calories	257
Protéines	30 g
Matières grasses	6 g
Glucides	18 g
Fibres	1 g
Fer	21 mg
Calcium	112 mg
Sodium	336 mg

Au total

306
calories

Gingembre ①
émincé
45 ml (3 c. à soupe)

Citronnelle ②
3 bâtons

Poulet ③
1 paquet de tranches
pour fondue de 240 g

1 carotte ④
émincée

Bébés épinards ⑤
500 ml (2 tasses)

PRÉVOIR AUSSI :
➤ **Bouillon de poulet**
1,25 litre (5 tasses)
➤ **Ail**
2 gousses émincées
➤ **2 oignons verts**
émincés

FACULTATIF :
➤ 1 petit **piment thaï**
émincé
➤ **Lime**
15 ml (1 c. à soupe)
de zestes

Soupe de poulet à la citronnelle et au gingembre

Préparation : **15 minutes** • Cuisson : **35 minutes** • Quantité : **4 portions**

Préparation

Dans une casserole, porter à ébullition le gingembre avec les bâtons de citronnelle, le bouillon de poulet et l'ail. Si désiré, ajouter le piment thaï. Laisser mijoter 30 minutes à feu doux-moyen.

Filtrer le bouillon, puis le remettre dans la casserole.

Porter à ébullition à feu moyen, puis ajouter le poulet et la carotte. Cuire 4 minutes.

Incorporer les bébés épinards. Si désiré, ajouter les zestes. Prolonger la cuisson de 2 à 3 minutes.

Garnir d'oignons verts au moment de servir.

PAR PORTION	
Calories	117
Protéines	19 g
Matières grasses	2 g
Glucides	7 g
Fibres	3 g
Fer	2 mg
Calcium	58 mg
Sodium	562 mg

Au total
295
calories

Idée pour accompagner

Petits pains au parmesan

Par pain: 178 calories

Dans un bol, mélanger 60 ml (¼ de tasse) de persil haché avec 10 ml (2 c. à thé) d'ail haché et 60 ml (¼ de tasse) de parmesan râpé. Mélanger avec 500 g (environ 1 lb) de pâte à pizza en pétrissant. Diviser la pâte en huit boules. Beurrer les alvéoles d'un moule à muffins, puis y répartir les boules de pâte. Laisser gonfler de 15 à 20 minutes à température ambiante. Cuire au four de 15 à 20 minutes à 205 °C (400 °F).

**Mélange de légumes
frais pour soupe**
500 ml (2 tasses) ①

Bouillon de légumes ②
1,5 litre (6 tasses)

Petites farfalles ③
250 ml (1 tasse)

Haricots blancs ④
rincés et égouttés
1 boîte de 540 ml

Pesto ⑤
30 ml (2 c. à soupe)

PRÉVOIR AUSSI :
➤ **Huile d'olive**
15 ml (1 c. à soupe)

➤ **Ail**
haché
10 ml (2 c. à thé)

FACULTATIF :
➤ **Roquette**
500 ml (2 tasses)

➤ **Parmesan**
quelques copeaux

Minestrone

Préparation : **15 minutes** • Cuisson : **10 minutes** • Quantité : **4 portions**

Préparation

Dans une casserole, chauffer l'huile à feu moyen.
Cuire le mélange de légumes de 2 à 3 minutes.

Ajouter l'ail et remuer. Cuire 1 minute.

Verser le bouillon et porter à ébullition.

Ajouter les pâtes et laisser mijoter 8 minutes
à feu doux-moyen.

Ajouter les haricots et poursuivre la cuisson
de 2 à 3 minutes.

Hors du feu, incorporer le pesto.

Répartir la soupe dans les bols. Si désiré, garnir
de roquette et de copeaux de parmesan.

PAR PORTION	
Calories	294
Protéines	15 g
Matières grasses	7 g
Glucides	43 g
Fibres	8 g
Fer	4 mg
Calcium	122 mg
Sodium	1 145 mg

▼

Au total
370
calories

Idée pour accompagner

Scones oignon et parmesan

Par scone: 76 calories

Dans un bol, mélanger 625 ml (2 ½ tasses) de farine avec
15 ml (1 c. à soupe) de poudre à pâte. Dans un autre bol,
fouetter 125 ml (½ tasse) de lait 2% avec 125 ml (½ tasse)
de yogourt nature 0%, 1 œuf, 15 ml (1 c. à soupe) de thym
haché, 3 oignons verts hachés et 125 ml (½ tasse) de
parmesan râpé. Saler et poivrer. Incorporer les ingrédients
secs. Façonner 18 boules de pâte, puis déposer sur une
plaque de cuisson tapissée d'une feuille de papier parchemin. Cuire au four de 20 à 25 minutes à 180°C (350°F).

Purée de tomates ①
500 ml (2 tasses)

Bouillon de légumes ②
1 litre (4 tasses)

Mélange de légumes
frais pour soupe ③
500 ml (2 tasses)

Pois chiches ④
rincés et égouttés
1 boîte de 540 ml

20 boulettes de viande ⑤

Soupe aux boulettes et pois chiches

Préparation : **15 minutes** • Cuisson : **35 minutes** • Quantité : **de 4 à 6 portions**

Préparation

Dans une casserole, chauffer l'huile à feu moyen. Faire dorer les oignons.

Ajouter la purée de tomates, le bouillon et, si désiré, la harissa. Porter à ébullition et, si désiré, ajouter le thym. Saler. Laisser mijoter 15 minutes.

Ajouter le mélange de légumes à la préparation. Poursuivre la cuisson 10 minutes.

Ajouter les pois chiches et les boulettes. Prolonger de nouveau la cuisson de 8 à 10 minutes, jusqu'à ce que les boulettes soient cuites.

PAR PORTION	
Calories	324
Protéines	15 g
Matières grasses	15 g
Glucides	35 g
Fibres	6 g
Fer	4 mg
Calcium	65 mg
Sodium	274 mg

Au total
387
calories

Idée pour accompagner

Pitas grillés à l'huile parfumée

Par pointe : 63 calories

Dans un bol, mélanger 45 ml (3 c. à soupe) d'huile d'olive avec 10 ml (2 c. à thé) de paprika, 30 ml (2 c. à soupe) de parmesan râpé, 10 ml (2 c. à thé) de thym haché et 15 ml (1 c. à soupe) d'origan haché. Saler et poivrer. Badigeonner les deux côtés de 4 pitas avec la préparation. Dans une poêle striée, cuire les pitas de 1 à 2 minutes de chaque côté. Couper en quartiers.

Mélange de légumes surgelés pour chili ①
500 ml (2 tasses)

Bouillon de légumes sans sel ajouté ②
1,5 litre (6 tasses)

Tomates en dés ③
1 boîte de 540 ml

Lentilles cuites ④
brunes ou vertes, rincées et égouttées
580 ml (2 ⅓ tasses)

Bébés épinards ⑤
1 litre (4 tasses)

PRÉVOIR AUSSI :
➤ **Huile d'olive**
15 ml (1 c. à soupe)

➤ **Cumin**
10 ml (2 c. à thé)

Chaudrée mexicaine

Préparation : **15 minutes** • Cuisson : **18 minutes** • Quantité : **4 portions**

Préparation

Dans une casserole, chauffer l'huile à feu moyen. Cuire le mélange de légumes de 2 à 3 minutes.

Ajouter le bouillon et le cumin. Porter à ébullition. Couvrir et laisser mijoter 10 minutes à feu moyen.

Ajouter les tomates et les lentilles. Prolonger la cuisson de 8 à 10 minutes.

Au moment de servir, incorporer les bébés épinards et, si désiré, les zestes de lime et les feuilles de coriandre.

PAR PORTION	
Calories	303
Protéines	15 g
Matières grasses	5 g
Glucides	55 g
Fibres	9 g
Fer	7 mg
Calcium	146 mg
Sodium	548 mg

▼

Au total
383
calories

Idée pour accompagner

Pains à la mexicaine

Par pain : 80 calories

Dans une poêle, faire revenir ½ poivron rouge taillé en petits dés dans 5 ml (1 c. à thé) d'huile d'olive 2 minutes à feu moyen. Laisser tiédir. Dans un grand bol, mélanger 250 ml (1 tasse) de farine de maïs avec 160 ml (⅔ de tasse) de farine tout usage, 10 ml (2 c. à thé) de poudre à pâte et 1,25 ml (¼ de c. à thé) de sel. Dans un autre bol, mélanger 180 ml (¾ de tasse) de yogourt grec nature 0% avec 30 ml (2 c. à soupe) de coriandre hachée, 10 ml (2 c. à thé) de paprika fumé, 2 œufs battus, 60 ml (¼ de tasse) de lait 1%, 30 ml (2 c. à soupe) d'huile d'olive et 30 ml (2 c. à soupe) d'eau. Mélanger avec les ingrédients secs, puis incorporer la préparation au poivron. Verser dans un plat de cuisson beurré de 20 cm (8 po). Cuire au four de 30 à 35 minutes à 180°C (350°F). Couper en 16 pains.

FACULTATIF :
➤ **Lime**
30 ml (2 c. à soupe) de zestes

➤ **Coriandre**
60 ml (¼ de tasse) de feuilles

Vermicelles de riz ①
225 g

Gingembre ②
haché
15 ml (1 c. à soupe)

Coriandre ③
hachée
30 ml (2 c. à soupe)

12 crevettes moyennes ④
(calibre 31/40)
cuites et décortiquées

Julienne de ⑤
légumes frais
de type Saladexpress
250 ml (1 tasse)

PRÉVOIR AUSSI :
➤ **Bouillon**
de légumes
1,5 litre (6 tasses)

➤ **Ail**
haché
10 ml (2 c. à thé)

FACULTATIF :
➤ **Sauce de poisson**
3 à 4 gouttes

➤ **Fèves germées**
500 ml (2 tasses)

➤ **2 limes**
coupées en
quartiers

Soupe tonkinoise aux crevettes

Préparation : **15 minutes** • Cuisson : **15 minutes** • Quantité : **4 portions**

Préparation

Faire cuire les vermicelles selon le mode de préparation indiqué sur l'emballage.

Dans une casserole, verser le bouillon et ajouter le gingembre, la moitié de la coriandre, l'ail et, si désiré, la sauce de poisson. Porter à ébullition, puis laisser mijoter 10 minutes à feu moyen.

Égoutter les vermicelles et les répartir dans quatre bols à soupe préalablement réchauffés sous l'eau chaude.

Répartir les crevettes, la julienne de légumes et le reste de la coriandre dans les bols.

Verser le bouillon chaud dans les bols. Si désiré, presser le jus d'un ou de deux quartiers de lime dans chaque portion.

PAR PORTION	
Calories	273
Protéines	17 g
Matières grasses	4 g
Glucides	45 g
Fibres	2 g
Fer	3 mg
Calcium	69 mg
Sodium	207 mg

Au total
341
calories

Idée pour accompagner

Rouleaux de printemps

Par rouleau : 68 calories

Déposer 500 ml (2 tasses) de vermicelles de riz dans un bol, puis couvrir d'eau très chaude. Laisser reposer 5 minutes, jusqu'à ce que les vermicelles soient tendres. Égoutter. Couper les vermicelles en morceaux d'environ 10 cm (4 po) de longueur. Trancher finement 6 fraises, puis tailler en julienne ½ concombre et ½ poivron orange. Tremper 8 feuilles de riz dans l'eau tiède, puis transférer sur une planche à découper. Déposer 15 ml (1 c. à soupe) de vermicelles au centre de chaque feuille de riz, puis garnir de tranches de fraises, de concombre et de poivron. Replier la portion inférieure de chaque feuille sur la garniture, puis rabattre les côtés vers le centre. Rouler en serrant bien.

Poulet ①
3 poitrines sans peau
de 150 g (⅓ de lb)
chacune, coupées
en dés

Mélange de légumes
frais pour soupe ②
500 ml (2 tasses)

Orzo ③
125 ml (½ tasse)

3 tomates italiennes ④
coupées en dés

Pesto ⑤
15 ml (1 c. à soupe)

PRÉVOIR AUSSI:
➤ **Bouillon de poulet**
sans sel ajouté
1,5 litre (6 tasses)

FACULTATIF:
➤ **1 poireau**
émincé
➤ **Basilic**
quelques feuilles

Soupe au poulet à l'italienne

Préparation: **15 minutes** • Cuisson: **18 minutes** • Quantité: **4 portions**

Préparation

Dans une casserole, porter à ébullition le bouillon
à feu moyen.

Ajouter le poulet, le mélange de légumes et, si désiré,
le poireau. Porter de nouveau à ébullition. Couvrir
et laisser mijoter 10 minutes à feu doux-moyen.

Ajouter l'orzo et les tomates. Prolonger la cuisson
de 8 à 10 minutes.

Au moment de servir, incorporer le pesto. Si désiré,
garnir de feuilles de basilic.

PAR PORTION	
Calories	276
Protéines	33 g
Matières grasses	4 g
Glucides	26 g
Fibres	2 g
Fer	1 mg
Calcium	41 mg
Sodium	206 mg

Au total
316
calories

Idée pour accompagner

Bouchées au parmesan

Par bouchée: 40 calories

Couper 6 muffins anglais en deux sur l'épaisseur. Hacher
4 gousses d'ail très finement, puis mélanger avec
250 ml (1 tasse) de mayonnaise « ½ moins de gras »,
250 ml (1 tasse) de parmesan râpé, 5 ml (1 c. à thé)
de persil haché et 5 ml (1 c. à thé) d'origan haché. Étaler
le mélange sur les muffins anglais. Déposer sur une plaque
de cuisson tapissée d'une feuille de papier d'aluminium
et faire dorer au four à la position « gril » (broil). Couper
chaque moitié de muffin en quatre bouchées.

Bœuf ①
450 g (1 lb) de bavette
coupée en cubes

2 tomates ②
pelées et coupées en dés

2 pommes de terre ③
pelées et coupées en dés
de type Russet ou
Yukon Gold

Pois verts ④
surgelés
500 ml (2 tasses)

Quinoa ⑤
250 ml (1 tasse)

PRÉVOIR AUSSI :
➤ **Huile de canola**
15 ml (1 c. à soupe)

➤ **½ oignon**
haché

➤ **Ail**
2 gousses hachées

FACULTATIF :
➤ **Cumin**
10 ml (2 c. à thé)

➤ **Paprika fumé**
5 ml (1 c. à thé)

Soupe au quinoa et bœuf

Préparation : **15 minutes** • Cuisson : **40 minutes** • Quantité : **6 portions**

Préparation

Éponger les cubes de bœuf à l'aide de papier absorbant.

Dans une grande casserole, chauffer l'huile à feu moyen. Déposer les cubes de bœuf et bien colorer chaque face. Retirer et réserver dans une assiette.

Dans la même casserole, cuire les tomates, l'oignon et l'ail 3 minutes, jusqu'à ce que l'oignon soit tendre. Si désiré, ajouter le cumin et le paprika. Saler et poivrer.

Ajouter 2,5 litres (10 tasses) d'eau et les pommes de terre. Porter à ébullition. Couvrir et cuire 20 minutes à feu doux-moyen.

Dans la casserole, ajouter les pois verts, le quinoa et les cubes de bœuf. Porter à ébullition, puis baisser le feu et laisser mijoter 20 minutes, jusqu'à ce que le quinoa soit tendre.

Rectifier l'assaisonnement au besoin. La soupe épaissira en refroidissant. Au besoin, la diluer avec de l'eau.

PAR PORTION	
Calories	283
Protéines	23 g
Matières grasses	6 g
Glucides	34 g
Fibres	5 g
Fer	4 mg
Calcium	37 mg
Sodium	75 mg

Au total
323
calories

Idée pour accompagner

Croûtons au cari et gingembre

Par croûton : 40 calories

Dans un bol, mélanger 30 ml (2 c. à soupe) d'huile d'olive avec 15 ml (1 c. à soupe) de beurre fondu, 15 ml (1 c. à soupe) de cari et 10 ml (2 c. à thé) de gingembre haché. Couper ¼ de baguette de pain en 12 tranches. Badigeonner les tranches avec la préparation. Déposer sur une plaque de cuisson et faire dorer au four de 1 à 2 minutes de chaque côté à la position « gril » (*broil*).

Recette de Ève Godin, nutritionniste

Mélange de légumes frais pour sauce à spaghetti
500 ml (2 tasses)

1

Bouillon de poulet
2 litres (8 tasses)

2

Riz à grains longs
80 ml (⅓ de tasse)

3

Chou frisé
coupé en dés
250 ml (1 tasse)

4

Poulet
2 poitrines sans peau de
180 g (environ ⅓ de lb)
chacune, cuites et
effilochées

5

PRÉVOIR AUSSI :
➤ **Beurre**
15 ml (1 c. à soupe)

➤ **Ail**
haché
10 ml (2 c. à thé)

FACULTATIF :
➤ **Thym**
1 tige

➤ **Laurier**
1 feuille

➤ 2 **tomates**
coupées en dés

Soupe au poulet, riz et chou frisé

Préparation : **15 minutes** • Cuisson : **20 minutes** • Quantité : de 4 à 6 portions

Préparation

Dans une casserole, faire fondre le beurre à feu moyen. Cuire les légumes pour sauce à spaghetti avec l'ail de 2 à 3 minutes.

Si désiré, ajouter le thym et le laurier et cuire à nouveau de 2 à 3 minutes.

Verser le bouillon, puis porter à ébullition. Ajouter le riz et le chou. Saler et poivrer. Couvrir et laisser mijoter 15 minutes à feu doux-moyen.

Ajouter le poulet et, si désiré, les tomates. Prolonger la cuisson de 5 minutes.

PAR PORTION	
Calories	159
Protéines	19 g
Matières grasses	3 g
Glucides	14 g
Fibres	3 g
Fer	1 mg
Calcium	52 mg
Sodium	596 mg

Au total
245
calories

Idée pour accompagner

Torsades feuilletées au pesto de tomates et pavot

Pour 2 torsades : 86 calories

Sur une surface farinée, abaisser 200 g (environ ½ lb) de pâte feuilletée en un rectangle d'environ 35 cm x 25 cm (14 po x 10 po). Tailler la pâte en deux rectangles et badigeonner avec 1 blanc d'œuf battu. Saupoudrer un premier rectangle de 30 ml (2 c. à soupe) de graines de pavot. Sur le second rectangle, étaler 30 ml (2 c. à soupe) de pesto aux tomates séchées, puis parsemer de 125 ml (½ tasse) de fromage suisse râpé. Réfrigérer 15 minutes. Déposer le rectangle saupoudré de pavot sur le rectangle au pesto, garnitures sur le dessus. À l'aide d'un rouleau à pâte, presser légèrement les rectangles pour les sceller. À l'aide d'un couteau, tailler 28 bandes de 1 cm (½ po) de large dans la pâte. En la tenant aux extrémités, tourner chaque bande de deux à trois fois sur elle-même afin de former une torsade. Déposer sur une plaque de cuisson tapissée de papier parchemin. Cuire au four de 10 à 12 minutes à 205 °C (400 °F).

Vermicelles de riz ❶
100 g

**Bouillon de bœuf
sans sel ajouté** ❷
1,25 litre (5 tasses)

**Mélange californien
de légumes surgelés** ❸
250 ml (1 tasse)

Gingembre ❹
haché
15 ml (1 c. à soupe)

Bœuf ❺
250 g (environ ½ lb) de
tranches à fondue

PRÉVOIR AUSSI :
➤ **Huile d'olive**
30 ml (2 c. à soupe)

➤ 1 **oignon**
haché

➤ **Ail**
haché
10 ml (2 c. à thé)

FACULTATIF :
➤ **Lime**
30 ml (2 c. à soupe)
de jus

Soupe au bœuf et gingembre

Préparation : **15 minutes** • Cuisson : **10 minutes** • Quantité : **4 portions**

Préparation

Réhydrater les vermicelles de riz selon le mode
de préparation indiqué sur l'emballage. Égoutter.

Dans une casserole, chauffer l'huile à feu moyen.
Cuire l'oignon et l'ail 1 minute.

Verser le bouillon et porter à ébullition.

Ajouter les légumes et le gingembre. Cuire 5 minutes
à feu moyen.

Ajouter le bœuf et cuire 1 minute.

Incorporer les vermicelles et, si désiré, le jus de lime.
Servir immédiatement.

PAR PORTION	
Calories	321
Protéines	20 g
Matières grasses	14 g
Glucides	30 g
Fibres	3 g
Fer	3 mg
Calcium	55 mg
Sodium	200 mg

Au total
380
calories

Idée pour accompagner

Croustilles de wontons au sésame

Par pointe : 59 calories

Préchauffer le four à 180 °C (350 °F). Badigeonner
12 feuilles de pâte à wontons avec 1 blanc d'œuf battu.
Parsemer les feuilles de 45 ml (3 c. à soupe) de graines
de sésame et presser afin qu'elles adhèrent bien à la pâte.
Couper chaque feuille en diagonale. Badigeonner de 30 ml
(2 c. à soupe) d'huile d'olive et déposer sur une plaque
de cuisson tapissée de papier parchemin. Cuire au four
de 8 à 10 minutes, jusqu'à ce que la pâte soit dorée.

Bœuf
et veau

Qui peut résister au crépitement et aux effluves
de ces deux viandes lorsqu'elles cuisent dans
la poêle ou au four ? Qu'on les préfère bien cuites,
mi-cuites ou saignantes, ces sources de fer
et de protéines savent rassasier tous les types
de carnivores !

Sauce teriyaki ①
du commerce
125 ml (½ tasse)

Bœuf ②
450 g (1 lb)
de bavette coupée
en lanières

1 poivron rouge ③
coupé en cubes

Brocoli ④
375 ml (1 ½ tasse)

2 pêches ⑤
coupées en quartiers

PRÉVOIR AUSSI :
➤ **Fécule de maïs**
10 ml (2 c. à thé)

➤ **Huile de sésame**
non grillé
30 ml (2 c. à soupe)

FACULTATIF :
➤ **Gingembre**
haché 15 ml (1 c. à soupe)

➤ 1 **oignon vert** émincé

Sauté de bœuf teriyaki aux pêches

Préparation : **15 minutes** • Cuisson : **7 minutes** • Quantité : **4 portions**

Préparation

Dans un bol, délayer la fécule de maïs dans la sauce teriyaki.

Dans une poêle, chauffer l'huile à feu moyen. Cuire les lanières de bœuf de 3 à 4 minutes, puis les déposer dans une assiette.

Dans la même poêle, cuire le poivron rouge, le brocoli et, si désiré, le gingembre de 2 à 3 minutes, en prenant soin de garder les légumes légèrement croquants. Transférer dans une assiette.

Dans la même poêle, faire dorer les pêches de 1 à 2 minutes de chaque côté.

Remettre les lanières de bœuf et les légumes dans la poêle. Verser la sauce teriyaki. Porter à ébullition en remuant.

Au moment de servir, garnir d'oignon vert si désiré.

PAR PORTION	
Calories	298
Protéines	29 g
Matières grasses	13 g
Glucides	16 g
Fibres	2 g
Fer	4 mg
Calcium	37 mg
Sodium	1 541 mg

Version minceur

Sauce teriyaki

Dans une casserole, porter à ébullition à feu doux moyen 60 ml (¼ de tasse) de bouillon de poulet avec 10 ml (2 c. à thé) de cassonade, 10 ml (2 c. à thé) de vinaigre de xérès ou de vinaigre de riz et 45 ml (3 c. à soupe) de sauce soya. Laisser mijoter de 3 à 5 minutes.

167 CALORIES
Du commerce

Pour 125 ml
(½ tasse)

55 CALORIES
Maison

Veau haché ❶
400 g (environ ¾ de lb)

4 petits pains à hamburger ❷

Confit de carotte et d'oignon perlé au porto Mylliam ❸
60 ml (¼ de tasse)

2 tomates ❹
coupées en tranches

½ laitue Boston ❺

FACULTATIF :
➤ **Moutarde de Dijon**
30 ml (2 c. à soupe)

➤ **Fromage suisse**
faible en gras
8 tranches

Burger de veau au confit de carotte et d'oignon perlé au porto

Préparation : **15 minutes** • Cuisson : **12 minutes** • Quantité : **4 portions**

Préparation

Préchauffer le four à la position « gril » (*broil*).

Dans un grand bol, déposer le veau. Saler et poivrer. Bien mélanger, puis façonner quatre galettes avec la viande.

Dans une grande poêle antiadhésive, chauffer l'huile à feu moyen-élevé. Cuire les galettes de veau de 8 à 10 minutes en les retournant à mi-cuisson, jusqu'à ce qu'elles soient bien cuites.

Faire griller les pains au four 1 minute, jusqu'à ce qu'ils soient légèrement dorés.

Si désiré, tartiner les burgers de moutarde de Dijon. Garnir chaque burger d'une galette de veau, de 15 ml (1 c. à soupe) de confit de carotte et d'oignon perlé, de 2 tranches de tomates, de 2 feuilles de laitue et, si désiré, de 2 tranches de fromage suisse.

PAR PORTION	
Calories	399
Protéines	30 g
Matières grasses	13 g
Glucides	37 g
Fibres	2 g
Fer	3 mg
Calcium	258 mg
Sodium	526 mg

Version minceur

Boulettes au tofu

Râper 1 bloc de tofu ferme de 300 g. Déposer dans un bol et mélanger avec 60 ml (¼ de tasse) d'oignon haché, 1 œuf battu, 15 ml (1 c. à soupe) de sauce soya, 15 ml (1 c. à soupe) de farine, 30 ml (2 c. à soupe) de parmesan râpé et 125 ml (½ tasse) de chapelure nature. Saler et poivrer. Façonner 4 boulettes avec la préparation. Dans une poêle allant au four, chauffer 15 ml (1 c. à soupe) d'huile d'olive à feu moyen. Faire dorer les boulettes de 2 à 3 minutes de chaque côté. Compléter la cuisson au four de 5 à 6 minutes à 180 °C (350 °F).

864 CALORIES

Du commerce pour 4 boulettes **Maison**

575 CALORIES

Veau ①
4 escalopes de 130 g
(environ ¼ de lb)
chacune

Échalotes sèches ②
hachées
30 ml (2 c. à soupe)

**Bouillon de poulet
sans sel ajouté** ③
180 ml (¾ de tasse)

Citron ④
½ coupé en fines
rondelles
+ 30 ml (2 c. à soupe)
de jus

Câpres ⑤
15 ml (1 c. à soupe)

PRÉVOIR AUSSI :
➤ **Farine**
45 ml (3 c. à soupe)
➤ **Huile d'olive**
15 ml (1 c. à soupe)
➤ **Sucre**
2,5 ml (½ c. à thé)
➤ **Beurre**
10 ml (2 c. à thé)

Escalopes de veau piccata

Préparation : **15 minutes** • Cuisson : **10 minutes** • Quantité : **4 portions**

Préparation

Fariner les escalopes de veau.

Dans une poêle, chauffer l'huile à feu moyen. Cuire les escalopes de 1 à 2 minutes de chaque côté. Transférer dans une assiette et couvrir d'une feuille de papier d'aluminium.

Dans la même poêle, cuire les échalotes 1 minute.

Verser le bouillon et racler le fond de la poêle à l'aide d'une cuillère en bois afin de détacher les sucs de cuisson.

Ajouter les rondelles de citron, le jus de citron, les câpres et le sucre. Cuire de 3 à 4 minutes.

Incorporer le beurre.

Au moment de servir, napper les escalopes de sauce.

PAR PORTION	
Calories	219
Protéines	31 g
Matières grasses	7 g
Glucides	7 g
Fibres	0 g
Fer	2 mg
Calcium	17 mg
Sodium	147 mg

Au total
391
calories

Idée pour accompagner

Spaghettis aux courgettes et fines herbes

Par portion: 172 calories

Dans une casserole d'eau bouillante salée, cuire 100 g de spaghettis *al dente*. Égoutter. Dans la même casserole, cuire 2 courgettes coupées en julienne dans 30 ml (2 c. à soupe) d'huile d'olive 2 minutes à feu moyen. Ajouter les pâtes, 30 ml (2 c. à soupe) de ciboulette hachée et 15 ml (1 c. à soupe) d'origan haché. Remuer.

Bœuf ❶
1 rôti de palette
avec os de 1,2 kg
(environ 2 ¾ lb)

Ail ❷
8 gousses
entières pelées

Vin rouge ❸
500 ml (2 tasses)

Orange ❹
250 ml (1 tasse) de jus

Sirop d'érable ❺
80 ml (⅓ de tasse)

PRÉVOIR AUSSI :
➤ **Huile d'olive**
15 ml (1 c. à soupe)

➤ 1 **oignon**
haché

FACULTATIF :
➤ 1 **poireau**
émincé

➤ **Pâte de tomates**
30 ml (2 c. à soupe)

➤ **Romarin**
1 tige

Bœuf braisé au vin rouge et à l'érable

Préparation : **15 minutes** • Cuisson : **3 heures** • Quantité : **de 6 à 8 portions**

Préparation

Préchauffer le four à 180 °C (350 °F). Parer le rôti
en retirant l'excédent de gras.

Dans une grande casserole allant au four, chauffer
l'huile à feu moyen. Saler et poivrer les deux côtés du
rôti. Saisir le rôti 2 minutes de chaque côté, puis retirer
de la casserole.

Ajouter les gousses d'ail, l'oignon et, si désiré, le poireau
dans la casserole. Cuire de 1 à 2 minutes. Déglacer avec
le vin et le jus d'orange.

Ajouter le sirop d'érable et, si désiré, la pâte de tomates
et le romarin, puis porter à ébullition en raclant le fond
de la casserole avec une cuillère en bois pour détacher
les sucs de cuisson.

Couvrir et cuire au four de 3 heures à 3 heures
30 minutes, jusqu'à ce que la viande se défasse
à la fourchette.

PAR PORTION	
Calories	334
Protéines	27 g
Matières grasses	11 g
Glucides	19 g
Fibres	1 g
Fer	3 mg
Calcium	50 mg
Sodium	103 mg

Au total
361
calories

Idée pour accompagner

Spaghettis de tofu
aux fines herbes

Par portion : 27 calories

Préparer 2 paquets de spaghettis de tofu (de
type Shirataki) de 226 g chacun selon les indications de
l'emballage. Mélanger avec 15 ml (1 c. à soupe) d'huile
d'olive, 30 ml (2 c. à soupe) de persil haché et 15 ml
(1 c. à soupe) d'origan haché. Saler et poivrer.

**Bœuf haché
extra-maigre**
450 g (1 lb)

1

**Assaisonnements
à chili**
30 ml (2 c. à soupe)

2

Salsa
250 ml (1 tasse)

3

Sauce tomate
500 ml (2 tasses)

4

Haricots rouges
rincés et égouttés
1 boîte de 540 ml

5

PRÉVOIR AUSSI :
➤ **Huile d'olive**
15 ml (1 c. à soupe)

➤ **Ail**
haché
15 ml (1 c. à soupe)

Chili au bœuf

Préparation : **15 minutes** • Cuisson : **30 minutes** • Quantité : **4 portions**

Préparation

Dans une grande casserole, chauffer l'huile à feu moyen. Cuire le bœuf haché de 3 à 4 minutes en égrainant la viande avec une cuillère en bois.

Ajouter les assaisonnements à chili et l'ail. Cuire 1 minute.

Ajouter la salsa et la sauce tomate. Saler.

Porter à ébullition et laisser mijoter de 25 à 30 minutes à feu doux-moyen.

Ajouter les haricots et remuer. Prolonger la cuisson de 5 minutes.

PAR PORTION	
Calories	383
Protéines	34 g
Matières grasses	13 g
Glucides	33 g
Fibres	3 g
Fer	6 mg
Calcium	96 mg
Sodium	1 594 mg

▼
Au total
400
calories

Idée pour accompagner

Tortillas aux épices à chili

Par pointe : 17 calories

Mélanger 2,5 ml (½ c. à thé) de chili moulu avec 2,5 ml (½ c. à thé) de cumin moulu, 2,5 ml (½ c. à thé) d'origan haché, 2,5 ml (½ c. à thé) de paprika, 2,5 ml (½ c. à thé) d'ail en poudre et 2,5 ml (½ c. à thé) de clous de girofle moulus. Avec 20 ml (4 c. à thé) d'huile d'olive, badigeonner un côté de 4 tortillas au blé entier moyennes. Saupoudrer du mélange d'épices. Couper chaque tortilla en huit pointes et déposer sur une plaque de cuisson tapissée d'une feuille de papier parchemin. Cuire au four de 8 à 10 minutes à 205 °C (400 °F).

Veau de lait ❶
1,3 kg (3 lb)
de rôti d'épaule
désossé et ficelé

Fenouil ❷
1 bulbe émincé

Vin blanc ❸
80 ml (⅓ de tasse)

Tomates broyées ❹
1 boîte de 540 ml

Bouillon de poulet ❺
180 ml (¾ de tasse)

PRÉVOIR AUSSI :
➤ **Huile d'olive**
15 ml (1 c. à soupe)

➤ 1 **oignon**
haché

➤ **Ail**
2 gousses
hachées

Rôti de veau braisé au fenouil

Préparation : **15 minutes** • Cuisson : **2 heures 30 minutes** • Quantité : **6 portions**

Préparation

Préchauffer le four à 170 °C (340 °F).

Dans une grande casserole, chauffer l'huile à feu moyen-vif. Faire dorer le veau sur toutes les faces. Retirer et réserver dans une assiette.

Dans la même casserole, cuire le fenouil, l'oignon et l'ail 4 minutes, jusqu'à ce que les légumes soient tendres.

Verser le vin blanc et chauffer jusqu'à réduction complète du liquide.

Ajouter les tomates broyées et le bouillon de poulet, puis déposer le veau sur les légumes. Saler et poivrer. Porter à ébullition. Couvrir et cuire 2 heures 30 minutes, jusqu'à ce que la chair se défasse à la fourchette.

PAR PORTION	
Calories	264
Protéines	39 g
Matières grasses	5 g
Glucides	13 g
Fibres	4 g
Fer	4 mg
Calcium	102 mg
Sodium	360 mg

Au total
371
calories

Idée pour accompagner

Riz aux courgettes jaunes et vertes

Par portion: 107 calories

Dans une casserole antiadhésive, faire fondre 5 ml (1 c. à thé) de beurre à feu moyen. Cuire 1 oignon haché de 1 à 2 minutes. Ajouter 175 ml (environ ¾ de tasse) de riz à grains longs étuvé (*converted*). Saler et poivrer. Verser 375 ml (1 ½ tasse) d'eau et porter à ébullition. Couvrir et cuire de 18 à 20 minutes à feu doux-moyen. Ajouter ½ courgette jaune et ½ courgette verte coupées en dés. Remuer. Couvrir et laisser reposer 5 minutes.

Recette de Ève Godin, nutritionniste

Mélange de légumes surgelés
de type Orléans
375 ml (1 ½ tasse) **1**

Bœuf
12 boulettes
du commerce **2**

Pâte de cari jaune **3**
30 ml (2 c. à soupe)

Curcuma **4**
5 ml (1 c. à thé)

Lait de coco léger **5**
1 boîte de 400 ml

PRÉVOIR AUSSI :
➤ **Huile de sésame**
non grillé
15 ml (1 c. à soupe)
➤ 1 **oignon**
haché

FACULTATIF :
➤ **Châtaignes d'eau**
entières, égouttées
½ boîte de 227 g

Cari thaï aux boulettes de bœuf et légumes

Préparation : **15 minutes** • Cuisson : **12 minutes** • Quantité : **4 portions**

Préparation

Dans une poêle, chauffer la moitié de l'huile à feu moyen. Cuire les légumes, l'oignon et, si désiré, les châtaignes d'eau 2 minutes. Déposer dans une assiette.

Dans la même poêle, faire dorer les boulettes avec le reste de l'huile de 4 à 5 minutes.

Ajouter la pâte de cari jaune et le curcuma. Cuire 30 secondes en remuant afin que les arômes se libèrent.

Verser le lait de coco et porter à ébullition. Laisser mijoter 5 minutes à feu doux-moyen.

Remettre les légumes dans la poêle et chauffer 1 minute.

PAR PORTION	
Calories	399
Protéines	15 g
Matières grasses	22 g
Glucides	35 g
Fibres	11 g
Fer	2 mg
Calcium	84 mg
Sodium	250 mg

Version minceur

Boulettes de bœuf

Dans un bol, mélanger 180 g (environ ⅓ de lb) de bœuf haché extra-maigre avec 20 ml (4 c. à thé) de chapelure nature, 5 ml (1 c. à thé) de gingembre haché, 2,5 ml (½ c. à thé) d'ail haché, 2,5 ml (½ c. à thé) de pâte de cari jaune, 1 oignon vert haché, 1 blanc d'œuf et ⅓ de piment thaï haché. Saler. Façonner 12 boulettes avec la préparation.

510 CALORIES

Du commerce   pour 12 boulettes   **Maison**

349 CALORIES

Bouillon de poulet ①
250 ml (1 tasse)

Mélange laitier pour cuisson 5 % ②
60 ml (¼ de tasse)

Moutarde à l'ancienne ③
15 ml (1 c. à soupe)

Moutarde de Dijon ④
15 ml (1 c. à soupe)

Veau ⑤
4 escalopes de 120 g
(environ ¼ de lb)
chacune

PRÉVOIR AUSSI :
➤ **Beurre**
15 ml (1 c. à soupe)

➤ **Farine**
15 ml (1 c. à soupe)

➤ **Huile de canola**
15 ml (1 c. à soupe)

FACULTATIF :
➤ **Échalotes sèches**
hachées
45 ml (3 c. à soupe)

Escalopes de veau aux deux moutardes

Préparation : **15 minutes** • Cuisson : **4 minutes** • Quantité : **4 portions**

Préparation

Dans une casserole, faire fondre le beurre à feu moyen. Si désiré, faire dorer les échalotes 1 minute.

Incorporer la farine et cuire 1 minute, sans laisser colorer. Ajouter le bouillon, le mélange laitier pour cuisson et les deux moutardes. Porter à ébullition en fouettant. Saler et poivrer. Réserver.

Dans une poêle, chauffer l'huile à feu moyen. Saisir les escalopes 2 minutes de chaque côté.

Au moment de servir, napper les escalopes de sauce.

PAR PORTION	
Calories	207
Protéines	27 g
Matières grasses	9 g
Glucides	4 g
Fibres	1 g
Fer	1 mg
Calcium	17 mg
Sodium	340 mg

Au total
275
calories

Idée pour accompagner

Brocoli à la pancetta et graines de tournesol

Par portion: 68 calories

Dans une casserole d'eau bouillante salée, blanchir 1 brocoli coupé en petits bouquets de 2 à 3 minutes. Égoutter. Dans une poêle, faire fondre 15 ml (1 c. à soupe) de beurre à feu moyen. Faire dorer 25 g de pancetta précuite coupée en dés et 30 ml (2 c. à soupe) de graines de tournesol de 1 à 2 minutes en remuant. Ajouter le brocoli et cuire 1 minute.

6 shiitakes ❶

6 champignons de Paris ❷

Bœuf ❸
4 biftecks de surlonge
de 150 g
(⅓ de lb) chacun
et de 2 cm (¾ de po)
d'épaisseur

Vinaigre balsamique ❹
30 ml (2 c. à soupe)

Café filtre ❺
tiède
125 ml (½ tasse)

PRÉVOIR AUSSI :
➤ **Huile d'olive**
15 ml (1 c. à soupe)

➤ **Cassonade**
5 ml (1 c. à thé)

➤ **Fécule de maïs**
5 ml (1 c. à thé)

FACULTATIF :
➤ **Ail**
2 gousses

➤ **2 échalotes sèches**

Biftecks sauce aux champignons et café

Préparation : **15 minutes** • Cuisson : **10 minutes** • Quantité : **4 portions**

Préparation

Retirer les pieds des shiitakes. Émincer les chapeaux des shiitakes, les champignons de Paris et, si désiré, les gousses d'ail et les échalotes.

Dans une poêle, chauffer l'huile à feu moyen. Cuire les biftecks de 2 à 3 minutes de chaque côté. Déposer dans une assiette. Saler et poivrer. Couvrir d'une feuille de papier d'aluminium.

Dans la même poêle, cuire les champignons avec, si désiré, l'ail et les échalotes de 2 à 3 minutes. Saupoudrer de cassonade et remuer. Cuire 1 minute.

Dans un bol, délayer la fécule de maïs dans le vinaigre balsamique. Incorporer le café, puis verser la préparation dans la poêle. Porter à ébullition en remuant.

Émincer finement les biftecks. Servir avec la sauce aux champignons.

PAR PORTION	
Calories	271
Protéines	36 g
Matières grasses	10 g
Glucides	10 g
Fibres	1 g
Fer	4 mg
Calcium	21 mg
Sodium	95 mg

Au total
366
calories

Idée pour accompagner

Purée de chou-fleur et parmesan

Par portion: 95 calories

Cuire 1 chou-fleur coupé en bouquets 15 minutes à la vapeur. Réduire le chou-fleur en purée à l'aide du mélangeur électrique. Incorporer 15 ml (1 c. à soupe) de beurre, 45 ml (3 c. à soupe) de parmesan râpé et 30 ml (2 c. à soupe) de lait. Poivrer.

Beurre
ramolli
60 ml (¼ de tasse) **1**

Échalotes sèches
hachées
30 ml (2 c. à soupe) **2**

Persil
haché
15 ml (1 c. à soupe) **3**

Poivre rose
10 ml (2 c. à thé)
de grains **4**

Bœuf
4 filets mignons
de 120 g
(environ ¼ de lb) et
de 2,5 cm (1 po)
d'épaisseur chacun **5**

PRÉVOIR AUSSI :
➤ **Huile de canola**
15 ml (1 c. à soupe)

FACULTATIF :
➤ **Ciboulette**
hachée
15 ml (1 c. à soupe)

Filets mignons au beurre parfumé

Préparation : **15 minutes** • Cuisson : **6 minutes** • Quantité : **4 portions**

Préparation

Dans un bol, mélanger le beurre avec les échalotes, le persil, les grains de poivre rose et, si désiré, la ciboulette. Saler et poivrer. Déposer sur une pellicule plastique et façonner un cylindre de 2,5 cm (1 po) de diamètre. Emballer le cylindre dans la pellicule. Placer au congélateur.

Dans une poêle, chauffer l'huile à feu moyen. Cuire les filets de bœuf de 4 à 5 minutes de chaque côté. Saler et poivrer.

Au moment de servir, déposer une rondelle de beurre parfumé sur chacun des filets.

PAR PORTION	
Calories	296
Protéines	27 g
Matières grasses	20 g
Glucides	1 g
Fibres	0,2 g
Fer	3 mg
Calcium	14 mg
Sodium	74 mg

Au total
383
calories

Idée pour accompagner

Salade de pêches grillées et feta

Par portion: 87 calories

Couper en quartiers 3 pêches et ½ oignon rouge. Dans une poêle striée, faire griller les quartiers de pêches et d'oignon rouge de 1 à 2 minutes de chaque côté à feu moyen. Dans un saladier, mélanger 15 ml (1 c. à soupe) d'huile d'olive avec 30 ml (2 c. à soupe) de jus de lime, 30 ml (2 c. à soupe) d'eau, 30 ml (2 c. à soupe) de menthe hachée et 30 ml (2 c. à soupe) de persil haché. Saler et poivrer. Ajouter les pêches et l'oignon grillés, 1 laitue frisée verte déchiquetée et 50 g de feta coupée en dés. Remuer.

Sauté de veau à l'asiatique

Préparation : **15 minutes** • Cuisson : **7 minutes** • Quantité : **de 4 à 6 portions**

Préparation

Préparer les nouilles de riz selon le mode de préparation indiqué sur l'emballage. Égoutter.

Dans un bol, fouetter le bouillon avec la sauce soya, le miel, la fécule de maïs et, si désiré, l'ail.

Dans une poêle, chauffer l'huile à feu moyen. Saisir les lanières de veau de 1 à 2 minutes.

Ajouter les légumes et cuire de 2 à 3 minutes.

Verser la sauce. Incorporer les nouilles. Porter à ébullition à feu moyen. Remuer jusqu'à épaississement.

PAR PORTION	
Calories	258
Protéines	18 g
Matières grasses	3 g
Glucides	38 g
Fibres	2 g
Fer	2 mg
Calcium	38 mg
Sodium	608 mg

Au total

309

calories

Idée pour accompagner

Œufs épicés à la coriandre

Par portion : 51 calories

Fouetter 2 œufs entiers et 4 blancs d'œufs avec 15 ml (1 c. à soupe) de coriandre hachée. Dans une poêle, chauffer 15 ml (1 c. à soupe) d'huile de sésame (non grillé) à feu moyen. Cuire 5 ml (1 c. à thé) d'ail haché de 1 à 2 minutes. Verser les œufs et 2,5 ml (½ c. à thé) de sauce sriracha et remuer jusqu'à ce que les œufs soient pris. Laisser tiédir et couper en dés. Parsemer le sauté d'œufs épicés au moment de servir.

Nouilles de riz ❶
225 g

Bouillon de bœuf ❷
375 ml (1 ½ tasse)

Sauce soya ❸
30 ml (2 c. à soupe)

Veau ❹
450 g (1 lb)
de bifteck de surlonge
coupé en lanières

Julienne de légumes frais ❺
250 ml (1 tasse)

PRÉVOIR AUSSI :
➤ **Miel**
15 ml (1 c. à soupe)
➤ **Huile de canola**
15 ml (1 c. à soupe)
➤ **Fécule de maïs**
30 ml (2 c. à soupe)

FACULTATIF :
➤ **Ail**
haché
5 ml (1 c. à thé)

Chou de Savoie ①
12 grandes feuilles

Veau haché ②
340 g (¾ de lb)

Lentilles cuites ③
rincées et égouttées
1 boîte de 540 ml

Sauce tomate ④
750 ml (3 tasses)

Bouillon de poulet ⑤
125 ml (½ tasse)

Cigares au chou à la viande et aux lentilles

Préparation : **15 minutes** • Cuisson : **40 minutes** • Quantité : **6 portions**

Préparation

Dans une grande casserole d'eau bouillante salée, blanchir les feuilles de chou 5 minutes, jusqu'à ce qu'elles soient tendres. Plonger les feuilles dans un bac d'eau très froide pour arrêter la cuisson. Égoutter sur un linge. Réserver.

Préchauffer le four à 180 °C (350 °F).

Dans une poêle antiadhésive, chauffer l'huile à feu moyen. Cuire le veau haché et l'oignon 3 minutes. Si désiré, ajouter l'ail et poursuivre la cuisson quelques secondes.

Transvider dans un grand bol. Incorporer les lentilles, 500 ml (2 tasses) de sauce tomate et, si désiré, le thym. Saler et poivrer.

Dans un moule en verre (de type pyrex) de 33 cm x 23 cm (13 po x 9 po), verser le reste de la sauce tomate et le bouillon de poulet. Remuer.

Au centre de chaque feuille de chou, déposer environ 80 ml (⅓ de tasse) de préparation à la viande. Replier les côtés de la feuille sur la garniture et rouler. Déposer les cigares côte à côte dans le plat de cuisson.

Couvrir le plat de papier d'aluminium. Cuire au four de 30 à 35 minutes, jusqu'à ce que les rouleaux soient tendres.

PAR PORTION	
Calories	242
Protéines	21 g
Matières grasses	6 g
Glucides	27 g
Fibres	9 g
Fer	4 mg
Calcium	98 mg
Sodium	104 mg

Au total
372
calories

Idée pour accompagner

Salade de roquette et ricotta

Par portion : 130 calories

Dans un saladier, mélanger 60 ml (¼ de tasse) d'huile d'olive avec 15 ml (1 c. à soupe) de vinaigre de xérès et 15 ml (1 c. à soupe) de moutarde à l'ancienne. Saler et poivrer. Ajouter 750 ml (3 tasses) de roquette, 125 ml (½ tasse) de ricotta et 12 tomates cerises de couleurs variées coupées en deux.

PRÉVOIR AUSSI :
➤ **Huile d'olive**
15 ml (1 c. à soupe)
➤ 1 **oignon**
haché

FACULTATIF :
➤ **Ail**
3 gousses hachées
➤ **Thym**
haché au goût

Recette de Ève Godin, nutritionniste

Bœuf ①
4 biftecks de faux-filet
de 120 g
(environ ¼ de lb)
chacun

10 champignons ②
émincés

Bouillon de bœuf ③
310 ml (1 ¼ tasse)

Vinaigre de vin rouge ④
15 ml (1 c. à soupe)

Sauce au poivre ⑤
1 sachet d'environ 34 g

PRÉVOIR AUSSI :
➤ **Huile de canola**
15 ml (1 c. à soupe)
➤ **½ oignon**
haché

FACULTATIF :
➤ **Thym séché**
5 ml (1 c. à thé)
➤ **Ail**
haché
5 ml (1 c. à thé)

Bifteck de faux-filet, sauce au poivre et champignons

Préparation : **15 minutes** • Cuisson : **4 minutes** • Quantité : **4 portions**

Préparation

Saler les biftecks et, si désiré, parsemer de thym.

Dans une poêle, chauffer l'huile à feu moyen-vif. Cuire les biftecks 2 minutes de chaque côté pour une cuisson saignante. Transférer les biftecks dans une assiette et couvrir d'une feuille de papier d'aluminium.

Dans la même poêle, faire dorer les champignons de 2 à 3 minutes avec l'oignon et, si désiré, l'ail.

Dans un bol, mélanger le bouillon avec le vinaigre, puis y délayer le contenu du sachet de sauce au poivre. Verser dans la poêle. Porter à ébullition en remuant. Servir avec les biftecks.

PAR PORTION	
Calories	279
Protéines	30 g
Matières grasses	14 g
Glucides	8 g
Fibres	1 g
Fer	3 mg
Calcium	20 mg
Sodium	876 mg

Au total
360
calories

Idée pour accompagner

Pommes de terre croustillantes à l'ail

Par portion : 81 calories

Couper de 16 à 20 pommes de terre grelots en deux. Déposer dans un bol et mélanger avec 15 ml (1 c. à soupe) d'huile d'olive, ½ oignon coupé en quartiers et 8 gousses d'ail entières non pelées. Saler et poivrer. Déposer sur une plaque de cuisson tapissée d'une feuille de papier parchemin. Faire rôtir au four de 20 à 25 minutes à 205 °C (400 °F).

Bœuf haché maigre ①
450 g (1 lb)

1 oignon ②
haché

Consommé de bœuf ③
1 ½ boîte de 284 ml

Macédoine de légumes ④
500 ml (2 tasses)

Vin rouge ⑤
125 ml (½ tasse)

FACULTATIF :
➤ **Persil**
haché
30 ml (2 c. à soupe)

➤ **Thym**
haché
15 ml (1 c. à soupe)

➤ **4 pommes de terre**
pelées et coupées
en dés

PRÉVOIR AUSSI :
➤ 1 œuf
➤ **Beurre**
15 ml (1 c. à soupe)

Ragoût de boulettes aux légumes

Préparation : **15 minutes** • Cuisson : **18 minutes** • Quantité : *de 4 à 6 portions*

Préparation

Dans un bol, mélanger le bœuf haché avec l'oignon, l'œuf et, si désiré, le persil et le thym. Façonner des boulettes en utilisant environ 30 ml (2 c. à soupe) de préparation pour chacune d'elles.

Dans une casserole, faire fondre le beurre à feu moyen. Faire dorer les boulettes sur toutes les faces.

Ajouter le consommé de bœuf, la macédoine, le vin rouge et, si désiré, les pommes de terre. Couvrir et cuire à feu doux-moyen de 18 à 20 minutes.

PAR PORTION	
Calories	262
Protéines	22 g
Matières grasses	9 g
Glucides	23 g
Fibres	6 g
Fer	3 mg
Calcium	64 mg
Sodium	224 mg

Au total
318
calories

Idée pour accompagner

Mâche et laitue frisée aux artichauts

Par portion : 56 calories

Dans un saladier, mélanger 15 ml (1 c. à soupe) d'huile d'olive avec 30 ml (2 c. à soupe) de jus de citron, 30 ml (2 c. à soupe) d'eau, 15 ml (1 c. à soupe) d'assaisonnements italiens et 15 ml (1 c. à soupe) de moutarde à l'ancienne. Ajouter le contenu de 1 boîte de fonds d'artichaut de 398 ml (égouttés et émincés), 500 ml (2 tasses) de mâche et ½ laitue frisée verte déchiquetée. Remuer.

Chop suey au bœuf

Préparation : **15 minutes** • Cuisson : **8 minutes** • Quantité : **de 4 à 6 portions**

Préparation

Dans une poêle, chauffer l'huile à feu moyen.
Cuire le bœuf haché 5 minutes.

Ajouter le mélange de légumes, le gingembre et,
si désiré, l'ail. Cuire de 2 à 3 minutes.

Ajouter la sauce soya, le ketchup et les fèves germées.
Saler et poivrer. Prolonger la cuisson de 1 minute.
Si désiré, parsemer de persil.

Bœuf haché mi-maigre ❶
650 g (environ 1 ½ lb)

Légumes frais pour sauce à spaghetti ❷
½ sac de 700 g

Gingembre ❸
haché
15 ml (1 c. à soupe)

Sauce soya ❹
45 ml (3 c. à soupe)

Fèves germées ❺
250 ml (1 tasse)

PAR PORTION	
Calories	290
Protéines	22 g
Matières grasses	19 g
Glucides	8 g
Fibres	1 g
Fer	3 mg
Calcium	40 mg
Sodium	410 mg

Au total
382
calories

Idée pour accompagner

Riz lime et coriandre

Par portion : 92 calories

Déposer 250 ml (1 tasse) de riz dans une casserole avec
500 ml (2 tasses) d'eau froide, 15 ml (1 c. à soupe) de
zestes de lime et 1 oignon haché. Saler et poivrer. Porter à
ébullition à feu moyen. Couvrir et cuire de 18 à 20 minutes
à feu doux-moyen. Au moment de servir, incorporer 45 ml
(3 c. à soupe) de coriandre émincée.

PRÉVOIR AUSSI :
➤ **Huile de canola**
15 ml (1 c. à soupe)
➤ **Ketchup**
30 ml (2 c. à soupe)

FACULTATIF :
➤ **Ail**
haché
10 ml (2 c. à thé)
➤ **Persil**
haché
30 ml (2 c. à soupe)

Veau
1
4 escalopes de 120 g
(environ ¼ de lb)
chacune

8 champignons
2
émincés

Ail
3
haché
10 ml (2 c. à thé)

Bouillon de poulet
4
250 ml (1 tasse)

Fromage à la crème léger
5
coupé en cubes
¾ de 1 paquet de 250 g

PRÉVOIR AUSSI :
➤ **Huile de canola**
15 ml (1 c. à soupe)

FACULTATIF :
➤ **Ciboulette**
hachée
30 ml (2 c. à soupe)

Escalopes de veau aux champignons et fines herbes

Préparation : **15 minutes** • Cuisson : **10 minutes** • Quantité : **4 portions**

Préparation

Dans une poêle, chauffer l'huile à feu moyen. Saisir les escalopes 1 minute de chaque côté. Transférer dans une assiette et réserver.

Dans la même poêle, faire dorer les champignons de 2 à 3 minutes.

Ajouter l'ail et le bouillon. Porter à ébullition. Réduire l'intensité du feu et laisser mijoter 2 minutes à feu moyen.

Incorporer graduellement le fromage à la crème. Remuer jusqu'à ce qu'il soit fondu. Si désiré, ajouter la ciboulette.

Au moment de servir, napper les escalopes de sauce.

PAR PORTION	
Calories	245
Protéines	30 g
Matières grasses	11 g
Glucides	5 g
Fibres	1 g
Fer	1 mg
Calcium	81 mg
Sodium	390 mg

Au total
345
calories

Idée pour accompagner

Riz pilaf aux poivrons

Par portion: 100 calories

Dans une casserole, chauffer 15 ml (1 c. à soupe) d'huile d'olive à feu moyen. Faire revenir ¼ d'oignon haché et ¼ de poivron rouge coupé en dés 1 minute. Ajouter 125 ml (½ tasse) de riz et remuer. Verser 250 ml (1 tasse) de bouillon de poulet. Saler et poivrer. Porter à ébullition. Couvrir et cuire de 15 à 18 minutes à feu doux. Garnir de 10 ml (2 c. à thé) de ciboulette hachée.

Bœuf braisé, miel aux épices

Préparation : **15 minutes** • Cuisson : **2 heures** • Quantité : **4 portions**

Préparation

Préchauffer le four à 190°C (375°F).

Dans un bol, mélanger le miel avec le jus de citron, les grains de coriandre et, si désiré, le cumin et le sumac.

Retirer l'excédent de gras du rôti de palette. Badigeonner généreusement toute la surface du rôti de miel aux épices.

Déposer le rôti dans une cocotte à fond épais. Ajouter la sauce demi-glace, le reste du miel aux épices, le bouillon, l'oignon et les gousses d'ail. Saler et poivrer.

Couvrir et cuire au four de 2 heures à 2 heures 30 minutes, jusqu'à ce que la viande se défasse à la fourchette.

Idée pour accompagner

Purée de chou-fleur à la ciboulette

Par portion : 84 calories

Dans une casserole, déposer 1 chou-fleur coupé en bouquets et 2 pommes de terre pelées et coupées en cubes. Couvrir d'eau froide et saler. Porter à ébullition et cuire jusqu'à tendreté. Égoutter et réduire en purée avec 30 ml (2 c. à soupe) de beurre. Incorporer 45 ml (3 c. à soupe) de ciboulette hachée. Saler et poivrer.

PAR PORTION	
Calories	309
Protéines	28 g
Matières grasses	10 g
Glucides	30 g
Fibres	2 g
Fer	4 mg
Calcium	46 mg
Sodium	789 mg

Au total
393
calories

Miel ❶
60 ml (¼ de tasse)

Citron ❷
60 ml (¼ de tasse)
de jus

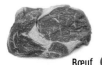

Coriandre ❸
15 ml (1 c. à soupe)
de grains concassés

Bœuf ❹
1 rôti de palette sans os
de 480 g (environ 1 lb)

Sauce demi-glace ❺
250 ml (1 tasse)

PRÉVOIR AUSSI :
➤ **Bouillon de bœuf**
180 ml (¾ de tasse)

➤ **1 oignon**
émincé

➤ **Ail**
4 gousses entières
pelées

FACULTATIF :
➤ **Cumin**
5 ml (1 c. à thé)
➤ **Sumac**
2,5 ml (½ c. à thé)

Poulet exquis

Ah, le poulet ! Pas étonnant qu'il fasse partie des viandes les plus appréciées au pays... Haut en protéines et faible en gras, il convient aussi bien pour les chics repas entre amis que pour les soirs pressés où l'on se rassemble autour d'une table en toute simplicité.

3 oranges ①
pelées et coupées en
quartiers
+ 30 ml (2 c. à soupe)
de zestes

Gingembre ②
haché
15 ml (1 c. à soupe)

**Assaisonnements
pour poulet** ③
15 ml (1 c. à soupe)

Poulet ④
4 poitrines sans peau

1 poivron rouge ⑤
émincé

PRÉVOIR AUSSI :
➤ **Miel**
30 ml (2 c. à soupe)
➤ **Huile d'olive**
30 ml (2 c. à soupe)

FACULTATIF :
➤ **Ail**
haché
10 ml (2 c. à thé)
➤ **½ oignon rouge**
émincé

Poitrines de poulet aux oranges, gingembre et miel

Préparation : **15 minutes** • Marinage : **2 heures** • Cuisson : **15 minutes** • Quantité : **4 portions**

Préparation

Dans un bol, mélanger les zestes d'orange avec le gingembre, les assaisonnements pour poulet, le miel, 15 ml (1 c. à soupe) d'huile d'olive et, si désiré, l'ail. Verser dans un sac hermétique. Ajouter les poitrines et laisser mariner de 2 à 3 heures au frais.

Dans une poêle, chauffer le reste de l'huile à feu moyen. Cuire les poitrines 6 minutes de chaque côté, jusqu'à ce que l'intérieur de la chair du poulet ait perdu sa teinte rosée. Déposer dans une assiette et couvrir d'une feuille de papier d'aluminium.

Dans la même poêle, cuire le poivron et, si désiré, l'oignon rouge de 1 à 2 minutes. Si désiré, verser la sauce orange-gingembre (voir recette ci-dessous) et porter à ébullition.

Ajouter les poitrines et les quartiers d'orange dans la poêle. Réchauffer 1 minute.

PAR PORTION	
Calories	257
Protéines	21 g
Matières grasses	8 g
Glucides	26 g
Fibres	3 g
Fer	1 mg
Calcium	63 mg
Sodium	763 mg

Au total
394
calories

Idée pour accompagner

Sauce orange-gingembre

Par portion : 137 calories

Mélanger 125 ml (½ tasse) de jus d'orange avec 30 ml (2 c. à soupe) de sauce soya, 45 ml (3 c. à soupe) de miel, 5 ml (1 c. à thé) de fécule de maïs et 80 ml (⅓ de tasse) de marmelade orange et gingembre. Saler et poivrer.

1 poivron rouge
émincé

16 pois mange-tout

1 petite mangue 3
émincée

Poulet 4
3 poitrines sans peau
coupées en lanières

Sauce aigre-douce 5
du commerce
180 ml (¾ de tasse)

PRÉVOIR AUSSI :
➤ **Huile de sésame**
non grillé
15 ml (1 c. à soupe)

➤ **1 oignon**
émincé

FACULTATIF :
➤ **Noix de cajou**
grillées
80 ml (⅓ de tasse)

Sauté de poulet aigre-doux à la thaï

Préparation : **15 minutes** • Cuisson : **8 minutes** • Quantité : **4 portions**

Préparation

Dans une poêle ou dans un wok, chauffer l'huile à feu moyen. Cuire les légumes et la mangue de 2 à 3 minutes. Déposer dans une assiette.

Dans la même poêle, cuire les lanières de poulet de 2 à 3 minutes de chaque côté en procédant par petites quantités.

Verser la sauce et porter à ébullition. Laisser mijoter 2 minutes à feu doux-moyen.

Remettre les légumes et la mangue dans la poêle. Prolonger la cuisson de 1 à 2 minutes.

Si désiré, parsemer de noix de cajou.

PAR PORTION	
Calories	288
Protéines	24 g
Matières grasses	11 g
Glucides	24 g
Fibres	2 g
Fer	2 mg
Calcium	32 mg
Sodium	231 mg

Version minceur

Sauce aigre-douce

Délayer 15 ml (1 c. à soupe) de miel dans 30 ml (2 c. à soupe) de vinaigre de riz. Incorporer 160 ml (⅔ de tasse) de sauce chili épicée thaï, 80 ml (⅓ de tasse) de bouillon de poulet et 60 ml (¼ de tasse) de sauce soya.

550 CALORIES

Du commerce

> pour 330 ml
(1 ⅓ tasse)

306 CALORIES

Maison

Farine ①
80 ml (⅓ de tasse)

2 œufs ②

Chapelure panko ③
250 ml (1 tasse)

**Noix de coco
non sucrée** ④
râpée
180 ml (¾ de tasse)

Poulet ⑤
3 poitrines sans peau
coupées en lanières

Doigts de poulet croustillants à la noix de coco

Préparation : **15 minutes** • Cuisson : **15 minutes** • Quantité : **4 portions (12 doigts de poulet)**

Préparation

Préchauffer le four à 190°C (375°F).

Préparer trois assiettes creuses. Dans la première, verser la farine. Dans la deuxième, battre les œufs. Dans la dernière, mélanger la chapelure panko avec la noix de coco et, si désiré, le piment de Cayenne. Saler et poivrer. Fariner les poitrines, puis secouer pour retirer l'excédent. Tremper dans les œufs battus, puis enrober de chapelure.

Déposer les morceaux de poulet sur une plaque de cuisson tapissée d'une feuille de papier parchemin. Cuire au four de 15 à 18 minutes, en retournant les lanières à mi-cuisson, jusqu'à ce que l'intérieur de la chair du poulet ait perdu sa teinte rosée.

PAR PORTION	
Calories	339
Protéines	27 g
Matières grasses	15 g
Glucides	24 g
Fibres	4 g
Fer	2 mg
Calcium	20 mg
Sodium	103 mg

Au total
381
calories

Idée pour accompagner

Sauce mangue et miel

Par portion: 42 calories

Dans le contenant du robot culinaire, réduire en purée ½ mangue émincée. Incorporer 125 ml (½ tasse) de yogourt grec nature 0%, 15 ml (1 c. à soupe) de zestes de lime, 15 ml (1 c. à soupe) de miel et 2,5 ml (½ c. à thé) de cari. Saler.

FACULTATIF :
➤ **Piment de Cayenne**
2 à 3 pincées

84

Citron ①
30 ml (2 c. à soupe)
de jus
+ 15 ml (1 c. à soupe)
de zestes

Menthe ②
hachée
30 ml (2 c. à soupe)

Origan ③
haché
15 ml (1 c. à soupe)

Miel ④
15 ml (1 c. à soupe)

Poulet ⑤
4 poitrines sans peau

PRÉVOIR AUSSI :
➤ **Huile d'olive**
60 ml (¼ de tasse)

➤ **Ail**
haché
10 ml (2 c. à thé)

Poitrines de poulet à la grecque

Préparation : **15 minutes** • Marinage : **1 heure** • Cuisson : **12 minutes** • Quantité : **4 portions**

Préparation

Dans un bol, mélanger tous les ingrédients, à l'exception du poulet.

Transférer le tiers de la préparation dans un sac hermétique. Réserver le reste de la préparation. Ajouter les poitrines de poulet dans le sac et secouer pour bien enrober le poulet de marinade. Laisser mariner 1 heure au frais, idéalement 8 heures.

Si désiré, dans un saladier, mélanger délicatement les ingrédients de la garniture à la grecque (voir recette ci-dessous) avec la marinade réservée.

Au moment de la cuisson, préchauffer le four à 205 °C (400 °F).

Égoutter le poulet et jeter la marinade. Déposer les poitrines sur une plaque de cuisson tapissée de papier parchemin. Cuire au four de 12 à 15 minutes en retournant les poitrines à mi-cuisson, jusqu'à ce que l'intérieur de la chair du poulet ait perdu sa teinte rosée.

Si désiré, servir les poitrines avec la garniture à la grecque.

PAR PORTION	
Calories	281
Protéines	28 g
Matières grasses	16 g
Glucides	7 g
Fibres	1 g
Fer	1 mg
Calcium	35 mg
Sodium	69 mg

▼
Au total
378
calories

Idée pour accompagner

Garniture à la grecque

Par portion: 97 calories

Mélanger 100 g de feta émiettée avec 16 tomates raisins coupées en deux, 60 ml (¼ de tasse) d'olives noires et ¼ d'oignon rouge émincé.

Poulet ①
4 cuisses avec peau
coupées en deux

Sauce hoisin ②
45 ml (3 c. à soupe)

Lime ③
30 ml (2 c. à soupe)
de jus
+ 15 ml (1 c. à soupe)
de zestes

Gingembre ④
haché
15 ml (1 c. à soupe)

2 anis étoilés ⑤

PRÉVOIR AUSSI :
➤ **Sauce soya**
60 ml (¼ de tasse)
➤ **Miel**
45 ml (3 c. à soupe)

FACULTATIF :
➤ **Ail**
haché
10 ml (2 c. à thé)

Poulet miel et lime à la chinoise

Préparation : **15 minutes** • Marinage : **30 minutes** • Cuisson : **40 minutes** • Quantité : **4 portions**

Préparation

Avec les doigts, soulever délicatement la peau du poulet afin d'aider la marinade à pénétrer la chair.

Dans un sac hermétique, mélanger tous les ingrédients, à l'exception du poulet. Si désiré, incorporer l'ail. Ajouter le poulet dans le sac et laisser mariner au moins 30 minutes au frais, idéalement de 1 à 2 heures.

Au moment de la cuisson, préchauffer le four à 205 °C (400 °F).

Déposer les cuisses de poulet et la marinade dans un plat de cuisson, sans superposer les morceaux de viande. Cuire au four 40 minutes, en arrosant le poulet de marinade à mi-cuisson, jusqu'à ce que les morceaux de poulet soient dorés et croustillants et que l'intérieur de la chair ait perdu sa teinte rosée.

PAR PORTION	
Calories	320
Protéines	16 g
Matières grasses	19 g
Glucides	21 g
Fibres	1 g
Fer	1 mg
Calcium	24 mg
Sodium	952 mg

Au total
395
calories

Idée pour accompagner

Salade de chou asiatique

Par portion: 75 calories

Dans un saladier, mélanger 45 ml (3 c. à soupe) de vinaigrette japonaise (de type Wafu) avec 15 ml (1 c. à soupe) de gingembre haché et 30 ml (2 c. à soupe) de jus de lime. Ajouter 10 pois mange-tout, ¼ de chou rouge et 1 carotte émincés finement. Saler, poivrer et remuer.

Poulet ①
4 poitrines sans peau

12 tomates cerises ②
coupées en quatre

1 poivron vert ③
émincé

Vinaigre de vin rouge ④
30 ml (2 c. à soupe)

Paprika ⑤
15 ml (1 c. à soupe)

FACULTATIF:
➤ **Ail**
haché
10 ml (2 c. à thé)

PRÉVOIR AUSSI:
➤ **Huile d'olive**
30 ml (2 c. à soupe)

➤ **Origan**
15 ml (1 c. à soupe)
de feuilles

➤ 1 **oignon**
haché

➤ 1 **piment thaï**
haché finement

Escalopes de poulet à la portugaise

Préparation: **15 minutes** • Cuisson: **10 minutes** • Quantité: **4 portions**

Préparation

Trancher les poitrines de poulet en deux sur l'épaisseur afin de former des escalopes.

Dans une poêle, chauffer l'huile à feu moyen. Cuire les escalopes de 1 à 2 minutes de chaque côté.

Ajouter l'oignon et, si désiré, l'ail dans la poêle. Cuire de 1 à 2 minutes.

Ajouter les tomates cerises, le poivron, le vinaigre et le paprika. Si désiré, parsemer d'origan et de piment thaï. Couvrir et cuire de 5 à 6 minutes à feu doux-moyen.

PAR PORTION	
Calories	228
Protéines	29 g
Matières grasses	9 g
Glucides	7 g
Fibres	2 g
Fer	2 mg
Calcium	42 mg
Sodium	72 mg

Au total
352
calories

Idée pour accompagner

Riz basmati aux herbes salées

Par portion: 124 calories

Rincer 250 ml (1 tasse) de riz basmati à l'eau froide. Déposer dans une casserole avec 500 ml (2 tasses) de bouillon de légumes et 30 ml (2 c. à soupe) d'herbes salées. Porter à ébullition à feu moyen. Couvrir et cuire à feu doux de 18 à 20 minutes.

Poulet
4 poitrines sans peau

①

Fromage de chèvre crémeux
115 g

②

8 tomates séchées
émincées

③

Bébés épinards
250 ml (1 tasse)

④

Huile d'olive
15 ml (1 c. à soupe)

⑤

Poitrines de poulet farcies au chèvre et tomates séchées

Préparation : **15 minutes** • Cuisson : **12 minutes** • Quantité : **4 portions**

Préparation

Inciser les poitrines en deux sur l'épaisseur, sans les couper complètement. Farcir les poitrines de fromage de chèvre, de tomates séchées et de bébés épinards. Maintenir les poitrines fermées à l'aide de cure-dents.

Dans une poêle, chauffer l'huile à feu moyen. Cuire les poitrines de 12 à 15 minutes, en les retournant à mi-cuisson, jusqu'à ce que l'intérieur de la chair du poulet ait perdu sa teinte rosée.

PAR PORTION	
Calories	289
Protéines	33 g
Matières grasses	15 g
Glucides	3 g
Fibres	1 g
Fer	1 mg
Calcium	57 mg
Sodium	364 mg

Au total
352
calories

Idée pour accompagner

Sauce tomate

Par portion : 63 calories

Dans une casserole, chauffer 15 ml (1 c. à soupe) d'huile d'olive à feu moyen. Cuire 1 oignon haché et 2 gousses d'ail hachées de 1 à 2 minutes. Ajouter le contenu de 1 boîte de tomates en dés de 540 ml, 1 tige de thym et 1 feuille de laurier. Saler et poivrer. Couvrir et laisser mijoter de 8 à 10 minutes à feu moyen.

Noix de cajou
180 ml (¾ de tasse)

1

Lait de coco léger
1 boîte de 400 ml

2

Bouillon de poulet
500 ml (2 tasses)

3

Poulet
750 g (1 ⅔ lb) de cubes

4

Pâte de cari rouge
30 ml (2 c. à soupe)

5

FACULTATIF :

➤ **Ail**
haché
15 ml (1 c. à soupe)

PRÉVOIR AUSSI :

➤ **Huile de canola**
15 ml (1 c. à soupe)

➤ **1 oignon**
haché

➤ **Gingembre**
haché
15 ml (1 c. à soupe)

➤ **Curcuma**
5 ml (1 c. à thé)

Cari de poulet à l'indienne

Préparation : **15 minutes** • Trempage : **1 heure** • Cuisson : **15 minutes** • Quantité : **de 6 à 8 portions**

Préparation

Dans un bol, déposer les noix de cajou et verser le lait de coco. Laisser tremper 1 heure au frais.

À l'aide du robot culinaire, réduire en purée les noix de cajou avec le lait de coco et le bouillon de poulet. Mélanger jusqu'à l'obtention d'une préparation lisse.

Dans une casserole, chauffer l'huile à feu moyen. Cuire les cubes de poulet de 3 à 4 minutes.

Ajouter l'oignon et, si désiré, l'ail et le gingembre. Cuire de 1 à 2 minutes.

Ajouter la pâte de cari et, si désiré, le curcuma. Cuire 30 secondes en remuant afin que les arômes se libèrent.

Verser la préparation aux noix de cajou. Porter à ébullition. Couvrir et cuire de 10 à 12 minutes à feu doux-moyen.

PAR PORTION	
Calories	313
Protéines	27 g
Matières grasses	19 g
Glucides	10 g
Fibres	1 g
Fer	2 mg
Calcium	24 mg
Sodium	422 mg

Au total
371
calories

Idée pour accompagner

Riz basmati

Par portion : 58 calories

À l'aide d'une passoire fine, rincer 250 ml (1 tasse) de riz basmati sous l'eau froide. Bien égoutter. Dans une casserole, déposer le riz et verser 500 ml (2 tasses) de bouillon de poulet. Saler et poivrer. Couvrir et porter à ébullition à feu moyen. Cuire 18 minutes à feu doux. Laisser reposer 5 minutes, puis remuer.

Cidre ①
250 ml (1 tasse)

Miel ②
30 ml (2 c. à soupe)

Thym ③
haché
15 ml (1 c. à soupe)

Poulet ④
4 tournedos non bardés

Prosciutto ⑤
4 tranches

PRÉVOIR AUSSI :
➤ 1 **oignon**
haché
➤ **Huile d'olive**
7,5 ml (½ c. à soupe)

FACULTATIF :
➤ **Romarin**
haché
10 ml (2 c. à thé)
➤ **Ail**
haché
10 ml (2 c. à thé)

Tournedos de poulet bardés de prosciutto

Préparation : **15 minutes** • Marinage : **3 heures** • Cuisson : **12 minutes** • Quantité : **4 portions**

Préparation

Dans un bol, mélanger le cidre avec le miel, le thym, l'oignon et, si désiré, le romarin et l'ail. Verser dans un sac hermétique et ajouter les tournedos de poulet. Laisser mariner de 3 à 4 heures au frais, idéalement 8 heures.

Plier les tranches de prosciutto en deux ou en trois sur la longueur, puis les enrouler autour des tournedos. Fixer avec des cure-dents.

Au moment de la cuisson, préchauffer le four à 205 °C (400 °F).

Égoutter les tournedos et jeter la marinade.

Dans une poêle, chauffer l'huile à feu moyen. Saisir les tournedos 2 minutes de chaque côté.

Déposer les tournedos sur une plaque de cuisson tapissée de papier parchemin. Cuire au four de 12 à 15 minutes en retournant les tournedos à mi-cuisson, jusqu'à ce que l'intérieur de la chair du poulet ait perdu sa teinte rosée.

PAR PORTION	
Calories	303
Protéines	27 g
Matières grasses	13 g
Glucides	20 g
Fibres	1 g
Fer	1 mg
Calcium	46 mg
Sodium	847 mg

Au total
389
calories

Idée pour accompagner

Sauce au cidre

Par portion : 86 calories

Dans une casserole, chauffer 250 ml (1 tasse) de sauce demi-glace avec 80 ml (⅓ de tasse) de gelée de pommes de 3 à 4 minutes à feu doux-moyen. Saler et poivrer.

Poulet ①
4 poitrines sans peau

Pesto de roquette ②
45 ml (3 c. à soupe)

Échalotes sèches ③
émincées
60 ml (¼ de tasse)

Tomates séchées ④
émincées
60 ml (¼ de tasse)

Parmesan ⑤
80 ml (⅓ de tasse)
de copeaux

PRÉVOIR AUSSI :
➤ **Huile d'olive**
15 ml (1 c. à soupe)

Escalopes de poulet au pesto de roquette

Préparation : **15 minutes** • Cuisson : **6 minutes** • Quantité : **4 portions**

Préparation

Couper les poitrines en deux sur l'épaisseur, afin de former des escalopes. Badigeonner les deux côtés des escalopes avec le pesto de roquette.

Dans une poêle, chauffer l'huile à feu moyen. Cuire les escalopes 3 minutes de chaque côté.

Ajouter les échalotes et les tomates séchées. Cuire 1 minute.

Répartir la préparation dans les assiettes. Parsemer chacune des portions de copeaux de parmesan.

PAR PORTION	
Calories	293
Protéines	39 g
Matières grasses	13 g
Glucides	4 g
Fibres	1 g
Fer	2 mg
Calcium	126 mg
Sodium	310 mg

Au total
390
calories

Idée pour accompagner

Salade de tomates et croûtons

Par portion: 97 calories

Dans un saladier, mélanger 30 ml (2 c. à soupe) d'huile d'olive avec 30 ml (2 c. à soupe) d'eau, 15 ml (1 c. à soupe) de jus de citron, 30 ml (2 c. à soupe) de basilic émincé et 15 ml (1 c. à soupe) de zestes de citron. Ajouter 24 tomates cerises de couleurs variées coupées en quatre et 125 ml (½ tasse) de croûtons. Saler et poivrer. Remuer.

Vinaigre de riz ❶
30 ml (2 c. à soupe)

Gingembre ❷
haché
15 ml (1 c. à soupe)

1 poivron rouge ❸

8 à 10 asperges ❹

Poulet ❺
4 poitrines sans peau

PRÉVOIR AUSSI :
➤ **Sauce soya**
60 ml (¼ de tasse)
➤ **Miel**
45 ml (3 c. à soupe)
➤ **Huile de sésame**
non grillé
30 ml (2 c. à soupe)

FACULTATIF :
➤ **Ail**
haché
10 ml (2 c. à thé)
➤ **Châtaignes d'eau**
1 boîte de 227 g

«Sauté» de poulet au four

Préparation : **15 minutes** • Cuisson : **15 minutes** • Quantité : **4 portions**

Préparation

Préchauffer le four à 205 °C (400 °F).

Dans un bol, mélanger le vinaigre de riz avec le gingembre, la sauce soya, le miel, l'huile de sésame et, si désiré, l'ail.

Couper le poivron en lanières et les asperges en morceaux.

Déposer les légumes, le poulet et, si désiré, les châtaignes d'eau dans le bol. Remuer.

Sur une plaque de cuisson couverte de papier parchemin, répartir les légumes et le poulet sans les superposer. Cuire au four de 15 à 18 minutes, jusqu'à ce que l'intérieur de la chair du poulet ait perdu sa teinte rosée.

PAR PORTION	
Calories	309
Protéines	30 g
Matières grasses	9 g
Glucides	28 g
Fibres	2 g
Fer	1 mg
Calcium	23 mg
Sodium	986 mg

Au total
400
calories

Idée pour accompagner

Vermicelles à la coriandre

Par portion: 91 calories

Réhydrater 150 g de vermicelles de riz selon les indications de l'emballage. Égoutter. Dans une poêle, chauffer 80 ml (⅓ de tasse) de bouillon de poulet à feu moyen. Ajouter les vermicelles et 30 ml (2 c. à soupe) de coriandre émincée. Saler et poivrer. Réchauffer 2 minutes en remuant.

4 pommes de terre ①
pelées et tranchées

Fenouil ②
1 bulbe émincé

Poulet ③
4 poitrines sans peau

Thym ④
haché
15 ml (1 c. à soupe)

Tomates en dés ⑤
1 boîte de 540 ml

PRÉVOIR AUSSI :
➤ 1 **oignon**
émincé
➤ **Huile d'olive**
30 ml (2 c. à soupe)

FACULTATIF :
➤ **Ail**
2 gousses émincées
➤ **Origan**
haché
15 ml (1 c. à soupe)

Poitrines de poulet à l'italienne et légumes au four

Préparation : **15 minutes** • Cuisson : **30 minutes** • Quantité : **4 portions**

Préparation

Préchauffer le four à 205 °C (400 °F).

Dans un plat de cuisson de 33 cm x 23 cm (13 po x 9 po), étaler les tranches de pommes de terre. Ajouter le fenouil, l'oignon et, si désiré, l'ail. Déposer les poitrines sur les légumes, puis parsemer de thym et, si désiré, d'origan.

Couvrir de tomates en dés et arroser d'huile d'olive. Saler et poivrer.

Cuire au four de 30 à 35 minutes, jusqu'à ce que l'intérieur de la chair du poulet ait perdu sa teinte rosée.

PAR PORTION	
Calories	334
Protéines	32 g
Matières grasses	9 g
Glucides	32 g
Fibres	6 g
Fer	3 mg
Calcium	89 mg
Sodium	111 mg

Au total

380

calories

Idée pour accompagner

Salade aux radis et concombre

Par portion : 46 calories

Dans un saladier, mélanger 80 ml (⅓ de tasse) de vinaigrette aux tomates séchées avec 6 radis émincés, ¼ de concombre anglais émincé finement et 500 ml (2 tasses) de mesclun.

1 poivron rouge ①

Poulet ②
4 poitrines sans peau
d'environ 150 g
(⅓ de lb) chacune

Tamari ③
60 ml (¼ de tasse)

Lime ④
30 ml (2 c. à soupe)
de jus

Vinaigre de riz ⑤
30 ml (2 c. à soupe)

PRÉVOIR AUSSI :
➤ **1 oignon**
➤ **Huile de sésame**
non grillé
15 ml (1 c. à soupe)
➤ **Miel**
15 ml (1 c. à soupe)

FACULTATIF :
➤ **Ail**
haché
15 ml (1 c. à soupe)
➤ **Sauce sriracha**
5 ml (1 c. à thé)

Brochettes de poulet
à la marinade thaï

Préparation : **15 minutes** • Marinage : **2 heures** • Cuisson : **12 minutes** • Quantité : **4 portions**

Préparation

Tailler le poivron et l'oignon en cubes. Tailler le poulet en cubes de 2,5 cm (1 po).

Dans un sac hermétique, mélanger le tamari avec le jus de lime, le vinaigre de riz, l'huile de sésame, le miel et, si désiré, l'ail et la sauce sriracha. Ajouter les cubes de poulet et de légumes dans le sac. Laisser mariner 2 heures au frais, idéalement 4 heures.

Au moment de la cuisson, préchauffer le four à 205 °C (400 °F). Égoutter les cubes de poulet et de légumes, puis jeter la marinade.

Piquer les cubes de poulet, de poivron et d'oignon sur quatre brochettes, en les faisant alterner.

Déposer les brochettes sur une plaque de cuisson tapissée d'une feuille de papier d'aluminium. Cuire au four de 12 à 15 minutes, en retournant les brochettes à mi-cuisson, jusqu'à ce que l'intérieur de la chair du poulet ait perdu sa teinte rosée.

PAR PORTION	
Calories	250
Protéines	37 g
Matières grasses	6 g
Glucides	10 g
Fibres	1 g
Fer	1 mg
Calcium	23 mg
Sodium	1 131 mg

Au total
377
calories

Idée pour accompagner

Riz au citron et fines herbes

Par portion: 127 calories

Rincer 250 ml (1 tasse) de riz basmati à l'eau froide. Déposer dans une casserole avec 30 ml (2 c. à soupe) de zestes de citron, 1 oignon haché et 1 tige de thym. Saler et poivrer. Porter à ébullition, puis laisser mijoter de 18 à 20 minutes à feu doux. Incorporer 30 ml (2 c. à soupe) de persil haché et 30 ml (2 c. à soupe) d'estragon haché.

Céréales de maïs ①
de type Corn Flakes
750 ml (3 tasses)

Parmesan ②
râpé
80 ml (⅓ de tasse)

Yogourt nature 0 % ③
160 ml (⅔ de tasse)

Moutarde de Dijon ④
15 ml (1 c. à soupe)

Poulet ⑤
8 pilons sans peau

PRÉVOIR AUSSI :
➤ **Huile de canola**
à vaporiser

FACULTATIF :
➤ **Thym**
haché
10 ml (2 c. à thé)

Pilons de poulet croustillants sans friture

Préparation : **15 minutes** • Cuisson : **45 minutes** • Quantité : **4 portions (8 pilons)**

Préparation

Préchauffer le four à 190 °C (375 °F).

Dans un sac hermétique, déposer les céréales. À l'aide d'un rouleau à pâte, écraser légèrement les flocons. Dans le sac, ajouter le parmesan et, si désiré, le thym. Secouer et verser dans une assiette creuse.

Dans une autre assiette creuse, mélanger le yogourt avec la moutarde de Dijon. Saler et poivrer. Tremper les pilons dans le mélange au yogourt, puis enrober de céréales.

Déposer les pilons sur une plaque de cuisson tapissée de papier parchemin. Vaporiser d'huile de canola. Cuire au four de 45 à 50 minutes, jusqu'à ce que la chair se détache de l'os.

PAR PORTION	
Calories	300
Protéines	29 g
Matières grasses	11 g
Glucides	20 g
Fibres	1 g
Fer	4 mg
Calcium	206 mg
Sodium	443 mg

Au total
322
calories

Idée pour accompagner

**Trempette au tofu
ni vu, ni connu**

Par portion (30 ml – 2 c. à soupe) : 22 calories

À l'aide du mélangeur électrique, réduire en purée 300 g de tofu mou avec 1 jaune d'œuf, 80 ml (⅓ de tasse) de yogourt nature 0 %, 15 ml (1 c. à soupe) de zestes de citron, 45 ml (3 c. à soupe) de jus de citron, 15 ml (1 c. à soupe) de miel, 10 ml (2 c. à thé) d'ail haché et 5 ml (1 c. à thé) de paprika fumé. Donne 450 ml (environ 1 ¾ tasse). Se conserve de 3 à 4 jours au frais.

Nouilles de riz larges ①
200 g

Brocoli chinois ②
ou brocolini
1 botte coupée en
morceaux

12 pois mange-tout ③
coupés en morceaux

Poulet ④
2 poitrines sans peau
coupées en cubes

Sauce miel et ail ⑤
du commerce
125 ml (½ tasse)

PRÉVOIR AUSSI :
➤ **Huile de sésame**
non grillé
15 ml (1 c. à soupe)

Pad sew au poulet

Préparation : **15 minutes** • Cuisson : **10 minutes** • Quantité : **4 portions**

Préparation

Réhydrater les nouilles de riz selon les indications de l'emballage. Égoutter.

Dans une poêle ou dans un wok, chauffer l'huile de sésame à feu moyen. Cuire le brocoli chinois et les pois mange-tout de 2 à 3 minutes. Déposer dans une assiette.

Dans la même poêle, faire dorer les cubes de poulet de 3 à 4 minutes en remuant.

Si désiré, ajouter l'ail et les oignons verts. Cuire 1 minute en remuant.

Ajouter la sauce, les nouilles, le brocoli chinois et les pois mange-tout. Réchauffer 1 minute en remuant.

PAR PORTION	
Calories	398
Protéines	18 g
Matières grasses	5 g
Glucides	71 g
Fibres	3 g
Fer	2 mg
Calcium	61 mg
Sodium	254 mg

Version minceur

Sauce miel et ail

Mélanger 60 ml (¼ de tasse) de sauce aux huîtres avec 60 ml (¼ de tasse) de sauce soya, 30 ml (2 c. à soupe) de miel, 30 ml (2 c. à soupe) de vinaigre de riz et 15 ml (1 c. à soupe) d'ail haché.

551 CALORIES

Du commerce

pour 180 ml
(¾ de tasse)

221 CALORIES

Maison

FACULTATIF :
➤ **Ail**
2 gousses émincées

➤ 2 **oignons verts**
émincés

Poulet
entier
1,5 kg (environ 3 lb)

①

Moutarde de Dijon
15 ml (1 c. à soupe)

②

12 pommes de terre grelots
coupées en deux

③

2 carottes
coupées en cubes

④

16 tomates cerises

⑤

PRÉVOIR AUSSI :
➤ **Sirop d'érable**
80 ml (⅓ de tasse)
➤ **Huile d'olive**
30 ml (2 c. à soupe)
➤ **Sauce soya**
30 ml (2 c. à soupe)

FACULTATIF :
➤ **Ail**
8 gousses entières pelées
➤ **½ oignon rouge**
coupé en morceaux

Casserole de poulet aux légumes caramélisés

Préparation : **15 minutes** • Cuisson : **43 minutes** • Quantité : **4 portions**

Préparation

Préchauffer le four à 205 °C (400 °F).

Couper le poulet en huit morceaux.

Dans un bol, fouetter la moutarde de Dijon avec le sirop d'érable, l'huile d'olive et la sauce soya. Saler et poivrer.

Ajouter les morceaux de poulet, les pommes de terre grelots, les carottes et, si désiré, les gousses d'ail et l'oignon rouge dans le bol. Remuer pour bien enrober les aliments de sauce.

Déposer le poulet et les légumes sur une plaque de cuisson tapissée d'une feuille de papier d'aluminium en prenant soin de ne pas superposer les morceaux de poulet. Cuire au four de 35 à 40 minutes.

Ajouter les tomates cerises et poursuivre la cuisson de 8 à 10 minutes.

PAR PORTION	
Calories	272
Protéines	27 g
Matières grasses	9 g
Glucides	21 g
Fibres	2 g
Fer	2 mg
Calcium	76 mg
Sodium	460 mg

Au total
358
calories

Idée pour accompagner

Salade colorée

Par portion : 86 calories

Dans un saladier, mélanger 30 ml (2 c. à soupe) d'huile d'olive avec 30 ml (2 c. à soupe) d'eau, 15 ml (1 c. à soupe) de jus de citron, 15 ml (1 c. à soupe) de moutarde à l'ancienne et 30 ml (2 c. à soupe) de parmesan râpé. Saler et poivrer. Ajouter 1 radicchio déchiqueté, ¼ d'oignon rouge émincé et 1 cœur de laitue romaine déchiqueté. Remuer.

Poulet
4 poitrines sans peau ➊

**Riz blanc
à grains longs** ➋
250 ml (1 tasse)

Lait de coco léger ➌
250 ml (1 tasse)

Ananas ➍
en dés avec le jus
⅔ de 1 boîte de 398 ml

**Mélange de légumes
frais pour sauce
à spaghetti** ➎
500 ml (2 tasses)

FACULTATIF :
➤ **Pâte de cari rouge**
30 ml (2 c. à soupe)

➤ **Amandes tranchées**
rôties
60 ml (¼ de tasse)

PRÉVOIR AUSSI :
➤ **Huile de canola**
15 ml (1 c. à soupe)

Poulet et riz à la noix de coco

Préparation : **15 minutes** • Cuisson : **25 minutes** • Quantité : **de 4 à 6 portions**

Préparation

Préchauffer le four à 190 °C (375 °F).

Dans une casserole, chauffer l'huile à feu moyen. Faire dorer les poitrines de poulet de 1 à 2 minutes de chaque côté. Déposer dans une assiette.

Si désiré, dans la même casserole, ajouter la pâte de cari et cuire 30 secondes en remuant afin que les arômes se libèrent.

Ajouter le riz, le lait de coco et les dés d'ananas avec le jus. Remuer et porter à ébullition.

Incorporer les légumes, puis remettre les poitrines dans la casserole. Couvrir et cuire au four de 25 à 30 minutes.

Au moment de servir, si désiré, parsemer d'amandes rôties.

PAR PORTION	
Calories	343
Protéines	26 g
Matières grasses	7 g
Glucides	43 g
Fibres	8 g
Fer	2 mg
Calcium	70 mg
Sodium	407 mg

Au total
391
calories

Idée pour accompagner

Salade fraîcheur à l'avocat

Par portion : 48 calories

Dans un saladier, mélanger 60 ml (¼ de tasse) de vinaigrette miel et moutarde faible en calories avec 30 ml (2 c. à soupe) de jus de lime. Saler et poivrer. Ajouter ½ oignon rouge émincé, 12 tomates cerises coupées en deux, 1 avocat coupé en quartiers, 375 ml (1 ½ tasse) de mesclun et 45 ml (3 c. à soupe) de feuilles de coriandre. Remuer.

Porc délectable

La réputation de cette savoureuse viande n'est plus à faire, puisqu'elle est appréciée autant pour sa valeur nutritive que pour son impressionnante polyvalence. Profitez des meilleures découpes de porc pour concocter ces recettes géniales qui vous feront saliver!

Porc haché maigre ❶
450 g (1 lb)

Chapelure nature ❷
60 ml (¼ de tasse)

Poivre de la Jamaïque ❸
(quatre-épices)
moulu
1,25 ml (¼ de c. à thé)

Bouillon de poulet ❹
500 ml (2 tasses)

Mélange laitier
pour cuisson 5 % ❺
80 ml (⅓ de tasse)

PRÉVOIR AUSSI :
➤ 1 **œuf**
battu
➤ **Lait**
30 ml (2 c. à soupe)
➤ **Huile de canola**
7,5 ml (½ c. à soupe)
➤ **Farine**
45 ml (3 c. à soupe)

FACULTATIF :
➤ 8 à 10 **champignons**
émincés

Ragoût de boulettes à la suédoise

Préparation : **15 minutes** • Cuisson : **15 minutes** • Quantité : **4 portions**

Préparation

Dans un bol, mélanger le porc haché avec la chapelure, le poivre de la Jamaïque, l'œuf battu et le lait. Façonner de 18 à 20 boulettes en utilisant environ 30 ml (2 c. à soupe) de préparation pour chacune d'elles.

Dans une casserole, chauffer l'huile à feu moyen. Faire dorer les boulettes de 4 à 5 minutes, en procédant par petites quantités. Réserver dans une assiette.

Dans la même poêle, cuire la farine de 1 à 2 minutes en remuant. Verser le bouillon et le mélange laitier. Porter à ébullition en raclant le fond de la poêle à l'aide d'une cuillère en bois afin de détacher les sucs de cuisson.

Ajouter les boulettes et, si désiré, les champignons dans la sauce. Cuire de 5 à 6 minutes à feu doux-moyen.

PAR PORTION	
Calories	369
Protéines	27 g
Matières grasses	22 g
Glucides	13 g
Fibres	1 g
Fer	2 mg
Calcium	51 mg
Sodium	365 mg

Au total
392
calories

Idée pour accompagner

Légumes colorés à la vapeur

Par portion: 23 calories

Déposer une marguerite dans une casserole et verser de l'eau jusqu'à hauteur de la marguerite. Déposer 2 carottes pelées et coupées en deux sur la longueur dans la marguerite. Couvrir et porter à ébullition. Cuire 3 minutes. Ajouter 150 g (⅓ de lb) de haricots verts et jaunes et poursuivre la cuisson de 4 à 5 minutes. Saler et poivrer.

Porc ①
755 g (1 ⅔ lb) de filets

Cassonade ②
30 ml (2 c. à soupe)

Coriandre ③
15 ml (1 c. à soupe)
de grains concassés

Cumin ④
5 ml (1 c. à thé)

Poivre de la Jamaïque ⑤
(quatre-épices)
2,5 ml (½ c. à thé)

Filets de porc à la marinade sèche

Préparation : **15 minutes** • Cuisson : **15 minutes** • Quantité : **4 portions**

Préparation

Préchauffer le four à 205 °C (400 °F). Parer les filets de porc en retirant la membrane blanche.

Préparer la marinade sèche. Dans un bol, mélanger la cassonade avec les épices. Frotter les filets de porc avec le mélange et presser afin qu'il adhère bien à la chair.

Déposer les filets dans un plat de cuisson. Cuire au four de 15 à 18 minutes, en retournant les filets à mi-cuisson.

Déposer les filets dans une assiette. Couvrir d'une feuille de papier d'aluminium et laisser reposer de 6 à 8 minutes avant de trancher.

PAR PORTION	
Calories	226
Protéines	42 g
Matières grasses	3 g
Glucides	6 g
Fibres	1 g
Fer	3 mg
Calcium	31 mg
Sodium	254 mg

Au total
376
calories

Idée pour accompagner

Salade croquante aux pommes et endives

Par portion: 150 calories

Dans un saladier, mélanger 45 ml (3 c. à soupe) d'huile d'olive avec 15 ml (1 c. à soupe) de jus de citron. Saler et poivrer. Détacher les feuilles de 3 endives. Déposer dans le saladier avec 1 oignon émincé, 2 pommes vertes émincées et de 6 à 8 feuilles de menthe. Remuer.

Côtelettes de porc aux épices

Préparation : **15 minutes** • Cuisson : **10 minutes** • Quantité : **4 portions**

Préparation

Préchauffer le four à 180°C (350°F). Parer les côtelettes de porc en retirant l'excédent de gras.

Dans un bol, mélanger la cassonade avec les épices. Saupoudrer les deux côtés des côtelettes de porc avec le mélange et presser légèrement afin que les épices adhèrent bien à la chair.

Dans une poêle allant au four, chauffer l'huile à feu moyen. Cuire les côtelettes de 1 à 2 minutes de chaque côté.

Compléter la cuisson au four de 8 à 10 minutes.

PAR PORTION	
Calories	213
Protéines	28 g
Matières grasses	10 g
Glucides	3 g
Fibres	0 g
Fer	1 mg
Calcium	23 mg
Sodium	70 mg

Au total
381
calories

Porc ❶
4 côtelettes sans os de 150 g (⅓ de lb) chacune et de 2,5 cm (1 po) d'épaisseur

Cassonade ❷
15 ml (1 c. à soupe)

Cumin ❸
2,5 ml (½ c. à thé) de grains

Poudre d'ail ❹
2,5 ml (½ c. à thé)

Poudre d'oignons ❺
2,5 ml (½ c. à thé)

Idée pour accompagner

Légumes rôtis à l'italienne

Par portion : 168 calories

Peler et couper en cubes 400 g (environ 1 lb) de pommes de terre. Déposer sur une plaque de cuisson et arroser de 15 ml (1 c. à soupe) d'huile d'olive. Saler et poivrer, puis remuer. Cuire au four 20 minutes à 180°C (350°F). Dans un bol, mélanger 1 poivron rouge avec 1 courgette et ½ oignon rouge coupés en cubes. Ajouter 2 gousses d'ail émincées et 15 ml (1 c. à soupe) d'huile d'olive. Déposer les légumes sur la plaque et poursuivre la cuisson au four de 8 à 10 minutes. Parsemer de 30 ml (2 c. à soupe) de basilic émincé.

PRÉVOIR AUSSI :
➤ **Huile d'olive**
15 ml (1 c. à soupe)

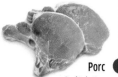

Porc ①
6 côtelettes
de longe sans os

1 poivron rouge ②
émincé

Brocoli ③
coupé en petits bouquets
375 ml (1 ½ tasse)

Sauce douce ④
aux piments
de type A Taste of Thaï
125 ml (½ tasse)

Mandarines ⑤
égouttées
1 boîte de 284 ml

PRÉVOIR AUSSI :
➤ **Huile de sésame**
non grillé
15 ml (1 c. à soupe)

➤ **Ail**
haché
10 ml (2 c. à thé)

➤ **Sauce soya**
60 ml (¼ de tasse)

FACULTATIF :
➤ **½ oignon rouge**
émincé

➤ **Gingembre**
haché
15 ml (1 c. à soupe)

Porc aigre-doux aux mandarines

Préparation : **15 minutes** • Cuisson : **10 minutes** • Quantité : **4 portions**

Préparation

Couper les côtelettes en lanières.

Dans une poêle, chauffer l'huile de sésame à feu moyen. Cuire les lanières de porc de 2 à 3 minutes de chaque côté. Déposer dans une assiette.

Dans la même poêle, cuire le poivron rouge, le brocoli et, si désiré, l'oignon rouge de 2 à 3 minutes.

Ajouter l'ail et, si désiré, le gingembre. Cuire 1 minute.

Remettre le porc dans la poêle. Verser la sauce aux piments et la sauce soya. Remuer, puis ajouter les mandarines. Cuire de 1 à 2 minutes.

PAR PORTION	
Calories	324
Protéines	34 g
Matières grasses	10 g
Glucides	23 g
Fibres	2 g
Fer	2 mg
Calcium	53 mg
Sodium	1 289 mg

Au total
398
calories

Idée pour accompagner

Riz basmati aux oignons verts

Par portion : 74 calories

Rincer 125 ml (½ tasse) de riz basmati à l'eau froide. Égoutter. Dans une casserole, faire fondre 15 ml (1 c. à soupe) de beurre léger à feu moyen. Ajouter le riz basmati, 2 oignons verts hachés et 250 ml (1 tasse) de bouillon de légumes. Saler et poivrer. Porter à ébullition, puis couvrir et cuire à feu doux-moyen de 18 à 20 minutes.

Bière blonde ❶
1 bouteille de 355 ml

Pamplemousse ❷
80 ml (⅓ de tasse)
de jus

Épices cajun ❸
45 ml (3 c. à soupe)

Moutarde de Dijon ❹
80 ml (⅓ de tasse)

Porc ❺
2 filets d'environ 450 g
(1 lb) chacun

PRÉVOIR AUSSI :
➤ **Huile d'olive**
15 ml (1 c. à soupe)

➤ **Cassonade**
80 ml (⅓ de tasse)

➤ **Ketchup**
125 ml (½ tasse)

➤ **Sauce Worcestershire**
45 ml (3 c. à soupe)

FACULTATIF :
➤ 2 **oignons**
émincés

Filets mignons de porc, style ribs

Préparation : **15 minutes** • Cuisson : **45 minutes** • Quantité : **6 portions**

Préparation

Préparer la sauce. Dans une casserole, chauffer la moitié de l'huile d'olive à feu doux. Si désiré, faire revenir les oignons 5 minutes. Ajouter la cassonade et remuer jusqu'à ce qu'elle soit fondue.

Incorporer la bière, le jus de pamplemousse, les épices cajun, le ketchup et la sauce Worcestershire. Laisser mijoter 25 minutes à feu doux-moyen.

Incorporer la moutarde de Dijon. Transférer la sauce dans le contenant du mélangeur. Mélanger jusqu'à l'obtention d'une sauce homogène. Laisser refroidir au réfrigérateur.

Badigeonner les filets de porc de sauce.

Dans une poêle, faire chauffer le reste de l'huile à feu moyen. Cuire les filets de 7 à 8 minutes de chaque côté. Retirer les filets du feu. Couvrir d'une feuille de papier d'aluminium et laisser reposer 7 minutes.

Tailler les filets en médaillons de 5 cm (2 po) d'épaisseur.

Si désiré, verser le reste de la sauce dans de petits ramequins.

PAR PORTION	
Calories	293
Protéines	35 g
Matières grasses	5 g
Glucides	21 g
Fibres	1 g
Fer	3 mg
Calcium	39 mg
Sodium	668 mg

Au total
379
calories

Idée pour accompagner

Papillote de pommes de terre grelots et choux de Bruxelles

Par portion: 86 calories

Dans un bol, mélanger 4 choux de Bruxelles avec 12 pommes de terre grelots rouges, 15 ml (1 c. à soupe) d'ail haché et 45 ml (3 c. à soupe) d'huile d'olive. Déposer sur une plaque de cuisson tapissée d'une feuille de papier parchemin. Cuire au four de 20 à 25 minutes à 180 °C (350 °F), jusqu'à ce que les pommes de terre soient cuites. Retirer du four, couper les pommes de terre en deux et effeuiller les choux de Bruxelles.

Orange
60 ml (¼ de tasse)
de jus **1**

Moutarde à l'ancienne
15 ml (1 c. à soupe) **2**

Moutarde de Dijon
10 ml (2 c. à thé) **3**

**Assaisonnements
pour porc**
15 ml (1 c. à soupe) **4**

Porc
4 côtelettes avec ou
sans os de 2 cm
(¾ de po) d'épaisseur **5**

PRÉVOIR AUSSI :
▶ **Huile d'olive**
7,5 ml (½ c. à soupe)

Côtelettes de porc orange et moutarde

Préparation : **15 minutes** • Cuisson : **8 minutes** • Quantité : **4 portions**

Préparation

Dans un bol, mélanger le jus d'orange avec la moutarde à l'ancienne, la moutarde de Dijon et les assaisonnements pour porc.

Badigeonner les côtelettes de porc de sauce.

Dans une poêle antiadhésive, chauffer l'huile à feu moyen. Cuire les côtelettes de 4 à 5 minutes de chaque côté, en les badigeonnant de sauce en cours de cuisson.

PAR PORTION	
Calories	164
Protéines	21 g
Matières grasses	6 g
Glucides	6 g
Fibres	0,2 g
Fer	1 mg
Calcium	21 mg
Sodium	928 mg

Au total

281
calories

Idée pour accompagner

Haricots verts et jaunes aux fines herbes

Par portion: 117 calories

Mélanger 30 ml (2 c. à soupe) d'huile d'olive avec 15 ml (1 c. à soupe) de beurre léger fondu, ½ oignon rouge émincé, 500 g (environ 1 lb) de haricots verts et jaunes, 1 tige de thym et 1 tige de romarin. Saler et poivrer. Déposer les légumes sur une grande feuille de papier d'aluminium. Plier la feuille de manière à former une papillote hermétique. Cuire au four de 8 à 10 minutes à 180°C (350°F).

**Riz blanc
à cuisson rapide**
125 ml (½ tasse) ①

1 poivron vert ②

2 tomates ③

Porc haché maigre ④
400 g (environ 1 lb)

**Sauce au cari rouge
et noix de coco** ⑤
du commerce
160 ml (⅔ de tasse)

PRÉVOIR AUSSI :
➤ **Huile de canola**
7,5 ml (½ c. à soupe)

FACULTATIF :
➤ **½ oignon rouge**
➤ **2 oignons verts**
hachés

Sauté de porc au cari rouge

Préparation : **12 minutes** • Cuisson : **8 minutes** • Quantité : **4 portions**

Préparation

Cuire le riz selon le mode de préparation indiqué sur l'emballage.

Émincer le poivron vert et, si désiré, l'oignon rouge. Couper les tomates en dés.

Dans une grande poêle ou dans un wok, chauffer l'huile à feu moyen-élevé. Cuire le porc haché de 4 à 5 minutes en l'égrainant à l'aide d'une cuillère en bois, jusqu'à ce que le porc ait perdu sa teinte rosée.

Ajouter le poivron vert et, si désiré, l'oignon rouge. Réchauffer 2 minutes en remuant.

Ajouter la sauce au cari rouge et les tomates. Cuire de 2 à 3 minutes jusqu'à évaporation complète du liquide.

Répartir le riz et le sauté de porc dans les assiettes. Si désiré, garnir d'oignons verts.

PAR PORTION	
Calories	378
Protéines	22 g
Matières grasses	19 g
Glucides	28 g
Fibres	2 g
Fer	2 mg
Calcium	38 mg
Sodium	292 mg

Version minceur

Sauce au cari rouge et noix de coco

Dans un bol, mélanger 125 ml (½ tasse) de bouillon de poulet avec 30 ml (2 c. à soupe) de jus de lime, 30 ml (2 c. à soupe) de cassonade, 15 ml (1 c. à soupe) de sauce de poisson, 15 ml (1 c. à soupe) d'ail haché, 15 ml (1 c. à soupe) de gingembre haché et 30 ml (2 c. à soupe) de pâte de cari rouge.

304 CALORIES
Du commerce

➤ Pour 200 ml
(environ ¾ de tasse)

184 CALORIES
Maison

Porc ①
650 g (environ 1 ½ lb)
de filets

Gelée de pommes ②
250 ml (1 tasse)

Orange ③
80 ml (⅓ de tasse)
de jus

Vinaigre de riz ④
45 ml (3 c. à soupe)

Gingembre ⑤
haché
15 ml (1 c. à soupe)

PRÉVOIR AUSSI :
➤ **Sauce soya**
60 ml (¼ de tasse)
➤ **Huile de canola**
15 ml (1 c. à soupe)
➤ **Fécule de maïs**
10 ml (2 c. à thé)

FACULTATIF :
➤ **Ail**
haché
15 ml (1 c. à soupe)
➤ **Coriandre**
15 ml (1 c. à soupe)
de grains

Filet de porc caramélisé
Préparation : **15 minutes** • Marinage : **2 heures** • Cuisson : **20 minutes** • Quantité : **6 portions**

Préparation

Parer le filet de porc en retirant la membrane blanche.

Mélanger la gelée de pommes avec le jus d'orange, le vinaigre de riz, le gingembre, la sauce soya et, si désiré, l'ail et les grains de coriandre. Transférer le tiers de la marinade dans un sac hermétique et réserver le reste au frais. Ajouter le filet de porc dans le sac. Laisser mariner de 2 à 4 heures au frais.

Au moment de la cuisson, préchauffer le four à 205 °C (400 °F). Égoutter le filet de porc et jeter la marinade.

Dans une poêle allant au four, chauffer l'huile à feu moyen. Saisir le filet de 2 à 3 minutes, puis cuire au four 18 minutes pour une cuisson rosée.

Régler le four à la position « gril » (*broil*). Prolonger la cuisson de 1 à 2 minutes, jusqu'à ce que la chair du porc soit caramélisée.

Déposer le filet sur une planche à découper et couvrir d'une feuille de papier d'aluminium, sans serrer. Laisser reposer de 6 à 8 minutes avant de trancher.

Verser la marinade réservée dans une casserole. Ajouter la fécule de maïs et remuer pour la délayer. Porter à ébullition à feu moyen en remuant jusqu'à épaississement. Servir avec le filet.

Idée pour accompagner

Nouilles au sésame

Par portion: 42 calories

Préparer 1 paquet de pâtes au tofu (de type Shirataki) de 226 g selon les indications de l'emballage. Dans une poêle, chauffer 15 ml (1 c. à soupe) d'huile de canola à feu moyen. Cuire 2 oignons verts émincés, 1 gousse d'ail hachée et 1 carotte coupée en julienne de 2 à 3 minutes. Ajouter les nouilles et faire sauter 1 minute. Incorporer 15 ml (1 c. à soupe) de graines de sésame. Saler et poivrer.

PAR PORTION	
Calories	298
Protéines	25 g
Matières grasses	4 g
Glucides	40 g
Fibres	1 g
Fer	2 mg
Calcium	19 mg
Sodium	673 mg

Au total
340
calories

Porc haché maigre ❶
450 g (1 lb)

**Flocons d'avoine
à cuisson rapide** ❷
45 ml (3 c. à soupe)

Sirop d'érable ❸
125 ml (½ tasse)

Vinaigre de riz ❹
30 ml (2 c. à soupe)

Sauce aux huîtres ❺
30 ml (2 c. à soupe)

PRÉVOIR AUSSI :
➤ **Sauce soya**
45 ml (3 c. à soupe)

➤ **1 œuf**
battu

➤ **Huile de sésame**
non grillé
15 ml (1 c. à soupe)

FACULTATIF :
➤ **Gingembre**
haché
15 ml (1 c. à soupe)

➤ **Graines de sésame**
15 ml (1 c. à soupe)

Boulettes glacées au sirop d'érable

Préparation : **15 minutes** • Cuisson : **15 minutes** • Quantité : **6 portions**

Préparation

Préchauffer le four à 205 °C (400 °F).

Dans un bol, mélanger le porc haché avec les flocons d'avoine, 15 ml (1 c. à soupe) de sauce soya et l'œuf battu. Façonner 16 boulettes en utilisant environ 30 ml (2 c. à soupe) de préparation pour chacune d'elles. Réserver au frais.

Préparer la sauce. Dans un bol, mélanger le sirop d'érable avec le vinaigre de riz, la sauce aux huîtres, le reste de la sauce soya et, si désiré, le gingembre.

Dans une poêle allant au four, chauffer l'huile de sésame à feu moyen. Faire dorer les boulettes de 2 à 3 minutes.

Verser la sauce et remuer. Terminer la cuisson au four de 8 à 10 minutes, jusqu'à ce que les boulettes soient légèrement caramélisées.

Retirer du four et, si désiré, parsemer de graines de sésame.

PAR PORTION	
Calories	316
Protéines	17 g
Matières grasses	16 g
Glucides	26 g
Fibres	1 g
Fer	2 mg
Calcium	60 mg
Sodium	684 mg

Au total
398
calories

Idée pour accompagner

Riz basmati carotte et lime

Par portion: 82 calories

Rincer 250 ml (1 tasse) de riz basmati sous l'eau froide. Égoutter. Dans une casserole, déposer le riz avec 1 carotte rapée, 15 ml (1 c. à soupe) de zestes de lime et 500 ml (2 tasses) de bouillon de poulet. Porter à ébullition à feu moyen. Couvrir et cuire de 18 à 20 minutes à feu doux-moyen. Retirer du feu et laisser reposer 5 minutes.

Porc ①
605 g (1 ⅓ lb) de filets

Bouillon de poulet ②
sans sel ajouté
80 ml (⅓ de tasse)

Orange ③
60 ml (¼ de tasse)
de jus

Marmelade au ④
gingembre
45 ml (3 c. à soupe)

Lime ⑤
30 ml (2 c. à soupe)
de jus

PRÉVOIR AUSSI :
➤ **Huile d'olive**
15 ml (1 c. à soupe)

FACULTATIF :
➤ 2 **anis étoilés**

Médaillons de porc aux agrumes

Préparation : **15 minutes** • Cuisson : **8 minutes** • Quantité : **4 portions**

Préparation

Parer le filet de porc en retirant la membrane blanche. Trancher le filet afin d'obtenir 8 médaillons.

Préparer la sauce. Dans un bol, mélanger le bouillon de poulet avec le jus d'orange, la marmelade, le jus de lime et, si désiré, l'anis étoilé.

Dans une poêle, chauffer l'huile à feu moyen. Cuire les médaillons de 2 à 3 minutes de chaque côté, en prenant soin de conserver la chair rosée. Transférer dans une assiette et couvrir d'une feuille de papier d'aluminium.

Au besoin, retirer l'excédent de gras de la poêle. Verser la sauce dans la poêle et porter à ébullition. Cuire en remuant 2 minutes à feu doux-moyen, jusqu'à l'obtention d'une consistance sirupeuse. Servir avec les médaillons.

PAR PORTION	
Calories	241
Protéines	34 g
Matières grasses	6 g
Glucides	13 g
Fibres	0 g
Fer	2 mg
Calcium	21 mg
Sodium	96 mg

Au total
347
calories

Idée pour accompagner

Salade de fenouil au miel

Par portion: 106 calories

Émincer 1 bulbe de fenouil et 2 carottes. Déposer dans un bol et mélanger avec 30 ml (2 c. à soupe) d'huile d'olive, 15 ml (1 c. à soupe) de jus de citron et 15 ml (1 c. à soupe) de miel. Saler et poivrer. Si désiré, ajouter quelques brins de feuillage du fenouil hachés finement.

Nouilles asiatiques ①
1 paquet de 300 g

Porc ②
4 côtelettes sans os

**Sauce noix de coco
et arachides
pour cuisson** ③
180 ml (¾ de tasse)

2 carottes ④
taillées en julienne

Brocoli ⑤
taillé en petits
bouquets
250 ml (1 tasse)

FACULTATIF :
➤ **Ail**
haché
15 ml (1 c. à soupe)

➤ **Gingembre**
haché
15 ml (1 c. à soupe)

➤ **2 oignons verts**
émincés

PRÉVOIR AUSSI :
➤ **Huile de sésame**
non grillé
7,5 ml (½ c. à soupe)

Nouilles épicées au porc, sauce aux arachides

Préparation : **15 minutes** • Cuisson : **10 minutes** • Quantité : **6 portions**

Préparation

Dans une casserole d'eau bouillante salée, cuire les nouilles asiatiques *al dente*. Égoutter.

Émincer les côtelettes de porc.

Dans une poêle antiadhésive, chauffer l'huile à feu moyen. Cuire les lanières de porc de 2 à 3 minutes.

Si désiré, ajouter l'ail et le gingembre. Cuire 1 minute en remuant.

Verser la sauce pour cuisson et porter à ébullition.

Ajouter les carottes, le brocoli, les nouilles asiatiques et, si désiré, les oignons verts. Réchauffer de 1 à 2 minutes.

Idée pour accompagner

Julienne de carottes, panais et haricots verts

Par portion: 43 calories

Tailler en julienne 2 carottes et 2 panais. Émincer 200 g (environ ½ lb) de haricots verts. Déposer les carottes, les panais, les haricots, 1 oignon haché et 1 gousse d'ail hachée sur une feuille de papier d'aluminium. Replier le papier de manière à former une papillote hermétique. Cuire au four de 8 à 10 minutes à 180 °C (350 °F). Incorporer 15 ml (1 c. à soupe) d'estragon haché. Saler et poivrer.

PAR PORTION	
Calories	348
Protéines	23 g
Matières grasses	9 g
Glucides	43 g
Fibres	4 g
Fer	1 mg
Calcium	34 mg
Sodium	431 mg

Au total
391
calories

Porc ❶
4 côtelettes désossées

Chapelure panko ❷
180 ml (¾ de tasse)

Parmesan ❸
râpé
80 ml (⅓ de tasse)

Romarin ❹
haché
5 ml (1 c. à thé)

Citron ❺
15 ml (1 c. à soupe)
de zestes

PRÉVOIR AUSSI :
➤ **Farine**
80 ml (⅓ de tasse)
➤ **1 œuf**
➤ **Huile d'olive**
15 ml (1 c. à soupe)

Côtelettes en croûte de panko et parmesan

Préparation : **15 minutes** • Cuisson : **6 minutes** • Quantité : **4 portions**

Préparation

Parer les côtelettes en retirant l'excédent de gras.

Préparer trois assiettes creuses. Dans la première, verser la farine. Dans la deuxième, battre l'œuf. Dans la troisième, mélanger la chapelure panko avec le parmesan, le romarin et les zestes de citron.

Fariner les côtelettes, les tremper dans l'œuf battu, puis les enrober du mélange de chapelure. Presser légèrement sur l'enrobage afin qu'il adhère bien à la chair.

Dans une poêle, chauffer l'huile à feu moyen. Cuire les côtelettes de 3 à 5 minutes de chaque côté.

PAR PORTION	
Calories	286
Protéines	28 g
Matières grasses	11 g
Glucides	17 g
Fibres	1 g
Fer	2 mg
Calcium	122 mg
Sodium	214 mg

Au total
387
calories

Idée pour accompagner

Salade de pois mange-tout et raisins

Par portion: 101 calories

Dans un saladier, mélanger 30 ml (2 c. à soupe) d'huile d'olive avec 30 ml (2 c. à soupe) d'eau, 15 ml (1 c. à soupe) de moutarde à l'ancienne, 30 ml (2 c. à soupe) de jus de citron et 30 ml (2 c. à soupe) de ciboulette hachée. Saler et poivrer. Ajouter 20 pois mange-tout coupés en lanières et 250 ml (1 tasse) de raisins rouges coupés en deux. Remuer.

Porc ❶
650 g (environ 1 ½ lb)
de filets

Sirop d'érable ❷
60 ml (¼ de tasse)

Moutarde à l'ancienne ❸
45 ml (3 c. à soupe)

1 citron ❹
jus

Vin blanc ❺
125 ml (½ tasse)

PRÉVOIR AUSSI :
➤ **Huile de canola**
15 ml (1 c. à soupe)

➤ **Fécule de maïs**
10 ml (2 c. à thé)

FACULTATIF :
➤ **Ail**
1 gousse émincée

➤ **½ oignon rouge**
émincé

Filets de porc érable et moutarde

Préparation : **15 minutes** • Marinage : **2 heures** • Cuisson : **15 minutes** • Quantité : **4 portions**

Préparation

Parer le filet de porc en retirant la membrane blanche. Tailler la chair en cubes.

Dans un bol, mélanger la moitié du sirop d'érable avec 15 ml (1 c. à soupe) de moutarde, le jus de citron et, si désiré, l'ail. Verser dans un sac hermétique et ajouter les cubes de porc. Réfrigérer de 2 à 3 heures.

Dans une poêle, chauffer l'huile à feu moyen. Faire dorer les cubes de porc et, si désiré, l'oignon rouge. Transférer dans une assiette et couvrir d'une feuille de papier d'aluminium.

Dans un bol, mélanger le vin blanc avec le reste de la moutarde, le reste du sirop d'érable et la fécule de maïs. Verser dans la poêle et chauffer 4 minutes à feu doux, jusqu'à ce que la sauce réduise un peu.

Ajouter le porc et, si désiré, l'oignon rouge. Saler et poivrer. Réchauffer de 1 à 2 minutes.

PAR PORTION	
Calories	283
Protéines	36 g
Matières grasses	6 g
Glucides	18 g
Fibres	0,3 g
Fer	2 mg
Calcium	42 mg
Sodium	309 mg

Au total
354
calories

Idée pour accompagner

Haricots verts et oignon rouge

Par portion : 71 calories

Dans une casserole d'eau bouillante salée, cuire 500 g (environ 1 lb) de haricots verts de 4 à 5 minutes, jusqu'à tendreté. Égoutter. Tailler ½ oignon rouge en rondelles minces. Dans une poêle, faire fondre 30 ml (2 c. à soupe) de beurre léger à feu moyen. Cuire les rondelles d'oignon rouge de 2 à 3 minutes. Ajouter les haricots et poursuivre la cuisson de 2 à 3 minutes. Saler et poivrer.

Porc ①
755 g (1 ⅔ lb) de longe
coupée en cubes

Pâte de cari rouge ②
30 ml (2 c. à soupe)

3 carottes ③
coupées en biseau

2 poivrons jaunes ④
coupés en lanières

Sauce coco-cari ⑤
250 ml (1 tasse)

PRÉVOIR AUSSI :
➤ **Huile de canola**
30 ml (2 c. à soupe)

➤ **1 oignon**
émincé

Cari de porc

Préparation : **15 minutes** • Cuisson : **10 minutes** • Quantité : **4 portions**

Préparation

Assécher la viande à l'aide de papier absorbant.

Dans un bol, mélanger les cubes de porc avec la pâte de cari rouge. Remuer afin de bien enrober la viande.

Dans une casserole à fond épais ou dans une cocotte, chauffer l'huile à feu moyen-vif. Saisir quelques cubes de viande à la fois, de 6 à 8 minutes, jusqu'à ce que chacune de leurs faces soit dorée. Déposer la viande dans une assiette.

Retirer l'excédent de gras de la casserole. Remettre la viande dans la casserole. Ajouter les carottes, les poivrons, la sauce et l'oignon. Chauffer jusqu'aux premiers bouillons.

PAR PORTION	
Calories	245
Protéines	30 g
Matières grasses	6 g
Glucides	17 g
Fibres	2 g
Fer	2 mg
Calcium	25 mg
Sodium	644 mg

Au total
302
calories

Idée pour accompagner

Riz au jasmin citron et coriandre

Par portion: 57 calories

Rincer 125 ml (½ tasse) de riz au jasmin sous l'eau froide jusqu'à ce que l'eau soit claire. Bien égoutter. Dans une casserole, porter à ébullition 180 ml (¾ de tasse) de bouillon de poulet avec 15 ml (1 c. à soupe) de zestes de citron. Ajouter le riz. Couvrir et cuire à feu doux-moyen de 15 à 18 minutes. Séparer les grains de riz à la fourchette et incorporer 15 ml (1 c. à soupe) de coriandre hachée.

Poisson et fruits de mer

Les joyaux de la mer sont les alliés parfaits des soirées réussies! Pâtes, pavés, salades, sautés et galettes simplissimes sont idéaux pour créer des tables festives qui sauront assurément charmer vos convives!

Lime
30 ml (2 c. à soupe)
de jus

1

Poivre de la Jamaïque
(quatre-épices)
moulu
2,5 ml (½ c. à thé)

2

Gingembre en poudre
2,5 ml (½ c. à thé)

3

Cannelle
1,25 ml (¼ de c. à thé)

4

Saumon
4 filets de 120 g
(environ ¼ de lb) chacun,
la peau enlevée

5

PRÉVOIR AUSSI :
➤ **Miel**
30 ml
(2 c. à soupe)

➤ **Huile d'olive**
30 ml
(2 c. à soupe)

Saumon grillé au miel épicé

Préparation : **15 minutes** • Réfrigération : **5 minutes** • Cuisson : **6 minutes** • Quantité : **4 portions**

Préparation

Dans un bol, mélanger le jus de lime avec le poivre de la Jamaïque, le gingembre en poudre, la cannelle, le miel et 15 ml (1 c. à soupe) d'huile d'olive.

Badigeonner les deux côtés des filets de saumon avec le mélange. Réfrigérer de 5 à 10 minutes.

Égoutter les filets de saumon. Dans une poêle, chauffer le reste de l'huile à feu moyen. Cuire les filets de 3 à 4 minutes de chaque côté.

PAR PORTION	
Calories	347
Protéines	25 g
Matières grasses	23 g
Glucides	10 g
Fibres	0,2 g
Fer	1 mg
Calcium	15 mg
Sodium	72 mg

Au total
395
calories

Idée pour accompagner

Salade de tomates cerises et gingembre

Par portion : 48 calories

Dans un bol, mélanger 15 ml (1 c. à soupe) d'huile d'olive avec 1 échalote sèche émincée, 15 ml (1 c. à soupe) de jus de citron, 30 ml (2 c. à soupe) de basilic haché et 5 ml (1 c. à thé) de gingembre haché. Saler et poivrer. Couper de 18 à 20 tomates cerises en deux ou en quatre et les ajouter dans le bol. Remuer.

Crevettes sauce au cari rouge

Préparation : **15 minutes** • Cuisson : **5 minutes** • Quantité : **4 portions**

Préparation

Dans une poêle, chauffer l'huile à feu moyen. Cuire les crevettes de 1 à 2 minutes de chaque côté.

Ajouter la sauce au cari rouge et la sauce soya. Cuire en remuant de 3 à 4 minutes, jusqu'à ce que la sauce soit chaude.

Répartir dans des assiettes creuses. Parsemer de piments thaï et de feuilles de coriandre. Servir avec un quartier de lime si désiré.

PAR PORTION	
Calories	231
Protéines	19 g
Matières grasses	14 g
Glucides	8 g
Fibres	1 g
Fer	2 mg
Calcium	58 mg
Sodium	1 041 mg

① Crevettes moyennes (calibre 31/40)
crues et décortiquées
1 sac de 340 g

② Sauce thaï au cari rouge pour cuisson
du commerce
1 pot de 355 ml

③ Sauce soya
30 ml (2 c. à soupe)

④ 2 piments thaï
émincés

⑤ Coriandre
30 ml (2 c. à soupe)
de feuilles

Version minceur

Sauce thaï

Dans une casserole, porter à ébullition à feu moyen le contenu de 1 boîte de lait de coco léger de 400 ml avec 30 ml (2 c. à soupe) de jus de lime, 45 ml (3 c. à soupe) de pâte de cari rouge, 15 ml (1 c. à soupe) de gingembre haché, 15 ml (1 c. à soupe) d'ail, 15 ml (1 c. à soupe) de zestes de lime et 2,5 ml (½ c. à thé) de curcuma.

412 CALORIES
Du commerce

Pour 500 ml
(2 tasses)

342 CALORIES
Maison

PRÉVOIR AUSSI :
➤ **Huile de sésame**
non grillé
30 ml (2 c. à soupe)

FACULTATIF :
➤ **1 lime**
coupée en quartiers

148

Tourte aux fruits de mer

Préparation : **15 minutes** • Cuisson : **45 minutes** • Quantité : **8 portions**

Préparation

Dans une grande casserole, porter à ébullition le vin et 500 ml (2 tasses) d'eau. Ajouter les fruits de mer et laisser mijoter 5 minutes à découvert à feu doux-moyen. À l'aide d'une passoire fine, filtrer le bouillon en prenant soin de réserver 250 ml (1 tasse) de liquide.

Dans la même casserole, faire fondre le beurre à feu moyen-vif. Cuire les échalotes jusqu'à ce qu'elles soient tendres. Si désiré, ajouter l'ail et cuire quelques secondes. Saupoudrer de farine et bien mélanger pour que la préparation devienne homogène. Verser le lait et le bouillon réservé en mélangeant au fouet jusqu'à ce que la préparation épaississe. Saler et poivrer.

Déposer les fruits de mer dans un plat de cuisson de 20 cm (8 po). Ajouter les pommes de terre et la sauce.

Préchauffer le four à 190 °C (375 °F).

Sur une surface farinée, abaisser la pâte feuilletée en un rectangle de 21 cm (8 ½ po). Déposer sur le plat. Dans un bol, mélanger le jaune d'œuf avec 10 ml (2 c. à thé) d'eau. Badigeonner le dessus de la pâte feuilletée de ce mélange.

Cuire au four 45 minutes, jusqu'à ce que la pâte soit dorée et bien gonflée.

PAR PORTION	
Calories	386
Protéines	20 g
Matières grasses	18 g
Glucides	29 g
Fibres	1 g
Fer	7 mg
Calcium	134 mg
Sodium	308 mg

Au total
400
calories

Vin blanc ❶
375 ml (1 ½ tasse)

Mélange de fruits de mer surgelés ❷
décongelés
2 sacs de 340 g chacun

2 échalotes sèches ❸
hachées

2 grosses pommes de terre ❹
pelées et coupées
en cubes

Pâte feuilletée ❺
240 g

PRÉVOIR AUSSI :
➤ **Beurre**
60 ml (¼ de tasse)
➤ **Farine tout usage**
non blanchie
80 ml (⅓ de tasse)
➤ **Lait**
500 ml (2 tasses)
➤ **Œuf**
1 jaune

FACULTATIF :
➤ **Ail**
2 gousses hachées

Idée pour accompagner

Salade de trévise, concombre et tomates cerises

Par portion : 14 calories

Dans un saladier, mélanger 60 ml (¼ de tasse) de vinaigrette italienne hypocalorique et 15 ml (1 c. à soupe) de ciboulette hachée. Saler et poivrer. Ajouter 1 trévise (ou 1 radicchio) déchiquetée, ¼ de concombre anglais émincé et 10 tomates cerises jaunes coupées en deux. Remuer.

Recette de Ève Godin, nutritionniste

2 oranges 1

1 fenouil 2

**20 gros pétoncles
(calibre U10)** 3

1 oignon 4
émincé

Bébés épinards 5
500 ml (2 tasses)

PRÉVOIR AUSSI :
➤ **Huile d'olive**
30 ml
(2 c. à soupe)

Pétoncles aux oranges et fenouil

Préparation : **15 minutes** • Cuisson : **6 minutes** • Quantité : **4 portions**

Préparation

Prélever les suprêmes des oranges en pelant d'abord l'écorce à vif, puis en tranchant de chaque côté des membranes. Parer le fenouil en retirant les tiges, puis émincer le bulbe. Si désiré, réserver quelques brins de fenouil pour garnir.

Dans une poêle, chauffer l'huile à feu moyen. En procédant par petites quantités, faire dorer les pétoncles de 1 à 2 minutes de chaque côté. Réserver dans une assiette.

Dans la même poêle, cuire l'oignon et le fenouil de 2 à 3 minutes.

Ajouter les bébés épinards et les suprêmes d'oranges. Cuire de 1 à 2 minutes.

Saler et poivrer, puis ajouter les pétoncles. Remuer quelques secondes pour les réchauffer.

Répartir dans les assiettes. Si désiré, parsemer de brins de fenouil hachés.

PAR PORTION	
Calories	190
Protéines	15 g
Matières grasses	8 g
Glucides	17 g
Fibres	4 g
Fer	1 mg
Calcium	95 mg
Sodium	165 mg

Au total

347
calories

Idée pour accompagner

Garniture aux pacanes

Par portion: 157 calories

Dans une casserole, cuire 60 ml (¼ de tasse) de sirop d'érable avec 125 ml (½ tasse) de pacanes en morceaux et 10 ml (2 c. à thé) de thym haché de 2 à 3 minutes à feu moyen, jusqu'à ce que les pacanes soient caramélisées.

Truite saumonée ❶
450 g (1 lb) de filets,
la peau enlevée

Couscous ❷
250 ml (1 tasse)

1 orange ❸

½ oignon rouge ❹

Menthe ❺
hachée
60 ml (¼ de tasse)

Taboulé de truite saumonée à l'orange

Préparation : **15 minutes** • Cuisson : **15 minutes** • Quantité : **4 portions**

Préparation

Préchauffer le four à 205 °C (400 °F).

Déposer les filets de truite sur une plaque de cuisson tapissée d'une feuille de papier parchemin. Parsemer de cumin et, si désiré, de grains de coriandre. Cuire au four de 15 à 18 minutes. Retirer du four et laisser tiédir.

Dans un saladier, verser le couscous et 250 ml (1 tasse) d'eau bouillante. Couvrir et laisser gonfler le couscous 5 minutes. Égrainer le couscous avec une fourchette. Laisser tiédir.

Prélever les suprêmes de l'orange en pelant d'abord l'écorce à vif, puis en tranchant de chaque côté des membranes. Tailler les suprêmes en cubes. Hacher l'oignon rouge et, si désiré, couper le concombre en dés. Dans le saladier, ajouter les dés d'orange, l'oignon rouge, la menthe et, si désiré, le concombre et le persil. Remuer. Saler et poivrer.

Émietter la truite et l'incorporer au taboulé. Servir immédiatement ou réserver de 1 à 2 heures au frais avant de déguster.

PAR PORTION	
Calories	375
Protéines	30 g
Matières grasses	8 g
Glucides	44 g
Fibres	4 g
Fer	3 mg
Calcium	98 mg
Sodium	69 mg

▼
Au total
398
calories

Idée pour accompagner

Chips de tortillas épicés

Pour 2 pointes : 23 calories

Mélanger 15 ml (1 c. à soupe) de beurre léger fondu avec 5 ml (1 c. à thé) d'assaisonnements à chili et 1,25 ml (¼ de c. à thé) de chipotle. Badigeonner 4 tortillas de blé entier moyennes avec la préparation. Couper chaque tortilla en huit pointes. Déposer sur une plaque de cuisson tapissée de papier parchemin et faire dorer au four de 8 à 10 minutes à 180 °C (350 °F).

FACULTATIF :

➤ **Coriandre**
5 ml (1 c. à thé)
de grains concassés

➤ **½ concombre anglais**

➤ **Persil**
haché
30 ml (2 c. à soupe)

PRÉVOIR AUSSI :
➤ **Cumin**
1,25 ml
(¼ de c. à thé)

Sauce pomodoro ①
500 ml (2 tasses)

Sole ②
8 filets de 100 g
(3 ½ oz) chacun

1 poivron jaune ③

Chapelure panko ④
125 ml (½ tasse)

Fromage romano ⑤
râpé
80 ml (⅓ de tasse)

FACULTATIF :
➤ **Ciboulette**
hachée
30 ml (2 c. à soupe)

➤ **Aneth**
haché
30 ml (2 c. à soupe)

Sole à la sauce pomodoro, poivron et romano

Préparation : **15 minutes** • Cuisson : **12 minutes** • Quantité : **4 portions**

Préparation

Préchauffer le four à 205 °C (400 °F).

Dans un plat de cuisson, étaler un peu de sauce. Superposer les filets de sole deux par deux et déposer dans le plat. Napper du reste de la sauce.

Couper le poivron en fines rondelles et déposer sur les filets de sole.

Dans un bol, mélanger la chapelure avec le fromage romano et, si désiré, les fines herbes. Parsemer les filets du mélange.

Cuire au four de 12 à 15 minutes.

PAR PORTION	
Calories	297
Protéines	43 g
Matières grasses	6 g
Glucides	18 g
Fibres	3 g
Fer	2 mg
Calcium	146 mg
Sodium	294 mg

Au total
375
calories

Idée pour accompagner

Spaghettis asperges et ciboulette

Par portion : 78 calories

Cuire 1 paquet de spaghettis de tofu (de type Shirataki) de 226 g selon les indications de l'emballage. Dans une casserole d'eau bouillante salée, cuire 10 asperges coupées en tronçons 5 minutes. Égoutter en prenant soin de réserver 60 ml (¼ de tasse) d'eau de cuisson. Dans la même casserole, chauffer 30 ml (2 c. à soupe) d'huile d'olive. Cuire 2 gousses d'ail émincées de 1 à 2 minutes. Ajouter les spaghettis, les asperges, l'eau de cuisson réservée et 45 ml (3 c. à soupe) de ciboulette hachée. Réchauffer de 1 à 2 minutes. Saler et poivrer.

Bouillon de poulet
180 ml (¾ de tasse)

1

1 poivron jaune
émincé

2

1 oignon
émincé

3

20 pois mange-tout
émincés

4

**Crevettes moyennes
(calibre 31/40)**
crues et décortiquées
1 sac de 340 g

5

PRÉVOIR AUSSI :
➤ **Sauce soya**
30 ml (2 c. à soupe)

➤ **Sucre**
15 ml (1 c. à soupe)

➤ **Fécule de maïs**
5 ml (1 c. à thé)

➤ **Huile de canola**
30 ml (2 c. à soupe)

FACULTATIF :
➤ **Sauce sriracha**
5 ml (1 c. à thé)

Sauté de crevettes

Préparation : **15 minutes** • Cuisson : **5 minutes** • Quantité : **4 portions**

Préparation

Dans un bol, fouetter le bouillon de poulet avec la sauce soya, le sucre, la fécule de maïs et, si désiré, la sauce sriracha. Réserver.

Dans une poêle ou dans un wok, chauffer l'huile à feu moyen. Cuire les légumes de 2 à 3 minutes. Déposer dans une assiette.

Dans la même poêle, cuire les crevettes de 2 à 3 minutes.

Remettre les légumes dans la poêle. Verser la sauce réservée et porter à ébullition en remuant jusqu'à épaississement.

Idée pour accompagner

Riz parfumé au lait de coco

Par portion : 86 calories

Rincer 125 ml (½ tasse) de riz au jasmin à l'eau froide. Déposer dans une casserole avec le contenu de ½ boîte de lait de coco léger de 400 ml, 125 ml (½ tasse) d'eau et 1 pincée de sel. Porter à ébullition. Couvrir et cuire de 20 à 25 minutes à feu doux-moyen, en remuant de temps en temps, jusqu'à ce que le riz soit cuit.

PAR PORTION	
Calories	195
Protéines	19 g
Matières grasses	9 g
Glucides	10 g
Fibres	1 g
Fer	3 mg
Calcium	63 mg
Sodium	681 mg

Au total
281
calories

Morue à la chermoula

Préparation : **15 minutes** • Réfrigération : **1 heure** • Cuisson : **15 minutes** • Quantité : **4 portions**

Préparation

Dans un bol, mélanger le jus de citron avec la coriandre, le cumin, l'huile d'olive et, si désiré, le paprika. Ajouter les filets de morue et les retourner pour bien les enrober. Couvrir et réfrigérer au moins 1 heure.

Au moment de la cuisson, préchauffer le four à 190°C (375°F).

Dans un plat de cuisson, déposer les tomates cerises, puis couvrir avec les filets de poisson et la marinade. Cuire au four de 15 à 20 minutes selon l'épaisseur des filets de morue, jusqu'à ce que le poisson se défasse facilement à la fourchette.

PAR PORTION	
Calories	175
Protéines	22 g
Matières grasses	7 g
Glucides	3 g
Fibres	1 g
Fer	1 mg
Calcium	28 mg
Sodium	73 mg

Au total

329
calories

Idée pour accompagner

Riz basmati à la courgette

Par portion: 154 calories

Dans une casserole, chauffer 15 ml (1 c. à soupe) d'huile d'olive à feu moyen. Cuire 1 courgette taillée en petits dés et 1 échalote sèche hachée finement 3 minutes. Ajouter 250 ml (1 tasse) de riz basmati rincé sous l'eau froide et remuer. Verser 375 ml (1 ½ tasse) d'eau et porter à ébullition. Couvrir et laisser mijoter à feu doux de 12 à 14 minutes, jusqu'à ce que le riz ait absorbé tout le liquide. Saler et poivrer.

Citron ①
45 ml (3 c. à soupe)
de jus

Coriandre ②
hachée
30 ml (2 c. à soupe)

Cumin ③
moulu
5 ml (1 c. à thé)

Morue ④
4 filets de 120 g
(environ ¼ de lb)
chacun

Tomates cerises ⑤
coupées en deux
500 ml (2 tasses)

PRÉVOIR AUSSI :
➤ **Huile d'olive**
30 ml
(2 c. à soupe)

FACULTATIF :
➤ **Paprika**
5 ml (1 c. à thé)

Recette de Ève Godin, nutritionniste

Orange ❶
30 ml (2 c. à soupe)
de jus

Fenouil ❷
1 bulbe
coupé en quartiers

1 poivron rouge ❸
coupé en quartiers

1 orange ❹
coupée en quartiers

Saumon ❺
4 filets de 120 g
(environ ¼ de lb) chacun
la peau enlevée

PRÉVOIR AUSSI:
➤ **Sirop d'érable**
45 ml (3 c. à soupe)
➤ **Huile d'olive**
30 ml (2 c. à soupe)

FACULTATIF:
➤ **Thym**
haché
15 ml (1 c. à soupe)

➤ **½ oignon rouge**
coupé en quartiers

Saumon à l'orange et légumes au four

Préparation: **15 minutes** • Cuisson: **12 minutes** • Quantité: **4 portions**

Préparation

Dans un saladier, mélanger le jus d'orange avec le sirop d'érable, l'huile et, si désiré, le thym. Saler et poivrer. Ajouter le fenouil, le poivron, les quartiers d'orange, les filets de saumon et, si désiré, l'oignon rouge. Remuer délicatement.

Sur une plaque de cuisson tapissée d'une feuille de papier parchemin, déposer les filets de saumon. Répartir les légumes et les quartiers d'orange autour des filets. Cuire au four de 12 à 15 minutes, jusqu'à ce que la chair du saumon se défasse à la fourchette.

PAR PORTION	
Calories	267
Protéines	16 g
Matières grasses	13 g
Glucides	22 g
Fibres	3 g
Fer	1 mg
Calcium	74 mg
Sodium	76 mg

Au total
323
calories

Idée pour accompagner

Riz basmati au zeste d'orange

Par portion: 56 calories

Rincer à l'eau froide 125 ml (½ tasse) de riz basmati. Dans une casserole, verser 250 ml (1 tasse) de bouillon de poulet et ajouter le riz. Saler et poivrer. Porter à ébullition. Couvrir et cuire de 18 à 20 minutes à feu doux-moyen. Ajouter 15 ml (1 c. à soupe) de zestes d'orange.

Échalotes sèches ➊
hachées
60 ml (¼ de tasse)

Muscade ➋
1,25 ml
(¼ de c. à thé)

Bébés épinards ➌
750 ml (3 tasses)

Tilapia ➍
4 filets de 150 g
(⅓ de lb) chacun

8 champignons ➎
émincés

PRÉVOIR AUSSI :
➤ **Beurre**
30 ml (2 c. à soupe)

➤ **Farine**
15 ml (1 c. à soupe)

➤ **Lait**
250 ml (1 tasse)

➤ **Huile d'olive**
15 ml (1 c. à soupe)

FACULTATIF :
➤ **Paprika**
au goût

Tilapia à la florentine

Préparation : **15 minutes** • Cuisson : **18 minutes** • Quantité : **4 portions**

Préparation

Préchauffer le four à 205 °C (400 °F).

Dans une casserole, faire fondre le beurre à feu moyen. Cuire les échalotes de 1 à 2 minutes. Ajouter la farine et remuer. Verser le lait et porter à ébullition en fouettant. Continuer de fouetter jusqu'à épaississement. Incorporer la muscade et les bébés épinards. Saler et poivrer.

Verser les trois quarts de la sauce dans un plat de cuisson. Déposer les filets de tilapia sur la sauce. Si désiré, saupoudrer de paprika.

Dans une poêle, chauffer l'huile à feu moyen. Cuire les champignons de 2 à 3 minutes. Saler et poivrer.

Napper les filets du reste de la sauce et garnir de champignons. Cuire au four de 15 à 18 minutes.

PAR PORTION	
Calories	285
Protéines	34 g
Matières grasses	13 g
Glucides	8 g
Fibres	1 g
Fer	2 mg
Calcium	123 mg
Sodium	171 mg

Au total
399
calories

Idée pour accompagner

Chips de patates douces au micro-ondes

Par portion (environ 10 chips) : 114 calories

Émincer finement 1 patate douce d'environ 250 g (environ ½ lb). Sur une assiette tapissée d'une feuille de papier parchemin, étaler quelques rondelles de patate douce, sans les superposer. Badigeonner d'un soupçon d'huile d'olive (calculer 30 ml - 2 c. à soupe d'huile pour l'ensemble des chips). Faire dorer de 4 à 5 minutes au micro-ondes à puissance élevée. Saler et poivrer. Procéder de la même manière avec le reste des rondelles de patate douce.

Tilapia
450 g (1 lb)
de filets ①

Gingembre ②
haché
15 ml (1 c. à soupe)

Ail ③
haché
10 ml (2 c. à thé)

3 oignons verts ④
hachés

Œuf ⑤
1 blanc battu

PRÉVOIR AUSSI :
➤ **Farine**
30 ml (2 c. à soupe)
➤ **Huile d'olive**
30 ml (2 c. à soupe)

Galettes de sole ail et gingembre

Préparation : **15 minutes** • Cuisson : **15 minutes** • Quantité : **4 portions**

Préparation

Couper les filets de tilapia en cubes. Dans le contenant du robot culinaire, hacher les cubes de poisson quelques secondes. Ajouter le reste des ingrédients, à l'exception de l'huile d'olive. Mélanger 30 secondes. Façonner 8 galettes de 2 cm (¾ de po) d'épaisseur avec la préparation.

Dans une poêle, chauffer l'huile à feu moyen. Cuire les galettes de 4 à 5 minutes de chaque côté, jusqu'à ce qu'elles soient dorées.

PAR PORTION	
Calories	133
Protéines	24 g
Matières grasses	2 g
Glucides	4 g
Fibres	0,4 g
Fer	1 mg
Calcium	17 mg
Sodium	73 mg

Au total
257
calories

Idée pour accompagner

Sauce miel et lime

Par portion : 124 calories

Dans un bol, mélanger 125 ml (½ tasse) de yogourt grec nature 0 % avec 15 ml (1 c. à soupe) de sauce soya et 15 ml (1 c. à soupe) de miel. Incorporer 15 ml (1 c. à soupe) de jus de lime, 10 ml (2 c. à thé) de zestes de lime et 60 ml (¼ de tasse) de noix de cajou hachées. Saler au goût.

Vinaigre de riz ①
30 ml (2 c. à soupe)

Miso ②
15 ml (1 c. à soupe)

Cassonade ③
10 ml (2 c. à thé)

Sauce sriracha ④
2,5 ml (½ c. à thé)

Saumon ⑤
4 filets avec la peau de
120 g (environ ¼ de lb)
chacun

PRÉVOIR AUSSI :
➤ **Huile de canola**
15 ml (1 c. à soupe)

Saumon à la thaï

Préparation : **15 minutes** • Cuisson : **10 minutes** • Quantité : **4 portions**

Préparation

Dans un bol, mélanger le vinaigre de riz avec le miso, la cassonade, la sauce sriracha et 30 ml (2 c. à soupe) d'eau.

Dans une poêle antiadhésive, chauffer l'huile à feu moyen. Faire dorer les filets de poisson côté peau environ 5 minutes.

Verser la sauce dans la poêle. Poursuivre la cuisson de 2 à 3 minutes en arrosant les filets de sauce afin qu'ils soient bien enrobés.

Au besoin, terminer la cuisson au four à la position « gril » (*broil*), sur la grille du haut, environ 3 minutes.

PAR PORTION	
Calories	193
Protéines	15 g
Matières grasses	13 g
Glucides	3 g
Fibres	0,2 g
Fer	0,4 mg
Calcium	11 mg
Sodium	217 mg

Au total
256
calories

Idée pour accompagner

Légumes sautés

Par portion: 63 calories

Couper 1 brocoli en bouquets et la tige en dés. Dans une grande poêle ou dans un wok, chauffer 15 ml (1 c. à soupe) d'huile de canola à feu moyen-vif. Cuire 1 grosse carotte taillée en biseau, 250 ml (1 tasse) de champignons coupés en quartiers et 250 ml (1 tasse) de pois mange-tout, en prenant soin de les conserver légèrement croquants. Incorporer 15 ml (1 c. à soupe) de sauce pad thaï (de type Thaï Kitchen) et 45 ml (3 c. à soupe) d'oignons verts hachés. Servir aussitôt.

Recette de Ève Godin, nutritionniste

Tilapia
4 filets de 150 g
(⅓ de lb) chacun ➊

Chapelure panko ➋
250 ml (1 tasse)

Parmesan ➌
râpé
125 ml (½ tasse)

Tomates séchées ➍
hachées
15 ml (1 c. à soupe)

Pesto aux
tomates séchées ➎
15 ml (1 c. à soupe)

PRÉVOIR AUSSI :
➤ **Mayonnaise
« ½ moins de gras »**
60 ml (¼ de tasse)

➤ **Ail**
haché
5 ml (1 c. à thé)

FACULTATIF :
➤ **Échalotes sèches**
hachées
15 ml (1 c. à soupe)

Tilapia en croûte de pesto et panko

Préparation : **15 minutes** • Cuisson : **10 minutes** • Quantité : **4 portions**

Préparation

Préchauffer le four à 190 °C (375 °F).

Huiler un plat de cuisson de 33 cm x 23 cm (13 po x 9 po). Déposer les filets de tilapia dans le plat, sans les superposer.

Dans un bol, mélanger le reste des ingrédients avec, si désiré, les échalotes. Étaler la préparation sur les filets et presser légèrement afin qu'elle adhère bien à la chair du poisson.

Cuire au four de 10 à 12 minutes, jusqu'à ce que la chair du poisson se défasse à la fourchette et que la croûte soit dorée.

PAR PORTION	
Calories	317
Protéines	37 g
Matières grasses	12 g
Glucides	15 g
Fibres	1 g
Fer	1 mg
Calcium	175 mg
Sodium	487 mg

Au total
387
calories

Idée pour accompagner

Salade de roquette aux fines herbes

Par portion : 70 calories

Dans un saladier, mélanger 30 ml (2 c. à soupe) d'huile d'olive avec 30 ml (2 c. à soupe) d'eau, 15 ml (1 c. à soupe) de vinaigre de riz, 30 ml (2 c. à soupe) de ciboulette hachée, 30 ml (2 c. à soupe) de persil haché et 15 ml (1 c. à soupe) d'estragon haché. Saler et poivrer. Ajouter 750 ml (3 tasses) de roquette. Remuer.

Bouillon de poulet ➊
625 ml (2 ½ tasses)

Orzo ➋
250 ml (1 tasse)

28 pétoncles moyens ➌
(calibre 20/30)

Roquette ➍
émincée
375 ml (1 ½ tasse)

Bacon précuit ➎
6 tranches coupées
en morceaux

PRÉVOIR AUSSI :
➤ **Huile d'olive**
15 ml (1 c. à soupe)

➤ **1 oignon**
haché

➤ **Ail**
haché
10 ml (2 c. à thé)

Pétoncles à l'orzo et roquette

Préparation : **15 minutes** • Cuisson : **15 minutes** • Quantité : **4 portions**

Préparation

Dans une casserole, porter le bouillon à ébullition. Ajouter l'orzo et cuire à feu doux-moyen 10 minutes, jusqu'à ce que l'orzo soit *al dente*. Égoutter.

Dans une poêle, chauffer l'huile à feu moyen. Saisir les pétoncles 1 minute de chaque côté. Transférer dans une assiette et réserver.

Dans la même poêle, cuire l'oignon et l'ail de 1 à 2 minutes.

Ajouter la roquette, les pétoncles et l'orzo. Saler et poivrer. Couvrir et cuire 1 minute.

Au moment de servir, répartir la préparation dans les assiettes et parsemer de bacon.

PAR PORTION	
Calories	332
Protéines	28 g
Matières grasses	7 g
Glucides	37 g
Fibres	2 g
Fer	1 mg
Calcium	64 mg
Sodium	568 mg

Au total
357
calories

Idée pour accompagner

Chips de pain au cari

Par croûton : 25 calories

Couper ¼ de baguette de pain en 12 tranches fines. Dans un bol, mélanger 30 ml (2 c. à soupe) de beurre léger ramolli avec 10 ml (2 c. à thé) de cari. Badigeonner les deux côtés des tranches de pain avec le beurre parfumé. Déposer sur une plaque de cuisson tapissée de papier parchemin et faire griller au four de 1 à 2 minutes de chaque côté à la position « gril » (*broil*).

Coriandre ❶
hachée
45 ml (3 c. à soupe)

Lime ❷
15 ml (1 c. à soupe)
de zestes

Gingembre ❸
haché
5 ml (1 c. à thé)

Saumon ❹
800 g (environ 1 ¾ lb)
de filets, la peau
enlevée et coupés
en 12 cubes

2 poivrons rouges ❺
coupés en cubes

PRÉVOIR AUSSI :
➤ **Huile d'olive**
60 ml (¼ de tasse)

➤ **Miel**
15 ml (1 c. à soupe)

➤ **Ail**
haché
10 ml (2 c. à thé)

Brochettes de saumon au gingembre

Préparation : **15 minutes** • Marinage : **30 minutes** • Cuisson : **8 minutes** • Quantité : **4 portions**

Préparation

Dans un bol, mélanger la coriandre avec les zestes de lime, le gingembre, l'huile d'olive, le miel et l'ail.

Verser la moitié de la marinade dans un sac hermétique et ajouter les cubes de saumon dans le sac. Laisser mariner 30 minutes au frais.

Au moment de la cuisson, préchauffer le four à 205 °C (400 °F).

Piquer les cubes de saumon et de poivrons rouges sur quatre brochettes, en les faisant alterner.

Sur une plaque de cuisson tapissée d'une feuille de papier parchemin, déposer les brochettes de saumon. Cuire au four de 12 à 15 minutes en retournant les brochettes à mi-cuisson et en les badigeonnant avec la marinade réservée.

PAR PORTION	
Calories	300
Protéines	15 g
Matières grasses	23 g
Glucides	8 g
Fibres	1 g
Fer	1 mg
Calcium	16 mg
Sodium	44 mg

Au total
397
calories

Idée pour accompagner

Salade de radis et concombres

Par portion: 97 calories

À l'aide d'une mandoline, couper en fines tranches 6 mini-concombres et 10 radis. Dans un saladier, mélanger 30 ml (2 c. à soupe) d'huile d'olive avec 30 ml (2 c. à soupe) d'eau, 20 ml (4 c. à thé) de sirop d'érable et 15 ml (1 c. à soupe) de moutarde à l'ancienne. Saler et poivrer. Ajouter les concombres, les radis et 2 oignons verts émincés. Remuer.

Crevettes nordiques ①
225 g (375 ml)

Ciboulette ②
hachée
30 ml (2 c. à soupe)

Citron ③
10 ml (2 c. à thé)
de zestes

Sole ④
8 filets de 90 g
(environ 3 ½ oz) chacun

**Fromage à la crème
au saumon fumé léger** ⑤
¾ de 1 contenant
de 250 g

PRÉVOIR AUSSI :
➤ **Lait**
60 ml (¼ de tasse)

Roulés de sole aux crevettes

Préparation : **15 minutes** • Cuisson : **10 minutes** • Quantité : **4 portions**

Préparation

Mélanger les crevettes avec la ciboulette et les zestes de citron. Répartir cette préparation sur la base des filets de sole et les rouler en serrant.

Dans une poêle, chauffer le fromage à la crème avec le lait à feu doux-moyen, jusqu'à ce que le fromage soit fondu.

Déposer les filets de sole dans la poêle, joint dessous. Couvrir et cuire de 10 à 12 minutes.

PAR PORTION	
Calories	306
Protéines	48 g
Matières grasses	10 g
Glucides	5 g
Fibres	0,2 g
Fer	1 mg
Calcium	131 mg
Sodium	733 mg

Au total
386
calories

Idée pour accompagner

Riz aux légumes

Par portion : 80 calories

Rincer à l'eau froide 125 ml (½ tasse) de riz basmati. Dans une casserole, chauffer 15 ml (1 c. à soupe) d'huile d'olive à feu moyen. Cuire 125 ml (½ tasse) de légumes frais pour sauce spaghetti de 2 à 3 minutes. Ajouter le riz et 250 ml (1 tasse) de bouillon de légumes. Saler et poivrer. Porter à ébullition. Couvrir et cuire de 18 à 20 minutes à feu doux-moyen. Ajouter 15 ml (1 c. à soupe) de zestes de lime et 30 ml (2 c. à soupe) d'aneth haché.

Pâtes gourmandes

Les plats de pâtes conviennent aussi bien pour les soupers en amoureux que pour les réunions familiales et amicales! Qu'on les préfère nappées de sauce tomate, de sauce Alfredo ou de pesto, les pastas sont toutes désignées pour créer des festins gourmands en un rien de temps!

Fettucines ❶
225 g

**8 à 10 choux
de Bruxelles** ❷
effeuillés

18 tomates cerises ❸
de couleurs variées
coupées en deux

Poulet ❹
2 poitrines sans peau
coupées en lanières

Vin blanc ❺
60 ml (¼ de tasse)

PRÉVOIR AUSSI :
➤ **Huile d'olive**
15 ml (1 c. à soupe)

➤ **Ail**
1 gousse émincée

FACULTATIF :
➤ **½ oignon rouge**
émincé

➤ **Piment d'Espelette**
30 ml (2 c. à soupe)

Fettucines au poulet, tomates cerises et choux de Bruxelles

Préparation : **15 minutes** • Cuisson : **5 minutes** • Quantité : **4 portions**

Préparation

Dans une casserole d'eau bouillante salée, cuire les pâtes *al dente*. Ajouter les feuilles de choux de Bruxelles dans la casserole de 1 à 2 minutes avant la fin de la cuisson des pâtes. Égoutter.

Dans une poêle antiadhésive, chauffer l'huile à feu moyen. Cuire les tomates cerises, l'ail et, si désiré, l'oignon rouge de 2 à 3 minutes. Transférer dans une assiette.

Dans la même poêle, cuire les lanières de poulet de 2 à 3 minutes de chaque côté. Saler et poivrer. Si désiré, saupoudrer de piment d'Espelette.

Ajouter les choux de Bruxelles, les pâtes et le vin blanc. Réchauffer de 1 à 2 minutes en remuant.

PAR PORTION	
Calories	363
Protéines	23 g
Matières grasses	6 g
Glucides	52 g
Fibres	5 g
Fer	3 mg
Calcium	50 mg
Sodium	54 mg

Au total

392
calories

Idée pour accompagner

Croûtons gratinés au fromage suisse

Par croûton : 29 calories

Mélanger 250 ml (1 tasse) de fromage suisse faible en gras râpé avec 15 ml (1 c. à soupe) de thym haché. Sur une plaque de cuisson, déposer 4 tranches de pain de blé réduit en calories (de type Weight Watchers) et les couvrir du mélange au fromage. Poivrer. Faire griller au four de 8 à 10 minutes à 205 °C (400 °F). Couper chaque tranche en quatre.

Farfalles ❶
225 g

2 courgettes ❷
émincées

Céleri ❸
2 branches
émincées

1 poivron jaune ❹
émincé

Thon blanc ❺
dans l'eau, égoutté
2 conserves de 120 g
chacune

FACULTATIF :
➤ **Citron**
   15 ml (1 c. à soupe)
   de zestes

PRÉVOIR AUSSI :
➤ **Huile d'olive**
15 ml (1 c. à soupe)

➤ **Basilic**
   émincé
   30 ml (2 c. à soupe)

Farfalles au thon

Préparation : **15 minutes** • Cuisson : **15 minutes** • Quantité : **4 portions**

Préparation

Dans une casserole d'eau bouillante salée, cuire les pâtes 4 minutes. Ajouter les courgettes et le céleri dans la casserole. Prolonger la cuisson de 4 à 5 minutes, jusqu'à ce que les pâtes soient *al dente*. Égoutter.

Dans la même casserole, chauffer l'huile à feu moyen. Cuire le poivron 2 minutes.

Si désiré, verser la sauce légère au chou-fleur (voir recette ci-dessous) et chauffer jusqu'aux premiers frémissements.

Incorporer le thon, les pâtes, les légumes et, si désiré, les zestes de citron et le basilic. Réchauffer 1 minute.

Idée pour accompagner

Béchamel légère au chou-fleur

Par portion : 69 calories

Dans une casserole, porter à ébullition 375 ml (1 ½ tasse) de bouillon de légumes sans sel ajouté avec 15 ml (1 c. à soupe) d'ail haché, 15 ml (1 c. à soupe) de moutarde de Dijon, 1 petit chou-fleur de 600 g coupé en bouquets, du sel et du poivre. Couvrir et laisser mijoter de 15 à 20 minutes à feu doux-moyen, jusqu'à ce que le chou-fleur soit tendre. Verser la préparation et 160 ml (⅔ de tasse) de lait 1 % chaud dans le contenant du mélangeur électrique. Mélanger de 1 à 2 minutes jusqu'à l'obtention d'une sauce lisse.

PAR PORTION	
Calories	328
Protéines	23 g
Matières grasses	6 g
Glucides	45 g
Fibres	3 g
Fer	3 mg
Calcium	30 mg
Sodium	46 mg

Au total
397
calories

6 lasagnes ①

Sauce marinara
1 pot de 650 ml ②

Bœuf haché extra-maigre
300 g (⅔ de lb) ③

Ricotta
180 ml (¾ de tasse) ④

Mozzarella
râpée
310 ml (1 ¼ tasse) ⑤

Lasagne dans le poêlon
Préparation : **15 minutes** • Cuisson : **10 minutes** • Quantité : **4 portions**

Préparation

Dans une casserole d'eau bouillante salée, cuire les lasagnes *al dente*. Égoutter.

Pendant la cuisson des lasagnes, réchauffer la sauce dans une casserole.

Dans un grand poêlon allant au four, chauffer l'huile à feu moyen. Cuire le bœuf de 2 à 3 minutes en l'égrainant à l'aide d'une cuillère en bois.

Si désiré, ajouter l'ail. Cuire de 1 à 2 minutes.

Couper les lasagnes en trois morceaux. Réserver six morceaux de lasagne et ajouter le reste dans le poêlon. Remuer. Déposer les six morceaux de lasagne réservés sur le dessus, puis couvrir de ricotta et de mozzarella.

Faire gratiner au four à la position « gril » (*broil*) de 2 à 3 minutes.

PAR PORTION	
Calories	395
Protéines	37 g
Matières grasses	13 g
Glucides	30 g
Fibres	2 g
Fer	3 mg
Calcium	488 mg
Sodium	382 mg

Version minceur

Sauce marinara

Dans une casserole, chauffer 15 ml (1 c. à soupe) d'huile d'olive à feu moyen. Cuire 1 oignon haché jusqu'à tendreté. Ajouter le contenu de 1 boîte de tomates en dés de 540 ml, 500 ml (2 tasses) de sauce tomate, 30 ml (2 c. à soupe) d'origan haché et 15 ml (1 c. à soupe) de thym haché. Saler et poivrer. Porter à ébullition, puis laisser mijoter de 10 à 12 minutes à feu doux-moyen en remuant de temps en temps.

652 CALORIES

Du commerce

pour 1,5 litre
(6 tasses)

325 CALORIES

Maison

PRÉVOIR AUSSI :
➤ **Huile d'olive**
15 ml (1 c. à soupe)

FACULTATIF :
➤ **Ail**
haché
15 ml (1 c. à soupe)

Linguines ①
250 g

**Pesto aux
tomates séchées** ②
30 ml (2 c. à soupe)

20 olives Kalamata ③
entières

Thon blanc ④
dans l'eau, égoutté
2 boîtes de 120 g
chacune

Roquette ⑤
500 ml (2 tasses)

FACULTATIF :
➤ 1 **citron**
   jus et zeste

Linguines aux olives, citron et thon

Préparation : **5 minutes** • Cuisson : **10 minutes** • Quantité : **4 portions**

Préparation

Dans une casserole d'eau bouillante salée, cuire les pâtes *al dente*. Égoutter en prenant soin de conserver environ 125 ml (½ tasse) d'eau de cuisson. Remettre les pâtes dans la casserole.

Dans un bol, mélanger le pesto avec les olives et, si désiré, le zeste et le jus de citron.

Dans la casserole contenant les pâtes, verser la sauce au pesto. Incorporer un peu d'eau de cuisson réservée au besoin.

Ajouter le thon et la roquette, puis mélanger délicatement. Saler et poivrer.

PAR PORTION	
Calories	327
Protéines	24 g
Matières grasses	12 g
Glucides	43 g
Fibres	3 g
Fer	3 mg
Calcium	3 mg
Sodium	120 mg

Au total
361
calories

Idée pour accompagner

Croûtons au basilic

Par croûton: 34 calories

Couper 4 tranches de pain en quatre. Faire dorer au four de 2 à 3 minutes à la position « gril » (*broil*). Dans un bol, mélanger 60 ml (¼ de tasse) de beurre fondu avec 30 ml (2 c. à soupe) de basilic émincé. Badigeonner les pains de beurre au basilic à la sortie du four.

Recette de Ève Godin, nutritionniste

Choux de Bruxelles
150 g

12 à 16 asperges ②

Rotinis de blé entier ③
300 g

10 à 12 tomates cerises ④
de couleurs variées

1 poivron jaune ⑤

PRÉVOIR AUSSI :
➤ **Ail**
1 gousse
entière pelée

➤ **Huile d'olive**
30 ml (2 c. à soupe)

FACULTATIF :
➤ ½ **oignon rouge**

➤ **Basilic**
émincé
30 ml (2 c. à soupe)

➤ **Persil**
haché
30 ml (2 c. à soupe)

Rotinis aux légumes et fines herbes

Préparation : **15 minutes** • Cuisson : **10 minutes** • Quantité : **6 portions**

Préparation

Couper les choux de Bruxelles en quatre et les asperges en morceaux.

Dans une casserole d'eau bouillante salée, cuire les pâtes *al dente*. Ajouter les choux de Bruxelles et les asperges dans la casserole 5 minutes avant la fin de la cuisson des pâtes. Égoutter.

Pendant ce temps, trancher les tomates cerises en deux. Émincer le poivron, l'ail et, si désiré, l'oignon rouge.

Dans la même casserole, chauffer l'huile à feu moyen. Cuire le poivron, l'ail et, si désiré, l'oignon rouge de 2 à 3 minutes.

Ajouter les tomates, les pâtes et, si désiré, les fines herbes. Saler et poivrer. Réchauffer de 1 à 2 minutes en remuant.

PAR PORTION	
Calories	364
Protéines	14 g
Matières grasses	8 g
Glucides	65 g
Fibres	9 g
Fer	4 mg
Calcium	69 mg
Sodium	20 mg

Au total
395
calories

Idée pour accompagner

Croûtons au fromage et à l'ail

Par croûton : 31 calories + 1 g de protéines

Couper ¼ de baguette de pain en 12 tranches. Mélanger 150 g de fromage à la crème léger avec 30 ml (2 c. à soupe) de persil haché et 15 ml (1 c. à soupe) d'ail haché. Tartiner les croûtons avec cette préparation. Déposer sur une plaque de cuisson tapissée d'une feuille de papier d'aluminium et faire dorer au four de 1 à 2 minutes à la position « gril » (*broil*).

Psst!
Permet d'atteindre 15 g de protéines

Pâte de cari rouge ①
30 ml (2 c. à soupe)

Bouillon de légumes ②
750 ml (3 tasses)

Lait de coco léger ③
1 boîte de 398 ml

Linguines fraîches ④
1 paquet de 350 g

Saumon ⑤
375 g (environ ¾ de lb)
de pavés d'environ 2,5 cm
(1 po) d'épaisseur,
la peau enlevée

PRÉVOIR AUSSI :
➤ **Huile d'olive**
15 ml (1 c. à soupe)

➤ 1 **oignon** haché

Saumon et linguines à l'asiatique

Préparation : **15 minutes** • Cuisson : **18 minutes** • Quantité : **6 portions**

Préparation

Dans une casserole, chauffer l'huile à feu moyen. Cuire l'oignon et, si désiré, l'ail de 1 à 2 minutes.

Ajouter la pâte de cari rouge et cuire 1 minute en remuant, jusqu'à ce que les arômes se libèrent.

Verser le bouillon et le lait de coco. Saler et poivrer. Porter à ébullition.

Ajouter les pâtes et remuer. Ajouter les pavés de saumon et, si désiré, les tomates cerises et le poivron. Couvrir et cuire 18 minutes à feu doux-moyen en remuant de temps en temps, jusqu'à ce que les pâtes soient *al dente*.

PAR PORTION	
Calories	359
Protéines	21 g
Matières grasses	12 g
Glucides	42 g
Fibres	3 g
Fer	3 mg
Calcium	35 mg
Sodium	414 mg

Au total
380
calories

Idée pour accompagner

Croûtons au pesto de tomates séchées

Par croûton : 21 calories

Couper ½ baguette de pain en 12 tranches. Badigeonner les tranches de pain avec 15 ml (1 c. à soupe) de pesto aux tomates séchées. Déposer sur une plaque de cuisson tapissée de papier parchemin et faire griller au four de 8 à 10 minutes à 205 °C (400 °F).

FACULTATIF :
➤ **Ail**
haché
15 ml (1 c. à soupe)

➤ 16 **tomates cerises**

➤ 1 **poivron rouge**
émincé

Nouilles aux œufs ❶
225 g

Pois verts ❷
250 ml (1 tasse)

Thon ❸
égoutté
1 boîte de 170 g

Parmesan ❹
râpé
45 ml (3 c. à soupe)

Mozzarella sans gras ❺
râpée
180 ml (¾ de tasse)

PRÉVOIR AUSSI :
➤ **Beurre léger**
45 ml (3 c. à soupe)
➤ **Farine**
45 ml (3 c. à soupe)
➤ **Lait 2 %**
500 ml (2 tasses)

FACULTATIF :
➤ **Ail**
haché
10 ml (2 c. à thé)

Gratin de nouilles au thon

Préparation : **15 minutes** • Cuisson : **20 minutes** • Quantité : **6 portions**

Préparation

Préchauffer le four à 205 °C (400 °F).

Dans une casserole d'eau bouillante salée, cuire les nouilles 7 minutes.

Ajouter les pois verts et poursuivre la cuisson 2 minutes. Les nouilles doivent demeurer *al dente*. Égoutter.

Dans la même casserole, faire fondre le beurre à feu moyen. Saupoudrer de farine, remuer et cuire 1 minute. Verser le lait et porter à ébullition en fouettant. Ajouter le thon, les nouilles, le parmesan et, si désiré, l'ail. Saler, poivrer et remuer.

Transférer la préparation dans un plat de cuisson de 20 cm (8 po).

Couvrir la préparation de mozzarella et cuire au four de 20 à 25 minutes, jusqu'à ce que le fromage soit gratiné.

Idée pour accompagner

Salade de roquette, pommes et parmesan

Par portion: 66 calories

Dans un saladier, mélanger 30 ml (2 c. à soupe) d'huile d'olive avec 30 ml (2 c. à soupe) d'eau, 15 ml (1 c. à soupe) de moutarde à l'ancienne et 30 ml (2 c. à soupe) de ciboulette hachée. Saler et poivrer. Ajouter 500 ml (2 tasses) de roquette et 2 pommes émincées. Remuer et parsemer de 60 ml (¼ de tasse) de copeaux de parmesan.

PAR PORTION	
Calories	317
Protéines	20 g
Matières grasses	9 g
Glucides	39 g
Fibres	3 g
Fer	3 mg
Calcium	307 mg
Sodium	220 mg

Au total
383
calories

Spaghetti aux boulettes de viande

Préparation : **15 minutes** • Cuisson : **15 minutes** • Quantité : **de 4 à 6 portions**

Préparation

Dans un bol, mélanger le porc haché avec la chapelure, le blanc d'œuf battu et, si désiré, 10 ml (2 c. à thé) d'ail haché. Ajouter un peu de chapelure si les boulettes ne se tiennent pas bien. Façonner 12 boulettes en utilisant environ 80 ml (⅓ de tasse) de préparation pour chacune d'elles.

Dans une casserole, chauffer l'huile à feu moyen. Faire dorer les boulettes de 2 à 3 minutes.

Ajouter l'oignon et, si désiré, le reste de l'ail. Cuire de 1 à 2 minutes en remuant.

Ajouter le jus de tomate et les tomates. Saler et poivrer. Porter à ébullition. Couvrir et laisser mijoter à feu doux-moyen de 10 à 12 minutes.

Pendant ce temps, cuire les spaghettis *al dente* dans une casserole d'eau bouillante salée. Égoutter. Répartir les pâtes dans les assiettes et napper de sauce aux boulettes.

PAR PORTION	
Calories	315
Protéines	20 g
Matières grasses	8 g
Glucides	41 g
Fibres	3 g
Fer	2 mg
Calcium	77 mg
Sodium	390 mg

Au total

377
calories

Porc haché mi-maigre ❶
350 g (environ ¾ de lb)

Chapelure nature ❷
80 ml (⅓ de tasse)

Jus de tomate ❸
1 boîte de 540 ml

Tomates en dés ❹
1 boîte de 540 ml

Spaghettis ❺
225 g

Idée pour accompagner

Salade d'asperges et épinards

Par portion: 62 calories

Dans une casserole d'eau bouillante salée, blanchir 250 g (environ ½ lb) d'asperges de 2 à 3 minutes. Rafraîchir sous l'eau très froide, puis égoutter. Dans un saladier, mélanger 30 ml (2 c. à soupe) d'huile d'olive avec 30 ml (2 c. à soupe) d'eau, 15 ml (1 c. à soupe) de moutarde à l'ancienne, 15 ml (1 c. à soupe) de zestes de citron, 15 ml (1 c. à soupe) de jus de citron et 15 ml (1 c. à soupe) de miel. Ajouter 500 ml (2 tasses) de bébés épinards et les asperges coupées en morceaux. Saler, poivrer et remuer.

PRÉVOIR AUSSI :
➤ **Œuf**
1 blanc battu
➤ **Huile d'olive**
15 ml (1 c. à soupe)
➤ ½ **oignon** haché

FACULTATIF :
➤ **Ail**
haché
25 ml (1 c. à soupe
+ 2 c. à thé)

Linguines frais aux épinards
ou nature
225 g
①

Lait 2 %
375 ml (1 ½ tasse)
②

Poivrons rôtis
égouttés
250 ml (1 tasse)
③

Parmesan
râpé
80 ml (⅓ de tasse)
④

**20 pétoncles moyens
(calibre 20/30)**
⑤

PRÉVOIR AUSSI :
➤ **Beurre**
45 ml (3 c. à soupe)

➤ **Farine**
30 ml (2 c. à soupe)

➤ **Huile d'olive**
15 ml (1 c. à soupe)

FACULTATIF :
➤ 1 **oignon** haché
➤ **Ail**
haché
10 ml (2 c. à thé)

Pétoncles et linguines, sauce aux poivrons rôtis

Préparation : **15 minutes** • Cuisson : **15 minutes** • Quantité : **6 portions**

Préparation

Dans une casserole d'eau bouillante salée, cuire les pâtes *al dente*. Égoutter.

Pendant ce temps, préparer la sauce. Dans une autre casserole, faire fondre le beurre à feu moyen. Si désiré, cuire l'oignon et l'ail de 1 à 2 minutes.

Ajouter la farine, remuer et cuire 1 minute. Verser le lait, puis porter à ébullition en fouettant. Ajouter les poivrons rôtis et le parmesan. Cuire 1 minute.

Transférer la préparation dans le contenant du mélangeur électrique. Mélanger 30 secondes, jusqu'à l'obtention d'une consistance lisse et onctueuse. Remettre la sauce dans la casserole et réserver à feu doux.

Dans une poêle, chauffer l'huile à feu moyen-élevé. Saisir les pétoncles 1 minute de chaque côté. Saler et poivrer.

Répartir les pâtes égouttées dans les assiettes. Napper de sauce et garnir de pétoncles.

PAR PORTION	
Calories	305
Protéines	20 g
Matières grasses	10 g
Glucides	33 g
Fibres	2 g
Fer	2 mg
Calcium	182 mg
Sodium	353 mg

Version minceur

Poivrons rôtis

Couper 3 poivrons en deux, puis retirer la membrane blanche et les pépins. Déposer les demi-poivrons sur une plaque de cuisson, peau vers le haut. Faire rôtir au four de 10 à 15 minutes à 205 °C (400 °F), jusqu'à ce que la peau soit noircie et gonflée. Retirer du four. Déposer dans un sac hermétique et laisser reposer 15 minutes. Peler les poivrons.

100 CALORIES
Du commerce

> pour 250 ml (1 tasse)

69 CALORIES
Maison

Cannellonis à la courge et aux fromages

Préparation : **15 minutes** • Cuisson : **35 minutes** • Quantité : **4 portions (8 rouleaux)**

Préparation

Préchauffer le four à 205 °C (400 °F).

Piquer la courge avec une fourchette en plusieurs endroits. Cuire au micro-ondes de 10 à 15 minutes, jusqu'à ce que la courge soit tendre.

Couper la courge en deux, puis retirer les graines. Prélever la chair à l'aide d'une cuillère. Déposer dans un plat de cuisson avec l'ail. Cuire au micro-ondes 5 minutes.

Pendant ce temps, cuire les lasagnes *al dente* dans une casserole d'eau bouillante salée. Égoutter.

Dans la même casserole, chauffer le mélange laitier à feu moyen jusqu'à ébullition. Incorporer la moitié du cheddar et le fromage de chèvre, puis saler et poivrer. Remuer jusqu'à ce que les fromages soient fondus.

Dans le contenant du mélangeur, réduire la courge et l'ail en purée.

Couper chaque lasagne en deux. Sur chaque morceau, déposer environ 80 ml (⅓ de tasse) de farce à la courge et rouler. Placer les rouleaux dans un plat de cuisson, joint dessous.

Napper les cannellonis de sauce et garnir du reste du cheddar. Cuire au four de 20 à 25 minutes.

PAR PORTION	
Calories	334
Protéines	22 g
Matières grasses	18 g
Glucides	25 g
Fibres	2 g
Fer	2 mg
Calcium	527 mg
Sodium	476 mg

Au total

382
calories

Courge Butternut ❶
petite
1 ½

4 lasagnes ❷

Mélange laitier pour cuisson 5 % ❸
175 ml (environ ¾ de tasse)

Cheddar faible en gras ❹
râpé
375 ml (1 ½ tasse)

Fromage de chèvre mou ❺
115 g

PRÉVOIR AUSSI :
➤ **Ail**
2 gousses entières pelées

Idée pour accompagner

Salade aux poires et canneberges

Par portion : 48 calories

Couper 2 poires en quartiers minces. Déposer dans un saladier et mélanger avec 45 ml (3 c. à soupe) de canneberges séchées, ½ laitue romaine déchiquetée, 250 ml (1 tasse) de roquette et 60 ml (¼ de tasse) de vinaigrette française sans gras. Saler et poivrer.

Nouilles asiatiques ①
230 g

½ oignon rouge ②

1 poivron jaune ③

Crevettes moyennes ④
(calibre 31/40)
crues et décortiquées
1 sac de 340 g

Sauce hoisin ⑤
160 ml (⅔ de tasse)

PRÉVOIR AUSSI :
➤ **Huile de sésame**
non grillé
15 ml (1 c. à soupe)

FACULTATIF :
➤ 12 **mini-bok choys**

Nouilles asiatiques aux crevettes

Préparation : **15 minutes** • Cuisson : **10 minutes** • Quantité : **de 4 à 6 portions**

Préparation

Dans une casserole d'eau bouillante salée, cuire les nouilles *al dente*. Égoutter.

Émincer l'oignon rouge et le poivron.

Dans une poêle, chauffer l'huile à feu moyen. Cuire l'oignon rouge, le poivron et, si désiré, les mini-bok choys de 2 à 3 minutes. Déposer dans une assiette.

Dans la même poêle, saisir les crevettes 1 minute de chaque côté.

Remettre les légumes dans la poêle et ajouter les nouilles. Verser la sauce et porter à ébullition. Cuire 2 minutes à feu doux-moyen en remuant.

PAR PORTION	
Calories	299
Protéines	18 g
Matières grasses	6 g
Glucides	43 g
Fibres	3 g
Fer	2 mg
Calcium	58 mg
Sodium	774 mg

Version minceur

Sauce asiatique

Mélanger 60 ml (¼ de tasse) de sauce soya légère avec 60 ml (¼ de tasse) de mirin, 15 ml (1 c. à soupe) d'huile de sésame grillé, 15 ml (1 c. à soupe) de vinaigre de riz et 10 ml (2 c. à thé) de sauce sriracha.

381 CALORIES

Du commerce

➤

349 CALORIES

pour 160 ml
(⅔ de tasse)

Maison

Linguines ①
225 g

Palourdes ②
égouttées
2 boîtes de 142 g
chacune

Bruschetta ③
250 ml (1 tasse)

Persil ④
haché
30 ml (2 c. à soupe)

Basilic ⑤
haché
30 ml (2 c. à soupe)

Linguines aux palourdes

Préparation : **15 minutes** • Cuisson : **10 minutes** • Quantité : **4 portions**

Préparation

Dans une casserole d'eau bouillante salée, cuire les pâtes *al dente*. Égoutter.

Dans la même casserole, chauffer les palourdes avec la bruschetta et les fines herbes de 2 à 3 minutes à feu moyen.

Ajouter les pâtes et remuer. Saler et poivrer.

PAR PORTION	
Calories	357
Protéines	21 g
Matières grasses	8 g
Glucides	49 g
Fibres	2 g
Fer	15 mg
Calcium	62 mg
Sodium	320 mg

Au total

381
calories

Idée pour accompagner

Croûtons aux fines herbes

Par croûton: 24 calories

Dans un bol, mélanger 30 ml (2 c. à soupe) de beurre léger avec 5 ml (1 c. à thé) de thym haché, 2,5 ml (½ c. à thé) de romarin haché, 2,5 ml (½ c. à thé) d'ail haché et 2,5 ml (½ c. à thé) de piment d'Espelette. Couper ¼ de baguette de pain en 12 tranches et les badigeonner de beurre parfumé. Déposer les tranches sur une plaque de cuisson et faire dorer au four de 2 à 3 minutes à la position « gril » (*broil*).

Tortellinis aux quatre fromages
1 paquet de 350 g

①

Sauce rosée
du commerce
375 ml (1 ½ tasse)

②

Roquette
250 ml (1 tasse)

③

Jambon
75 g (2 ½ oz)
de tranches coupées
en morceaux

④

Basilic
1 bouquet

⑤

Tortellinis au jambon et basilic, sauce rosée

Préparation : **10 minutes** • Cuisson : **10 minutes** • Quantité : **4 portions**

Préparation

Dans une casserole d'eau bouillante salée, cuire les tortellinis *al dente*. Égoutter.

Pendant ce temps, chauffer la sauce rosée à feu moyen jusqu'aux premiers frémissements dans une autre casserole.

Incorporer la roquette et le jambon. Réchauffer de 1 à 2 minutes en remuant.

Incorporer les tortellinis et les feuilles de basilic. Réchauffer de 1 à 2 minutes en remuant.

PAR PORTION	
Calories	386
Protéines	15 g
Matières grasses	12 g
Glucides	55 g
Fibres	4 g
Fer	2 mg
Calcium	169 mg
Sodium	839 mg

Version minceur

Sauce rosée

Dans une poêle, chauffer 15 ml (1 c. à soupe) d'huile d'olive à feu doux. Saisir ½ oignon avec 5 ml (1 c. à thé) d'ail haché de 2 à 3 minutes. Ajouter 8 tomates italiennes épépinées et coupées en morceaux et 1 tige de thym. Laisser mijoter de 8 à 10 minutes à feu doux, jusqu'à l'obtention d'une consistance de compote. À l'aide du mélangeur électrique, broyer jusqu'à l'obtention d'une consistance homogène et lisse. Incorporer 80 ml (⅓ de tasse) de mélange laitier pour cuisson 5 %.

413 CALORIES
Du commerce

> pour 375 ml (1 ½ tasse)

182 CALORIES
Maison

Capellinis ① 225 g

20 tomates raisins ② coupées en deux

Crevettes nordiques ③ 225 g (375 ml)

Citron ④ 15 ml (1 c. à soupe) de zestes

Roquette ⑤ 500 ml (2 tasses)

PRÉVOIR AUSSI :
➤ **Huile d'olive** 15 ml (1 c. à soupe)

➤ **Ail** haché 10 ml (2 c. à thé)

FACULTATIF :
➤ **½ oignon rouge** émincé

Capellinis aux crevettes nordiques et roquette

Préparation : **15 minutes** • Cuisson : **10 minutes** • Quantité : **4 portions**

Préparation

Dans une casserole d'eau bouillante salée, cuire les pâtes *al dente*. Égoutter.

Dans la même casserole, chauffer l'huile à feu moyen. Cuire l'ail et, si désiré, l'oignon rouge de 1 à 2 minutes.

Ajouter les tomates raisins et les crevettes. Cuire de 2 à 3 minutes en remuant.

Ajouter les pâtes et les zestes. Saler et poivrer. Réchauffer 1 minute en remuant.

Répartir la préparation dans les assiettes. Garnir chacune des portions de feuilles de roquette.

PAR PORTION	
Calories	312
Protéines	18 g
Matières grasses	5 g
Glucides	48 g
Fibres	3 g
Fer	2 mg
Calcium	59 mg
Sodium	387 mg

Au total

350
calories

Idée pour accompagner

Croûtons aux fines herbes et fromage

Par croûton : 38 calories

Couper ½ pain baguette en 12 tranches fines. Badigeonner avec 30 ml (2 c. à soupe) de beurre léger fondu, puis parsemer de 15 ml (1 c. à soupe) de thym haché et de 5 ml (1 c. à thé) de romarin haché. Répartir 125 ml (½ tasse) de cheddar faible en gras râpé sur les tranches. Déposer sur une plaque de cuisson couverte d'une feuille de papier d'aluminium. Faire gratiner au four de 2 à 3 minutes à la position « gril » (*broil*).

Salades-repas

Envie de profiter d'un généreux repas sans culpabiliser? Optez pour l'une de ces superbes salades-repas légères, mais nutritives, qui sauront vous rassasier! À base de laitue, mais aussi de vermicelles, d'orzo, de quinoa ou de riz, elles vous permettent de vous délecter sans faire grimper les calories!

Vermicelles de riz ①
200 g

½ concombre anglais ②

½ oignon rouge ③
émincé

1 carotte ④
coupée en julienne

Poulet ⑤
2 poitrines sans peau
coupées en tranches de
1 cm (½ po) d'épaisseur

PRÉVOIR AUSSI :
➤ **Huile de canola**
7,5 ml (½ c. à soupe)

FACULTATIF :
➤ **Basilic thaï**
30 ml (2 c. à soupe)
de feuilles

Salade tiède au poulet thaï et vermicelles de riz

Préparation : **15 minutes** • Quantité : **4 portions**

Préparation

Réhydrater les vermicelles de riz selon les indications de l'emballage. Égoutter et laisser tiédir.

Couper le concombre en deux sur la longueur, puis l'émincer. Déposer les légumes dans le saladier.

Dans une poêle antiadhésive, chauffer l'huile à feu moyen-vif. Cuire les tranches de poulet 2 minutes de chaque côté. Saler et poivrer.

Répartir les vermicelles de riz dans les assiettes.

Dans le saladier, ajouter les tranches de poulet et remuer.

Répartir la salade de légumes et de poulet sur les vermicelles. Si désiré, garnir de feuilles de basilic thaï.

PAR PORTION	
Calories	221
Protéines	17 g
Matières grasses	3 g
Glucides	31 g
Fibres	1 g
Fer	1 mg
Calcium	28 mg
Sodium	50 mg

Au total
292
calories

Idée pour accompagner

Vinaigrette lait de coco et arachide

Par portion : 71 calories

Dans le contenant du mélangeur électrique, déposer 60 ml (¼ de tasse) de lait de coco léger, 30 ml (2 c. à soupe) de jus de lime, 15 ml (1 c. à soupe) d'huile de sésame (non grillé), 10 ml (2 c. à thé) de miel, 10 ml (2 c. à thé) de beurre d'arachide faible en gras, 5 ml (1 c. à thé) de zestes de lime, 5 ml (1 c. à thé) d'ail haché, 5 ml (1 c. à thé) de gingembre haché et ½ piment thaï haché. Mélanger quelques secondes jusqu'à l'obtention d'une consistance crémeuse et homogène. Saler au goût.

Couscous ①
250 ml (1 tasse)

1 pomme verte ②
émincée

10 radis ③
émincés

Noix de Grenoble ④
hachées grossièrement
60 ml (¼ de tasse)

Crevettes nordiques ⑤
300 g (500 ml)

Salade de couscous aux crevettes nordiques et pomme verte

Préparation : **15 minutes** • Quantité : **4 portions**

Préparation

Dans un bol, déposer le couscous. Saler et poivrer, puis verser 250 ml (1 tasse) d'eau bouillante. Couvrir et laisser gonfler de 5 à 6 minutes.

Égrainer le couscous à l'aide d'une fourchette et laisser tiédir.

Dans un saladier, déposer la pomme, les radis, les noix et le couscous. Remuer, puis incorporer les crevettes.

PAR PORTION	
Calories	299
Protéines	20 g
Matières grasses	6 g
Glucides	42 g
Fibres	4 g
Fer	1 mg
Calcium	38 mg
Sodium	507 mg

Au total
382
calories

Idée pour accompagner

Vinaigrette au pesto de tomates séchées

Par portion : 83 calories

Fouetter 30 ml (2 c. à soupe) d'huile d'olive avec 30 ml (2 c. à soupe) de ciboulette hachée, 15 ml (1 c. à soupe) de pesto aux tomates séchées et 15 ml (1 c. à soupe) de vinaigre de cidre. Saler et poivrer.

Salade de pâtes au jambon et légumes

Préparation : **15 minutes** • Cuisson : **10 minutes** • Quantité : **4 portions**

Rotinis de blé entier ❶
200 g

Brocoli ❷
coupé en petits bouquets
250 ml (1 tasse)

Vinaigrette miel et moutarde faible en calories ❸
du commerce
125 ml (½ tasse)

Jambon ❹
coupé en cubes
180 ml (¾ de tasse)

10 tomates cerises ❺
de couleurs variées
coupées en deux

PRÉVOIR AUSSI :
➤ **Cheddar jaune réduit en gras**
coupé en cubes
180 ml (¾ de tasse)

FACULTATIF :
➤ **Maïs en grains**
125 ml (½ tasse)

Préparation

Dans une casserole d'eau bouillante salée, cuire les pâtes *al dente*. Ajouter le brocoli dans la casserole 3 minutes avant la fin de la cuisson des pâtes. Rafraîchir sous l'eau froide et égoutter.

Dans un saladier, mélanger la vinaigrette avec le jambon, les tomates, le fromage, les pâtes, le brocoli et, si désiré, le maïs. Saler, poivrer et remuer.

PAR PORTION	
Calories	385
Protéines	22 g
Matières grasses	10 g
Glucides	56 g
Fibres	6 g
Fer	3 mg
Calcium	287 mg
Sodium	803 mg

Version minceur

Vinaigrette miel et moutarde

Mélanger 125 ml (½ tasse) de yogourt grec nature 0 % avec 15 ml (1 c. à soupe) de vinaigre balsamique, 15 ml (1 c. à soupe) de miel et 15 ml (1 c. à soupe) de moutarde de Dijon.

378 CALORIES > **165** CALORIES

Du commerce   Pour 180 ml (¾ de tasse)   **Maison**

Salade estivale au poulet grillé

Préparation : **15 minutes** • Marinage : **4 heures** • Cuisson : **12 minutes** • Quantité : **4 portions**

Citron
15 ml (1 c. à soupe)
de zestes + 30 ml
(2 c. à soupe) de jus ➊

Poulet
4 poitrines sans peau ➋

12 fraises ➌

1 pomme ➍

2 laitues Boston ➎
ou 1 laitue frisée

Préparation

Dans un sac hermétique, mélanger les zestes avec le jus de citron, l'huile d'olive, l'ail et, si désiré, le thym. Ajouter les poitrines et laisser mariner de 4 à 8 heures au frais.

Au moment de la cuisson, préchauffer le four à 205 °C (400 °F).

Égoutter le poulet et jeter la marinade.

Dans une poêle allant au four, chauffer 15 ml (1 c. à soupe) d'huile d'olive à feu moyen. Saisir les poitrines de 1 à 2 minutes de chaque côté.

Cuire au four de 10 à 13 minutes, jusqu'à ce que l'intérieur des poitrines ait perdu sa teinte rosée. Laisser tiédir sur une planche à découper, puis émincer.

Émincer les fraises, la pomme et, si désiré, les oignons verts.

Dans chaque assiette, répartir les feuilles de laitue. Garnir de fraises, de pomme, d'une poitrine émincée et, si désiré, d'oignons verts et d'amandes.

PAR PORTION	
Calories	296
Protéines	31 g
Matières grasses	15 g
Glucides	10 g
Fibres	2 g
Fer	2 mg
Calcium	68 mg
Sodium	72 mg

Au total
363
calories

Idée pour accompagner

Vinaigrette crémeuse au miel et pavot

Par portion : 67 calories

Délayer 30 ml (2 c. à soupe) de miel dans 15 ml (1 c. à soupe) de jus de lime. Incorporer 80 ml (⅓ de tasse) de crème sure légère 5 % et 15 ml (1 c. à soupe) de graines de pavot. Saler et poivrer.

PRÉVOIR AUSSI :
➤ **Huile d'olive**
30 ml (2 c. à soupe)

➤ **Ail**
haché
15 ml (1 c. à soupe)

FACULTATIF :
➤ **Thym**
haché
5 ml (1 c. à thé)

➤ **2 oignons verts**

➤ **Amandes** tranchées
80 ml (⅓ de tasse)

½ oignon rouge ①

12 tomates raisins ②

Mozzarella fraîche ③
2 boules de 226 g
chacune

Pois chiches ④
rincés et égouttés
1 boîte de 540 ml

Raisins secs ⑤
60 ml (¼ de tasse)

Salade de pois chiches à la méditerranéenne

Préparation : **15 minutes** • Quantité : **6 portions**

Préparation

Hacher finement l'oignon rouge. Couper les tomates raisins en deux et les boules de mozzarella en cubes.

Dans un saladier, déposer tous les ingrédients. Remuer.

PAR PORTION	
Calories	316
Protéines	19 g
Matières grasses	17 g
Glucides	24 g
Fibres	4 g
Fer	2 mg
Calcium	263 mg
Sodium	96 mg

▼

Au total
400
calories

Idée pour accompagner

Vinaigrette citronnée

Par portion : 84 calories

Mélanger 60 ml (¼ de tasse) d'huile d'olive avec le zeste et le jus de 1 citron, 30 ml (2 c. à soupe) de persil haché, 30 ml (2 c. à soupe) de ciboulette hachée et 5 ml (1 c. à thé) d'ail haché. Saler et poivrer.

Thon
2 boîtes de 170 g
chacune, égoutté

1

1 laitue romaine
déchiquetée

2

2 pommes Cortland
émincées

3

Raisins rouges
coupés en deux
250 ml (1 tasse)

4

Noix de Grenoble
80 ml (⅓ de tasse)

5

Salade Waldorf au thon

Préparation : **15 minutes** • Quantité : **4 portions**

Préparation

Dans un saladier, mélanger le thon avec la laitue et les pommes.

Ajouter les raisins et les noix, puis remuer.

PAR PORTION	
Calories	224
Protéines	22 g
Matières grasses	9 g
Glucides	14 g
Fibres	3 g
Fer	2 mg
Calcium	42 mg
Sodium	47 mg

Au total

289
calories

Idée pour accompagner

Vinaigrette miel et citron

Par portion: 65 calories

Délayer 15 ml (1 c. à soupe) de miel dans 15 ml (1 c. à soupe) de jus de citron. Incorporer 125 ml (½ tasse) de yogourt nature 0 %, 45 ml (3 c. à soupe) de mayonnaise « ½ moins de gras », 30 ml (2 c. à soupe) de persil haché, 30 ml (2 c. à soupe) de ciboulette hachée et 15 ml (1 c. à soupe) de zestes de citron. Saler et poivrer.

2 pêches ①

10 fraises ②

Mesclun ③
250 ml (1 tasse)

Roquette ④
500 ml (2 tasses)

Prosciutto fumé ⑤
14 tranches

Salade dolce vita

Préparation : **15 minutes** • Quantité : **4 portions**

Préparation

Couper les pêches et les fraises en quartiers.

Répartir le mesclun et la roquette dans quatre assiettes.

Garnir chacune des portions de fruits, de tranches de prosciutto et, si désiré, d'oignon rouge.

PAR PORTION	
Calories	156
Protéines	15 g
Matières grasses	6 g
Glucides	9 g
Fibres	2 g
Fer	1 mg
Calcium	48 mg
Sodium	1238 mg

Au total

326
calories

Idée pour accompagner

Vinaigrette basilic et parmesan

Par portion: 170 calories

Fouetter 60 ml (¼ de tasse) d'huile d'olive avec 30 ml (2 c. à soupe) de vinaigre balsamique. Incorporer 45 ml (3 c. à soupe) de basilic émincé, 30 ml (2 c. à soupe) de parmesan râpé et 30 ml (2 c. à soupe) de noix de pin grillées. Saler et poivrer.

FACULTATIF :
➤ **½ oignon rouge**
émincé

Lait de coco léger
125 ml (½ tasse) ①

**Riz blanc
à grains longs** ②
80 ml (⅓ de tasse)

**Petites crevettes
(calibre 61/70)** ③
crues et décortiquées
1 sac de 450 g

Poudre de chili ④
7,5 ml (½ c. à soupe)

1 poivron orange ⑤
coupé en julienne

PRÉVOIR AUSSI :
➤ **Huile d'olive**
15 ml (1 c. à soupe)
➤ **Citron**
30 ml (2 c. à soupe)
de jus

FACULTATIF :
➤ **Ciboulette**
hachée
45 ml (3 c. à soupe)

Salade aux crevettes, riz et lait de coco

Préparation : **15 minutes** • Cuisson : **18 minutes** • Quantité : **4 portions**

Préparation

Dans une casserole, mélanger le lait de coco avec 375 ml (1 ½ tasse) d'eau et le riz. Porter à ébullition à feu moyen. Couvrir et cuire à feu doux-moyen de 18 à 20 minutes. Égoutter et laisser tiédir.

Préchauffer le four à 180 °C (350 °F).

Dans un bol, mélanger les crevettes avec la poudre de chili, l'huile et le jus de citron. Répartir les crevettes sur une plaque de cuisson tapissée de papier d'aluminium. Cuire au four de 8 à 10 minutes. Retirer du four et laisser tiédir.

Dans un bol, mélanger le riz avec les crevettes, le poivron et, si désiré, la ciboulette. Saler et poivrer.

Idée pour accompagner

Vinaigrette lime-coco

Par portion : 68 calories

Mélanger 30 ml (2 c. à soupe) d'huile de canola avec 30 ml (2 c. à soupe) de jus de lime, 15 ml (1 c. à soupe) de lait de coco léger et 2 à 3 gouttes d'huile de sésame grillé.

PAR PORTION	
Calories	216
Protéines	24 g
Matières grasses	8 g
Glucides	11 g
Fibres	1 g
Fer	3 mg
Calcium	69 mg
Sodium	184 mg

Au total
284
calories

Recette de Ève Godin, nutritionniste

¼ de baguette
de pain
coupée en cubes

1

Bacon précuit **2**
10 tranches
coupées en morceaux

Tomates cerises **3**
rouges et jaunes
16 à 20

Poulet **4**
cuit et émincé
500 ml (2 tasses)

2 laitues Boston **5**

PRÉVOIR AUSSI :
➤ **Huile d'olive**
7,5 ml (½ c. à soupe)

Salade club sandwich

Préparation : **15 minutes** • Quantité : **4 portions**

Préparation

Dans une poêle, chauffer l'huile à feu moyen. Cuire les
cubes de pain de 2 à 3 minutes en remuant. Réserver
dans une assiette.

Dans la même poêle, réchauffer le bacon de 1 à
2 minutes. Éponger sur du papier absorbant.

Dans un saladier, mélanger les tomates avec le poulet,
le bacon et les croûtons.

Dans chacune des assiettes, répartir les feuilles de laitue
Boston et garnir du mélange au poulet.

PAR PORTION	
Calories	244
Protéines	31 g
Matières grasses	7 g
Glucides	13 g
Fibres	2 g
Fer	2 mg
Calcium	43 mg
Sodium	379 mg

Au total
293
calories

Idée pour accompagner

Vinaigrette dijonnaise

Par portion: 49 calories

Fouetter 60 ml (¼ de tasse) de mayonnaise
« ½ moins de gras » avec 45 ml (3 c. à soupe) de lait
2 % et 15 ml (1 c. à soupe) de moutarde de Dijon.
Saler et poivrer au goût.

Saumon ①
1 filet de 800 g
(environ 1 ¾ lb)
la peau enlevée

10 choux de Bruxelles ②
coupés en quatre

1 poivron rouge ③
coupé en cubes

1 laitue frisée verte ④
déchiquetée

**12 tomates
cerises jaunes** ⑤
coupées en deux

Salade de saumon et légumes grillés

Préparation : **15 minutes** • Cuisson : **12 minutes** • Quantité : **4 portions**

Préparation

Préchauffer le four à 205 °C (400 °F).

Sur une plaque de cuisson tapissée de papier d'aluminium, déposer le filet de saumon, les choux de Bruxelles et les cubes de poivron, sans les superposer.

Cuire au four de 12 à 15 minutes, jusqu'à ce que la chair du saumon se défasse à la fourchette et que les choux de Bruxelles soient dorés.

Retirer la plaque du four et laisser le four allumé à la même température.

Pendant la cuisson du saumon, si désiré, préparer les croûtons de pain. Dans un bol, mélanger les cubes de pain avec l'huile. Sur une plaque de cuisson tapissée de papier parchemin, déposer les cubes de pain. Faire dorer au four de 8 à 10 minutes.

Défaire la chair du saumon en gros flocons. Dans quatre assiettes, répartir la laitue, le saumon, les légumes rôtis et les tomates cerises. Si désiré, garnir de croûtons.

PAR PORTION	
Calories	258
Protéines	19 g
Matières grasses	13 g
Glucides	18 g
Fibres	4 g
Fer	2 mg
Calcium	53 mg
Sodium	155 mg

Au total
383
calories

Idée pour accompagner

Vinaigrette pesto et citron

Par portion: 125 calories

Délayer 15 ml (1 c. à soupe) de miel dans 15 ml (1 c. à soupe) de jus de citron. Incorporer 15 ml (1 c. à soupe) de pesto, 45 ml (3 c. à soupe) d'huile d'olive, 15 ml (1 c. à soupe) d'eau, 10 ml (2 c. à thé) de zestes de citron, 30 ml (2 c. à soupe) de ciboulette hachée et 5 ml (1 c. à thé) d'ail haché. Saler et poivrer.

FACULTATIF :
➤ ¼ de **baguette de pain**
coupée en cubes
➤ **Huile d'olive**
15 ml (1 c. à soupe)

Poulet ①
2 poitrines sans peau
de 150 g (⅓ de lb)
chacune

Flocons d'avoine ②
180 ml (¾ de tasse)

**Céréales
croustillantes au riz** ③
(de type Special K
Originales) écrasées
250 ml (1 tasse)

1 laitue Boston ④

Mandarines ⑤
1 boîte de 284 ml

PRÉVOIR AUSSI :
➤ **Farine**
60 ml (¼ de tasse)

➤ **1 œuf**

➤ **Huile d'olive**
30 ml (2 c. à soupe)

FACULTATIF :
➤ ¼ de **chou rouge**
émincé

➤ **Nouilles frites**
160 ml (⅔ de tasse)

Salade thaï au poulet croustillant

Préparation : **15 minutes** • Cuisson : **12 minutes** • Quantité : **4 portions**

Préparation

Préchauffer le four à 205 °C (400 °F).

Couper les poitrines de poulet en deux sur l'épaisseur pour obtenir quatre escalopes.

Préparer trois assiettes creuses. Dans la première, verser la farine. Dans la deuxième, battre l'œuf. Dans la troisième, mélanger les flocons d'avoine avec les céréales.

Fariner les escalopes, puis les tremper dans l'œuf battu. Enrober du mélange aux céréales.

Déposer les escalopes sur une plaque de cuisson tapissée de papier parchemin. Arroser d'un filet d'huile d'olive. Cuire au four de 12 à 15 minutes, en retournant les escalopes à mi-cuisson, jusqu'à ce que l'intérieur de la chair ait perdu sa teinte rosée.

Pendant ce temps, répartir la laitue, les mandarines et, si désiré, le chou rouge dans les assiettes. Si désiré, parsemer de nouilles frites.

Une fois la cuisson du poulet terminée, émincer les escalopes. Répartir les morceaux de poulet dans les assiettes.

PAR PORTION	
Calories	351
Protéines	25 g
Matières grasses	12 g
Glucides	36 g
Fibres	4 g
Fer	4 mg
Calcium	63 mg
Sodium	160 mg

Au total
380
calories

Idée pour accompagner

**Vinaigrette aux piments
et gingembre**

Par portion : 29 calories

Mélanger 60 ml (¼ de tasse) de sauce douce aux piments avec 30 ml (2 c. à soupe) de coriandre hachée, 15 ml (1 c. à soupe) de gingembre haché, 15 ml (1 c. à soupe) de jus de lime et 5 ml (1 c. à thé) d'ail haché.

Mesclun ①
625 ml (2 ½ tasses)

2 tomates ②

2 pommes ③

3 gros œufs ④
cuits dur

Thon blanc ⑤
ou thon pâle
égoutté
2 boîtes de 120 g
chacune

Salade multicolore au thon

Préparation : **15 minutes** • Quantité : **4 portions**

Préparation

Répartir le mesclun dans les assiettes.

Si désiré, émincer l'oignon rouge et le céleri, puis répartir au centre des assiettes.

Couper en quartiers les tomates, les pommes et les œufs cuits dur. Répartir dans les assiettes.

Garnir chacune des portions de thon et, si désiré, d'olives.

PAR PORTION	
Calories	178
Protéines	16 g
Matières grasses	8 g
Glucides	13 g
Fibres	3 g
Fer	2 mg
Calcium	81 mg
Sodium	333 mg

Au total
375
calories

Idée pour accompagner

Vinaigrette citron, sésame et tamari

Par portion: 197 calories

Fouetter 60 ml (¼ de tasse) d'huile d'olive avec 30 ml (2 c. à soupe) d'huile de canola, 30 ml (2 c. à soupe) de vinaigre de riz, 30 ml (2 c. à soupe) de jus de citron, 15 ml (1 c. à soupe) de tamari, 5 ml (1 c. à thé) de sirop d'érable, 2,5 ml (½ c. à thé) d'huile de sésame grillé, 2,5 ml (½ c. à thé) de basilic séché et 1 gousse d'ail hachée. Saler et poivrer.

FACULTATIF :
➤ ½ **oignon rouge**
➤ **Céleri**
  2 branches
➤ 12 **olives Kalamata**
  entières ou émincées

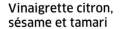

Orzo ①
1 sac de 350 g

Poivrons ②
1 jaune et ½ rouge

1 tomate ③

Crabe ④
300 g (⅔ de lb) de chair

Feta ⑤
émiettée
60 ml (¼ de tasse)

FACULTATIF :
➤ **Basilic**
émincé
125 ml (½ tasse)

➤ **Grenade**
125 ml (½ tasse)
de grains

➤ **Câpres**
30 ml (2 c. à soupe)

Salade d'orzo au crabe

Préparation : **15 minutes** • Quantité : **6 portions**

Préparation

Dans une casserole d'eau bouillante salée, cuire l'orzo *al dente*. Égoutter, puis rincer sous l'eau froide. Égoutter de nouveau.

Couper en dés les poivrons et la tomate.

Dans un saladier, mélanger l'orzo avec les poivrons, la tomate, le crabe et la feta.

Au moment de servir, ajouter le basilic, les grains de grenade et les câpres si désiré.

PAR PORTION	
Calories	283
Protéines	16 g
Matières grasses	3 g
Glucides	48 g
Fibres	2 g
Fer	1 mg
Calcium	88 mg
Sodium	469 mg

Au total

382
calories

Idée pour accompagner

Vinaigrette balsamique aux herbes

Par portion: 99 calories

Fouetter 60 ml (¼ de tasse) d'huile de canola avec 10 ml (2 c. à thé) d'huile de noix, 15 ml (1 c. à soupe) de jus de citron, 7,5 ml (½ c. à soupe) de vinaigre balsamique, 7,5 ml (½ c. à soupe) de vinaigre de vin rouge, 7,5 ml (½ c. à soupe) de thym haché, 7,5 ml (½ c. à soupe) de basilic haché, 2,5 ml (½ c. à thé) de poivre noir fraîchement moulu et 5 ml (1 c. à thé) d'ail haché finement. Saler.

Canard confit ➊
4 cuisses

3 oranges ➋

½ concombre ➌
émincé

Bébés épinards ➍
500 ml (2 tasses)

Coriandre ➎
30 ml (2 c. à soupe)
de feuilles

FACULTATIF :
➤ **Chou nappa**
émincé
375 ml (1 ½ tasse)

➤ 3 **oignons verts**
émincés

➤ **Céleri**
2 branches
émincées

Salade tiède au canard confit et suprêmes d'oranges

Préparation : **15 minutes** • Cuisson : **12 minutes** • Quantité : **6 portions**

Préparation

Préchauffer le four à 205 °C (400 °F).

Sur une plaque de cuisson tapissée de papier parchemin, déposer les cuisses de canard, côté peau dessus. Cuire au four 12 minutes. Laisser tiédir, puis retirer la peau des cuisses et effilocher la chair.

Prélever les suprêmes des oranges en pelant d'abord l'écorce à vif, puis en tranchant de chaque côté des membranes. Presser les membranes au-dessus d'un saladier afin d'en récupérer le jus.

Dans le saladier, déposer les suprêmes d'oranges, le concombre et, si désiré, le chou nappa, les oignons verts et le céleri. Remuer, puis incorporer les bébés épinards.

Répartir la salade dans les assiettes. Garnir chacune des portions de canard confit et de feuilles de coriandre.

PAR PORTION	
Calories	219
Protéines	18 g
Matières grasses	12 g
Glucides	11 g
Fibres	2 g
Fer	2 mg
Calcium	66 mg
Sodium	229 mg

Au total
367
calories

Idée pour accompagner

Vinaigrette à la thaï

Par portion : 148 calories

Délayer 30 ml (2 c. à soupe) de miel dans 30 ml (2 c. à soupe) de jus de lime. Incorporer 80 ml (⅓ de tasse) d'huile de sésame (non grillé), 30 ml (2 c. à soupe) de sauce soya, 15 ml (1 c. à soupe) de gingembre haché, 15 ml (1 c. à soupe) d'ail haché et 15 ml (1 c. à soupe) de graines de sésame. Saler, puis ajouter du piment thaï haché.

Salade de crevettes à l'asiatique

Préparation : **15 minutes** • Quantité : **4 portions**

Edamames ①
(fèves de soya)
surgelés
250 ml (1 tasse)

1 mangue ②

**Crevettes moyennes
(calibre 31/40)** ③
crues et décortiquées
1 sac de 340 g

Bébés épinards ④
500 ml (2 tasses)

Noix de cajou ⑤
rôties
60 ml (¼ de tasse)

Préparation

Dans une casserole d'eau bouillante salée, cuire les edamames 5 minutes. Égoutter et rincer sous l'eau froide.

Couper la mangue en deux, puis émincer finement chacune des moitiés. Si désiré, râper la carotte ou la tailler en julienne.

Dans une poêle, chauffer l'huile de sésame à feu moyen. Cuire les crevettes de 2 à 3 minutes. Retirer du feu et laisser tiédir.

Dans un saladier, mélanger les edamames avec les bébés épinards, les noix de cajou, les crevettes et, si désiré, la carotte râpée et le chou rouge.

Répartir la salade dans les assiettes. Garnir chacune des portions de tranches de mangue.

PAR PORTION	
Calories	298
Protéines	28 g
Matières grasses	12 g
Glucides	22 g
Fibres	5 g
Fer	6 mg
Calcium	215 mg
Sodium	167 mg

Au total
381
calories

Idée pour accompagner

Vinaigrette sésame et lime

Par portion: 83 calories

Mélanger 30 ml (2 c. à soupe) d'huile de sésame (non grillé) avec 15 ml (1 c. à soupe) de jus de lime, 15 ml (1 c. à soupe) de mirin, 7,5 ml (½ c. à soupe) de gingembre haché, 7,5 ml (½ c. à soupe) de graines de sésame, 5 ml (1 c. à thé) d'ail haché, 1 oignon vert haché finement et 1 piment thaï haché finement. Saler.

PRÉVOIR AUSSI :
➤ **Huile de sésame**
non grillé
7,5 ml (½ c. à soupe)

FACULTATIF :
➤ **1 carotte**
➤ **Chou rouge**
émincé
250 ml (1 tasse)

Bébés épinards ①
1 litre (4 tasses)

1 poivron rouge ②
coupé en cubes

Chorizo ③
coupé en tranches
minces
150 g (⅓ de lb)

Pois chiches ④
rincés et égouttés
250 ml (1 tasse)

Persil ⑤
haché
60 ml (¼ de tasse)

Salade de pois chiches, poivron et chorizo

Préparation : **15 minutes** • Quantité : **4 portions**

Préparation

Dans un saladier, mélanger les bébés épinards avec le poivron, le chorizo, les pois chiches et le persil.

PAR PORTION	
Calories	211
Protéines	16 g
Matières grasses	10 g
Glucides	16 g
Fibres	4 g
Fer	3 mg
Calcium	59 mg
Sodium	706 mg

Au total
273
calories

Idée pour accompagner

Vinaigrette au piment d'Espelette et vinaigre de vin rouge

Par portion : 62 calories

Mélanger 30 ml (2 c. à soupe) d'huile d'olive avec 15 ml (1 c. à soupe) de vinaigre de vin rouge, 15 ml (1 c. à soupe) de jus de citron et 2,5 ml (½ c. à thé) de piment d'Espelette.

Recette de Ève Godin, nutritionniste

Pizzas, burgers & Cie

Vous raffolez de la nourriture de type bistro,
mais vous avez l'impression d'engraisser rien qu'à
y penser ? Cette section vous offre des versions
minceur faciles à réaliser qui vous donneront
le sentiment de vous gâter… sans tricher !

Tomates cerises ①
de 20 à 25

Pâte à pizza ②
du commerce
350 g (environ ¾ de lb)

Semoule de maïs ③
20 ml (4 c. à thé)

Mozzarella di bufala ④
égouttée et
émincée finement
1 boule de 200 g

Origan ⑤
haché
15 ml (1 c. à soupe)

PRÉVOIR AUSSI :
➤ **Ail**
3 gousses émincées

➤ **Sucre**
15 ml (1 c. à soupe)

➤ **Huile d'olive**
15 ml (1 c. à soupe)

FACULTATIF :
➤ **Thym**
haché
10 ml (2 c. à thé)

Pizza margarita aux tomates confites

Préparation : **15 minutes** • Cuisson des tomates confites : **35 minutes** • Cuisson de la pizza : **18 minutes**
Quantité : **4 portions (1 pizza de 28 cm – 11 po)**

Préparation

Préchauffer le four à 180°C (350°F).

Sur une plaque de cuisson tapissée de papier parchemin, déposer les tomates cerises et l'ail. Saupoudrer de sucre et napper d'huile. Remuer avec les doigts. Saler et poivrer. Cuire au four 35 minutes. Laisser tiédir.

Sur une surface farinée, étirer la pâte en un cercle d'environ 28 cm (11 po) de diamètre.

Saupoudrer le cercle de pâte de semoule de maïs. Déposer sur une plaque de cuisson, côté garni de semoule de maïs dessous.

Hausser la température du four à 205°C (400°F).

Garnir la pâte à pizza de tomates confites, de mozzarella di bufala, d'origan et, si désiré, de thym. Cuire au four de 18 à 20 minutes.

PAR PORTION	
Calories	400
Protéines	18 g
Matières grasses	13 g
Glucides	54 g
Fibres	4 g
Fer	4 mg
Calcium	309 mg
Sodium	409 mg

Version minceur

Pâte à pizza au blé

Dissoudre 30 ml (2 c. à soupe) de sucre dans 250 ml (1 tasse) d'eau tiède. Saupoudrer du contenu de 1 sachet de levure sèche instantanée à levée rapide de 8 g. Laisser reposer 5 minutes, jusqu'à ce que des bulles se forment.

1688 CALORIES
Du commerce

Pour 1 boule
de 675 g
(environ 1 ½ lb)

1368 CALORIES
Maison

Ajouter 15 ml (1 c. à soupe) d'huile d'olive. Dans le contenant du robot culinaire, mélanger 600 ml (environ 2 ⅔ tasses) de farine de blé entier avec 10 ml (2 c. à thé) de sel. À vitesse moyenne, incorporer graduellement la préparation liquide. Mélanger 30 secondes, jusqu'à ce que la pâte décolle des parois du contenant et qu'elle forme une boule élastique. Sur une surface farinée, pétrir la pâte de 1 à 2 minutes jusqu'à l'obtention d'une boule lisse. Déposer la pâte dans un bol badigeonné d'huile. Couvrir d'une pellicule plastique. Laisser gonfler à température ambiante de 1 à 2 heures, jusqu'à ce que la pâte ait doublé de volume. Une fois la pâte levée, y enfoncer le poing pour la faire dégonfler. Diviser la pâte en deux boules (la pâte non cuite peut être congelée jusqu'à 1 mois dans un sac hermétique). Sur une surface, étaler la pâte en un cercle de 28 cm (11 po). Laisser reposer 5 minutes.

Burgers au porc effiloché

Préparation : **15 minutes** • Cuisson : **5 minutes** • Quantité : **6 portions**

Porc effiloché ①
du commerce
600 g (environ 1 ⅓ lb)

Sauce barbecue ②
30 ml (2 c. à soupe)

Fromage suisse ③
ou emmenthal
6 tranches

6 pains à burger ④
coupés en deux

Salade de chou
traditionnelle ⑤
180 ml (¾ de tasse)

Préparation

Préchauffer le four à 150°C (300°F).

Réchauffer le porc effiloché selon les indications de l'emballage.

Dans un bol, mélanger le porc effiloché avec la sauce barbecue.

Déposer une tranche de fromage sur la base des pains. Badigeonner l'autre moitié des pains de moutarde. Griller au four.

Garnir les pains de porc, de salade de chou et, si désiré, de tranches de pommes.

PAR PORTION	
Calories	399
Protéines	28 g
Matières grasses	13 g
Glucides	35 g
Fibres	2 g
Fer	2 mg
Calcium	224 mg
Sodium	980 mg

Version minceur

Porc effiloché

Mélanger 10 ml (2 c. à thé) de paprika avec 15 ml (1 c. à soupe) d'assaisonnements à chili, 10 ml (2 c. à thé) de poudre d'ail, 10 ml (2 c. à thé) de moutarde en poudre, 10 ml (2 c. à thé) de thym haché et 10 ml (2 c. à thé) d'huile de canola. Dans un plat de cuisson, déposer 1 kg (2,2 lb) d'épaule de porc et la frotter avec le mélange d'épices. Couvrir et cuire au four 4 heures à 150°C (300°F).

1087 CALORIES > **884** CALORIES

Du commerce

Pour 600 g
(environ 1 ⅓ lb)

Maison

PRÉVOIR AUSSI :
➤ **Moutarde**
à l'ancienne
30 ml (2 c. à soupe)

FACULTATIF :
➤ **2 pommes vertes**
tranchées finement

4 pains ciabatta ①
ou à panini

**Fromage crémeux ail
et fines herbes** ②
du commerce
120 g (environ ¼ de lb)

Saumon fumé ③
1 paquet de 170 g

1 avocat ④
émincé

Roquette ⑤
500 ml (2 tasses)

PRÉVOIR AUSSI :
➤ ¼ d'**oignon rouge**
émincé
➤ **Câpres**
15 ml (1 c. à soupe)

Paninis au saumon fumé, avocat et roquette

Préparation : **15 minutes** • Cuisson : **5 minutes** • Quantité : **4 portions**

Préparation

Préchauffer le gril à panini à température moyenne.

Couper les pains en deux sur l'épaisseur. Tartiner l'intérieur des pains avec le fromage crémeux. Garnir la base des pains de saumon fumé, d'avocat, d'oignon rouge et de câpres. Poivrer, puis ajouter la roquette. Couvrir avec le dessus des pains, côté tartiné à l'intérieur.

Cuire dans le gril à panini de 5 à 6 minutes.

PAR PORTION	
Calories	370
Protéines	21 g
Matières grasses	20 g
Glucides	28 g
Fibres	3 g
Fer	1 mg
Calcium	109 mg
Sodium	726 mg

Version minceur

Sauce ail et fines herbes

Mélanger 125 ml (½ tasse) de yogourt grec nature 0 % avec 10 ml (2 c. à thé) d'ail haché, 10 ml (2 c. à thé) de ciboulette hachée, 10 ml (2 c. à thé) de persil haché et 10 ml (2 c. à thé) d'origan haché.

264 CALORIES

Du commerce

Pour 125 ml
(½ tasse)

79 CALORIES

Maison

Pâte à pizza ①
du commerce
350 g (environ ¾ de lb)

Sauce chili épicée thaï ②
du commerce
80 ml (⅓ de tasse)

**12 crevettes moyennes
(calibre 31/40)** ③
cuites et décortiquées

Arachides ④
30 ml (2 c. à soupe)

Cheddar ⑤
râpé
180 ml (¾ de tasse)

PRÉVOIR AUSSI :
➤ **Huile de sésame**
non grillé
10 ml (2 c. à thé)

➤ **Sauce soya**
5 ml (1 c. à thé)

FACULTATIF :
➤ 1 **poivron rouge**
émincé

➤ 1 **oignon rouge**
émincé

➤ **Fèves germées**
60 ml (¼ de tasse)

Pizza thaï aux crevettes

Préparation : **15 minutes** • Cuisson : **20 minutes** • Quantité : **4 portions (1 pizza de 28 cm - 11 po)**

Préparation

Préchauffer le four à 205 °C (400 °F).

Sur une surface farinée, étirer la pâte en un cercle de 28 cm (11 po) de diamètre. Déposer sur une plaque de cuisson.

Étaler la sauce chili sur la pâte en réservant un pourtour de 1 cm (½ po). Garnir de crevettes, d'arachides, de cheddar et, si désiré, de poivron et d'oignon rouge. Arroser d'un filet d'huile de sésame et de sauce soya.

Cuire au four de 20 à 25 minutes, jusqu'à ce que la pâte soit dorée et croustillante.

À la sortie du four, parsemer de fèves germées si désiré.

PAR PORTION	
Calories	393
Protéines	19 g
Matières grasses	10 g
Glucides	55 g
Fibres	3 g
Fer	4 mg
Calcium	222 mg
Sodium	1 140 mg

Version minceur

Sauce chili épicée

Dans un bol, mélanger 60 ml (¼ de tasse) de sauce tomate avec 5 ml (1 c. à thé) de sauce sriracha, 7,5 ml (½ c. à soupe) de cassonade et 7,5 ml (½ c. à soupe) de vinaigre de riz.

104 CALORIES

Du commerce

Pour 80 ml
(⅓ de tasse)

39 CALORIES

Maison

1 pomme Cortland ①

Poulet ②
cuit
3 poitrines sans peau
de 120 g (environ
¼ de lb) chacune

Cheddar marbré ③
faible en gras
coupé en cubes
250 ml (1 tasse)

Canneberges séchées ④
80 ml (⅓ de tasse)

2 pitas pochettes ⑤

FACULTATIF :
➤ **Céleri**
1 branche
➤ **Laitue frisée verte**
4 feuilles
➤ **2 oignons verts**
hachés

Pitas au poulet, pomme, cheddar et canneberges

Préparation : **15 minutes** • Quantité : **4 portions**

Préparation

Tailler la pomme, le poulet et, si désiré, le céleri en dés. Déposer dans un saladier et mélanger avec le cheddar et les canneberges. Saler et poivrer.

Couper les pitas en deux. Garnir chaque demi-pita de la préparation au poulet et, si désiré, de laitue et d'oignons verts.

Idée pour accompagner

Sauce miel et citron

Par portion : 39 calories

Dans un saladier, mélanger 75 ml (¼ de tasse + 1 c. à soupe) de crème sure légère 5 % avec 10 ml (2 c. à thé) de miel et 10 ml (2 c. à thé) de jus de citron.

PAR PORTION	
Calories	358
Protéines	35 g
Matières grasses	10 g
Glucides	33 g
Fibres	2 g
Fer	2 mg
Calcium	350 mg
Sodium	500 mg

Au total
397
calories

Moutarde à l'ancienne ①
10 ml (2 c. à thé)

Crabe ②
1 paquet de chair
de 200 g, égouttée

Crevettes nordiques ③
150 g (250 ml)

2 pommes vertes ④
coupées en julienne

8 pains à hot dog ⑤

PRÉVOIR AUSSI :
➤ **Yogourt grec
nature 0 %**
125 ml (½ tasse)
➤ **Ail**
haché
5 ml (1 c. à thé)

FACULTATIF :
➤ **Persil**
haché
30 ml (2 c. à soupe)
➤ **Piment d'Espelette**
2,5 ml (½ c. à thé)

Guedilles au crabe et crevettes nordiques

Préparation : **15 minutes** • Réfrigération : **1 heure** • Quantité : **4 portions**

Préparation

Dans un saladier, mélanger la moutarde avec le yogourt et l'ail. Incorporer la chair de crabe, les crevettes et la julienne de pommes. Si désiré, ajouter le persil et le piment d'Espelette. Réfrigérer 1 heure.

Ouvrir les pains et les déposer sur une plaque de cuisson. Faire griller au four à la position « gril » (*broil*) environ 1 minute.

Garnir les pains de la préparation au crabe.

Idée pour accompagner

Chips santé

Par portion: 104 calories

À l'aide d'une mandoline ou d'un couteau, couper en fines tranches 2 pommes de terre à chair jaune ou Yukon Gold. Déposer une feuille de papier parchemin dans une assiette et la badigeonner légèrement d'environ 5 ml (1 c. à thé) d'huile d'olive. Étaler quelques tranches de pomme de terre sur la feuille et badigeonner de 10 ml (2 c. à thé) d'huile. Cuire au micro-ondes de 4 à 6 minutes à intensité élevée. Répéter pour le reste des tranches. Saupoudrer de fleur de sel et de poivre du moulin.

PAR PORTION	
Calories	284
Protéines	24 g
Matières grasses	3 g
Glucides	46 g
Fibres	7 g
Fer	3 mg
Calcium	151 mg
Sodium	985 mg

Au total
388
calories

Pâte à pizza ①
350 g (environ ¾ de lb)

Sauce marinara ②
125 ml (½ tasse)

Pepperoni végétarien ③
de type Yves
Veggie Cuisine
60 g (environ
20 tranches)

½ poivron jaune ④
émincé

Mozzarella ⑤
sans gras
râpée
125 ml (½ tasse)

PRÉVOIR AUSSI :
> 1 **petit oignon**
émincé

FACULTATIF :
> 8 **champignons**
émincés

256

Pizza toute garnie

Préparation : **15 minutes** • Cuisson : **18 minutes** • Quantité : **4 portions (1 pizza de 28 cm – 11 po)**

Préparation

Préchauffer le four à 220 °C (425 °F).

Sur une surface légèrement farinée, étirer la pâte en un cercle de 28 cm (11 po) de diamètre. Déposer la pâte sur une plaque de cuisson ou sur une plaque à pizza.

Étaler la sauce sur la pâte en réservant un pourtour de 1 cm (½ po). Garnir de pepperoni végétarien, de poivron, d'oignon et, si désiré, de champignons. Couvrir de mozzarella.

Cuire au four de 18 à 20 minutes, jusqu'à ce que la pâte et le fromage soient dorés.

PAR PORTION	
Calories	308
Protéines	16 g
Matières grasses	3 g
Glucides	54 g
Fibres	4 g
Fer	5 mg
Calcium	178 mg
Sodium	728 mg

Au total
386
calories

Idée pour accompagner

Salade mesclun et concombre

Par portion : 78 calories

Mélanger 30 ml (2 c. à soupe) d'huile d'olive avec 10 ml (2 c. à thé) de vinaigre balsamique, 10 ml (2 c. à thé) d'ail haché, 10 ml (2 c. à thé) de moutarde de Dijon et 30 ml (2 c. à soupe) de ciboulette hachée. Saler et poivrer. Ajouter 500 ml (2 tasses) de mesclun et ½ concombre coupé en rondelles. Mélanger.

**Bœuf haché
extra-maigre**
340 g (¾ de lb)

1

**Assaisonnements
à tacos**
15 ml (1 c. à soupe)

2

4 pains à hamburger
réduits en calories
(de type Weight
Watchers)

3

Cheddar léger
4 tranches

4

Salsa
180 ml (¾ de tasse)

5

Hamburgers à la mexicaine

Préparation : **15 minutes** • Cuisson : **12 minutes** • Quantité : **4 portions**

Préparation

Dans un bol, mélanger le bœuf avec les assaisonnements à tacos. Façonner quatre galettes d'environ 2 cm (¾ de po) d'épaisseur avec le mélange.

Dans une poêle, chauffer l'huile à feu moyen. Cuire les galettes 6 minutes de chaque côté, jusqu'à ce que l'intérieur de la chair ait perdu sa teinte rosée.

Préchauffer le four à la position « gril » (*broil*). Diviser les pains en deux et les faire griller au four.

Garnir les pains d'une galette de viande, de cheddar, de salsa et, si désiré, de laitue.

PAR PORTION	
Calories	319
Protéines	25 g
Matières grasses	13 g
Glucides	26 g
Fibres	4 g
Fer	3 mg
Calcium	70 mg
Sodium	1 110 mg

Au total

389
calories

Idée pour accompagner

Salade de chou de Savoie et endives à la sauce crémeuse

Par portion : 70 calories

Dans un saladier, mélanger 60 ml (¼ de tasse) de mayonnaise avec 60 ml (¼ de tasse) de yogourt grec nature 0 %, 15 ml (1 c. à soupe) de moutarde à l'ancienne et 45 ml (3 c. à soupe) de persil plat haché. Ajouter 3 endives émincées, ¼ de chou de Savoie émincé et 1 pomme coupée en dés. Saler, poivrer et remuer.

PRÉVOIR AUSSI :
➤ **Huile d'olive**
15 ml (1 c. à soupe)

FACULTATIF :
➤ **Laitue frisée verte**
4 feuilles

Crevettes nordiques ①
250 g (416 ml)

½ céleri-rave ②
pelé et taillé
en julienne

½ pomme verte ③
taillée en julienne

Crème sure légère 4 % ④
80 ml (⅓ de tasse)

**4 petits pains ciabatta
de blé entier** ⑤

FACULTATIF :
➤ **Citron**
15 ml (1 c. à soupe)
de jus

➤ **Persil**
quelques feuilles
hachées

PRÉVOIR AUSSI :
➤ **Moutarde de Dijon**
5 ml (1 c. à thé)

Sandwich aux crevettes et rémoulade

Préparation : **15 minutes** • Quantité : **4 portions**

Préparation

Dans un bol, mélanger les crevettes avec le céleri-rave, la pomme, la crème sure, la moutarde de Dijon et, si désiré, le jus de citron et le persil.

Ouvrir les pains en deux et les garnir de la préparation aux crevettes.

Idée pour accompagner

Poêlée de brocoli et tomates cerises

Par portion : 58 calories

Dans une poêle, chauffer 15 ml (1 c. à soupe) d'huile de sésame (non grillé) à feu moyen. Cuire ½ oignon haché avec 5 ml (1 c. à thé) d'ail haché de 1 à 2 minutes. Ajouter 500 ml (2 tasses) de brocoli coupé en petits bouquets et de 8 à 10 tomates cerises. Saler, poivrer et cuire de 3 à 4 minutes en remuant de temps en temps.

PAR PORTION	
Calories	169
Protéines	16 g
Matières grasses	2 g
Glucides	20 g
Fibres	2 g
Fer	2 mg
Calcium	74 mg
Sodium	199 mg

Au total
227
calories

Recette de Ève Godin, nutritionniste

Pâte à pizza ①
du commerce
350 g (environ ¾ de lb)

Crème sure légère 5 % ②
125 ml (½ tasse)

Fromage fouetté ③
à la crème léger
ramolli
1 contenant de 150 g

Câpres ④
15 ml (1 c. à soupe)

Saumon fumé ⑤
coupé en morceaux
1 paquet de 120 g

FACULTATIF :
➤ **Citron**
15 ml (1 c. à soupe)
de zestes

➤ **Aneth**
haché
30 ml (2 c. à soupe)

PRÉVOIR AUSSI :
➤ **½ oignon rouge**
émincé

Tarte flammée au saumon fumé

Préparation : **15 minutes** • Cuisson : **18 minutes** • Quantité : **4 portions**

Préparation

Préchauffer le four à 205 °C (400 °F).

Sur une surface légèrement farinée, étendre la pâte en un rectangle de 33 cm x 23 cm (13 po x 9 po). Déposer la pâte sur une plaque de cuisson.

Dans un bol, mélanger la crème sure avec le fromage fouetté et, si désiré, les zestes de citron. Étaler la préparation sur la pâte à pizza. Garnir de câpres, de saumon fumé et d'oignon rouge.

Cuire au four de 18 à 20 minutes, jusqu'à ce que la croûte soit dorée.

À la sortie du four, poivrer et parsemer d'aneth si désiré.

PAR PORTION	
Calories	396
Protéines	19 g
Matières grasses	13 g
Glucides	51 g
Fibres	2 g
Fer	3 mg
Calcium	81 mg
Sodium	878 mg

Version minceur

Pâte à pizza au chou-fleur

Couper ½ chou-fleur en bouquets. À l'aide du robot culinaire, réduire le chou-fleur en granules. Verser dans un bol et couvrir de pellicule plastique. Cuire 3 minutes au micro-ondes. Retirer la pellicule plastique, remuer et laisser tiédir 5 minutes. Verser le chou-fleur sur un linge, puis le plier pour former un baluchon. Serrer au-dessus de l'évier pour enlever l'excédent de liquide. Dans un bol, mélanger le chou-fleur avec 1 œuf, 125 ml (½ tasse) de parmesan râpé et 30 ml (2 c. à soupe) d'origan séché jusqu'à l'obtention d'une boule homogène. Étendre le mélange sur une plaque à pizza couverte de papier parchemin. Presser fermement pour retirer l'air. Cuire au four 15 minutes, puis retirer délicatement le papier parchemin. Poursuivre la cuisson sur la plaque 15 minutes, jusqu'à ce que la croûte soit dorée et légèrement croustillante. Garnir la croûte selon les indications de la recette et cuire au four 12 minutes à 205 °C (400 °F).

1000 CALORIES
Du commerce

404 CALORIES
Maison

Pour 400 g (environ 1 lb)

Porc ①
1 filet de 300 g
(⅔ de lb)

Sauce hoisin ②
45 ml (3 c. à soupe)

Vinaigre de riz ③
45 ml (3 c. à soupe)

**Mélange de légumes
pour salade de chou** ④
1 litre (4 tasses)

Tortillas de blé ⑤
4 moyennes

PRÉVOIR AUSSI :
➤ **Ail**
2 gousses
hachées

➤ **Huile de sésame**
non grillé
15 ml (1 c. à soupe)

FACULTATIF :
➤ **Shiitakes**
le pied enlevé
et chapeaux émincés
250 g (environ ½ lb)

➤ 2 **oignons verts**
émincés

Sandwich au porc moo shu

Préparation : **15 minutes** • Marinage : **15 minutes** • Cuisson : **15 minutes** • Quantité : **4 portions**

Préparation

Parer le filet de porc en retirant la membrane blanche. Couper le filet en lanières de 1 cm (½ po) d'épaisseur.

Dans un grand bol, mélanger la sauce hoisin avec le vinaigre de riz et l'ail. Ajouter le porc et remuer. Laisser mariner 15 minutes au frais.

Dans une poêle antiadhésive, chauffer la moitié de l'huile de sésame à feu moyen. Égoutter le porc et jeter la marinade. Cuire quelques lanières de porc à la fois de 4 à 5 minutes. Transférer dans une assiette.

Dans la même poêle, verser le reste de l'huile. Cuire la salade de chou avec, si désiré, les shiitakes de 2 à 3 minutes. Saler et poivrer.

Chauffer les tortillas au micro-ondes 1 minute. Garnir les tortillas avec la préparation. Si désiré, garnir d'oignons verts.

PAR PORTION	
Calories	380
Protéines	25 g
Matières grasses	8 g
Glucides	59 g
Fibres	10 g
Fer	6 mg
Calcium	51 mg
Sodium	403 mg

Au total
399
calories

Idée pour accompagner

Salade asiatique aux fèves germées

Par portion: 19 calories

Dans un saladier, mélanger 30 ml (2 c. à soupe) de coriandre hachée avec 180 ml (¾ de tasse) de fèves germées, ¼ de concombre anglais émincé et 1 carotte coupée en julienne. Remuer.

Poireaux ①
émincés
1 sac de 250 g
(environ ½ lb)

4 pitas de blé entier ②

Pesto ③
30 ml (2 c. à soupe)

Jambon ④
tranché
150 g (⅓ de lb)

Brie ⑤
tranché
150 g (⅓ de lb)

FACULTATIF :

➤ **Basilic**
émincé
30 ml (2 c. à soupe)

➤ **Origan**
30 ml (2 c. à soupe)
de feuilles

Pizza au jambon, brie et poireaux

Préparation : **15 minutes** • Cuisson : **8 minutes** • Quantité : **4 portions**

Préparation

Préchauffer le four à 205 °C (400 °F).

Dans une casserole, blanchir les poireaux dans l'eau bouillante 2 minutes. Égoutter.

Napper les pitas de pesto. Répartir les poireaux, le jambon et le brie sur les pitas. Poivrer.

Déposer les pizzas sur une plaque de cuisson tapissée de papier parchemin. Cuire au four de 8 à 10 minutes.

À la sortie du four, parsemer de basilic et d'origan si désiré.

PAR PORTION	
Calories	308
Protéines	17 g
Matières grasses	16 g
Glucides	28 g
Fibres	4 g
Fer	3 mg
Calcium	128 mg
Sodium	869 mg

Au total
386
calories

Idée pour accompagner

Salade de bébés épinards aux suprêmes d'oranges

Par portion : 78 calories

Prélever les suprêmes de 2 oranges en pelant d'abord l'écorce à vif, puis en tranchant de chaque côté des membranes. Réserver les suprêmes. Au-dessus d'un saladier, presser les membranes afin d'en récupérer le jus. Incorporer 15 ml (1 c. à soupe) d'huile d'olive, 15 ml (1 c. à soupe) d'eau et 10 ml (2 c. à thé) de miel. Saler et poivrer. Ajouter 410 ml (1 ⅔ tasse) de bébés épinards et les suprêmes des oranges. Remuer.

Poudre de chili ①
5 ml (1 c. à thé)

32 crevettes moyennes (calibre 31/40) ②
crues et décortiquées

Tortillas au blé entier ③
8 moyennes

2 avocats ④
émincés

Yogourt grec nature 0 % ⑤
125 ml (½ tasse)

PRÉVOIR AUSSI :
➤ **Cassonade**
5 ml (1 c. à thé)
➤ **Huile d'olive**
15 ml (1 c. à soupe)

Fajitas aux crevettes et avocats

Préparation : **15 minutes** • Quantité : **4 portions**

Préparation

Dans un bol, mélanger la poudre de chili avec la cassonade et, si désiré, le cumin et les zestes. Saler. Assaisonner les crevettes avec ce mélange.

Dans une poêle antiadhésive, chauffer l'huile à feu moyen. Faire revenir les crevettes de 2 à 3 minutes.

Envelopper les tortillas dans un linge humide et faire chauffer au micro-ondes de 1 à 2 minutes.

Garnir les tortillas de crevettes, d'avocat, de yogourt grec et, si désiré, de laitue.

Idée pour accompagner

Salsa mexicaine

Par portion : 14 calories

Tailler ½ oignon rouge, 1 tomate et ½ poivron rouge en dés. Mélanger avec 30 ml (2 c. à soupe) de coriandre hachée, 30 ml (2 c. à soupe) de sauce chili, 15 ml (1 c. à soupe) de jus de lime, 5 ml (1 c. à thé) d'ail haché et 1,25 ml (¼ de c. à thé) de chipotle. Saler et remuer.

PAR PORTION	
Calories	384
Protéines	26 g
Matières grasses	16 g
Glucides	37 g
Fibres	7 g
Fer	4 mg
Calcium	105 mg
Sodium	671 mg

Au total
398
calories

FACULTATIF :
➤ **Cumin**
1,25 ml (¼ de c. à thé)
➤ **Lime**
15 ml (1 c. à soupe)
de zestes
➤ ¼ de **laitue iceberg**
émincée

1 poivron rouge ①

Tortillas au blé entier ②
4 moyennes

Houmous ③
125 ml (½ tasse)

Dinde fumée ④
12 tranches

Laitue frisée verte ⑤
ou romaine
4 feuilles

Wrap à la dinde et houmous

Préparation : **15 minutes** • Quantité : **4 portions**

Préparation

Tailler le poivron et, si désiré, le concombre en bâtonnets.

Tartiner les tortillas avec le houmous. Garnir les tortillas de dinde fumée, de laitue et de bâtonnets de poivron et de concombre.

Rouler les tortillas.

PAR PORTION	
Calories	233
Protéines	17 g
Matières grasses	8 g
Glucides	26 g
Fibres	5 g
Fer	2 mg
Calcium	38 mg
Sodium	1 215 mg

Au total
387
calories

Idée pour accompagner

Salade de légumes grillés à la grecque

Par portion : 154 calories

Préchauffer le four à 205 °C (400 °F) ou le barbecue à puissance moyenne-élevée. Dans un plateau en aluminium, cuire 1 courgette émincée, 3 demi-poivrons de couleurs variées, ½ oignon rouge coupé en quartiers et 6 asperges de 4 à 6 minutes. Dans un saladier, mélanger 30 ml (2 c. à soupe) d'huile d'olive avec 30 ml (2 c. à soupe) d'eau, 15 ml (1 c. à soupe) de jus de citron et 30 ml (2 c. à soupe) d'origan haché. Saler et poivrer. Incorporer les légumes grillés coupés en morceaux et le contenu de 1 pot de feta coupée en dés de 200 g.

FACULTATIF :
➤ ¼ de **concombre anglais**

Végé et savoureux

Êtes-vous de ceux qui croient que les plats végétariens sont ennuyants? Ces recettes décadentes et colorées ont tout ce qu'il faut pour vous faire changer d'idée! Et qui sait, peut-être prendrez-vous l'habitude de troquer quelques pièces de viande par semaine pour une option végé?

Tomates en dés
2 boîtes de 398 ml
chacune

Poudre de chili
15 ml (1 c. à soupe)

Haricots rouges
rincés et égouttés
1 boîte de 540 ml

12 coquilles à tacos

Feta
émiettée
250 ml (1 tasse)

Tacos aux haricots rouges

Préparation : **10 minutes** • Cuisson : **15 minutes** • Quantité : **12 tacos (6 portions)**

Préparation

Dans une casserole, chauffer l'huile à feu moyen. Ajouter la gousse d'ail et cuire jusqu'à ce qu'elle soit légèrement colorée. Retirer la gousse d'ail de la casserole.

Dans la même casserole, mélanger les tomates avec le chili et, si désiré, le cari et le cumin. Saler et poivrer. Laisser mijoter 10 minutes à feu doux.

Ajouter les haricots et poursuivre la cuisson 5 minutes à feu doux. Rectifier l'assaisonnement au besoin.

Garnir les coquilles de garniture aux haricots et de feta.

PAR PORTION	
Calories	295
Protéines	15 g
Matières grasses	11 g
Glucides	37 g
Fibres	8 g
Fer	3 mg
Calcium	200 mg
Sodium	498 mg

Au total
336
calories

Idée pour accompagner

Salade de tomates

Par portion : 41 calories

Dans un saladier, mélanger 15 ml (1 c. à soupe) d'huile d'olive avec 15 ml (1 c. à soupe) de jus de citron. Saler et poivrer. Couper 12 tomates cocktail de couleurs variées en quartiers. Ajouter dans le saladier avec 15 ml (1 c. à soupe) d'origan haché. Remuer, puis parsemer de 45 ml (3 c. à soupe) de copeaux de parmesan.

PRÉVOIR AUSSI :
> **Huile d'olive**
5 ml (1 c. à thé)

> **Ail**
1 gousse
entière pelée

FACULTATIF :
> **Cari**
2,5 ml (½ c. à thé)

> **Cumin**
moulu
2,5 ml (½ c. à thé)

Recette de Ève Godin, nutritionniste

Tofu ferme
1 bloc de 454 g

Chapelure panko ②
ou chapelure nature
250 ml (1 tasse)

Épices italiennes ③
10 ml (2 c. à thé)

Sauce tomate ④
250 ml (1 tasse)

Mozzarella ⑤
râpée
250 ml (1 tasse)

PRÉVOIR AUSSI :
➤ **Ail**
1 gousse hachée finement

➤ **2 œufs**

➤ **Huile d'olive**
30 ml (2 c. à soupe)

FACULTATIF :
➤ **Parmesan**
râpé
60 ml (¼ de tasse)

Tofu parmigiana

Préparation : **15 minutes** • Cuisson : **10 minutes** • Quantité : **4 portions**

Préparation

Couper le bloc de tofu en tranches d'environ 0,5 cm (¼ de po) d'épaisseur. Éponger les tranches à l'aide de papier absorbant.

Dans un bol, mélanger la chapelure avec les épices italiennes, l'ail et, si désiré, 30 ml (2 c. à soupe) de parmesan. Saler et poivrer.

Dans un autre bol, battre les œufs.

Déposer les tranches de tofu dans les œufs battus, puis les enrober de chapelure.

Dans une poêle antiadhésive, chauffer l'huile à feu moyen. Faire dorer les tranches de tofu de 2 à 3 minutes de chaque côté.

Déposer les tranches de tofu dans un plat de cuisson et couvrir de sauce tomate. Parsemer de mozzarella et, si désiré, du reste du parmesan. Faire gratiner au four 5 minutes à la position « gril » (*broil*).

PAR PORTION	
Calories	284
Protéines	18 g
Matières grasses	18 g
Glucides	12 g
Fibres	1 g
Fer	2 mg
Calcium	299 mg
Sodium	319 mg

Au total
330
calories

Idée pour accompagner

Salade de roquette aux tomates séchées et parmesan

Par portion: 46 calories

Dans un saladier, mélanger 80 ml (⅓ de tasse) de tomates séchées émincées avec 60 ml (¼ de tasse) de vinaigrette italienne faible en calories et 45 ml (3 c. à soupe) de parmesan râpé. Ajouter 750 ml (3 tasses) de roquette et remuer.

Recette de Ève Godin, nutritionniste

Tofu ferme
égoutté
1 bloc de 450 g ①

Beurre d'amande
60 ml (¼ de tasse) ②

Vinaigre de riz ③
30 ml (2 c. à soupe)

Mélange asiatique de légumes surgelés ④
500 ml (2 tasses)

Bébés épinards ⑤
500 ml (2 tasses)

PRÉVOIR AUSSI:
➤ **Miel**
15 ml (1 c. à soupe)
➤ **Huile de canola**
30 ml (2 c. à soupe)

FACULTATIF:
➤ **Sambal oelek**
10 ml (2 c. à thé)

Sauté de tofu au beurre d'amande

Préparation : **15 minutes** • Marinage : **30 minutes (facultatif)** • Cuisson : **10 minutes** • Quantité : **4 portions**

Préparation

Couper le tofu en cubes et, si désiré, ajouter à la marinade (voir recette ci-dessous) et faire mariner 30 minutes au frais.

Dans un bol, fouetter le beurre d'amande avec le vinaigre de riz, le miel, 125 ml (½ tasse) d'eau froide et, si désiré, le sambal oelek.

Dans une poêle ou dans un wok, chauffer l'huile à feu moyen-vif. Si nécessaire, égoutter le tofu et jeter la marinade. Faire dorer le tofu de 2 à 3 minutes. Déposer dans une assiette.

Dans la même poêle, cuire les légumes de 3 à 4 minutes.

Verser la sauce au beurre d'amande et remettre le tofu dans la poêle. Réchauffer de 1 à 2 minutes en remuant.

PAR PORTION	
Calories	315
Protéines	17 g
Matières grasses	18 g
Glucides	23 g
Fibres	5 g
Fer	8 mg
Calcium	323 mg
Sodium	72 mg

Au total

357
calories

Idée pour accompagner

Marinade pour tofu

Par portion: 42 calories

Mélanger 15 ml (1 c. à soupe) de sauce soya légère avec 15 ml (1 c. à soupe) d'huile de sésame (non grillé), 15 ml (1 c. à soupe) de gingembre haché, 10 ml (2 c. à thé) d'ail haché et 5 ml (1 c. à thé) de miel.

Tofu soyeux mou
1 bloc de 300 g ①

Parmesan ②
râpé
30 ml (2 c. à soupe)

Spaghettis ③
115 g

**Mélange de légumes
frais pour sauce
à spaghetti** ④
375 ml (1 ½ tasse)

Mozzarella sans gras ⑤
râpée
500 ml (2 tasses)

PRÉVOIR AUSSI :
➤ **Lait 1 %**
60 ml (¼ de tasse)
➤ **Huile de canola**
7,5 ml (½ c. à soupe)

FACULTATIF :
➤ **Champignons
tranchés**
1 paquet de 227 g

Gratin tetrazzini

Préparation : **15 minutes** • Cuisson : **25 minutes** • Quantité : **4 portions**

Préparation

Dans le contenant du robot culinaire ou du mélangeur, réduire en purée lisse le tofu avec le parmesan et le lait. Saler et poivrer.

Dans une casserole d'eau bouillante salée, cuire les spaghettis *al dente*. Égoutter.

Préchauffer le four à 190 °C (375 °F).

Dans une poêle antiadhésive, chauffer l'huile à feu moyen. Cuire le mélange de légumes jusqu'à tendreté. Si désiré, ajouter les champignons, puis poursuivre la cuisson quelques minutes.

Dans un plat de cuisson d'environ 20 cm (8 po), déposer les légumes. Ajouter les spaghettis et mélanger légèrement. Verser la sauce au tofu et garnir de mozzarella.

Cuire au four de 25 à 30 minutes, jusqu'à ce que le dessus soit doré.

PAR PORTION	
Calories	301
Protéines	30 g
Matières grasses	5 g
Glucides	33 g
Fibres	4 g
Fer	2 mg
Calcium	675 mg
Sodium	523 mg

Au total
381
calories

Idée pour accompagner

Salade de mâche, vinaigrette au miso

Par portion: 80 calories

Mélanger 30 ml (2 c. à soupe) d'huile d'olive avec 30 ml (2 c. à soupe) d'eau, 15 ml (1 c. à soupe) de vinaigre de riz, 15 ml (1 c. à soupe) de miso et 30 ml (2 c. à soupe) d'oignons verts émincés. Ajouter 750 ml (3 tasses) de mâche. Saler, poivrer et remuer.

Recette de Ève Godin, nutritionniste

**Fusillis tricolores
aux légumes**
1 paquet de 225 g ①

Olives noires ②
tranchées
1 boîte de 398 ml

Tomates raisins ③
coupées en deux
180 ml (¾ de tasse)

Feta ④
coupée en dés
80 ml (⅓ de tasse)

**Vinaigrette grecque
faible en calories** ⑤
80 ml (⅓ de tasse)

Salade de pâtes à la grecque

Préparation : **10 minutes** • Cuisson : **10 minutes** • Quantité : **4 portions**

Préparation

Dans une casserole d'eau bouillante salée, cuire les pâtes *al dente*. Égoutter et rincer à l'eau froide. Égoutter de nouveau.

Dans un saladier, mélanger les olives avec les tomates, la feta, les pâtes et, si désiré, les oignons verts. Verser la vinaigrette et remuer.

PAR PORTION	
Calories	353
Protéines	12 g
Matières grasses	14 g
Glucides	7 g
Fibres	5 g
Fer	4 mg
Calcium	147 mg
Sodium	880 mg

Au total
396
calories

Idée pour accompagner

Galettes de courge au fromage suisse

Par portion : 43 calories + 3 g de protéines

Couper 1 courge spaghetti en deux sur la longueur, puis retirer les graines. Déposer les moitiés de courge dans un plat de cuisson, côté chair dessus. Verser un peu d'eau dans le plat et couvrir d'une pellicule plastique. Cuire au micro-ondes 15 minutes à intensité élevée, jusqu'à tendreté. À l'aide d'une fourchette, gratter la chair de la courge, puis laisser tiédir dans une passoire fine. Dans un bol, mélanger la chair de la courge avec 1 œuf battu, 180 ml (¾ de tasse) de fromage suisse faible en gras râpé, 30 ml (2 c. à soupe) de farine, 45 ml (3 c. à soupe) de ciboulette hachée, 5 ml (1 c. à thé) d'ail haché et 125 ml (½ tasse) de chapelure panko. Saler et poivrer. Dans une poêle, faire fondre 15 ml (1 c. à soupe) de beurre à feu moyen. Déposer environ 80 ml (⅓ de tasse) de préparation par galette, en l'écrasant légèrement. Cuire 2 minutes de chaque côté.

Psst !

Permet d'atteindre 15 g de protéines

FACULTATIF :
➤ 3 **oignons verts**
émincés

Recette de Véronique Robidoux

Lait de coco léger ❶
1 boîte de 400 ml

Yogourt grec nature 0 % ❷
60 ml (¼ de tasse)

Cari ❸
30 ml (2 c. à soupe)

Chou-fleur ❹
taillé en petits bouquets
400 g

Pois chiches ❺
rincés et égouttés
½ boîte de 540 ml

PRÉVOIR AUSSI :
➤ **Huile de canola**
15 ml (1 c. à soupe)

➤ 1 **oignon**
haché

Cari indien

Préparation : **15 minutes** • Cuisson : **15 minutes** • Quantité : **4 portions**

Préparation

Dans un bol, mélanger le lait de coco avec le yogourt.

Dans une casserole, chauffer l'huile à feu moyen.
Cuire l'oignon de 1 à 2 minutes.

Ajouter le cari et, si désiré, le gingembre, puis cuire quelques secondes en remuant.

Ajouter le chou-fleur et, si désiré, les tomates. Cuire de 2 à 3 minutes.

Incorporer la préparation au lait de coco et yogourt.
Porter à ébullition. Couvrir et laisser mijoter à feu doux-moyen de 8 à 10 minutes.

Ajouter les pois chiches et réchauffer 1 minute.
Si désiré, garnir de noix de cajou.

PAR PORTION	
Calories	297
Protéines	11 g
Matières grasses	16 g
Glucides	31 g
Fibres	7 g
Fer	4 mg
Calcium	108 mg
Sodium	77 mg

Au total
382
calories

Idée pour accompagner

Houmous aux poivrons grillés

Par portion: 85 calories
+ 4 g de protéines

Dans une poêle, chauffer 15 ml (1 c. à soupe) d'huile de sésame (non grillé) à feu moyen. Cuire 1 oignon haché et 5 ml (1 c. à thé) d'ail haché de 2 à 3 minutes. Ajouter le contenu de 1 boîte de pois chiches de 540 ml (rincés et égouttés), 5 ml (1 c. à thé) de cumin, 250 ml (1 tasse) de poivrons rouges grillés et émincés, 30 ml (2 c. à soupe) d'eau et de 2 à 3 gouttes de tabasco. Cuire de 1 à 2 minutes. Déposer dans le contenant du robot culinaire et réduire en purée lisse. Saler et poivrer.

Psst!
Permet d'atteindre 15 g de protéines

FACULTATIF :
➤ **Gingembre**
haché
15 ml (1 c. à soupe)

➤ 2 **tomates italiennes**
coupées en dés

➤ 12 **noix de cajou**

Tofu ferme ①
1 paquet de 350 g

Chapelure panko ②
375 ml (1 ½ tasse)

**Yogourt grec
nature 0 %** ③
80 ml (⅓ de tasse)

Fleur d'ail ④
dans l'huile
10 ml (2 c. à thé)

**4 pains à hamburger
de blé entier** ⑤

PRÉVOIR AUSSI :
➢ **1 œuf**
➢ **Huile d'olive**
15 ml (1 c. à soupe)
➢ **Sauce soya**
5 ml (1 c. à thé)

FACULTATIF :
➢ **Parmesan**
râpé
60 ml (¼ de tasse)

Burgers croustillants au tofu

Préparation : **15 minutes** • Cuisson : **10 minutes** • Quantité : **4 portions**

Préparation

Éponger le tofu avec du papier absorbant. Émietter le tofu et déposer dans le contenant du robot culinaire.

Ajouter la moitié de la chapelure et l'œuf. Mélanger jusqu'à l'obtention d'une texture pâteuse. Transférer la préparation dans un bol. Si désiré, incorporer le parmesan. Avec la préparation, façonner 4 galettes d'environ 2 cm (¾ de po) d'épaisseur.

Verser le reste de la chapelure dans une assiette creuse et en enrober les galettes.

Dans une poêle, chauffer l'huile à feu moyen. Cuire les galettes de 4 à 5 minutes de chaque côté, jusqu'à ce qu'elles soient bien dorées.

Dans un autre bol, mélanger le yogourt avec la fleur d'ail et la sauce soya.

Ouvrir les pains et les faire griller au four de 1 à 2 minutes à la position « gril » (*broil*).

Garnir chacun des pains d'une galette de tofu et de sauce.

PAR PORTION	
Calories	308
Protéines	18 g
Matières grasses	10 g
Glucides	40 g
Fibres	4 g
Fer	3 mg
Calcium	170 mg
Sodium	444 mg

Au total
371
calories

Idée pour accompagner

Salsa au maïs et poivrons

Par portion : 63 calories

Dans un bol, mélanger 5 ml (1 c. à thé) d'ail haché avec 15 ml (1 c. à soupe) d'huile d'olive et 30 ml (2 c. à soupe) de coriandre hachée. Couper en dés ¼ de poivron rouge, ¼ d'oignon rouge et 1 tomate. Déposer dans le bol et mélanger avec 125 ml (½ tasse) de maïs en grains. Saler et poivrer.

4 gros panais ②

6 grosses carottes ③

1 navet ④

Parmesan ⑤
râpé
125 ml (½ tasse)

PRÉVOIR AUSSI :
➤ 4 **œufs**
➤ **Huile d'olive**
7,5 ml (½ c. à soupe)
➤ 1 **oignon**
haché

Carbonara de légumes racines

Préparation : **15 minutes** • Cuisson : **10 minutes** • Quantité : **4 portions**

Préparation

Dans un bol, fouetter la pâte d'ail avec les œufs.

Dans une grande poêle, chauffer l'huile à feu moyen. Cuire l'oignon 5 minutes, jusqu'à ce qu'il soit très tendre.

Peler les légumes racines. À l'aide d'une mandoline et de sa lame effileuse (large), tailler de longs rubans dans chacun des légumes.

Dans une casserole d'eau bouillante salée, cuire les rubans de légumes de 4 à 5 minutes, jusqu'à ce qu'ils soient *al dente*. Égoutter en prenant soin de réserver un peu d'eau de cuisson.

Remettre les légumes dans la casserole, puis incorporer l'oignon et le parmesan.

Incorporer la sauce aux œufs en remuant rapidement, jusqu'à ce que les légumes soient bien enrobés de sauce. Saler et poivrer. Si la préparation est sèche, ajouter un peu d'eau de cuisson réservée.

PAR PORTION	
Calories	330
Protéines	15 g
Matières grasses	11 g
Glucides	46 g
Fibres	10 g
Fer	2 mg
Calcium	267 mg
Sodium	358 mg

Au total

373
calories

Idée pour accompagner

Croûtons aux fines herbes et pesto de tomates

Par croûton : 43 calories

Couper ¼ de baguette de pain en fines tranches. Dans un bol, mélanger 60 ml (¼ de tasse) de beurre léger fondu avec 15 ml (1 c. à soupe) de pesto aux tomates séchées, 30 ml (2 c. à soupe) de ciboulette hachée et 5 ml (1 c. à thé) de thym haché. Badigeonner les tranches de pain avec cette préparation. Déposer sur une plaque de cuisson tapissée de papier parchemin et faire griller au four de 8 à 10 minutes à 205 °C (400 °F).

Recette de Ève Godin, nutritionniste

Nouilles asiatiques au blé
de type Haiku
200 g ①

Tofu ferme ②
1 bloc de 300 g

1 poivron rouge ③

Pois mange-tout ④
200 g (environ ½ lb)

Sauce pour pad thaï ⑤
du commerce
125 ml (½ tasse)

PRÉVOIR AUSSI :
➤ **1 oignon**
➤ **Huile de canola**
15 ml (1 c. à soupe)

FACULTATIF :
➤ **Fèves germées**
250 ml (1 tasse)
➤ **Arachides**
hachées
30 ml (2 c. à soupe)

Pad thaï au tofu

Préparation : **15 minutes** • Cuisson : **10 minutes** • Quantité : **4 portions**

Préparation

Dans une casserole d'eau bouillante salée, cuire les nouilles selon les indications de l'emballage. Égoutter.

Éponger le tofu à l'aide de papier absorbant. Couper le tofu en cubes.

Émincer le poivron, les pois mange-tout et l'oignon.

Dans une poêle ou dans un wok, chauffer l'huile à feu moyen-élevé. Faire dorer le tofu de 2 à 3 minutes en remuant.

Ajouter les légumes émincés et, si désiré, les fèves germées. Cuire de 2 à 3 minutes en remuant.

Ajouter la sauce et les nouilles. Cuire 2 minutes.

Au moment de servir, parsemer d'arachides si désiré.

PAR PORTION	
Calories	385
Protéines	20 g
Matières grasses	12 g
Glucides	57 g
Fibres	5 g
Fer	5 mg
Calcium	209 mg
Sodium	454 mg

Version minceur

Sauce pour pad thaï

Mélanger 60 ml (¼ de tasse) de jus de lime avec 45 ml (3 c. à soupe) de sauce soya réduite en sodium, 15 ml (1 c. à soupe) de sauce de poisson et 15 ml (1 c. à soupe) de miel.

327 CALORIES

Du commerce

Pour 125 ml (½ tasse)

113 CALORIES

Maison

Pennes au blé entier ①
225 g

Sauce au fromage ②
du commerce
250 ml (1 tasse)

Citron ③
30 ml (2 c. à soupe)
de zestes

Bébés épinards ④
750 ml (3 tasses)

Noix de Grenoble ⑤
hachées grossièrement
80 ml (⅓ de tasse)

Pennes sauce au fromage et épinards

Préparation : **15 minutes** • Cuisson : **10 minutes** • Quantité : **4 portions**

Préparation

Dans une casserole d'eau bouillante salée, cuire les pennes *al dente*. Égoutter.

Dans une autre casserole, chauffer la sauce au fromage et les zestes de citron à feu moyen.

Incorporer les bébés épinards et les pâtes. Saler et poivrer. Réchauffer 1 minute en remuant.

Répartir les pâtes dans les assiettes et garnir de noix de Grenoble.

PAR PORTION	
Calories	374
Protéines	15 g
Matières grasses	14 g
Glucides	51 g
Fibres	6 g
Fer	3 mg
Calcium	76 mg
Sodium	424 mg

Version minceur

Sauce au fromage de chèvre

Dans une casserole, chauffer 500 ml (2 tasses) de mélange laitier pour cuisson 5 % à feu moyen jusqu'aux premiers frémissements. Ajouter 80 ml (⅓ de tasse) de parmesan râpé et 200 g de fromage de chèvre crémeux (de type Capriny). Remuer jusqu'à ce que les fromages soient fondus.

1373 CALORIES ➤ **1087** CALORIES

Du commerce
Pour 780 ml (environ 3 ¼ tasses)
Maison

Cumin
15 ml (1 c. à soupe) ①

Tomates entières ②
2 boîtes de 796 ml
chacune

1 petite courge ③
musquée
pelée et coupée
en petits dés

2 grosses carottes ④
pelées et coupées
en petits dés

Pois chiches ⑤
rincés et égouttés
1 ½ boîte de 540 ml

PRÉVOIR AUSSI :
➤ **Huile d'olive**
7,5 ml (½ c. à soupe)

➤ 1 **oignon**
haché

➤ **Ail**
2 gousses hachées

FACULTATIF :
➤ **Cannelle**
5 ml (1 c. à thé)

➤ **Gingembre**
râpé
2,5 ml (½ c. à thé)

Tajine de pois chiches et couscous

Préparation : **15 minutes** • Cuisson : **35 minutes** • Quantité : **6 portions**

Préparation

Dans une grande casserole, chauffer l'huile à feu moyen-vif. Cuire l'oignon jusqu'à ce qu'il soit tendre.

Ajouter le cumin, l'ail et, si désiré, la cannelle et le gingembre. Cuire 30 secondes en remuant.

Ajouter les tomates et écraser à l'aide d'une cuillère. Ajouter les dés de courge et de carottes.

Diminuer l'intensité du feu et laisser mijoter 30 minutes à feu doux en remuant de temps en temps, jusqu'à ce que la sauce ait épaissi et que les dés de légumes soient tendres.

Ajouter les pois chiches et poursuivre la cuisson 5 minutes. Saler et poivrer.

PAR PORTION	
Calories	255
Protéines	12 g
Matières grasses	5 g
Glucides	56 g
Fibres	9 g
Fer	7 mg
Calcium	182 mg
Sodium	413 mg

Au total
369
calories

Idée pour accompagner

Couscous au gingembre et échalotes

Par portion : 114 calories + 4 g de protéines

Dans une poêle, faire fondre 7,5 ml (½ c. à soupe) de beurre léger à feu moyen. Ajouter 60 ml (¼ de tasse) d'échalotes sèches émincées et 30 ml (2 c. à soupe) de gingembre haché. Cuire de 1 à 2 minutes. Transférer dans un bol et incorporer 250 ml (1 tasse) de couscous. Verser 250 ml (1 tasse) de bouillon de poulet bouillant. Saler et poivrer. Couvrir et laisser la semoule gonfler 5 minutes. Égrainer le couscous à l'aide d'une fourchette, puis incorporer 30 ml (2 c. à soupe) de coriandre hachée.

Psst!
Permet d'atteindre 15 g de protéines

Recette de Ève Godin, nutritionniste

Pesto ①
30 ml (2 c. à soupe)

Tofu ferme ②
1 bloc de 350 g

Pennes ③
ou autres pâtes courtes
225 g

Rapini ④
tiges retirées et feuilles
hachées grossièrement
1 botte

**Tomates séchées
dans l'huile** ⑤
hachées
30 ml (2 c. à soupe)

Salade de pâtes, tofu et rapini

Préparation : **15 minutes** • Marinage : **1 heure** • Cuisson : **10 minutes** • Quantité : **4 portions**

Préparation

Dans un saladier, mélanger le pesto avec 60 ml (¼ de tasse) d'eau.

Couper le bloc de tofu en deux sur l'épaisseur et sur la largeur, puis tailler en tranches de 0,5 cm (¼ de po) d'épaisseur. Déposer dans le pesto et laisser mariner 1 heure au frais.

Dans une casserole d'eau bouillante salée, cuire les pâtes *al dente*. Ajouter le rapini dans la casserole 7 minutes avant la fin de la cuisson. Égoutter en prenant soin de réserver environ 125 ml (½ tasse) d'eau de cuisson. Rincer les pâtes et le rapini sous l'eau froide. Égoutter de nouveau.

Dans le saladier, mélanger les tomates séchées avec les pâtes et le rapini. Ajouter un peu d'eau de cuisson des pâtes au besoin si la salade est trop sèche. Saler et poivrer.

Au moment de servir, garnir de copeaux de parmesan si désiré.

PAR PORTION	
Calories	362
Protéines	26 g
Matières grasses	15 g
Glucides	44 g
Fibres	3 g
Fer	4 mg
Calcium	293 mg
Sodium	277 mg

Au total
391
calories

Idée pour accompagner

Jus de légumes épicé

Par portion : 29 calories

Dans le contenant du mélangeur, émulsionner ½ concombre pelé et épépiné avec 1 branche de céleri, 500 ml (2 tasses) de jus de tomate, 30 ml (2 c. à soupe) de jus de citron, des flocons de piment ou du piment de Cayenne au goût ainsi que du sel de céleri au goût.

FACULTATIF :
➤ **Parmesan**
125 ml (½ tasse)
de copeaux

Recette de Ève Godin, nutritionniste

Aneth
haché
30 ml (2 c. à soupe)

1

3 courgettes
râpées

2

Feta
émiettée
100 g

3

Fromage suisse
faible en gras
râpé
180 ml (¾ de tasse)

4

Maïs
250 ml (1 tasse)

5

PRÉVOIR AUSSI :

➤ 3 **œufs**

➤ 1 **oignon**
haché finement

➤ **Farine**
250 ml (1 tasse)

➤ **Huile de canola**
15 ml (1 c. à soupe)

FACULTATIF :

➤ **Ail**
haché
10 ml (2 c. à thé)

Galettes de courgettes, maïs et feta

Préparation : **15 minutes** • Cuisson : **6 minutes** • Quantité : **4 portions (12 galettes)**

Préparation

Dans un bol, fouetter l'aneth avec les œufs, l'oignon et, si désiré, l'ail. Saler et poivrer.

Ajouter les courgettes, la feta, le fromage suisse, le maïs et la farine. Remuer jusqu'à l'obtention d'une préparation homogène.

Dans une poêle antiadhésive, chauffer l'huile à feu moyen. Verser environ 60 ml (¼ de tasse) de préparation par galette. Cuire de 3 à 4 minutes de chaque côté. Égoutter sur du papier absorbant.

PAR PORTION	
Calories	352
Protéines	19 g
Matières grasses	14 g
Glucides	38 g
Fibres	3 g
Fer	3 mg
Calcium	356 mg
Sodium	383 mg

Au total

399
calories

Idée pour accompagner

Salade d'avocats et tomates

Par portion: 47 calories

Dans un saladier, mélanger 30 ml (2 c. à soupe) d'huile d'olive avec 30 ml (2 c. à soupe) d'eau, 30 ml (2 c. à soupe) de jus de lime et 30 ml (2 c. à soupe) de coriandre hachée. Saler et poivrer. Ajouter 1 avocat coupé en quartiers, ½ oignon rouge émincé et 12 tomates cerises coupées en deux. Remuer.

Riz basmati ①
250 ml (1 tasse)

Bouillon de légumes ②
500 ml (2 tasses)

Pâte de cari rouge ③
30 ml (2 c. à soupe)

**Mélange de légumes
asiatiques surgelés** ④
375 ml (1 ½ tasse)

Lait de coco léger ⑤
1 boîte de 400 ml

PRÉVOIR AUSSI :
➤ **Huile de canola**
7,5 ml (½ c. à soupe)

➤ **Œufs**
6 blancs

➤ **Sauce soya**
30 ml (2 c. à soupe)

FACULTATIF :
➤ **1 courgette**
émincée

➤ **Noix de cajou**
60 ml (¼ de tasse)

Cari de riz aux légumes

Préparation : **15 minutes** • Cuisson : **18 minutes** • Quantité : **4 portions**

Préparation

À l'aide d'une passoire fine, rincer le riz sous l'eau froide jusqu'à ce que l'eau soit claire. Égoutter. Déposer le riz dans une casserole avec le bouillon. Porter à ébullition à feu moyen. Couvrir et laisser mijoter à feu doux de 18 à 20 minutes, jusqu'à ce que le riz ait complètement absorbé le liquide.

Dans une casserole, chauffer l'huile à feu moyen. Faire revenir la pâte de cari de 1 à 2 minutes.

Ajouter les blancs d'œufs. Lorsqu'ils sont bien cuits, ajouter les légumes asiatiques et, si désiré, la courgette. Cuire 1 minute.

Verser le lait de coco et la sauce soya. Porter à ébullition et laisser mijoter de 4 à 5 minutes.

Incorporer le riz cuit et, si désiré, les noix de cajou. Servir immédiatement.

PAR PORTION	
Calories	337
Protéines	13 g
Matières grasses	14 g
Glucides	36 g
Fibres	2 g
Fer	2 mg
Calcium	38 mg
Sodium	944 mg

Au total
398
calories

Idée pour accompagner

Pain naan au cari

Pour 1 morceau : 61 calories
+ 2 g de protéines

Mélanger 15 ml (1 c. à soupe) de beurre léger sans sel fondu avec 5 ml (1 c. à thé) de cari et 1,25 ml (¼ de c. à thé) de piment thaï haché. Badigeonner un côté de 3 pains naan avec la préparation. Couper chaque pain en quatre morceaux. Déposer sur une plaque de cuisson tapissée de papier parchemin et cuire au four de 5 à 8 minutes à 205 °C (400 °F).

Psst!

Permet d'atteindre 15 g de protéines

Gemellis ❶
ou pennes
225 g

2 petites courgettes ❷

18 tomates cerises ❸
de couleurs variées

**Pesto aux
tomates séchées** ❹
30 ml (2 c. à soupe)

Mini-bocconcinis ❺
160 g (environ
32 unités)

PRÉVOIR AUSSI :
➤ 1 petit **oignon**
➤ **Huile d'olive**
7,5 ml (½ c. à soupe)
➤ **Ail**
haché
10 ml (2 c. à thé)

Pâtes aux courgettes, tomates et bocconcinis

Préparation : **15 minutes** • Cuisson : **10 minutes** • Quantité : **4 portions**

Préparation

Dans une casserole d'eau bouillante salée, cuire les pâtes *al dente*. Égoutter.

Émincer les courgettes et l'oignon.

Dans la casserole ayant servi à cuire les pâtes, chauffer l'huile à feu moyen. Cuire les courgettes, les tomates, l'oignon et l'ail de 2 à 3 minutes.

Ajouter le pesto et les pâtes. Saler et poivrer. Remuer et cuire 1 minute.

Incorporer les bocconcinis. Servir immédiatemin.

PAR PORTION	
Calories	384
Protéines	19 g
Matières grasses	13 g
Glucides	50 g
Fibres	4 g
Fer	2 mg
Calcium	248 mg
Sodium	57 mg

Au total
399
calories

Idée pour accompagner

Tomates rôties au sirop d'érable et vinaigre balsamique

Pour ½ tomate : 15 calories

Déposer 8 petites tomates coupées en deux sur une plaque de cuisson tapissée de papier parchemin. Arroser de 30 ml (2 c. à soupe) de sirop d'érable et de 15 ml (1 c. à soupe) de vinaigre balsamique. Parsemer de 5 ml (1 c. à thé) de romarin haché et de 15 ml (1 c. à soupe) de parmesan râpé. Cuire au four de 8 à 10 minutes à 205 °C (400 °F).

Index des recettes

Une réalisation de

Pratico
pratiques

Éditeur de

     Gabrielle